KU-260-191

David Hume was born in Edinburgh in 1711. He was educated at Edinburgh University where he matriculated in 1723 and stayed for two or three years. He then spent seven years at home, nominally studying law, but in fact reading voraciously, particularly philosophy and criticism. In 1734, after a brief period as a clerk in Bristol, he went to France for three years, where he composed the *Treatise of Human Nature* which was published in London in 1739. In 1740 he settled at Ninewells and in the following years he produced *Essays Moral and Political* and *Philosophical Essays Concerning Human Understanding* which in subsequent editions became *An Enquiry Concerning Human Understanding*.

In 1744 he failed to obtain the chair of Ethics and Pneumatical Philosophy at Edinburgh University; in 1745-6 he was companion to the Marquess of Annandale, and he then spent two years as secretary to General St Clair. In 1749 he returned to Edinburgh where he became Keeper of the Advocate's Library and began work on his *History of Great Britain*. In 1763-5 he was private secretary to the British Ambassador in Paris, Embassy Secretary and, for a short period, chargé d'affaires. In 1767-8 he was in London as Under-Secretary of State, Northern Department. Then, in 1768, he returned to Edinburgh where he settled.

David Hume, described by Adam Smith as 'approaching as nearly to the idea of a perfectly wise and virtuous man, as perhaps the nature of human frailty will admit' died in 1776. His *Dialogues on Natural Religion* were published posthumously in 1779.

A TREATISE
OF HUMAN NATURE

*Being an attempt to introduce
the experimental method of reasoning
into moral subjects*

BOOK II Of the Passions
BOOK III Of Morals

DAVID HUME

Edited with an introduction by
PÁLL S. ÁRDAL
Professor of Philosophy, Queen's University,
at Kingston, Ontario

FONTANA/COLLINS

Books I and II of *A Treatise of Human Nature*
were first published in 1739

Book III and the Appendix
were first published in 1740

Book I first issued in Fontana in 1962
Books II and III first issued in Fontana in 1972

Second Impression September 1978

Printed in Great Britain
for the Publishers Wm. Collins Sons & Co Ltd,
14 St James's Place, London, S.W.1.,
by William Collins Sons & Co Ltd, Glasgow

Contents

Advertisement
to Books I and II

My design in the present work is sufficiently explained in the *Introduction*. The reader must only observe, that all the subjects I have there planned out to myself are not treated in these two volumes. The subjects of the *Understanding* and *Passions* make a complete chain of reasoning by themselves; and I was willing to take advantage of this natural division, in order to try the taste of the public. If I have the good fortune to meet with success, I shall proceed to the examination of *Morals*, *Politics* and *Criticism*, which will complete this *Treatise of Human Nature*. The approbation of the public I consider as the greatest reward of my labours; but am determined to regard its judgment, whatever it be, as my best instruction.

Editor's Note

The text in this edition follows that of the original edition except that certain archaisms of spelling, punctuation and the use of capital letters have been modernised.

Numbers in the text of the *Treatise* refer readers to the Editor's Notes, which begin on page 336.

A correlation of the page numbers in this edition with those in the OUP edition of *A Treatise of Human Nature* edited by L. A. Selby-Bigge is given on pages 366–7.

Introduction
by Páll S. Árdal

I. Why Study These Books Together?

The two books of Hume's *Treatise* contained in this volume
were originally published separately. The first edition of
Book I, *Of the Understanding*, and Book II, *Of the Passions*,
appeared together in 1739 because, as the author says in the
advertisement, 'The subjects of the *understanding* and *passions* make a complete chain of reasoning by themselves.'
A year later appeared the third volume, *Of Morals*. Although
this volume contains some discussion of politics the advertisement to Book I leads one to believe that Hume originally
intended in the *Treatise* to discuss that topic at much greater
length. It seems that the work was also planned to include a
volume on criticism which was never written.

In an advertisement for the volume *Of Morals* Hume
stresses that it is not necessary to understand 'all the abstract
reasonings' of the first two books to master the content of
Book III. It would be a serious error to infer from Hume's
statements in the two advertisements that there is no important relation between his discussion of the passions and his
moral theory. Some of Hume's most basic contentions with
regard to the nature of evaluation in general, and moral
evaluation in particular, can be understood only if due
emphasis is given to some of the most neglected parts of
Book II. The reason for this, once seen, is simple. Hume is
attempting to give an account of evaluation that makes it
unnecessary to postulate special faculties, relations or qualities. At the same time he does not maintain that moral conceptions are reducible to non-moral conceptions; he has some
harsh things to say about those rationalists who attempt to
reduce morality to truth and immorality to contradiction. His
is an alternative metaphysical interpretation of evaluations.
We are all agreed that human beings are capable of love and
hatred directed to others and that they also have similar
emotions directed towards themselves, emotions that Hume
calls pride and humility. We can explain how these passions

or emotions arise, and a large part of *Of the Passions* is concerned with this topic. These passions are generally biased and they do not as such constitute evaluations that could be properly expressed as 'X is good' or 'X is bad.' Hume tries to show how an adequate psychological explanation can be given of the way in which we come to be capable of an objectified version of these passions. The occurrence of evaluations in the world is no more mysterious essentially than the occurrence of love and hatred, pride and humility. So-called evaluations are not thoughts that can be true or false; they are emotions.

Hume's reinterpretation of the nature of evaluations can be easily missed if *Of the Passions* is totally neglected. Insufficient attention to this work is also undoubtedly partly responsible for the radically erroneous view that Hume's moral theory can be fully understood from reading the *Enquiry Concerning the Principles of Morals,* where the psychological explanation of the nature of evaluation is not reproduced.[1]

People may claim Hume's own authority for preferring to study his moral theory as expressed in his later and more popular work. Did not Hume himself disown the *Treatise* and describe the *Enquiry Concerning the Principles of Morals* as 'incomparably the best' of his works? But no serious student of Hume's thought would now maintain that Hume was right to disown the *Treatise* as a whole, and if Hume was basing his judgment of the *Enquiry* upon its philosophical merits one can only say that he was an exceptionally inept judge of the quality of his own work. There is no very good reason to believe that Hume had abandoned his views about the nature of evaluation before he wrote the *Enquiry.* Yet it is most confusing to quote the two works side by side in an attempt to support an interpretation of

1. An excellent discussion of the relation between the *Enquiries* and the *Treatise* is contained in John B. Stewart, *The Moral and Political Philosophy of David Hume,* Appendix: The Recastings, pp. 325–39. See also Vinding Kruse, *Hume's Philosophy in his Principal Work A Treatise of Human Nature and in his Essays,* Selby-Bigge's introduction to the Oxford edition of the *Enquiries,* John Laird's criticism of Selby-Bigge's views in Chapter VIII of his *Hume's Philosophy of Human Nature* and Part IV, Chapter XXIV, of Kemp Smith's *The Philosophy of David Hume.*

Hume's theory; for some of the central technical terms in the *Treatise*, such as 'sympathy', 'confined benevolence' and 'general benevolence' are used with very much less precision in the *Enquiry*. *The Dissertation of the Passions* (1757) is such an abbreviated and uninteresting version of Book II of the *Treatise* that it cannot be recommended to students.

Another reason for preferring Books II and III of the *Treatise* to the *Enquiry* is the immensely more important account the earlier work gives of the reasons why virtues such as justice, faithfulness to promises and allegiance to government are properly called artificial. And it is mostly in the course of his discussion of these virtues in the *Treatise* that Hume states his interesting views about the nature of obligation and duty. It is only by reading the *Treatise*, rather than the relatively superficial *Enquiry*, that Hume's greatness as a moral philosopher can be understood. For there is little in the *Enquiry* which is not at least as adequately treated in the *Treatise* whereas much is either omitted from the later work or much less interestingly discussed.

II. Rejection of Rationalism

Hume contends that both in philosophy and in ordinary life it is common to 'talk of the combat of passion and reason.'[2] According to this view, we ought to follow reason rather than the passions because of its 'eternity, invariableness and divine origin,' whereas the passions are blind, inconstant and deceitful. Hume claims that this has been the most common view in moral philosophy both in ancient and modern times.[3]

Hume describes this view as fallacious and claims to be able to prove this. He maintains (1) 'that reason alone can never be a motive to any action of the will';[4] and (2) 'that it can never oppose passion in the direction of the will.'

Notice that here Hume seems to be insisting only that reason needs assistance from something other than reason if

2. *T.H.N.*, Book II, p. 154.
3. For Hume's arguments against the Rationalists, see *T.H.N.*, Book II, Part III, Section III, and Book III, Part I, Section I.
4. *T.H.N.*, Book II, p. 155.

it is to be a motive. But this, by itself, would be sufficient to show that the model described above is a faulty one; at least it needs some modification because it appears to attribute motivating force to unaided reason, in its battle with the passions.

Hume begins his criticism of the traditional model by telling the reader that the understanding 'exerts' itself in judging either relations between ideas or probabilities.[5] Hume is referring to a doctrine that he thinks he has already established in Book I of the *Treatise*. Judgments about relations between ideas, such as we get in arithmetic, are, as such, irrelevant to conduct. It is only when we apply arithmetic, or any other abstract or demonstrative reasoning, in practice, that it affects our actions. We apply mathematics in engineering, or accountancy, and this has importance for practice, in that it assists us in making causal judgments. In making up an account we discover what sort of action would constitute squaring the account. In engineering we use calculation to help us discover how to achieve certain ends, such as the rigidity of structures needed in the building of a bridge. We are in applied mathematics using our calculations 'to some designed end or purpose,' other than simply getting the calculation right. This could of course be said of a person who sits an examination in pure mathematics with a view to obtaining a degree. But such a person is not *applying* mathematics to the solution of a practical problem, although he is *using* his mathematical skills to achieve a practical end. Thus it is only in so far as demonstrative reasoning helps us to discover causal properties that it has an influence upon conduct. But the discovery of causal connections in no way affects our conduct, unless we are interested in one or other of the objects between which the relation holds. 'Where the objects themselves do not affect us, their connection can

5. Hume here misleadingly suggests that it is proper to talk of a faculty of understanding that has different operations. He sometimes writes of reason in a similar way. His considered opinion, however, seems to be that faculty talk cannot be accepted as ultimate and has to be cashed in terms of actual, possible and probable occurrences. Hume is attempting to explain human experience and human conduct without referring to anything hidden behind, or beyond, experience. And what are faculties but hidden powers? See Árdal, *Passion and Value in Hume's Treatise*, Chapter 4.

never give them any influence; and it is plain that, as reason is nothing but the discovery of this connection, it cannot be by its means that the objects are able to affect us.'[6] Notice that Hume here equates reason with the *discovery* of causal connection and does not give it the status of a faculty for discovering such a connection. It is thus open to Hume to deny that *the same faculty* of the mind both discovers relations between ideas and causal connections. Reason would *be* the discovery of necessary connections in the one case and causal connections in the other.

That Hume uses the term 'discovery' is significant. To discover something entails that what is discovered is the case. You cannot *discover* that someone has broken into your house unless someone has broken into your house. Leif Ericsson could not have *discovered* America if no such place had existed. The logic of 'discover' is like the logic of 'know' in that one cannot be mistaken about what is discovered any more than one can be mistaken about what one knows. According to this use of 'reason,' it is illegitimate to ascribe mistaken causal inferences or erroneous deductive reasoning to reason. It would thus be a mistake to attribute to reason all judgments that can be either true or false for the false ones are not a discovery but a failure to discover something.

There are good reasons for believing that Hume is not talking here of reason as a faculty of judgment. We should normally maintain that our action was unreasonable, or contrary to reason, if it were based upon poor evidence. But he maintains that our actions can be contrary to reason only in so far as they are based upon *false* beliefs about the nature an end or *false* beliefs about the means to that end.[7] This use of 'reason' also makes it easy to see why reason cannot by itself be a motive to the will; for it is the belief and not the truth of what is believed that determines our conduct. Thus the fact that the belief is a discovery makes no difference to its practical effect.

To be 'contrary to reason' is to be inconsistent with some truth and in the chapter under discussion Hume even equates

6. *T.H.N.*, Book II, p. 156.
7. Hume's divergence from ordinary usage has been clearly pointed out by J. **Kemp** in his *Reason, Action and Morality*, Chapter 4.

reason with truth. He says: 'nothing can be contrary to truth or reason, except what has a reference to it ...' The use of the pronoun 'it' makes it obvious that 'truth' and 'reason' here refer to the same thing. Truth or reason has no 'special impulse' attached to it and it follows from this that it cannot counteract, or be in conflict with, the passions. The truth of the first proposition Hume sets out to prove entails the truth of the second one.

To say that reason as truth does not influence conduct is quite different from saying that it is not important for conduct. For a man who bases his behaviour upon true beliefs, whether he knows them to be true or not, is more likely to succeed in his activities than one who bases his actions upon false beliefs.

In the view Hume is here concerned to refute there is a strong suggestion, to put it mildly, that reason is infallible. But, of two beliefs, one true and the other false, both may influence conduct in quite the same degree; the fact that only one of them is to be attributed to reason is irrelevant to determining the influence of the beliefs upon conduct. Thus the causal efficacy even of the discovery of truth is not derived from the fact that it *is a discovery*, and thus the work of reason, for our conduct would have been equally affected by a false belief, and the falsehood of a belief entails that it is not a discovery. Hume, however, does not always mean by 'reason' 'the discovery of truth.' He sometimes equates reason with the *belief* in the truth of a proposition. Thus he writes: 'I may desire any fruit as of an excellent relish; but whenever you convince me of my mistake, my longing ceases.' This is described as our passion 'yielding to reason.' Although this seems to indicate that reason and passion may be in opposition, Hume does not treat this as a counter-example to his general thesis because *the passion is not supposed to offer any resistance*. It looks as if it is passion and not reason that is inert in this case. But the inconsistency is superficial only, for Hume never wants to deny that our *beliefs* about the world determine our emotions, and thus our actions. If by 'reason' we mean 'beliefs about matters of fact' rather than 'the discovery of truth,' then of course reason determines conduct. But we must remember that our belief may be equally involved whether we are interested in what is believed or not. Our conduct is affected only if what we believe arouses, or is connected with, our desires or our interests; thus it is also true of reason, in the sense we are not concerned with, that reason alone has no effects. It is the world, as we believe it to be, that affects us, and not reason as such. Our desires are not, generally speaking, blind; they are for things of a certain character. To come to believe that the thing does not have this character suffices to destroy the desire.

If conformity to reason is equivalent to truth, and moral principles are eternal and immutable, then there is but a short move to the view that to say something inconsistent with eternal moral principles is to say something self-contradictory. But it was the foundation of morality that Hume's opponents were seeking and to seek it in reason was to claim that immoral behaviour somehow contradicted or was inconsistent with necessary moral principles. It is with this in view that one must read statements such as 'It is not contrary to reason to prefer the destruction of the whole world to the scratching of my finger. It is not contrary to reason for me to choose my total ruin, to prevent the least uneasiness to an Indian, or person wholly unknown to me. It is as little contrary to reason to prefer even my own acknowledged lesser good to my greater, and have a more ardent affection for the former than the latter.'[8]

All these actions we should call either immoral or imprudent, or both. Hume chooses them because he agrees with this estimate of them. But their immorality is not based upon reason. A man whose preferences are shown in these choices is not contradicting himself, nor is he necessarily being inconsistent. Our criticism of him is moral disapproval and this, according to Hume, is totally different in nature from the criticism of a person for an intellectual error, such as is shown in self-contradiction.

It is fortunate that we know who the thinkers are that Hume specifically has in mind when he argues against rationalism in ethics. In 'A Letter from a Gentleman'[9] he explicitly mentions Samuel Clarke and William Wollaston.[10]

8. *T.H.N.*, Book II, p. 157.
9. Eds. Ernest C. Mossner and John V. Price, Edinburgh University Press, 1967, p. 30.
10. See also D. D. Raphael, *British Moralists 1650–1800*, OUP, 1969, pp. 243–4.

There is no doubt that Wollaston attempted to reduce all morality to truth and immorality to falsehood. To speak truly is to speak comformably to the nature of things and to speak falsely is to deny things to be what they are. Similarly moral action is action in conformity with the nature of things and amounts to the assertion in practice of a true proposition. Immorality consists in asserting false propositions in practice. He writes: '*A true proposition may be denied, or things may be denied to be what they are, by deeds, as well as by express words or another proposition,*'[11] and a little later he uses as an example the firing on one body of soldiers by another. This would amount to announcing them to be enemies. If they are not enemies, then the action has asserted what is false and is immoral. Things may be denied to be what they are in deeds as well as in words. Wollaston writes: 'Things cannot be denied to be what they are, in any instance or manner whatsoever, without contradicting axioms and truths eternal.'[12] Thus all immorality is contradiction in practice.

Wollaston's view is a species of reductivism and has to be distinguished from intuitionism as the doctrine that 'moral attributes are non-natural, objective properties, apprehended by reason.'[13] The intuitionist takes these properties, or relations, to be *sui generis*, unique and incapable of analysis in more fundamental terms. They certainly cannot be reduced to apparently non-moral characteristics, such as truth. Clarke certainly maintained that morality consisted in eternal relations apprehended by reason but the germ of Wollaston's view can still be found in his writings. In so far as this is the case he holds, according to Hume, two incompatible theories. For Hume distinguished between the view that morality is the object of reason and the doctrine that reason is the foundation of morality. Arguing that incest in animals and in men consists in the same relation he concludes that if morality and immorality consist in relations, then morality must be the object rather than the effect of reason. The view that morality is the effect of reason must be the reductivist thesis Wollaston advances and this Hume now claims to be inconsistent with intuitionism.

11. Raphael, *British Moralists*, p. 275.
12. Raphael, *British Moralists*, p. 282.
13. W. D. Hudson, 'Hume on *Is* and *Ought*,' *The Philosophical Quarterly*, XIV (1964), and in Chappell (ed.), *Hume*.

In reading Hume's arguments against the rationalists one must bear in mind that some of his arguments are aimed at the reductivist thesis and others at the intuitionist view. There is not a clear distinction between these two positions in the writings of people like Clarke. Thus he writes: 'He that refuses to deal with all men equitably, and with every man as he desires they should deal with him, is guilty of the very same unreasonableness and contradiction in one case, as he that in another case should affirm one number or quantity to be equal to another, and yet that other at the same time not to be equal to the first.'[14] And a little later he writes: 'All wilful wickedness and perversion of right, is the very same insolence and absurdity in moral matters, as it would be in natural things, for a man to pretend to alter the certain proportions of numbers, to take away the demonstrable relations and properties of mathematical figures, to make light darkness, and darkness light, or to call sweet bitter, and bitter sweet.'[15] Contradiction is here represented as trying to make the nature of things other than it is and this is precisely what happens in immoral action. Moral action is action conformable to the nature of things, immoral action attempts to make the world other than it is. It is a contradiction in practice.

It is not easy for us to understand this kind of rationalism, based as it is upon the notion that the natural order must somehow be seen to incorporate the moral order. A confusion undoubtedly made it easier for Clarke to conceive of immorality as a kind of contradiction: he tended to be insufficiently alive to the difference between calling white something which is, in fact, black, and calling black white.[16] A man who says of something which is in fact good that it is bad is not guilty of the absurdity of equating goodness with badness. Once you do get confused on this point it is very much easier to see immorality as a kind of intellectual error, akin to contradiction.

The strain involved in this assimilation of right and wrong to truth and falsity can be seen in the following quotations from the works of John Balguy, who writes: 'To treat men in the same way we treat brutes, and to treat brutes in the same way we do sticks and stones, is manifestly as disagree-

14. Raphael, *British Moralists*, p. 232.
15. Raphael, *British Moralists*, p. 232.
16. See John Kemp, *Reason, Action and Morality*.

able and dissonant to the natures of things, as it would be to attempt the forming of an angle with two parallel lines. I would not call such a conduct *acting a lie*, because that is confounding objective and subjective truth, and introducing needless perplexities.'[17] And a little later, in explaining how far it is proper to call a morally good action conformable to truth, he adds: 'If by truth be meant the *truth of things*, then I think it may properly be said, that the moral goodness of an action consists in a conformity thereto. It may therefore be called either a *true* or *right* action; though for distinction's sake, and the avoiding of ambiguity and confusion, I should constantly prefer the latter.'[18] It does not seem to have struck Balguy that the 'ambiguity' and 'confusion' is due to the use of the same terms for disparate phenomena. He, like Clarke, saw truth and moral goodness as agreement with reality, as saying what is fitting and doing what is fitting. But the notion of fitness in the case of actions is not equivalent to truth. It may or it may not be a moral concept. Compare 'It is fitting that university lecturers should wear gowns,' and, 'It is fitting that virtue should be rewarded.' The moral notion of fittingness or propriety may also be applied to statements; 'It is sometimes fitting to say what is false' would be a self-contradiction if by 'fitting' we meant 'true.' But that would be a most unusual interpretation of this statement. The notion of fittingness or propriety in this context is already a moral notion and therefore cannot be used to explain the foundation of the whole of morality without begging the question. Hume contends that the attempt to reduce the fundamental concepts of morality to truths of reason is bound to fail and can only begin to appear plausible by becoming circular. This is one of the justifications for counting Hume among those who insist upon the autonomy of morality. But this does not mean that there is a moral sphere in addition to the natural sphere. Nor does it mean that we have a sense for perceiving values already existing in nature. Moral conceptions arise with the dispositions human beings acquire to have certain emotional reactions to each other's actions and the qualities of character from which these arise. Hume thinks he can give an intelligible account of the way in which these emotions come to be

17. Raphael, *British Moralists*, p. 452.
18. Raphael, *British Moralists*, p. 452.

aroused. He produces an account of the foundation of morality, but not by defining moral notions in terms of truth, or reason, or indeed, in any other terms. No, his account of the foundation of morality is unashamedly psychological; it shows how we can explain the occurrence of moral emotions by reference to psychological principles that need to be referred to in explaining other emotions, such as love, hatred, pride and humility. Thus, in a sense he combines naturalism with the belief in the autonomy of morality, whereas there is some reason for classifying the rationalists he was arguing against as reductivists and anti-autonomists. One is so used to equating rationalism with the belief in a special moral faculty of intuition whereby we intuit non-natural qualities, or relations, that the reduction of morality to conformity to truth, and immorality to contradiction hardly enters our head. There is some point in characterizing both these rationalists and also Hume as naturalists. But Hume, in substituting a morally neutral conception of nature for a rational divinely guided order that includes all values, attempts to show how even in a value-neutral universe evaluations can still be made intelligible.

III. Moral 'Judgments' are Emotions

If moral characteristics are neither natural nor non-natural features of the objects of moral judgment, what then are they? If the goodness of a virtuous man is not in the man, where then can it be? It is tempting to suggest that if goodness is not a quality of the person thought of then it must be a characteristic of the person who is doing the thinking. Hume himself tells us that you can never find virtue or vice until you introspect and find a sentiment of approval or disapproval. This has led commentators to attribute to him the view that 'John is a good man' means 'I have a feeling of approval on contemplating John's character.' 'John is a bad man' is, in like fashion, taken to mean 'I have a feeling of disapproval on contemplating John's character.' This view has come to be known as subjectivism. But is this not an absurd view? Does it not entail the mistaken view that two people who appear to be making value judgments about John's character are really each thinking about his own feelings?[19]

Of course, one cannot argue that because this subjectivist view is absurd Hume could not have held it. But it is unnecessary for us to opt for this interpretation of his words for the whole trend of Books II and III of the *Treatise* suggests a much more plausible and interesting interpretation. To have a sense of virtue is to have a feeling, he tells us; and the feeling constitutes our assessment. Hume is providing us with an alternative metaphysics of value, if I may put it thus. Evaluations, according to this new way of looking at the matter, are not thoughts of any kind but emotional responses. Moral judgments, so called, are not true or false and thus do not attribute any sorts of characteristics to objects. Hume's is a non-propositional theory of moral judgment.

At this point one may feel like objecting that Hume is not making an impartial use of Occam's razor. Why does he use it so ruthlessly on faculties and special qualities and relations when he is prepared to allow special moral emotions? Is he not here allowing that special emotions can be arbitrarily produced like rabbits out of a conjurer's hat? To answer this charge the importance of certain aspects of Book II must be stressed.

In *Of the Passions* Hume insists that each passion is a simple impression. By this he means that no passion can be thought of as constructed out of separate elements. A man has to experience anger to understand what anger is; to be incapable of experiencing emotions entails total incapacity for understanding the meaning of terms referring to emotions. Each has to be learnt by coming to be associated with the appropriate passion. Hume's account of the passions cannot be thought of as an analysis of them, for each of them is unanalysable and indefinable. What he does provide us with is a description of the causal conditions that give rise to different passions. It is true that the account he gives of the conditions that give rise to some of the passions is illuminating when read as conceptual analysis; e.g. pride.[20]

19. For an extended discussion of the content of this section, see Ardal, *Passion and Value in Hume's Treatise*, Chapters 6 and 9.
20. For discussions of Hume's views on the passions, see in particular Páll S. Árdal, *Passion and Value in Hume's Treatise*,

But this is incidental; Hume is attempting to provide an account of causal conditions. He is engaged in writing part of his science of man.

Hume's discussion of pride and humility, love and hatred has sometimes been considered of little importance for the rest of his philosophy. But it is from these passions that his theory of morals takes its departure. For these are best considered as the four possible basic ways of valuing: love is having a favourable attitude to another, hatred the opposite, and pride and humility are the corresponding forms of self-evaluating.

Approval and disapproval are simple impressions like all other passions. Although simple impressions cannot be thought of as composed of parts, various resemblances between them may still be described, and an account can be given of the principles and circumstances from which they arise. Hume does not take the trouble to do this with *all* the different species of indirect passions, deeming it 'not necessary to give any particular account of them.' But the approval and disapproval of persons are of such central importance in accounting for the nature of evaluation that a special examination of these passions is necessary. It is only when we take up an 'objective' point of view that these emotions arise, although we sometimes mistake the love and hatred aroused because of a close relation of their object to ourselves for a 'calmer' or more imperceptible variety.

There are, Hume contends, passions that involve little or no 'disturbance in the soul' and are 'more known by their effects than by their immediate feeling or sensation.' These he calls calm passions. They turn out to be in many respects more like attitudes than emotions or passions. Hume nevertheless insists that when you are on a particular occasion conscious of your approval of a person, your approval is an emotion, though there may be little conscious 'disturbance in the

Chapters 1 and 2; P. L. Gardiner, 'Hume's Theory of the Passions'; *David Hume. A Symposium*; Anthony Kenny, *Action, Emotion and Will*, Routledge, 1963, Chapter 1; John B. Stewart, *The Moral and Political Philosophy of David Hume*, Chapter 3; John Laird in *Hume's Philosophy of Human Nature*, Chapter VII; Paul Dietl, 'Hume on The Passions,' *Philosophy and Phenomenological Research*, XXVIII (1967–8); Norman Kemp Smith, *The Philosophy of David Hume*, Chapters VI to VIII.

soul.' Moral approval and disapproval and the aesthetic sentiments usually involve such low conscious emotional intensity. Our evaluations may, in spite of this, sometimes determine our actions even when in conflict with a particular
violent passion that involves much greater conscious excite-
ment. Strength of motivating power and intensity of conscious
feeling do not always coincide. Passion in Hume's usage
covers the calm emotions. This wide usage characteristically
prompted Thomas Reid to charge him with a misuse of
language. We must, however, remember that if Hume thought
we were expressing a passion in voicing our approval of a
person, he did not mean we were feeling a passion *for* that
person in the ordinary sense of that term.

One of the things that characterizes passions such as love
and pride is their biased nature. The closeness of the related
object to the person who has these passions is a factor which
partly determines their strength. But I have no business to
say that a man *is a good man* unless I am abstracting from
the fact that he *happens* to be closely related to *me*.

It has been suggested that the principle of sympathy suffices to explain how we come to evaluate morally. This principle operates universally among human beings. It is described
as essentially a principle of communication of passions. Hume
puts it thus: 'As in strings equally wound up, the motion
of one communicates itself to the rest, so all the affections
readily pass from one person to another, and beget correspondent movements in every human creature.'[21]

There is a sense in which it would seem logically impossible for us to have another's experience. If I have a pain
exactly like yours, it still would be my pain. But it is, Hume
thinks, equally impossible for us to *observe* directly another's
experience. When I observe someone in pain, I do not
observe his pain. Behavioural signs are the only data we have
for inferring what the nature of another's experience is. In
Hume's view the signs lead us first of all to have an idea of
the experience of another. This idea or belief is then enlivened into a real impression through the influence of the
impression of the self. On Hume's view, my belief that
another person is in pain comes to be a real pain.

It is generally agreed that the principle of sympathy is
important for Hume's account of moral evaluation. Thus

21. *T.H.N.*, Book III, p. 296.

some people believe Hume *reduces* the moral sentiments to a species of sympathetic consciousness. To evaluate, on this view, is to sympathize. It is, however, *the cause* of what I sympathize with that I approve of. Sympathy with those affected by a man's character may partly be responsible for my love of him. My pride in my garden may be partly explained by sympathy with those who enjoy it and admire it. But the love or the pride are not constituted by sympathy. The feelings sympathized with and the object of the passion are different.

Thus, talking of the causes that lead us to call objects beautiful or ugly, Hume emphasizes that it is to a considerable extent the tendency of objects to produce pleasures and pains that determines the aesthetic valuing of them. Sympathy with the effects leads to the valuing of the cause. The principles involved are the same in moral evaluation.

But sympathy alone is not sufficient to account for the origin of morality for we can see its presence among animals also, though they have no morality and are incapable of moral judgment. Sympathy furthermore varies with relations. Thus the bias of the passions is accentuated by sympathy. The closeness of relations, however, is considered to be irrelevant to judgments about the virtuous or vicious nature of a person. Hume's problem thus is: how can we claim that a principle which contributes to a biased view of qualities of character is *the foundation* of morality? Though the capacity to be affected through sympathy by the feelings of others is a necessary condition of morality it is not a sufficient condition.

Moral evaluations are objective in a way in which love and hatred are not. Objectivity consists in discounting your own special relation to the object or your own special condition. The emotions that arise from such a point of view are proper evaluations. Hume attempts to explain how we come to take up this objective point of view in terms of known human motives that operate throughout human life, in our understanding as well as in practical affairs.

To judge of situations objectively is an acquired habit. The following may help to explain how it is acquired: We find that our situation in regard to objects varies from time to time and our moods may also change the effect the same object has upon us at different times. We discover that changes in our situation change the appearances of things. An object looks small at a distance but appears to become larger as one approaches nearer to it. It is fairly obvious that if we tried to base our actions upon the momentary appearances of things we should be much more often thwarted than we are in seeking the satisfaction of our needs and wants.

We learn that we cannot describe as delicious a stale sandwich we enjoy when famished, for this would suggest that it would have been enjoyable in ordinary circumstances. Differences in the apparent colours of objects similarly come to be attributed to changes in the light or to a change in our sense organs. Thus we begin to differentiate in general between a change of qualities in the object and changes due to our special situation or condition, which is perhaps not shared by others. Basic convenience is the main motive for judging of things from a special point of view, distinguishing the subjective appearance from the objective reality.

The importance of the distinction between appearance and reality is made even more obvious when we consider language, the value of which depends largely upon the furtherance of communication between people. Our interest is often in *an object* and not at all in the appearance of an object to a person who may be specially related to it. To learn the language we use to describe objects is to learn to abstract from our own special relation to them. We fix a general standard or a rule for the application of our expressions. In judging of size we have standards of comparison that must be applied in the same way by those using the language if communication is to be achieved. It would of course be wrong to suggest that someone has invented the standard for the use of words. Experience teaches us the advantages of language and a tacit agreement to abide by the rules of language grows up.

A similar account must be given of objectivity in moral evaluation. We form the habit of looking upon a situation in which an individual finds himself in such a way as to take into account only those characteristics that are independent of the special relation in which he stands to us. Only when we do this does *approval* or *disapproval*, as opposed to one or other of the biased passions, arise. Though Hume puts this in causal terms it is obvious that he helps us to see that we cannot legitimately claim to *morally* approve if the evaluation of a person is determined by the fact that he is a close relative or otherwise specially related to us.

It must be admitted that the language of love undoubtedly has its place, but it has also certain drawbacks. If someone says 'I love Jean' we are informed about the speaker, but the qualities we could expect Jean to have we cannot infer with any accuracy unless we know a great deal more about the speaker and his relation to Jean. But when a man says 'John is a good man' or 'I approve of John's moral character' we ought to be able to assume that the special relation the speaker has to John has been ignored. This is not merely a matter of language. To learn to take up an objective, impartial point of view in regard to situations and people marks our moral development. We may hate and love, be angry and benevolent, and yet be incapable of moral judgment. The source of our moral life is nevertheless to be found in these passions. When our hatred is directed by an objective view of the qualities of a man we call it moral indignation. When our love arises from a like objective view of a character it is moral approval.

Though a habit of objective evaluation may help to counteract our tendency to favour our friends there is of course no guarantee that our moral feelings will be strong enough to determine our conduct. Thus when we have learnt the language of objective evaluation we may speak in accordance with generally accepted standards of value and we may ourselves come to count as equally virtuous a historical character for whom we have little feeling, and a close friend for whom we have a warm love because of his qualities.

Though we may use evaluative expressions according to settled rules, and may not feel approval on every occasion on which we praise actions, Hume, I think, would say that unless we have at some time felt approval, we cannot be said to *know* the meaning of the value expressions we use, although we may praise all the right things. It is possible to use moral language, the language of praise and blame, correctly, but in a purely mechanical fashion. Yet, to be a moral being one must on occasion also *feel* approval or disapproval. To be moral entails having the capacity for moral emotions, but we may often, on particular occasions, reveal our moral attitudes in word and deed, without having specifically adopted an objective point of view on that occasion.

Sometimes we may be quite sincere in pronouncing a person vicious or virtuous, but our moral valuation may still be biased. We may have tried to be impartial, but due to the similarity between that love and that hatred which arises from objective reflection and the biased variety, we may mistake the latter for the former. We may think we really approve or disapprove when in fact we only like or dislike, love or hate. Hume quite often mentions how we may mistake one passion for another which is similar, despite the fact that a passion is a simple impression and thus revealed in consciousness just as it is. We may still classify it wrongly, fail to recognize it for what it is.

Hume no doubt thinks that we shall all more or less agree in our *evaluations* if only we learn the habit of true objectivity in looking at actions and persons. Human nature is much the same, he thinks, in all times and places, and we are all through sympathy affected in some measure by the feelings of our fellow-men. Even when we overlook our own relation to the object of our evaluation, sympathy with the feelings of others may still arouse our passions.

In describing the way sympathy operates I have talked as if the thought of *somebody's* pain or pleasure comes through sympathy to be enlivened in such a way as to pain or please us. It would thus seem that we can only sympathize with actual pains and pleasures, or at least pains and pleasures believed to be actual. If therefore it is sympathy with the *effects of qualities of mind* that leads us to approve or disapprove, it would seem that our approvals and disapprovals must be determined by the actual consequences of actions, or at least by those consequences we expect actions to have.

But virtue for Hume is a *quality* of mind or character and this can remain the same, although its beneficial effects may be prevented by special circumstances. 'Virtue in rags is still virtue; and the love which it procures attends a man into a dungeon or desert, where the virtue can no longer be exerted in action, and is lost to all the world.' This appears to be inconsistent with Hume's system for, to use his own words, 'if sympathy were the source of our esteem for virtue, that sentiment of approbation could only take place where the virtue actually attained its end, and was beneficial to mankind.'[22]

But we approve of a building that is well adapted to its

22. *T.H.N.*, Book III, pp. 303–4.

purpose, and value a fertile soil and a good climate even though the soil is uncultivated and the climate belongs to a desert island. A man may be deemed generous although he has little to give, and when a hero is imprisoned we do not cease to call him heroic, although he has no opportunity to display his courage. This is because we judge of the character by reflection upon the beneficial effects these qualities *would* have *if* their normal effects were not prevented.

It should now be clear that in so far as sympathy operates in accounting for approval and disapproval one cannot take literally its description as a principle of communication, for we are affected by sympathy in cases where the pain or pleasure sympathized with is not actual. 'When I run over a book with my eye, I imagine I hear it all; and also, by the force of the imagination, enter into the uneasiness which the delivery of it *would give the speaker*.'[23] The uneasiness is not real.'[24] We are, however, pained by the reading of the book because of the tendency of the expressions used to cause pain, and we consequently talk of the style as 'harsh and disagreeable'. These terms express our disapproval of the style and are not to be taken as an expression of *personal preference* only, for my evaluation is determined by the effect the book would have as a general rule.

Aesthetic evaluations may be objective in precisely the same way as moral evaluations. But were it not for the fact that the thought of the pleasures or pains of others pleased or pained us through sympathy, our passions would not be aroused when we take up an objective point of view, for we are then disregarding what we as individuals have to gain or lose by the character of the person we are evaluating.

We may also remind ourselves that love and hatred are not as such motives. We may love someone, as we may approve of him, without giving any thought to his happiness. These passions are different from the desire for the happiness or unhappiness of another, though related to these. We *tend* to want the happiness of a person we love and the unhappiness of a person we hate. This also makes it clear that Hume could not give an analysis of approval and disapproval in terms of a disposition to act in a particular way. The point is in some ways important for its bearing upon the problem

23. My italics.
24. *T.H.N.*, Book III, p. 305.

of testing sincerity.

If a man disapproves of the foreign policies of his government one has a certain uneasiness about the view that he cannot *really* disapprove unless he is willing to do something positive to change these policies. Would the man's lack of action be conclusive evidence that he was insincere? One may hesitate to accept this view because a person may, through weakness of will, or laziness, fail *to live up to* his standards of value. The problem is complicated by the fact that it is recognized that a man may deceive himself as to what he values and that in some cases people may act against their 'better judgment'.

I must not be taken to deny that watching a man's behaviour is on the whole a better guide to what he values than listening to what he says his values are. It is at least certain that a man is not always himself the best judge as to how *strongly* he approves or disapproves. He may not be able to decide this by simple introspection. It may be necessary to put him to the test. He may genuinely believe he would be willing to make considerable sacrifices for the sake of his convictions. Yet we may know his character better than he himself does and realize that his approval or disapproval is half-hearted. These considerations show, I think, the weakness of construing approval and disapproval as *occurrent feelings* whose nature and strength a man can determine by attending to his state of mind. I would, on the other hand, hesitate to say that a man *disapproved strongly* of, for example, racial discrimination, unless there were certain conditions under which he were both prepared to take action and also became emotionally perturbed. It is not only that there are other possible motives for the person's behaviour than disapproval of racial discrimination. Even though we might approve of *what he does* his lack of feeling might seem to us monstrous. But Hume, by introducing the notion of calm passions, seems to be at least partly aware of the fact that some passions may be *known more by their effects* than their immediate conscious impression. Since the moral sentiments are counted among the calm passions he might perhaps have agreed that the *strength* of our approvals and disapprovals cannot be fully ascertained by attention to our conscious emotional state. (Whether this is consistent with calling the passions simple impressions is much more doubtful.)

We must, I think, admit that, on some occasions, we know *what it feels like to approve or disapprove strongly* of something, and yet when the question as to the *strength* of our feelings arises, we may accept behaviour as a test of this. If this is admitted, we see that neither analysis in purely behavioural terms nor the construction of approval and disapproval simply as feelings can be counted as wholly satisfactory. We may perhaps think that Hume misconstrues the issue in so far as he treats passions such as approval as simple impressions, and thinks of the motives connected with these passions as contingently related to them. This would make it *possible* that genuine approval or disapproval might be consistent with *any behaviour*. But though the criteria based on behaviour may not always decide the issue, the fact that they are sometimes taken to be decisive would throw doubt upon the adequacy of this analysis.

Hume is aware that we may praise and blame simply because we approve or disapprove. We *need* not be doing this in order to change people's behaviour. Many people like expressing their moral views, with no ulterior motive, and Hume of course insists that the evaluations themselves are not matters of free decision. We cannot decide to approve or not to approve of a man in the sense in which this would be correctly expressed as praise or condemnation. We find ourselves approving or disapproving of things just as we find we love some things and hate others. 'What is your purpose in loving her?' is odd. 'What is your purpose in saying to her "I love you"?' is not odd at all.

It is thus of great importance to distinguish between Hume's doctrine, which I should like to call emotionism, and the doctrine that, in this century, has come to be known as emotivism, in so far as the latter is a doctrine about the function of evaluative language.[25] Hume is not primarily concerned with language. He is, however, asking us to reconsider our view about the nature of our evaluation of character. To think that a man is a virtuous man is not to think that he possesses special characteristics over and above his natural qualities. It is, on the contrary, to love him in a certain way.

25. For a further discussion of this point, see Árdal, *Passion and Value*, Chapter 9.

IV. Obligations are Based Upon, but not Inferred from, Beliefs

It is sometimes mistakenly thought that Hume had no theory of obligation, that he was exclusively concerned with virtue and vice.[26] It is true that he does not say much about obligation and that most of what he does say is to be found in the *Treatise*. But there one finds an explicitly stated view about the nature of obligation, a view which is in complete conformity with Hume's account of the evaluation of virtue.

Hume stresses that no action can be called virtuous unless it can be done from a motive other than the motive of duty or the sense of obligation. The reason for this is that all moral evaluation is of actions only in so far as they are seen to issue from some quality in a person. But he thinks that it is nevertheless possible for one to do the action a virtuous man would do from a natural motive although one lacks that motive. One may come to hate oneself for the lack of a certain virtue, and this hatred may lead one to perform the actions of the virtuous man in the hope that one will acquire the virtue from practice. An observer may approve of the actions resulting from this self-hatred, or sense of obligation, because these actions are usually a sign of a valuable quality of character.[27] It is of some interest that Hume should refer to the sense of obligation as self-hatred, and that he should insist that actions for which there are natural motives can be done from a sense of duty. But Hume develops his account of obligation or duty, mainly in dealing with the artificial virtues. Promise-keeping is one of the artificial virtues and the following quotation from the chapter on promises gives us a short but clear statement of the essence of Hume's account of moral judgments, including judgments of obligation: 'All morality depends upon our sentiments; and when any action, or quality of the mind, pleases us *after a certain manner*, we say it is virtuous; and when the neglect, or non-performance of it, displeases us *after a like manner*, we say that we

26. For an excellent discussion of Hume's views about obligation, see Bernard Wand, 'Hume's Account of Obligation,' *The Philosophical Quarterly*, VI (1956) and in Chappell (ed.), *Hume*.

27. See *T.H.N.*, Book III, Part II, Section I.

lie under an obligation to perform it.'[28]

It is in the light of this account of the nature of obligation that one must understand the following passage: 'We blame a father for neglecting his child. Why? Because it shows a want of natural affection, which is the duty of every parent.'[29] Here we have the case of a natural virtue and we blame the father for the lack of it. We may express this moral condemnation by saying that he has failed in his duty. This expresses our pain at the thought of the non-performance of what we call the man's duty. But the special pain constituting the thought that a person has neglected his obligation is caused by the man's disposition rather than by his actual deeds. Thus a man may be unable to care for his children because of a lack of funds. He has not failed morally. We do not accuse him of not having done his duty. To take a different example: If the man wanted to maltreat the child and was forcibly restrained from doing so we should be pained at the thought of the absence of parental affection and consequently say that the man has failed in his duty. Our feelings are not those of moral condemnation if they are entirely determined by the external features of the deed. We morally require of people that they should love their children. We feel pained at the thought of a man's lack of love for his children even though he may look after them; he might do this for purely selfish reasons. Hume's account of the nature of thinking someone obliged helps one to see a reason why he does not take the view that we are obliged only to do certain deeds, and are not obliged to do them from any particular motive. One must remember that the person himself may look after his child from a sense of duty, in the absence of parental affection, because he hates himself for not having love for his child. Hume's view may be unusual, indefensible, or both; but his account of obligation certainly makes it more intelligible why he should maintain that we have a duty to love our children, and not only to care for them.

The motive of duty or obligation plays a vital role in Hume's explanation of our conduct in conformity with what he calls artificial virtues. Taking our present situation there are no natural motives that could explain our adherence to the patterns of conduct we call just, honest, chaste or loyal.

28. *T.H.N.*, Book III, pp. 245–6.
29. *T.H.N.*, Book III, p. 211.

These patterns often demand that we should act against our strongest motives, particular desires, self-love and confined benevolence. Hume tells a complex story about the way in which one may explain the origin of the conventions underlying these practices. People come to see that it is to their mutual benefit to adopt the conventions that give rise to property, that certain forms of words should count as promises, etc. But how can we explain the fact that people feel they ought to adhere to these conventions when no one seems to be the gainer? In the case of justice, there are those who might be sophisticated enough to see that it is vital not to weaken the practice in any way; but most people surely never think of the general utility of justice and the effect of their individual acts of honesty upon the general welfare. Only a sense of duty or obligation can explain why so many people still behave justly in spite of strong personal motives not to do so. A similar account must be given of our adherence to the other artificial virtues mentioned above. The question now arises: how do we acquire this sense of duty? The answer is that most people acquire it in part through social conditioning: education and political propaganda condition us to feel pained at the thought of not doing an honest deed, and the feelings we have about natural virtues are transferred to the artificial ones. This is achieved partly by the use of the term 'virtue' for honesty as well as for kindness.

I am not concerned with the merit of Hume's view but it may be noted that, for him, there is no such thing as really having an obligation independent of people's thinking that they are obliged; for to think that you are obliged simply amounts to having a certain emotional reaction to the world. No statements of fact can entail an obligation, but people will tend to agree in their emotions, if they agree about the facts; and, in the case of the artificial virtues, if they have been similarly brought up.

Bernard Wand makes this criticism of Hume's view: 'As an attitude which has been developed by habit and social conditioning, Hume's view of moral obligation precludes the possibility of our recognizing, after deliberate reflection, that within any specific situation a certain action is right, and that our failure to carry it out makes us morally responsible for it. For Hume, moral obligation is passively determined upon us by others.'[30]

In spite of very general agreement with Professor Wand's account, I think Hume's view is rather the following: we could not have justice, or any of the artificial virtues, if we were to depend upon the rational decisions of individuals in particular cases. People would break the rules far too often; social stability would be threatened. I think Hume could still allow that it is possible that a thorough and objective consideration of a situation may lead a man to feel pained in a special way at the thought of the absence of a quality of character. Hume never claims that social conditioning is a necessary condition for having a sense of obligation at all. The sense of obligation of the ideal moral character would be, like the sense of virtue, determined by an unbiased objective reflection upon the person concerned, whether this be himself or another. But such reflective perspicuity, and conscious concern for the public, can be expected of only a few individuals. Hume clearly doubted whether social stability could be maintained if allegiance to the artificial virtues were left to the reflective decisions of each member of a community.

Notice that in the passage quoted from the *Treatise*[31] Hume is describing the conditions that lead one to say that someone is obliged. The account is a causal one, and much in conformity with the importance Hume gives to association in his philosophy. When one has a certain feeling at the thought of the non-performance of an action, then, because of the association formed between that feeling and certain words, one has a tendency to utter them. One must be very careful not to take Hume to be giving an analysis of the meaning of 'X is obliged.' Hume is not saying that 'X is obliged' means 'I have a feeling, etc.' The conditions that give rise to an utterance must not be confused with an analysis of its meaning.[32] Although when we say 'I am obliged' or 'he is obliged' we give the information that we have a feeling, we are not thereby stating that we have the feeling. We convey informa-

30. 'Hume's Account of Obligation', in Chappell (ed.), *Hume*, p. 327.

31. *T.H.N.*, Book III, pp. 245–6.

32. See Árdal, *Passion and Value*, Chapter 9 and Peter Jones, 'Another Look at Hume's Views of Aesthetic and Moral Judgments,' *The Philosophical Quarterly*, XX (1970). Jones comes to the conclusion that Hume holds a causal associationist theory of

tion to others in so far as they have come to associate certain expressions with the same situations as we have done. An exactly parallel account must be given of judgments about virtue: we say that a person is virtuous when we have a feeling of approval in contemplating his character.

I appreciate that I have not fully explicated Hume's views about obligation and duty. However, I hope to have said enough to reveal some widespread misinterpretations of the famous 'is–ought' passage.[33]

There is a traditional interpretation, and those who accept it are right to insist that Hume is denying that evaluations can be entailed by non-evaluative premises. However, they fail to appreciate the reason for this, which is that evaluations are emotional reactions to the world, and that they cannot therefore be entailed by any premises.

The traditionalist is also wrong in thinking that there is no sense in which Hume thinks morals have a foundation. He is trying to show us the causal conditions that underlie the emotional reactions that constitute evaluations. On the other hand he thinks these emotions are of a unique character: moral evaluation is *sui generis* and cannot be reduced to more fundamental conceptions. Approval and disapproval are simple impressions, different from all other impressions. There is thus a sense in which Hume is an autonomist, at least compared to some of the rationalists that he seems to have had in mind. Wollaston certainly was attempting to analyse moral conceptions in terms of truth, conformity to reason, falsehood, contradiction. People often seem to assume that all Hume's rationalist predecessors believed in non-natural moral qualities that were intuited by a special, rational moral faculty. What they were, at least sometimes, trying to show was that immoral action involved a contradiction, that the morality and the conformity to reason of an action, or its truth, amounted to the same thing. There is thus a sense in which they are the anti-autonomists, when compared with Hume.

A. C. MacIntyre has rightly insisted that it is totally ab-

---

meaning largely by an analysis of works other than the *Treatise*, although he rightly finds the theory in the *Treatise* as well.

33. *T.H.N.* Final paragraph of Book III, Part I, Section I.

surd to maintain that Hume could be classified with R. M.
Hare as a philosopher who insists that a moral conclusion
can be reached only from premises at least one of which is
moral. He proposes an ingenious alternative interpretation
of Hume's position. Hume, he thinks, is not denying that
one may derive statements of obligation from purely factual
premises, for this is what Hume himself proceeds to do.
Hume is saying only that the derivation is very difficult.
MacIntyre is entirely right to insist that Hume must be
taken to hold that our beliefs about facts determine our
obligation, but he is wrong to think that the derivation is
an inference.[34]

No evaluations are true or false thoughts and Hume's
emotional reaction theory of the nature of evaluation is meant
to explain how we come to be determined to evaluate and
feel obliged in a world in which, independently of our emotional reactions, there are neither any values nor any obligations.

34. For a discussion of the 'is–ought' passage, see the following:
A. C. MacIntyre, 'Hume on "Is" and "Ought",' *The Philosophical
Review*, Vol. LXVIII (1959), and Chappell (ed.); R. F. Atkinson,
'Hume on "Is" and "Ought"': A Reply to Mr. MacIntyre', *The
Philosophical Review*, Vol. LXX (1961) and Chappell; Antony
Flew, 'On the Interpretation of Hume,' *Philosophy*, Vol.
XXXVIII (1963), and Chappell; Geoffrey Hunter, 'Reply to
Professor Flew,' *Philosophy*, Vol. XXXVIII (1963), and Chap-
pell; Antony Flew, ' "Not Proven"—At Most,' in Chappell, ed.;
W. D. Hudson, 'Hume on *Is* and *Ought*,' *The Philosophical
Quarterly*, Vol. XIV (1964) and Chappell; M. J. Scott-Taggart,
'MacIntyre's Hume', *The Philosophical Review*, Vol. LXX (1961).

A Treatise of Human Nature

Books II and III

Book II *Of the Passions*

PART I *Of Pride and Humility*

SECTION I *Division of the Subject*

As all the perceptions of the mind may be divided into *impressions* and *ideas*, so the impressions admit of another division into *original* and *secondary*. This division of the impressions is the same with that which I formerly made use of when I distinguished them into impressions of *sensation* and *reflection*.* Original impressions or impressions of sensation are such as without any antecedent perception arise in the soul, from the constitution of the body, from the animal spirits, or from the application of objects to the external organs. Secondary, or reflective impressions are such as proceed from some of these original ones, either immediately or by the interposition of its idea. Of the first kind are all the impressions of the senses, and all bodily pains and pleasures; of the second are the passions, and other emotions resembling them.

It is certain, that the mind, in its perceptions, must begin somewhere; and that since the impressions precede their correspondent ideas, there must be some impressions, which without any introduction make their appearance in the soul. As these depend upon natural and physical causes, the examination of them would lead me too far from my present subject, into the sciences of anatomy and natural philosophy. For this reason I shall here confine myself to those other impressions, which I have called secondary and reflective, as arising either from the original impressions, or from their ideas. Bodily pains and pleasures are the source of many passions, both when felt and considered by the mind; but arise originally in the soul, or in the body, whichever you please to call it, without any preceding thought or perception. A fit of the gout produces a long train of passions, as grief, hope, fear; but is not derived immediately from any affection or idea.

The reflective impressions may be divided into two kinds,

* Book I. Part I. sect. 2.

viz. the *calm* and the *violent*. Of the first kind is the sense of beauty and deformity in action, composition, and external objects. Of the second are the passions of love and hatred, grief and joy, pride and humility. This division is far from being exact. The raptures of poetry and music frequently rise to the greatest height; while those other impressions, properly called *passions*, may decay into so soft an emotion, as to become, in a manner, imperceptible. But as in general the passions are more violent than the emotions arising from beauty and deformity, these impressions have been commonly distinguished from each other. The subject of the human mind being so copious and various, I shall here take advantage of this vulgar and specious division, that I may proceed with the greater order; and having said all I thought necessary concerning our ideas, shall now explain these violent emotions or passions, their nature, origin, causes, and effects.

When we take a survey of the passions, there occurs a division of them into *direct* and *indirect*. By direct passions I understand such as arise immediately from good or evil, from pain or pleasure. By indirect such as proceed from the same principles, but by the conjunction of other qualities. This distinction I cannot at present justify or explain any farther. I can only observe in general, that under the indirect passions I comprehend pride, humility, ambition, vanity, love, hatred, envy, pity, malice, generosity, with their dependants. And under the direct passions, desire, aversion, grief, joy, hope, fear, despair and security. I shall begin with the former.

SECTION II *Of pride and humility; their objects and causes*

The passions of *pride* and *humility* being simple and uniform impressions, it is impossible we can ever, by a multitude of words, give a just definition of them, or indeed of any of the passions.[1] The utmost we can pretend to is a description of them, by an enumeration of such circumstances, as attend them; but as these words, *pride* and *humility*, are of general use, and the impressions they represent the most common of any, every one, of himself, will be able to form a just idea of them, without any danger of mistake. For which reason, not to lose time upon preliminaries, I shall immediately enter upon the examination of these passions.

It is evident, that pride and humility, though directly contrary, have yet the same *object*. This object is self, or that succession of related ideas and impressions, of which we have an intimate memory and consciousness. Here the view always fixes when we are actuated by either of these passions. According as our idea of ourself is more or less advantageous, we feel either of those opposite affections, and are elated by pride, or dejected with humility. Whatever other objects may be comprehended by the mind, they are always considered with a view to ourselves; otherwise they would never be able either to excite these passions, or produce the smallest increase or diminution of them. When self enters not into the consideration, there is no room either for pride or humility.

But tho' that connected succession of perceptions, which we call *self*, be always the object of these two passions, it is impossible it can be their *cause*, or be sufficient alone to excite them. For as these passions are directly contrary, and have the same object in common; were their object also their cause; it could never produce any degree of the one passion, but at the same time it must excite an equal degree of the other; which opposition and contrariety must destroy both. It is impossible a man can at the same time be both proud and humble; and where he has different reasons for these passions, as frequently happens, the passions either take place alternately; or if they encounter, the one annihilates the other, as far as its strength goes, and to the remainder only of that, which is superior, continues to operate upon the mind. But in the present case neither of the passions could ever become superior; because supposing it to be the view only of ourself, which excited them, that being perfectly indifferent to either, must produce both in the very some proportion; or in other words, can produce neither. To excite any passion, and at the same time raise an equal share of its antagonist, is immediately to undo what was done, and must leave the mind at last perfectly calm and indifferent.[2]

We must, therefore, make a distinction betwixt the cause and the object of these passions; betwixt that idea, which excites them, and that to which they direct their view, when excited. Pride and humility, being once raised, immediately turn our attention to ourself, and regard that as their ultimate and final object; but there is something farther requisite in order to raise them; something, which is peculiar to one of the passions, and produces not both in the very same degree. The first idea, that is presented to the mind, is that of the cause or productive principle. This excites the passion, connected with it; and that passion, when excited, turns our view to another idea, which is that of self. Here then is a passion placed betwixt two ideas, of which the one produces it, and the other is produced by it. The first idea, therefore, represents the *cause*, the second the *object* of the passion.

To begin with the causes of pride and humility; we may observe, that their most obvious and remarkable property is the vast variety of *subjects*, on which they may be placed. Every valuable quality of the mind, whether of the imagination, judgment, memory or disposition; wit, good sense, learning, courage, justice, integrity; all these are the causes of pride; and their opposites of humility. Nor are these passions confined to the mind, but extend their view to the body likewise. A man may be proud of his beauty, strength, agility, good mien, address in dancing, riding, fencing, and of his dexterity in any manual business or manufacture. But this is not all. The passion looking farther, comprehends whatever objects are in the least allied or related to us. Our country, family, children, relations, riches, houses, gardens, horses, dogs, clothes; any of these may become a cause either of pride or of humility.

From the consideration of these causes, it appears necesary we should make a new distinction in the causes of the passion, betwixt that *quality*, which operates, and the *subject*, on which it is placed. A man, for instance, is vain of a beautiful house, which belongs to him, or which he has himself built and contrived. Here the object of the passion is himself, and the cause is the beautiful house; which cause again is sub-divided into two parts, *viz.* the quality, which operates upon the passion, and the subject, in which the quality inheres. The quality is the beauty, and the subject is the house, considered as his property or contrivance. Both these parts are essential, nor is the distinction vain and chimerical. Beauty, considered merely as such, unless placed upon something related to us, never produces any pride or vanity; and the strongest relation alone, without beauty, or something else in its place, has as little influence on that passion. Since, therefore, these two particulars are easily separated, and there is a necessity for their conjuction, in order to produce the passion, we ought to consider them as component parts of the cause; and infix in our minds an exact idea of this distinction.

SECTION III *Whence these objects and causes are derived*

Being so far advanced as to observe a difference betwixt the *object* of the passions and their *cause*, and to distinguish in the cause the *quality*, which operates on the passions, from the *subject*, in which it inheres; we now proceed to examine what determines each of them to be what it is, and assigns such a particular object, and quality, and subject to these affections. By this means we shall fully understand the origin of pride and humility.

It is evident in the first place, that these passions are determined to have self for their *object*, not only by a natural but also by an original property. No one can doubt but this property is *natural* from the constancy and steadiness of its operations. It is always self, which is the object of pride and humility; and whenever the passions look beyond, it is still with a view to ourselves, nor can any person or object otherwise have any influence upon us.

That this proceeds from an *original* quality or primary impulse, will likewise appear evident, if we consider that it is the distinguishing characteristic of these passions. Unless nature had given some original qualities to the mind, it could never have any secondary ones; because in that case it would have no foundaton for action, nor could it ever begin to exert itself. Now these qualities, which we must consider as original, are such as are most inseparable from the soul, and can be resolved into no other; and such is the quality, which determines the object of pride and humility.

We may, perhaps, make it a greater question, whether the *causes*, that produce the passion, be as *natural* as the object, to which it is directed, and whether all that vast variety proceeds from caprice or from the constitution of the mind. This doubt we shall soon remove, if we cast our eye upon human nature, and consider that in all nations and ages, the same objects still give rise to pride and humility; and that upon the view even of a stranger, we can know pretty nearly, what will either increase or diminish his passions of this kind. If there be any variation in this particular, it proceeds from nothing but a difference in the tempers and complexions of men; and is besides very inconsiderable. Can we imagine it possible, that while human nature remains the same, men will ever become entirely indifferent to their power, riches, beauty or personal merit, and that their pride and vanity will not be affected by these advantages?

But though the causes of pride and humility be plainly *natural*, we shall find upon examination, that they are not *original*, and that it is utterly impossible they should each of them be adapted to these passions by a particular provision, and primary constitution of nature. Beside their prodigious number, many of them are the effects of art, and arise partly from the industry, partly from the caprice, and partly from the good fortune of men. Industry produces houses, furniture, clothes. Caprice determines their particular kinds and qualities. And good fortune frequently contributes to all this, by discovering the effects that result from the different mixtures and combinations of bodies. It is absurd, therefore, to imagine, that each of these was foreseen and provided for by nature, and that every new production of art, which causes pride or humility; instead of adapting itself to the passion by partaking of some general quality, that naturally operates on the mind; is itself the object of an original principle, which till then lay concealed in the soul, and is only by accident at last brought to light. Thus the first mechanic, that invented a fine scritoire, produced pride in him, who became possessed of it, by principles different from those, which made him proud of handsome chairs and tables. As this appears evidently ridiculous, we must conclude, that each cause of pride and humility is not adapted to the passions by a distinct original quality; but that there are some one or more circumstances common to all of them, on which their efficacy depends.

Besides, we find in the course of nature, that though the effects be many, the principles, from which they arise, are commonly but few and simple, and that it is the sign of an unskilful naturalist to have recourse to a different quality, in order to explain every different operation. How much more must this be true with regard to the human mind, which being so confined a subject may justly be thought incapable of containing such a monstrous heap of principles, as would be necessary to excite the passions of pride and humility, were each distinct cause adapted to the passion of a distinct set of principles?

Here, therefore, moral philosophy is in the same condition as natural, with regard to astronomy before the time of *Copernicus*. The ancients, though sensible of that maxim, *that nature does nothing in vain*, contrived such intricate systems of the heavens, as seemed inconsistent with true philosophy, and gave place at last to something more simple and natural. To invent without scruple a new principle to every new phenomenon, instead of adapting it to the old; to overload our hypotheses with a variety of this kind; are certain proofs, that none of these principles is the just one, and that we only desire, by a number of falsehoods, to cover our ignorance of the truth.

SECTION IV *Of the relations of impressions and ideas*

Thus we have established two truths without any obstacle or difficulty, *that it is from natural principles this variety of causes excite pride and humility*, and *that it is not by a different principle each different cause is adapted to its passion*. We shall now proceed to enquire how we may reduce these principles to a lesser number, and find among the causes something common, on which their influence depends.

In order to this we must reflect on certain properties of human nature, which though they have a mighty influence on every operation both of the understanding and passions, are not commonly much insisted on by philosophers. The *first* of these is the association of ideas, which I have so often observed and explained. It is impossible for the mind to fix itself steadily upon one idea for any considerable time; nor can it by its utmost efforts ever arrive at such a constancy. But however changeable our thoughts may be, they are not entirely without rule and method in their changes. The rule, by which they proceed, is to pass from one object to what is resembling, contiguous to, or produced by it. When one idea is present to the imagination, any other, united by these relations, naturally follows it, and enters with more facility by means of that introduction.

The *second* property I shall observe in the human mind is a like association of impressions. All resembling impressions are connected together, and no sooner one arises than the rest immediately follow. Grief and disappointment give rise to anger, anger to envy, envy to malice, and malice to grief again, till the whole circle be completed. In like manner our temper, when elevated with joy, naturally throws itself into love, generosity, pity, courage, pride, and the other resembling affections. It is difficult for the mind, when actuated by any passion, to confine itself to that passion alone, without any change or variation. Human nature is too inconstant to admit of any such regularity. Changeableness is essential to it. And to what can it so naturally change as to affections or emotions, which are suitable to the temper, and agree with that set of passions, which then prevail? It is evident, then, there is an attraction or association among impressions, as well as among ideas; though with this remarkable difference, that ideas are associated by resemblance, contiguity, and causation; and impressions only by resemblance.[3]

In the *third* place, it is observable of these two kinds of association, that they very much assist and forward each other, and that the transition is more easily made where they both concur in the same object. Thus a man, who, by any injury from another, is very much discomposed and ruffled in his temper, is apt to find a hundred subjects of discontent, impatience, fear, and other uneasy passions; especially if he can discover these subjects in or near the person, who was the cause of his first passion. Those principles, which forward the transition of ideas, here concur with those, which operate on the passions; and both uniting in one action, bestow on the mind a double impulse. The new passion, therefore, must arise with so much greater violence, and the transition to it must be rendered so much more easy and natural.

Upon this occasion I may cite the authority of an elegant writer, who expresses himself in the following manner. 'As the fancy delights in everything that is great, strange, or beautiful, and is still more pleased the more it finds of these perfections in the *same* object, so it is capable of receiving a new satisfaction by the assistance of another sense. Thus any continued sound, as the music of birds, or a fall of waters, awakens every moment the mind of the beholder, and makes him more attentive to the several beauties of the place, that lie before him. Thus if there arises a fragrancy of smells or perfumes, they heighten the pleasure of the imagination, and make even the colours and verdure of the landscape appear more agreeable; for the ideas of both senses recommend each other, and are pleasanter together than when they enter the mind separately; as the different colours of a picture, when they are well disposed, set off one another, and receive an additional beauty from the advantage of the situation.'⁴ In this phenomenon we may remark the association both of impressions and ideas, as well as the mutual assistance they lend each other.

SECTION V *Of the influence of these relations on pride and humility*

These principles being established on unquestionable experience, I begin to consider how we shall apply them, by revolving over all the causes of pride and humility, whether these causes be regarded, as the qualities, that operate, or as the subjects, on which the qualities are placed. In examining these *qualities* I immediately find many of them to concur in producing the sensation of pain and pleasure, independent of those affections, which I here endeavour to explain. Thus the beauty of our person, of itself, and by its very appearance, gives pleasure, as well as pride; and its deformity, pain as well as humility. A magnificent feast delights us, and a sordid one displeases. What I discover to be true in some instances, I *suppose* to be so in all; and take it for granted at present, without any farther proof, that every cause of pride, by its peculiar qualities, produces a separate pleasure, and of humility a separate uneasiness.

Again, in considering the *subjects*, to which these qualities adhere, I make a new *supposition*, which also appears probable from many obvious instances, *viz.* that these subjects are either parts of ourselves, or something nearly related to us. Thus the good and bad qualities of our actions and manners constitute virtue and vice, and determine our personal character, than which nothing operates more strongly on these passions. In like manner, it is the beauty or deformity of our person, houses, equipage, or furniture, by which we are rendered either vain or humble. The same qualities, when transferred to subjects, which bear us no relation, influence not in the smallest degree either of these affections.

Having thus in a manner supposed two properties of the causes of these affections, *viz.* that the *qualities* produce a separate pain or pleasure, and that the *subjects*, on which the qualities are placed, are related to self; I proceed to examine the passions themselves, in order to find something in them, correspondent to the supposed properties of their causes. *First*, I find, that the peculiar object of pride and humility is determined by an original and natural instinct, and that it is absolutely impossible, from the primary constitution of the mind, that these passions should ever look beyond self, or that individual person, of whose actions and sentiments each of us is intimately conscious. Here at last the view always rests, when we are actuated by either of these passions; nor can we, in that situation of mind, ever lose sight of this object. For this I pretend not to give any reason; but consider such a peculiar direction of the thought as an original quality.

The *second* quality, which I discover in these passions, and which I likewise consider as an original quality, is their sensations, or the peculiar emotions they excite in the soul, and which constitute their very being and essence. Thus pride is a pleasant sensation, and humility a painful; and upon the removal of the pleasure and pain, there is in reality no pride nor humility. Of this our very feeling convinces us; and beyond our feeling, it is here in vain to reason or dispute.

If I compare, therefore, these two *established* properties of the passions, *viz.* their object, which is self, and their sensation, which is either pleasant or painful, to the two *supposed* properties of the causes, *viz.* their relation to self, and their tendency to produce a pain or pleasure, independent of the passion; I immediately find, that taking these suppositions to be just, the true system breaks in upon me with an irresistible evidence. That cause, which excites the passion, is related to the object, which nature has attributed to the passion; the sensation of the passion; from this double relation of ideas and impressions, the passion is derived. The one idea is easily converted into its correlative; and the one impression into that, which resembles and corresponds to it: with how much greater facility must this transition be made, where these movements mutually assist each other, and the mind receives a double impulse from the relations both of its impressions and ideas?

That we may comprehend this the better, we must suppose, that nature has given to the organs of the human mind, a certain disposition fitted to produce a peculiar impression or emotion, which we call *pride*; to this emotion she has assigned a certain idea, *viz.* that of *self*, which it never fails to produce. This contrivance of nature is easily conceived. We have many instances of such a situation of affairs. The nerves of the nose and palate are so disposed, as in certain circumstances to convey such peculiar sensations to the mind; the sensations of lust and hunger always produce in us the idea of those peculiar objects, which are suitable to each appetite. These two circumstances are united in pride. The organs are so disposed as to produce the passion; and the passion, after its production, naturally produces a certain idea. All this needs no proof. It is evident we never should be possessed of that passion, were there not a disposition of mind proper for it; and it is as evident, that the passion always turns our view to ourselves, and makes us think of our own qualities and circumstances.[5]

This being fully comprehended, it may now be asked *whether nature produces the passion immediately, of herself; or whether she must be assisted by the co-operation of other causes?* For it is observable, that in this particular her conduct is different in the different passions and sensations. The palate must be excited by an external object, in order to produce any relish; but hunger arises internally, without the concurrence of any external object. But however the case may stand with other passions and impressions, it is certain, that pride requires the assistance of some foreign object, and that the organs, which produce it, exert not themselves like the heart and arteries, by an original internal movement. For *first*, daily experience convinces us, that pride requires certain causes to excite it, and languishes when unsupported by some excellency in the character, in bodily accomplishments, in clothes, equipage or fortune. *Secondly*, it is evident pride would be perpetual, if it arose imediately from nature; since the object is always the same, and there is no disposition of body peculiar to pride, as there is to thirst and hunger. *Thirdly,* humility is in the very same situation with pride; and therefore, either must, upon this supposition, be perpetual likewise, or must destroy the contrary passion from the very first moment; so that none of them could ever make its appearance. Upon the whole, we may rest satisfied with the foregoing conclusion, that pride must have a cause, as well as an object, and that the one has no influence without the other.

The difficulty, then, is only to discover this cause, and find what it is that gives the first motion to pride, and sets those organs in action, which are naturally fitted to produce that emotion. Upon my consulting experience, in order to resolve this difficulty, I immediately find a hundred different causes, that produce pride; and upon examining these causes, I suppose, what at first I perceive to be probable, that all of them concur in two circumstances; which are, that of themselves they produce an impression, allied to the passion, and are placed on a subject, allied to the object of the passion. When I consider after this the nature of *relation*, and its effects both on the passions and ideas, I can no longer doubt, upon these suppositions, that it is the very principle, which gives rise to pride, and bestows motion on those organs, which being naturally disposed to produce that affection, require only a first impulse or beginning to their action. Anything, that gives a pleasant sensation, and is related to self, excites the passion of pride, which is also agreeable, and has self for its object.

What I have said of pride is equally true of humility. The sensation of humility is uneasy, as that of pride is agreeable; for which reason the separate sensation, arising from the causes, must be reversed, while the relation to self continues the same. Though pride and humility are directly contrary in their effects, and in their sensations, they have notwithstanding the same object; so that it is requisite only to change the relation of impressions, without making any change upon that of ideas. Accordingly we find, that a beautiful house, belonging to ourselves, produces pride; and that the same house, still belonging to ourselves, produces humility, when by any accident its beauty is changed into deformity, and thereby the sensation of pleasure, which corresponded to pride, is transformed into pain, which is related to humility.

The double relation between the ideas and impressions subsists in both cases, and produces an easy transition from the one emotion to the other.

In a word, nature has bestowed a kind of attraction on certain impressions and ideas, by which one of them, upon its appearance, naturally introduces its correlative. If these two attractions or associations of impressions and ideas concur on the same object, they mutually assist each other, and the transition of the affections and of the imagination is made with the greatest ease and facility. When an idea produces an impression, related to an impression, which is connected with an idea, related to the first idea, these two impressions must be in a manner inseparable, nor will the one in any case be unattended with the other. It is after this manner, that the particular causes of pride and humility are determined. The quality, which operates on the passion, produces separately an impression resembling it; the subject, to which the quality adheres, is related to self, the object of the passion; no wonder the whole cause, consisting of a quality and of a subject, does so unavoidably give rise to the passion.

To illustrate this hypothesis, we may compare it to that, by which I have already explained the belief attending the judgments, which we form from causation. I have observed, that in all judgments of this kind, there is always a present impression, and a related idea; and that the present impression gives a vivacity to the fancy, and the relation conveys this vivacity, by an easy transition, to the related idea. Without the present impression, the attention is not fixed, nor the spirits excited. Without the relation, this attention rests on its first object, and has no farther consequence. There is evidently a great analogy betwixt that hypothesis, and our present one of an impression and idea, that transfuse themselves into another impression and idea by means of their double relation; which analogy must be allowed to be no despicable proof of both hypotheses.

SECTION VI *Limitations of this system*

But before we proceed farther in this subject, and examine particularly all the causes of pride and humility, it will be proper to make some limitations to the general system, *that all agreeable objects, related to ourselves, by an association of ideas and of impression, produce pride, and disagreeable ones, humility;* and these limitations are derived from the very nature of the subject.

I. Suppose an agreeable object to acquire a relation to self, the first passion, that appears on this occasion, is joy; and this passion discovers itself upon a slighter relation than pride and vainglory. We may feel joy upon being present at a feast, where our senses are regaled with delicacies of every kind; but it is only the master of the feast, who, beside the same joy, has the additional passion of self-applause and vanity. It is true, men sometimes boast of a great entertainment, at which they have only been present; and by so small a relation convert their pleasure into pride; but however, this must in general be owned, that joy arises from a more inconsiderable relation than vanity, and that many things, which are too foreign to produce pride, are yet able to give us a delight and pleasure. The reason of the difference may be explained thus. A relation is requisite to joy, in order to approach the object to us, and make it give us any satisfaction. But beside this, which is common to both passions, it is requisite to pride, in order to produce a transition from one passion to another, and convert the satisfaction into vanity. As it has a double task to perform, it must be endowed with double force and energy. To which we may add, that where agreeable objects bear not a very close relation to ourselves, they commonly do to some other person; and this latter relation not only excels, but even diminishes, and sometimes destroys the former, as we shall see afterwards.*

Here then is the first limitation, we must make to our general position, *that everything related to us, which produces pleasure or pain, produces likewise pride or humility.* There is not only a relation required, but a close one, and a closer than is required to joy.

II. The second limitation is, that the agreeable or disagreeable object be not only closely related, but also peculiar to ourselves, or at least common to us with a few persons. It is a quality observable in human nature, and which we shall endeavour to explain afterwards, that everything, which is often presented, and to which we have been long accus-

* Part II. sect. 4.

tomed loses its value in our eyes, and is in a little time despised and neglected. We likewise judge of objects more from comparison than from their real and intrinsic merit; and where we cannot by some contrast enhance their value, we are apt to overlook even what is essentially good in them. These qualities of the mind have an effect upon joy as well as pride; and it is remarkable, that goods, which are common to all mankind, and have become familiar to us by custom, give us little satisfaction; though perhaps of a more excellent kind, than those on which, for their singularity, we set a much higher value. But though this circumstance operates on both these passions, it has a much greater influence on vanity. We are rejoiced for many goods, which, on account of their frequency, give us no pride. Health, when it returns after a long absence, affords us a very sensible satisfaction; but is seldom regarded as a subject of vanity, because it is shared with such vast numbers.

The reason, why pride is so much more delicate in this particular than joy, I take to be, as follows. In order to excite pride, there are always two objects we must contemplate, *viz.* the *cause* or that object which produces pleasure; and self, which is the real object of the passion. But joy has only one object necessary to its production, *viz.* that which gives pleasure; and though it be requisite, that this bear some relation to self, yet that is only requisite in order to render it agreeable; nor is self, properly speaking, the object of this passion. Since, therefore, pride has in a manner two objects, to which it directs our view; it follows, that where neither of them have any singularity, the passion must be more weakened upon that account, than a passion, which has only one object. Upon comparing ourselves with others, as we are every moment apt to do, we find we are not in the least distinguished; and upon comparing the object we possess, we discover still the same unlucky circumstance. By two comparisons so disadvantageous the passion must be entirely destroyed.

III. The third limitation is, that the pleasant or painful object be very discernible and obvious, and that not only to ourselves, but to others also. This circumstance, like the two foregoing, has an effect upon joy, as well as pride. We fancy ourselves more happy, as well as more virtuous or beautiful, when we appear so to others; but are still more ostentatious of our virtues than of our pleasures. This proceeds from causes, which I shall endeavour to explain afterwards.

IV. The fourth limitation is derived from the inconstancy of the cause of these passions, and from the short duration of its connection with ourselves. What is casual and inconstant gives but little joy, and less pride. We are not much satisfied with the thing itself; and are still less apt to feel any new degrees of self-satisfaction upon its account. We foresee and anticipate its change by the imagination; which makes us little satisfied with the thing; we compare it to ourselves, whose existence is more durable; by which means its inconstancy appears still greater. It seems ridiculous to infer an excellency in ourselves from an object, which is of so much shorter duration, and attends us during so small a part of our existence. It will be easy to comprehend the reason, why this cause operates not with the same force in joy as in pride; since the idea of self is not so essential to the former passion as to the latter.

V. I may add as a fifth limitation, or rather enlargement of this system, that *general rules* have a great influence upon pride and humility, as well as on all the other passions. Hence we form a notion of different ranks of men, suitable to the power or riches they are possessed of; and this notion we change not upon account of any peculiarities of the health or temper of the persons, which may deprive them of all enjoyment in their possessions. This may be accounted for from the same principles, that explained the influence of general rules on the understanding. Custom readily carries us beyond the just bounds in our passions, as well as in our reasonings.

It may not be amiss to observe on this occasion, that the influence of general rules and maxims on the passions very much contributes to facilitate the effects of all the principles, which we shall explain in the progress of this treatise. For it is evident, that if a person full-grown, and of the same nature with ourselves, were on a sudden transported into our world, he would be very much embarrassed with every object, and would not readily find what degree of love or hatred, pride or humility, or any other passion he ought to attribute to it. The passions are often varied by very inconsiderable principles; and these do not always play with a perfect regularity, especially on the first trial. But as custom and practice have brought to light all these principles, and have settled the just value of everything; this must certainly contribute to the easy production of the passions, and guide us, by means of general established maxims, in the proportions we ought to observe in preferring one object to another. This remark may, perhaps, serve to obviate difficulties, that may arise concerning some causes, which I shall hereafter ascribe to particular passions, and which may be esteemed too refined to operate so universally and certainly, as they are found to do.

I shall close this subject with a reflection derived from these five limitations. This reflection is, that the persons, who are proudest, and who in the eye of the world have most reason for their pride, are not always the happiest; nor the most humble always the most miserable, as may at first sight be imagined from this system. An evil may be real, though its cause has no relation to us; it may be real, without being peculiar; it may be real, without showing itself to others; it may be real, without being constant; and it may be real, without falling under the general rules. Such evils as these will not fail to render us miserable, though they have little tendency to diminish pride; and perhaps the most real and the most solid evils of life will be found of this nature.

Section VII *Of vice and virtue*

Taking these limitations along with us, let us proceed to examine the causes of pride and humility; and see, whether in every case we can discover the double relations, by which they operate on the passions. If we find that all these causes are related to self, and produce a pleasure or uneasiness separate from the passion, there will remain no farther scruple with regard to the present system. We shall principally endeavour to prove the latter point; the former being in a manner self-evident.

To begin with *vice* and *virtue*, which are the most obvious causes of these passions; it would be entirely foreign to my present purpose to enter upon the controversy, which of late years has so much excited the curiosity of the public, *whether these moral distinctions be founded on natural and original principles, or arise from interest and education.* The examination of this I reserve for the following book; and in the meantime shall endeavour to show, that my system maintains its ground upon either of these hypotheses; which will be a strong proof of its solidity.

For granting that morality had no foundation in nature, it must still be allowed, that vice and virtue, either from self-interest or the prejudices of education, produce in us a real pain and pleasure; and this we may observe to be strenuously asserted by the defenders of that hypothesis. Every passion, habit, or turn of character (say they) which has a tendency to our advantage or prejudice, gives a delight or uneasiness; and it is from thence the approbation or disapprobation arises. We easily gain from the liberality of others, but are always in danger of losing by their avarice; courage defends us, but cowardice lays us open to every attack; justice is the support of society, but injustice, unless checked, would quickly prove its ruin; humility exalts; but pride mortifies us. For these reasons the former qualities are esteemed virtues, and the latter regarded as vices. Now since it is granted there is a delight or uneasiness still attending merit or demerit of every kind, this is all that is requisite for my purpose.

But I go farther, and observe, that this moral hypothesis and my present system not only agree together, but also that, allowing the former to be just, it is an absolute and invincible proof of the latter. For if all morality be founded on the pain or pleasure, which arises from the prospect of any loss or advantage, that may result from our own characters, or from those of others, all the effects of morality must be derived from the same pain or pleasure, and among the rest, the passions of pride and humility. The very essence of virtue, according to this hypothesis, is to produce pleasure, and that of vice to give pain. The virtue and vice must be part of our character in order to excite pride or humility. What farther proof can we desire for the double relation of impressions and ideas?

The same unquestionable argument may be derived from the opinion of those, who maintain that morality is something real, essential, and founded on nature. The most probable hyopthesis, which has been advanced to explain the distinction betwixt vice and virtue, and the origin of moral rights and obligations, is, that from a primary constitution of nature certain characters and passions, by the very view and contemplation, produce a pain, and others in like manner excite a pleasure. The uneasiness and satisfaction are not only inseparable from vice and virtue, but constitute their very nature and essence. To approve of a character is to feel an original delight upon its appearance. To disapprove of it is to be sensible of an uneasiness. The pain and pleasure, therefore, being the primary causes of vice and virtue, must also be the causes of all their effects, and consequently of pride and humility, which are the unavoidable attendants of that distinction.

But supposing this hypothesis of moral philosophy should be allowed to be false, it is still evident, that pain and pleasure, if not the causes of vice and virtue, are at least inseparable from them. A generous and noble character affords a satisfaction even in the survey; and when presented to us, though only in a poem or fable, never fails to charm and delight us. On the other hand cruelty and treachery displease from their very nature; nor is it possible ever to reconcile us to these qualities, either in ourselves or others. Thus one hypothesis of morality is an undeniable proof of the foregoing system, and the other at worst agrees with it.

But pride and humility arise not from these qualities alone of the mind, which, according to the vulgar systems of ethics, have been comprehended as parts of moral duty, but from any other that has a connection with pleasure and uneasiness. Nothing flatters our vanity more than the talent of pleasing by our wit, good humour, or any other accomplishment; and nothing gives us a more sensible mortification than a disappointment in any attempt of that nature. No one has ever been able to tell what *wit* is, and to show why such a system of thought must be received under that denomination, and such another rejected. It is only by taste we can decide concerning it, nor are we possessed of any other standard, upon which we can form a judgment of this kind. Now what is this *taste*, from which true and false wit in a manner receive their being, and without which no thought can have a title to either of these denominations? It is plainly nothing but a sensation of pleasure from true wit, and of uneasiness from false, without our being able to tell the reasons of that pleasure or uneasiness. The power of bestowing these opposite sensations is, therefore, the very essence of true and false wit; and consequently the cause of that pride or humility, which arises from them.

There may, perhaps, be some, who being accustomed to the style of the schools and pulpit, and having never considered human nature in any other light, than that in which *they* place it, may here be surprised to hear me talk of virtue as exciting pride, which they look upon as a vice; and of vice as producing humility, which they have been taught to consider as a virtue. But not to dispute about words, I observe, that by *pride* I understand that agreeable impression, which arises in the mind, when the view either of our virtue, beauty, riches or power makes us satisfied with ourselves; and that by *humility* I mean the opposite impression. It is evident the former impression is not always vicious, nor the latter virtuous. The most rigid morality allows us to receive a pleasure from reflecting on a generous action; and it is by none esteemed a virtue to feel any fruitless remorses upon the thoughts of past villainy and baseness. Let us, therefore, examine these impressions, considered in themselves; and enquire into their causes, whether placed on the mind or body, without troubling ourselves at present with that merit or blame, which may attend them.

Section VIII *Of beauty and deformity*

Whether we consider the body as a part of ourselves, or assent to those philosophers, who regard it as something external, it must still be allowed to be near enough connected with us to form one of these double relations, which I have asserted to be necessary to the causes of pride and humility. Wherever, therefore, we can find the other relation of impressions to join to this of ideas, we may expect with assurance either of these passions, according as the impression is pleasant or uneasy. But *beauty* of all kinds gives us a peculiar delight and satisfaction; as *deformity* produces pain, upon whatever subject it may be placed, and whether surveyed in an animate or inanimate object. If the beauty or deformity, therefore, be placed upon our own bodies, this pleasure or uneasiness must be converted into pride or humility, as having in this case all the circumstances requisite to produce a perfect transition of impressions and ideas. These opposite sensations are related to the opposite passions. The beauty or deformity is closely related to self, the object of both these passions. No wonder, then, our own beauty becomes an object of pride, and deformity of humility.

But this effect of personal and bodily qualities is not only a proof of the present system, by showing that the passions arise not in this case without all the circumstances I have required, but may be employed as a stronger and more convincing argument. If we consider all the hypotheses, which have been formed either by philosophy or common reason, to explain the difference betwixt beauty and deformity, we shall find that all of them resolve into this, that beauty is such an order and construction of parts, as either by the *primary constitution* of our nature, by *custom*, or by *caprice*, is fitted to give a pleasure and satisfaction to the soul. This is the distinguishing character of beauty, and forms all the difference betwixt it and deformity, whose natural tendency is to produce uneasiness. Pleasure and pain, therefore, are not only necessary attendants of beauty and deformity, but constitute their very essence. And indeed, if we consider, that a great part of the beauty, which we admire either in animals or in other objects, is derived from the idea of convenience and utility, we shall make no scruple to assent to this opinion. That shape, which produces strength, is beautiful in one animal; and that which is a sign of agility in another. The order and convenience of a palace are no less essential to its beauty, than its mere figure and appearance. In like manner the rules of architecture require, that the top of a pillar should be more slender than its base, and that because such a figure conveys to us the idea of security, which is pleasant; whereas the contrary form gives us the apprehension of danger, which is uneasy. From innumerable instances of this kind, as well as from considering that beauty like wit, cannot be defined, but is discerned only by a taste or sensation, we may conclude, that beauty is nothing but a form, which produces pleasure, as deformity is a structure of parts, which conveys pain; and since the power of producing pain and pleasure make in this manner the essence of beauty and deformity, all the effects of these qualities must be derived from the sensation; and among the rest pride and humility, which of all their effects are the most common and remarkable.[6]

This argument I esteem just and decisive; but in order to give greater authority to the present reasoning, let us suppose it false for a moment, and see what will follow. It is certain, then, that if the power of producing pleasure and pain forms not the essence of beauty and deformity, the sensations are at least inseparable from the qualities, and it is even difficult to consider them apart. Now there is nothing common to natural and moral beauty, (both of which are the causes of pride) but this power of producing pleasure; and as a common effect supposes always a common cause, it is plain the pleasure must in both cases be the real and influencing cause of the passion. Again, there is nothing originally different betwixt the beauty of our bodies and the beauty of external and foreign objects, but that the one has a near relation to ourselves, which is wanting in the other. This original difference, therefore, must be the cause of all their other differences, and among the rest, of their different influence upon the passion of pride, which is excited by the beauty of our person, but is not affected in the least by that of foreign and external objects. Placing, then, these two conclusions together, we find they compose the preceding system betwixt them, *viz.* that pleasure, as a related or resembling impression, when placed on a related object, by a natural transition, produces pride; and its contrary, humility. This system, then, seem already sufficiently confirmed by experience; though we have not yet exhausted all our arguments.

It is not the beauty of the body alone that produces pride, but also its strength and force. Strength is a kind of power; and therefore the desire to excel in strength is to be considered as an inferior species of *ambition*. For this reason the present phenomenon will be sufficiently accounted for, in explaining that passion.

Concerning all other bodily accomplishments we may observe in general, that whatever in ourselves is either useful, beautiful, or surprising, is an object of pride; and its contrary, of humility. Now it is obvious, that every thing useful, beautiful or surprising, agrees in producing a separate pleasure, and agrees in nothing else. The pleasure, therefore, with the relation to self must be the cause of the passion.

Though it should be questioned, whether beauty be not something real, and different from the power of producing pleasure, it can never be disputed, that as surprise is nothing but a pleasure arising from novelty, it is not, properly speaking, a quality in any object, but merely a passion or impression in the soul. It must, therefore, be from that impression, that pride by a natural transition arises. And it arises so naturally, that there is nothing *in us or belonging to us*, which produces surprise, that does not at the same time excite that other passion. Thus we are vain of the surprising adventures we have met with, the escapes we have made, and dangers we have been exposed to. Hence the origin of vulgar lying; where men without any interest, and merely out of vanity, heap up a number of extraordinary events, which are either the fictions of their brain, or if true, have at least no connection with themselves. Their fruitful invention supplies them with a variety of adventures; and where that talent is wanting, they appropriate such as belong to others, in order to satisfy their vanity.

In this phenomenon are contained two curious experiments, which if we compare them together, according to the known rules, by which we judge of cause and effect in anatomy, natural philosophy, and other sciences, will be an undeniable argument for that influence of the double relations above-mentioned. By one of these experiments we find, that an object produces pride merely by the interposition of pleasure; and that because the quality, by which it produces pride, is in reality nothing but the power of producing pleasure. By the other experiment we find, that the pleasure produces the pride by a transition along related ideas; because when we cut off that relation the passion is immediately destroyed. A surprising adventure, in which we have been ourselves engaged, is related to us, and by that means produces pride. But the adventures of others, though they may cause pleasure, yet for want of this relation of ideas, never excite that passion. What farther proof can be desired for the present system?

There is only one objection to this system with regard to our body; which is, that though nothing be more agreeable than health, and more painful than sickness, yet commonly men are neither proud of the one, nor fortified with the other. This will easily be accounted for, if we consider the *second* and *fourth* limitations, proposed to our general system. It was observed, that no object ever produces pride or humility, if it has not something *peculiar* to ourself; as also, that every cause of that passion must be in some measure *constant*, and hold some proportion to the duration of ourself, which is its object. Now as health and sickness vary incessantly to all men, and there is none, who is *solely* or *certainly* fixed in either, these accidental blessings and calamities are in a manner separated from us, and are never considered as connected with our being and existence. And that this account is just appears hence, that wherever a malady of any kind is so rooted in our constitution, that we no longer entertain any hopes of recovery, from that moment it becomes an object of humility; as is evident in old men, whom nothing mortifies more than the consideration of their age and infirmities. They endeavour, as long as possible, to conceal their blindness and deafness, their rheums and gouts; nor do they ever confess them without reluctance and uneasiness. And though young men are not ashamed of every headache or cold they fall into, yet no topic is so proper to mortify human pride, and make us entertain a mean opinion of our nature, than this, that we are every moment of our lives subject to such infirmities. This sufficiently proves that bodily pain and sickness are in themselves proper causes of humility; though the custom of estimating everything by comparison more than by its intrinsic worth and value, makes us overlook these calamities, which we find to be incident to everyone, and causes us to form an idea of our merit and character independent of them.

We are ashamed of such maladies as affect others, and are either dangerous or disagreeable to them. Of the epilepsy, because it gives a horror to every one present; of the itch, because it is infectious; of the king's-evil, because it commonly goes to posterity. Men always consider the sentiments of others in their judgment of themselves. This has evidently appeared in some of the foregoing reasonings; and will appear still more evidently, and be more fully explained afterwards.

SECTION IX *Of external advantages and disadvantages*

But though pride and humility have the qualities of our mind and body, that is *self*, for their natural and more immediate causes, we find by experience, that there are many other objects, which produce these affections, and that the primary one is, in some measure, obscured and lost by the multiplicity of foreign and extrinsic. We found a vanity upon houses, gardens, equipages, as well as upon personal merit and accomplishments; and though these external advantages be in themselves widely distant from thought or a person, yet they considerably influence even a passion, which is directed to that as its ultimate object. This happens when external objects acquire any particular relation to ourselves, and are associated or connected with us. A beautiful fish in the ocean, an animal in a desert, and indeed anything that neither belongs, nor is related to us, has no manner or influence on our vanity, whatever extraordinary qualities it may be endowed with, and whatever degree of surprise and admiration it may naturally occasion. It must be some way associated with us in order to touch our pride. Its idea must hang in a manner, upon that of ourselves; and the transition from the one to the other must be easy and natural.

But here it is remarkable, that though the relation of *resemblance* operates upon the mind in the same manner as contiguity and causation, in conveying us from one idea to another, yet it is seldom a foundation either of pride or of humility. If we resemble a person in any of the valuable parts of his character, we must, in some degree, possess the quality, in which we resemble him; and this quality we always choose to survey directly in ourselves rather than by reflection in another person, when we would found upon it any degree of vanity. So that though a likeness may occasionally produce that passion by suggesting a more advantageous idea of ourselves, it is there the view fixes at last, and the passion finds its ultimate and final cause.

There are instances, indeed, wherein men show a vanity in resembling a great man in his countenance, shape, air, or other minute circumstances, that contribute not in any degree to his reputation; but it must be confessed, that this extends not very far, nor is of any considerable moment in these affections. For this I assign the following reason. We can never have a vanity of resembling in trifles any person, unless he be possessed of very shining qualities, which give us a respect and veneration for him. These qualities, then, are, properly speaking, the causes of our vanity, by means of their relation to ourselves. Now after what manner are they related to ourselves? They are parts of the person we value, and consequently connected with these trifles; which are also supposed to be parts of him. These trifles are connected with the resembling qualities in us; and these qualities in us, being parts, are connected with the whole; and by that means form a chain of several links betwixt ourselves and the shining qualities of the person we resemble. But besides that this multitude of relations must weaken the connection; it is evident the mind, in passing from the shining qualities to the trivial ones, must by that contrast the better perceive the minuteness of the latter, and be in some measure ashamed of the comparison and resemblance.

The relation, therefore, of contiguity, or that of causation, betwixt the cause and object of pride and humility, is alone requisite to give rise to these passions; and these relations are nothing else but qualities, by which the imagination is conveyed from one idea to another. Now let us consider what effect these can possibly have upon the mind, and by what means they become so requisite to the production of the passions. It is evident, that the association of ideas operates in so silent and imperceptible a manner, that we are scarce sensible of it, and discover it more by its effects than by any immediate feeling or perception. It produces no emotion, and gives rise to no new impression of any kind, but only modifies those ideas, of which the mind was formerly possessed, and which it could recall upon occasion. From this reasoning, as well as from undoubted experience, we may conclude, that an association of ideas, however necessary, is not alone sufficient to give rise to any passion.

It is evident, then, that when the mind feels the passion either of pride or humility upon the appearance of a related object, there is, beside the relation or transition of thought, an emotion or original impression produced by some other principle. The question is, whether the emotion first produced be the passion itself, or some other impression related to it. This question we cannot be long in deciding. For besides all the other arguments with which this subject abounds, it must evidently appear, that the relation of ideas, which experience shows to be so requisite a circumstance to the production of the passion, would be entirely superfluous, were it not to second a relation of affections, and facilitate the transition from one impression to another. If nature produced immediately the passion of pride or humility, it wou'd be completed in itself, and would require no farther addition or increase from any other affection. But supposing the first emotion to be only related to pride or humility, it is easily conceived to what purpose the relation of objects may serve, and how the two different associations, of impressions and ideas, by uniting their forces, may assist each other's operation. This is not only easily conceived, but I will venture to affirm it is the only manner, in which we can conceive this subject. An easy transition of ideas, which, of itself, causes no emotion, can never be necessary, or even useful to the passions, but by forwarding the transition betwixt some related impressions. Not to mention, that the same object causes a greater or smaller degree of pride, not only in proportion to the increase or decrease of its qualities, but also to the distance or nearness of the relation; which is a clear argument for the transition of affections along the relation of ideas; since every change in the relation produces a proportionable change in the passion. Thus one part of the preceding system, concerning the relations of ideas is a sufficient proof of the other, concerning that of impressions; and is itself so evidently founded on experience, that it would be lost time to endeavour farther to prove it.

This will appear still more evidently in particular instances. Men are vain of the beauty of their country, of their county, of their parish. Here the idea of beauty plainly produces a pleasure. This pleasure is related to pride. The object or cause of this pleasure is, by the supposition, related to self, or the object of pride. By this double relation of impressions and ideas, a transition is made from the one impression to the other.

Men are also vain of the temperature of the climate, in which they were born; of the fertility of their native soil; of the goodness of the wines, fruits or victuals, produced by it; of the softness or force of their language; with other particulars of that kind. These objects have plainly a reference to the pleasures of the senses, and are originally considered as agreeable to the feeling, taste or hearing. How is it possible they could ever become objects of pride, except by means of that transition above-explained?

There are some, that discover a vanity of an opposite kind, and affect to depreciate their own country, in comparison of those, to which they have travelled. These persons find, when they are at home, and surrounded with their countrymen, that the strong relation betwixt them and their own nation is shared with so many, that it is in a manner lost to them; whereas their distant relation to a foreign country, which is formed by their having seen it and lived in it, is augmented by their considering how few there are who have done the same. For this reason they always admire the beauty, utility and rarity of what is abroad, above what is at home.

Since we can be vain of a country, climate or any inanimate object, which bears a relation to us, it is no wonder we are vain of the qualities of those, who are connected with us by blood or friendship. Accordingly we find, that the very same qualities, which in ourselves produce pride, produce also in a lesser degree the same affection, when discovered in persons related to us. The beauty, address, merit, credit and honours of their kindred are carefully displayed by the proud, as some of their most considerable sources of their vanity.

As we are proud of riches in ourselves, so to satisfy our vanity we desire that every one, who has any connection with us, should likewise be possessed of them, and are ashamed of anyone, that is mean or poor, among our friends and relations. For this reason we remove the poor as far from us as possible; and as we cannot prevent poverty in some distant collaterals, and our forefathers are taken to be our nearest relations; upon this account everyone affects to be of a good family, and to be descended from a long succession of rich and honourable ancestors.

I have frequently observed, that those, who boast of the antiquity of their families, are glad when they can join this circumstance, that their ancestors for many generations have been uninterrupted proprietors of the same portion of land, and that their family has never changed its possessions, or been transplanted into any other county or province. I have also observed, that it is an additional subject of vanity, when they can boast, that these possessions have been transmitted through a descent composed entirely of males, and that the honours and fortune have never past through any female. Let us endeavour to explain these phenomena by the foregoing system.

It is evident, that when anyone boasts of the antiquity of his family, the subjects of his vanity are not merely the extent of time and number of ancestors, but also their riches and credit, which are supposed to reflect a lustre on himself on account of his relation to them. He first considers these objects; is affected by them in an agreeable manner; and then returning back to himself, through the relation of parent and child, is elevated with the passion of pride, by means of the double relation of impressions and ideas. Since therefore the passion depends on these relations, whatever strengthens any of the relations must also increase the passion, and whatever weakens the relations must diminish the passion. Now it is certain the identity of the possession strengthens the relation of ideas arising from blood and kindred, and conveys the fancy with great facility from one generation to another, from the remotest ancestors to their posterity, who are both their heirs and their descendants. By this facility the impression is transmitted more entire, and excites a greater degree of pride and vanity.

The case is the same with the transmission of the honours and fortune through a succession of males without their passing through any female. It is a quality of human nature, which we shall consider afterwards,* that the imagination naturally turns to whatever is important and considerable; and where two objects are presented to it, a small and a great one, usually leaves the former, and dwells entirely upon the latter. As in the society of marriage, the male sex has the advantage above the female, the husband first engages our attention; and whether we consider him directly, or reach him by passing through related objects, the thought both rests upon him with greater satisfaction, and arrives at him with greater facility than his consort. It is easy to see, that this property must strengthen the child's relation to the father, and weaken that to the mother. For as all relations are nothing but a propensity to pass from one idea to another, whatever

* Part II. sect. 2.

strengthens the propensity strengthens the relation; and as
we have a stronger propensity to pass from the idea of the
children to that of the father, than from the same idea to that
of the mother, we ought to regard the former relation as the
closer and more considerable. This is the reason why children
commonly bear their father's name, and are esteemed to be
of nobler or baser birth, according to *his* family. And though
the mother should be possessed of a superior spirit and genius
to the father, as often happens, the *general rule* prevails, notwithstanding the exception, according to the doctrine above-
explained. Nay even when a superiority of any kind is so
great, or when any other reasons have such an effect, as to
make the children rather represent the mother's family than
the father's, the general rule still retains such an efficacy that
it weakens the relation, and makes a kind of break in the line
of ancestors. The imagination runs not along them with
facility, nor is able to transfer the honour and credit of the
ancestors to their posterity of the same name and family
so readily, as when the transition is conformable to the
general rules, and passes from father to son, or from brother
to brother.

SECTION X *Of property and riches*

But the relation, which is esteemed the closest, and which of
all others produces most commonly the passion of pride, is
that of *property*. This relation it will be impossible for me
fully to explain before I come to treat of justice and the other
moral virtues. It is sufficient to observe on this occasion,
that property may be defined, *such a relation betwixt a person
and an object as permits him, but forbids any other, the free
use and possession of it, without violating the laws of justice
and moral equity.* If justice, therefore, be a virtue, which has
a natural and original influence on the human mind, property
may be looked upon as a particular species of *causation*;
whether we consider the liberty it gives the proprietor to
operate as he please upon the object, or the advantages, which
he reaps from it. It is the same case, if justice, according to
the system of certain philosophers, should be esteemed an
artificial and not a natural virtue. For then honour, and custom, and civil laws supply the place of natural conscience, and

produce, in some degree, the same effects. This in the meantime is certain, that the mention of the property naturally carries our thought to the proprietor, and of the proprietor to the property; which being a proof of a perfect relation of ideas is all that is requisite to our present purpose. A relation of ideas, joined to that of impressions, always produces a transition of affections; and therefore, whenever any pleasure or pain arises from an object, connected with us by property, we may be certain, that either pride or humility must arise from this conjunction of relations; if the foregoing system be solid and satisfactory. And whether it be so or not, we may soon satisfy ourselves by the most cursory view of human life.

Everything belonging to a vain man is the best that is anywhere to be found. His houses, equipage, furniture, clothes, horses, hounds, excel all others in his conceit; and it is easy to observe, that from the least advantage in any of these, he draws a new subject of pride and vanity. His wine, if you'll believe him, has a finer flavour than any other; his cookery is more exquisite; his table more orderly; his servants more expert; the air, in which he lives, more healthful; the soil he cultivates more fertile; his fruits ripen earlier and to great perfection; such a thing is remarkable for its novelty; such another for its antiquity. This is the workmanship of a famous artist, that belonged once to such a prince or great man; all objects, in a word, that are useful beautiful or surprising, or are related to such, may, by means of property, give rise to this passion. These agree in giving pleasure, and agree in nothing else. This alone is common of them; and therefore must be the quality that produces the passion, which is their common effect. As every new instance is a new argument, and as the instances are here without number, I may venture to affirm, that scarce any system was ever so fully proved by experience, as that which I have here advanced.

If the property of anything, that gives pleasure either by its utility, beauty or novelty, produces also pride by a double relation of impressions and ideas; we need not be surprised, that the power of acquiring this property, shou'd have the same effect. Now riches are to be considered as the power of acquiring the property of what pleases; and it is only in this view they have any influence on the passions. Paper will, on many occasions, be considered as riches, and that because it may convey the power of acquiring money. And money is not riches, as it is a metal endowed with certain qualities of solidity, weight and fusibility; but only as it has a relation to the pleasures and conveniences of life. Taking then this for granted, which is in itself so evident, we may draw from it one of the strongest arguments I have yet employed to prove the influence of the double relations on pride and humility.

It has been observed in treating of the understanding, that the distinction, which we sometimes make betwixt a *power* and the *exercise* of it, is entirely frivolous, and that neither man nor any other being ought ever to be thought possessed of any ability, unless it be exerted and put in action. But though this be strictly true in a just and *philosophical* way of thinking, it is certain it is not *the philosophy* of our passions; but that many things operate upon them by means of the idea and supposition of power, independent of its actual exercise. We are pleased when we acquire an ability of procuring pleasure, and are displeased when another acquires a power of giving pain. This is evident from experience; but in order to give a just explication of the matter, and account for this satisfaction and uneasiness, we must weigh the following reflections.

It is evident the error of distinguishing power from its exercise proceeds not entirely from the scholastic doctrine of *free-will*, which, indeed, enters very little into common life, and has but small influence on our vulgar and popular ways of thinking. According to that doctrine, motives deprive us not of free-will, nor take away our power of performing or forbearing any action. But according to common notions a man has no power, where very considerable motives lie betwixt him and the satisfaction of his desires, and determine him to forbear what he wishes to perform. I do not think I have fallen into my enemies power, when I see him pass me in the streets with a sword by his side, while I am unprovided of any weapon. I know that the fear of the civil magistrate is as strong a restraint as any of iron, and that I am in as perfect safety as if he were chained or imprisoned. But when a person acquires such an authority over me, that not only there is no external obstacle to his actions; but also that he may punish or reward me as he pleases, without any dread of punishment in his turn, I then attribute a full power to him, and consider myself as his subject or vassal.

Now if we compare these two cases, that of a person, who has very strong motives of interest or safety to forbear any action, and that of another, who lies under no such obligation, we shall find, according to the philosophy explained in the foregoing book, that the only *known* difference betwixt them lies in this, that in the former case we conclude from *past experience*, that the person never will perform that action, and in the latter, that he possibly or probably will perform it. Nothing is more fluctuating and inconstant on many occasions, than the will of man; nor it there anything but strong motives, which can give us an absolute certainty in pronouncing concerning any of his future actions. When we see a person free from these motives, we suppose a possibility either of his acting or forbearing; and though in general we may conclude him to be determined by motives and causes, yet this removes not the uncertainty of our judgment concerning these causes, nor the influence of that uncertainty on the passions. Since therefore we ascribe a power of performing an action to everyone, who has no very powerful motive to forbear it, and refuse it to such as have; it may justly be concluded, that *power* has always a reference to its *exercise*, either actual or probable, and that we consider a person as endowed with any ability when we find from past experience, that it is probable, or at least possible, he may exert it. And indeed, as our passions always regard the real existence of objects, and we always judge of this reality from past instances; nothing can be more likely of itself, without any farther reasoning, than that power consists in the possibility or probability of any action, as discovered by experience and the practice of the world.

Now it is evident, that wherever a person is in such a situation with regard to me, that there is no very powerful motive to deter him from injuring me, and consequently it is *uncertain* whether he will injure me or not, I must be uneasy in such a situation, and cannot consider the possibility or probability of that injury without a sensible concern. The passions are not only affected by such events as are certain and infallible, but also in an inferior degree by such as are possible and contingent. And though perhaps I never really feel any harm, and discover by the event, that, philosophically speaking, the person never had any power of harming me; since he did not exert any; this prevents not my uneasiness from the preceding uncertainty. The agreeable passions may here operate as well as the uneasy, and convey a pleasure when I perceive a good to become either possible or probable by the possibility or probability of another's bestowing it on me, upon the removal of any strong motives, which might formerly have hindered him.

But we may farther observe, that this satisfaction increases, when any good approaches in such a manner that it is in one's *own* power to take or leave it, and there neither is any physical impediment, nor any very strong motive to hinder our enjoyment. As all men desire pleasure, nothing can be more probable, than its existence when there is no external obstacle to the producing it, and men perceive no danger in following their inclinations. In that case their imagination easily anticipates the satisfaction, and conveys the same joy, as if they were persuaded of its real and actual existence.

But this accounts not sufficiently for the satisfaction, which attends riches. A miser receives delight from his money; that is, from the *power* it affords him of precuring all the pleasures and conveniences of life, though he knows he has enjoyed his riches for forty years without ever employing them; and consequently cannot conclude by any species of reasoning, that the real existence of these pleasures is nearer, than if he were entirely deprived of all his possessions. But though he cannot form any such conclusion in a way of reasoning concerning the nearer approach of the pleasure, it is certain he *imagines* it to approach nearer, whenever all external obstacles are removed, along with the more powerful motives of interest and danger, which oppose it. For farther satisfaction on this head I must refer to my account of the will, where I shall explain that false sensation of liberty, which makes us imagine we can perform any thing, that is not very dangerous or destructive.* Whenever any other person is under no strong obligations of interest to forbear any pleasure, we judge from *experience*, that the pleasure will exist, and that he will probably obtain it. But when ourselves are in that situation, we judge from an *illusion of the fancy*, that the pleasure is still closer and more immediate. The will seems to move easily every way, and casts a shadow or image

* Part III. sect. 2.

of itself, even to that side, on which it did not settle. By means of this image the enjoyment seems to approach nearer to us, and gives us the same lively satisfaction, as if it were perfectly certain and unavoidable.

It will now be easy to draw this whole reasoning to a point, and to prove, that when riches produce any pride or vanity in their possessors, as they never fail to do, it is only by means of a double relation of impressions and ideas. The very essence of riches consists in the power of procuring the pleasures and conveniences of life. The very essence of this power consists in the probability of its exercise, and in its causing us to anticipate, by a *true* or *false* reasoning, the real existence of the pleasure. This anticipation of pleasure is, in itself, a very considerable pleasure; and as its cause is some possession or property, which we enjoy, and which is thereby related to us, we here clearly see all the parts of the foregoing system most exactly and distinctly drawn out before us.

For the same reason, that riches cause pleasure and pride, and poverty excites uneasiness and humility, power must produce the former emotions, and slavery the latter. Power or an authority over others makes us capable of satisfying all our desires; as slavery, by subjecting us to the will of others, exposes us to a thousand wants, and mortifications.

It is here worth observing, that the vanity of power, or shame of slavery, are much augmented by the consideration of the persons, over whom we exercise our authority, or who exercise it over us. For supposing it possible to frame statues of such an admirable mechanism, that they could move and act in obedience to the will; it is evident the possession of them would give pleasure and pride, but not to such a degree, as the same authority, when exerted over sensible and rational creatures, whose condition, being compared to our own, makes it seem more agreeable and honourable. Comparison is in every case a sure method of augmenting our esteem of anything. A rich man feels the felicity of his condition better by opposing it to that of a beggar. But there is a peculiar advantage in power, by the contrast, which is, in a manner, presented to us, betwixt ourselves and the person we command. The comparison is obvious and natural; the imagination finds it in the very subject; the passage of the thought to its conception is smooth and easy. And that this circumstance has a considerable effect in augmenting its influence, will appear afterwards in examining the nature of *malice* and *envy*.[7]

SECTION XI *Of the love of fame*

But beside these original causes of pride and humility, there is a secondary one in the opinions of others, which has an equal influence on the affections. Our reputation, our character, our name are considerations of vast weight and importance; and even the other causes of pride; virtue, beauty and riches; have little influence, when not seconded by the opinions and sentiments of others. In order to account for this phenomenon it will be necessary to take some compass, and first explain the nature of *sympathy*.

No quality of human nature is more remarkable, both in itself and in its consequences, than that propensity we have to sympathize with others, and to receive by communication their inclinations and sentiments, however different from, or even contrary to our own. This is not only conspicuous in children, who implicitly embrace every opinion proposed to them; but also in men of the greatest judgment and understanding, who find it very difficult to follow their own reason or inclination, in opposition to that of their friends and daily companions. To this principle we ought to ascribe the great uniformity we may observe in the humours and turn of thinking of those of the same nation; and it is much more probable, that this resemblance arises from sympathy, than from any influence of the soil and climate, which, though they continue invariably the same, are not able to preserve the character of a nation the same for a century together. A good-natur'd man finds himself in an instant of the same humour with his company; and even the proudest and most surly take a tincture from their countrymen and acquaintance. A cheerful countenance infuses a sensible complacency and serenity into my mind; as an angry or sorrowful one throws a sudden damp upon me. Hatred, resentment, esteem, love, courage, mirth and melancholy; all these passions I feel more from communication than from my own natural temper and disposition. So remarkable a phenomenon merits our attention, and must be traced up to its first principles.

When any affection is infused by sympathy, it is at first

known only by its effects, and by those external signs in the countenance and conversation, which convey an idea of it. This idea is presently converted into an impression, and acquires such a degree of force and vivacity, as to become the very passion itself, and produce an equal emotion, as any original affection. However instantaneous this change of the idea into an impression may be, it proceeds from certain views and reflections, which will not escape the strict scrutiny of a philosopher, though they may the person himself, who makes them.

It is evident, that the idea, or rather impression of ourselves is always intimately present with us, and that our consciousness gives us so lively a conception of our own person, that it is not possible to imagine, that anything can in this particular go beyond it. Whatever object, therefore, is related to ourselves must be conceived with a like vivacity of conception, according to the foregoing principles; and though this relation should not be so strong as that of causation, it must still have a considerable influence. Resemblance and contiguity are relations not to be neglected; especially when by an inference from cause and effect, and by the observation of external signs, we are informed of the real existence of the object, which is resembling or contiguous.

Now it is obvious, that nature has preserved a great resemblance among all human creatures, and that we never remark any passion or principle in others, of which, in some degree or other, we may not find a parallel in ourselves. The case is the same with the fabric of the mind, as with that of the body. However the parts may differ in shape or size, their structure and composition are in general the same. There is a very remarkable resemblance, which preserves itself amidst all their variety; and this resemblance must very much contribute to make us enter into the sentiments of others, and embrace them with facility and pleasure. Accordingly we find, that where, beside the general resemblance of our natures, there is any peculiar similarity in our manners, or character, or country, or language, it facilitates the sympathy. The stronger the relation is betwixt ourselves and any object, the more easily does the imagination make the transition, and convey to the related idea the vivacity of conception, with which we always form the idea of our own person.

Nor is resemblance the only relation, which has this effect, but receives new force from other relations, that may accompany it. The sentiments of others have little influence, when far removed from us, and require the relation of contiguity, to make them communicate themselves entirely. The relations of blood, being a species of causation, may sometimes contribute to the same effect; as also acquaintance, which operates in the same manner with education and custom; as we shall see more fully afterwards.* All these relations, when united together, convey the impression or consciousness of our own person to the idea of the sentiments or passions of others, and makes us conceive them in the strongest and most lively manner.

It has been remarked in the beginning of this treatise, that all ideas are borrowed from impressions, and that these two kinds of perceptions differ only in the degrees of force and vivacity, with which they strike upon the soul. The component parts of ideas and impressions are precisely alike. The manner and order of their appearance may be the same. The different degrees of their force and vivacity are, therefore, the only particulars, that distinguish them; and as this difference may be removed, in some measure, by a relation betwixt the impressions and ideas, it is no wonder an idea of a sentiment or passion, may by this means be so enlivened as to become the very sentiment or passion. The lively idea of any object always approaches its impression; and it is certain we may feel sickness and pain from the mere force of imagination, and make a malady real by often thinking of it. But this is most remarkable in the opinions and affections; and it is there principally that a lively idea is converted into an impression. Our affections depend more upon ourselves, and the internal operations of the mind, than any other impressions; for which reason they arise more naturally from the imagination, and from every lively idea we form of them. This is the nature and cause of sympathy; and it is after this manner we enter so deep into the opinions and affections of others, whenever we discover them.

What is principally remarkable in this whole affair is the strong confirmation these phenomena give to the foregoing system concerning the understanding, and consequently to the present one concerning the passions; since these are analogous to each other. It is indeed evident, that when we

* Part II. sect. 4.

sympathize with the passions and sentiments of others, these movements appear at first in *our* mind as mere ideas, and are conceived to belong to another person, as we conceive any other matter of fact. It is also evident, that the ideas of the affections of others are converted into the very impressions they represent, and that the passions arise in conformity to the images we form of them. All this is an object of the plainest experience, and depends not on any hypothesis of philosophy. That science can only be admitted to explain the phenomena; though at the same time it must be confest, they are so clear of themselves, that there is but little occasion to employ it. For besides the relation of cause and effect, by which we are convinced of the reality of the passion, with which we sympathize; besides this, I say, we must be assisted by the relations of resemblance and contiguity, in order to feel the sympathy in its full perfection. And since these relations can entirely convert an idea into an impression, and convey the vivacity of the latter into the former, so perfectly as to lose nothing of it in the transition, we may easily conceive how the relation of cause and effect alone, may serve to strengthen and enliven an idea. In sympathy there is an evident conversion of an idea into an impression. This conversion arises from the relation of objects to ourself. Ourself is always intimately present to us. Let us compare all these circumstances, and we shall find, that sympathy is exactly correspondent to the operations of our understanding; and even contains something more surprising and extraordinary.

It is now time to turn our view from the general consideration of sympathy, to its influence on pride and humility, when these passions arise from praise and blame, from reputation and infamy. We may observe, that no person is ever praised by another for any quality, which would not, if real, produce, of itself, a pride in the person possessed of it. The eulogisms either turn upon his power, or riches, or family, or virtue; all of which are subjects of vanity, that we have already explained and accounted for. It is certain, then, that if a person considered himself in the same light, in which he appears to his admirer, he would first receive a separate pleasure, and afterwards a pride or self-satisfaction, according to the hypothesis above explained. Now nothing is more natural than for us to embrace the opinions of others in this particular; both from *sympathy*, which renders all their sentiments intimately present to us; and from *reasoning,* which makes us regard their judgment, as a kind of argument for what they affirm. These two principles of authority and sympathy influence almost all our opinions; but must have a peculiar influence, when we judge of our own worth and character. Such judgments are always attended with passion;* and nothing tends more to disturb our understanding, and precipitate us into any opinions, however unreasonable, than their connection with passion; which diffuses itself over the imagination, and gives an additional force to every related idea. To which we may add, that being conscious of great partiality in our own favour, we are peculiarly pleased with anything, that confirms the good opinion we have of ourselves, and are easily shocked with whatever opposes it.

All this appears very probable in theory; but in order to bestow a full certainty on this reasoning, we must examine the phenomena of the passions, and see if they agree with it.

Among these phenomena we may esteem it a very favourable one to our present purpose, that though fame in general be agreeable, yet we receive a much greater satisfaction from the approbation of those, whom we ourselves esteem and approve of, than of those, whom we hate and despise. In like manner we are principally mortified with the contempt of persons, upon whose judgment we set some value, and are, in a great measure, indifferent about the opinions of the rest of mankind. But if the mind received from any original instinct a desire of fame, and aversion to infamy, fame and infamy would influence us without distinction; and every opinion, according as it were favourable or unfavourable, would equally excite that desire or aversion. The judgment of a fool is the judgment of another person, as well as that of a wise man, and is only inferior in its influence on our own judgment.

We are not only better pleased with the approbation of a wise man than with that of a fool, but receive an additional satisfaction from the former, when it is obtained after a long and intimate acquaintance. This is accounted for after the same manner.

The praises of others never give us much pleasure, unless they concur with our own opinion, and extol us for those qualities, in which we chiefly excel. A mere soldier little

* Book I. Part III. sect. 10.

values the character of eloquence; a gownman of courage; a bishop of humour; or a merchant of learning. Whatever esteem a man may have for any quality, abstractedly considered; when he is conscious he is not possessed of it; the opinions of the whole world will give him little pleasure in that particular, and that because they never will be able to draw his own opinion after them.

Nothing is more usual than for men of good families, but narrow circumstances, to leave their friends and country, and rather seek their livelihood by mean and mechanical employments among strangers, than among those, who are acquainted with their birth and education. We shall be unknown, say they, where we go. Nobody will suspect from what family we are sprung. We shall be removed from all our friends and acquaintance, and our poverty and meanness will by that means fit more easy upon us. In examining these sentiments, I find they afford many very convincing arguments for my present purpose.

First, we may infer from them, that the uneasiness of being contemned depends on sympathy, and that sympathy depends on the relation of objects to ourselves; since we are most uneasy under the contempt of persons, who are both related to us by blood, and contiguous in place. Hence we seek to diminish this sympathy and uneasiness by separating these relations, and placing ourselves in a contiguity to strangers, and at a distance from relations.

Secondly, we may conclude, that relations are requisite to sympathy, not absolutely considered as relations, but by their influence in converting our ideas of the sentiments of others into the very sentiments, by means of the association betwixt the idea of their persons, and that of our own. For here the relations of kindred and contiguity both subsist; but not being united in the same persons, they contribute in a less degree to the sympathy.

Thirdly, this very circumstance of the diminution of sympathy by the separation of relations is worthy of our attention. Suppose I am placed in a poor condition among strangers, and consequently am but lightly treated; I yet find myself easier in that situation, than when I was every day exposed to the contempt of my kindred and countrymen. Here I feel a double contempt; from my relations, but they are absent; from those about me, but they are strangers.

This double contempt is likewise strengthened by the two relations of kindred and contiguity. But as the persons are not the same, who are connected with me by those two relations, this difference of ideas separates the impressions arising from the contempt, and keeps them from running into each other. The contempt of my neighbours has a certain influence; as has also that of my kindred. But these influences are distinct, and never unite; as when the contempt proceeds from persons who are at once both my neighbours and kindred. This phenomenon is analogous to the system of pride and humility above-explained, which may seem so extraordinary to vulgar apprehensions.

Fourthly, a person in these circumstances naturally conceals his birth from those among whom he lives, and is very uneasy, if anyone suspects him to be of a family, much superior to his present fortune and way of living. Everything in this world is judged of by comparison. What is an immense fortune for a private gentleman is beggary for a prince. A peasant would think himself happy in what cannot afford necessaries for a gentleman. When a man has either been accustomed to a more splendid way of living, or thinks himself entitled to it by his birth and quality, everything below is disagreeable and even shameful; and it is with the greatest industry he conceals his pretensions to a better fortune. Here he himself knows his misfortunes; but as those, with whom he lives, are ignorant of them, he has the disagreeable reflection and comparison suggested only by his own thoughts, and never receives it by a sympathy with others; which must contribute very much to his ease and satisfaction.

If there be any objections to this hypothesis, *that the pleasure, which we receive from praise, arises from a communication of sentiments,* we shall find, upon examination, that these objections, when taken in a proper light, will serve to confirm it. Popular fame may be agreeable even to a man, who despises the vulgar; but it is because their multitude gives them additional weight and authority. Plagiaries are delighted with praises, which they are conscious they do not deserve; but this is a kind of castle-building, where the imagination amuses itself with its own fictions, and strives to render them firm and stable by a sympathy with the sentiments of others. Proud men are most shock'd with contempt, though they do not most readily assent to it; but it is because of the opposition betwixt the passion, which is natural to them, and that received by sympathy. A violent lover in like manner is very much displeas'd when you blame and condemn his love; though it is evident your opposition can have no influence, but by the hold it takes of himself, and by his sympathy with you. If he despises you, or perceives you are in jest, whatever you say has no effect upon him.[8]

SECTION XII *Of the pride and humility of animals*

Thus in whatever light we consider this subject, we may still observe, that the causes of pride and humility correspond exactly to our hypothesis, and that nothing can excite either of these passions, unless it be both related to ourselves, and produces a pleasure or pain independent of the passion. We have not only proved, that a tendency to produce pleasure or pain is common to all the causes of pride or humility, but also that it is the only thing, which is common; and consequently is the quality, by which they operate. We have farther proved, that the most considerable causes of these passions are really nothing but the power of producing either agreeable or uneasy sensations; and therefore that all their effects, and amongst the rest, pride and humility, are derived solely from that origin. Such simple and natural principles, founded on such solid proofs, cannot fail to be received by philosophers, unless opposed by some objections, that have escaped me.

It is usual with anatomists to join their observations and experiments on human bodies to those on beasts, and from the agreement of these experiments to derive an additional argument for any particular hypothesis. It is indeed certain, that where the structure of parts in brutes is the same as in men, and the operation of these parts also the same, the causes of that operation cannot be different, and that whatever we discover to be true of the one species, may be concluded without hesitation to be certain of the other. Thus though the mixture of humours and the composition of minute parts may justly be presumed to be somewhat different in men from what it is in mere animals; and therefore any experiment we make upon the one concerning the effects of medicines will not always apply to the other; yet as the structure of the veins and muscles, the fabric and situation of the heart, of the lungs, the stomach, the liver and other parts, are the same or nearly the same in all animals, the very same hypothesis, which in one species explains muscular motion, the progress of the chyle, the circulation of the blood, must be applicable to every one; and according as it agrees or disagrees with the experiments we may make in any species of creatures, we may draw a proof of its truth or falsehood on the whole. Let us, therefore, apply this method of enquiry, which is found so just and useful in reasonings concerning the body, to our present anatomy of the mind, and see what discoveries we can make by it.

In order to this we must first show the correspondence of *passions* in men and animals, and afterwards compare the *causes*, which produce these passions.

It is plain, that almost in every species of creatures, but especially of the nobler kind, there are many evident marks of pride and humility. The very port and gait of a swan, or turkey, or peacock show the high idea he has entertained of himself, and his contempt of all others. This is the more remarkable, that in the two last species of animals, the pride always attends the beauty, and is discovered in the male only. The vanity and emulation of nightingales in singing have been commonly remarked; as likewise that of horses in swiftness, of hounds in sagacity and smell, of the bull and cock in strength, and of every other animal in his particular excellency. Add to this, that every species of creatures, which approach so often to man, as to familiarize themselves with him, show an evident pride in his approbation, and are pleased with his praises and caresses, independent of every other consideration. Nor are they the caresses of everyone without distinction, which give them this vanity, but those principally of the persons they know and love; in the same manner as that passion is excited in mankind. All these are evident proofs, that pride and humility are not merely human passions, but extend themselves over the whole animal creation.

The *causes* of these passions are likewise much the same in beasts as in us, making a just allowance for our superior knowledge and understanding. Thus animals have little or no sense of virtue or vice; they quickly lose sight of the relations of blood; and are incapable of that of right and property. For which reason the causes of their pride and humility must lie solely in the body, and can never be placed either in the mind or external objects. But so far as regards the body, the same qualities cause pride in the animal as in the human kind; and it is on beauty, strength, swiftness or some other useful or agreeable quality that this passion is always founded.[9]

The next question is, whether, since those passions are the same, and arise from the same causes through the whole creation, the *manner*, in which the causes operate, be also the same. According to all rules of analogy, this is justly to be expected; and if we find upon trial, that the explication of these phenomena, which we make use of in one species, will not apply to the rest, we may presume that that explication, however specious, is in reality without foundation.

In order to decide this question, let us consider, that there is evidently the same *relation* of ideas, and derived from the same causes, in the minds of animals as in those of men. A dog, that has hid a bone, often forgets the place; but when brought to it, his thought passes easily to what he formerly concealed, by means of the contiguity, which produces a relation among his ideas. In like manner, when he has been heartily beat in any place, he will tremble on his approach to it, even though he discover no signs of any present danger. The effects of resemblance are not so remarkable; but as that relation makes a considerable ingredient in causation, of which all animals show so evident a judgment. we may conclude that the three relations of resemblance, contiguity and causation operate in the same manner upon beasts as upon human creatures.

There are also instances of the relation of impressions, sufficient to convince us, that there is an union of certain affections with each other in the inferior species of creatures as well as in the superior, and that their minds are frequently conveyed through a series of connected emotions. A dog, when elevated with joy, runs naturally into love and kindness, whether of his master or of the sex. In like manner, when full of pain and sorrow, he becomes quarrelsome and ill-natured; and that passion, which at first was grief, is by the smallest occasion converted into anger.

Thus all the internal principles, that are necessary in us to produce either pride or humility, are common to all creatures; and since the causes, which excite these passions, are likewise the same, we may justly conclude, that these causes operate after the same *manner* through the whole animal creation. My hypothesis is so simple, and supposes so little reflection and judgment, that it is applicable to every sensible creature; which must not only be allowed to be a convincing proof of its veracity, but, I am confident, will be found an objection to every other system.

PART II *Of Love and Hatred*

SECTION I *Of the objects and causes of love and hatred*

It is altogether impossible to give any definition of the passions of *love* and *hatred*; and that because they produce merely a simple impression, without any mixture or composition. It would be as unnecessary to attempt any description of them, drawn from their nature, origin, causes and objects; and that both because these are the subjects of our present enquiry, and because these passions of themselves are sufficiently known from our common feeling and experience. This we have already observed concerning pride and humility, and here repeat it concerning love and hatred; and indeed there is so great a resemblance betwixt these two sets of passions, that we shall be obliged to begin with a kind of abridgment of our reasonings concerning the former, in order to explain the latter.

As the immediate *object* of pride and humility is self or that identical person, of whose thoughts, actions, and sensations we are intimately conscious; so the *object* of love and hatred is some other person, of whose thoughts, actions, and sensations we are not conscious. This is sufficiently evident from experience. Our love and hatred are always directed to some sensible being external to us; and when we talk of *self-love*, it is not in a proper sense, nor has the sensation it produces anything in common with that tender emotion, which is excited by a friend or mistress. It is the same case with hatred. We may be mortified by our own faults and follies; but never feel any anger or hatred, except from the injuries of others.[10]

But though the object of love and hatred be always some other person, it is plain that the object is not, properly speaking, the *cause* of these passions, or alone sufficient to excite them. For since love and hatred are directly contrary in their sensation, and have the same object in common, if that object were also their cause, it would produce these opposite passions in an equal degree; and as they must, from the very first moment, destroy each other, none of them would ever be able to make its appearance. There must, therefore, be some cause different from the object.

If we consider the causes of love and hatred, we shall find they are very much diversified, and have not many things in common. The virtue, knowledge, wit, good sense, good humour of any person, produce love and esteem; as the opposite qualities, hatred and contempt. The same passions arise from bodily accomplishments, such as beauty, force, swiftness, dexterity; and from their contraries; as likewise from the external advantages and disadvantages of family, possessions, clothes, nation and climate. There is not one of these objects, but what by its different qualities may produce love and esteem, or hatred and contempt.

From the view of these causes we may derive a new distinction betwixt the *quality* that operates, and the *subject* on which it is placed. A prince, that is possessed of a stately palace, commands the esteem of the people upon that account; and that *first*, by the beauty of the palace, and *secondly*, by the relation of property, which connects it with him. The removal of either of these destroys the passion; which evidently proves that the cause is a compounded one.

It would be tedious to trace the passions of love and hatred, through all the observations which we have formed concerning pride and humility, and which are equally applicable to both sets of passions. It will be sufficient to *remark* in general, that the object of love and hatred is evidently some thinking person; and that the sensation of the former passion is always agreeable, and of the latter uneasy. We may also *suppose* with some show of probability, *that the cause of both these passions is always related to a thinking being,* and *that the cause of the former produce a separate pleasure, and of the latter a separate uneasiness.*[11]

One of these suppositions, *viz.* that the cause of love and hatred must be related to a person or thinking being, in order to produce these passions, is not only probable, but too evident to be contested. Virtue and vice, when considered in the abstract; beauty and deformity, when placed on inanimate objects; poverty and riches, when belonging to a third person, excite no degree of love or hatred, esteem or contempt towards those, who have no relation to them. A person looking out at a window, sees me in the street, and beyond me a beautiful palace, with which I have no concern:

I believe none will pretend, that this person will pay me the same respect, as if I were owner of the palace.

It is not so evident at first sight, that a relation of impressions is requisite to these passions, and that because in the transition the one impression is so much confounded with the other, that they become in a manner undistinguishable. But as in pride and humility, we have easily been able to make the separation, and to prove, that every cause of these passions produces a separate pain or pleasure, I might here observe the same method with the same success, in examining particularly the several causes of love and hatred. But as I hasten to a full and decisive proof of these systems, I delay this examination for a moment. And in the meantime shall endeavour to convert to my present purpose all my reasonings concerning pride and humility, by an argument that is founded on unquestionable experience.

There are few persons, that are satisfied with their own character, or genius, or fortune, who are not desirous of showing themselves to the world, and of acquiring the love and approbation of mankind. Now it is evident, that the very same qualities and circumstances, which are the causes of pride or self-esteem, are also the causes of vanity or the desire of reputation; and that we always put to view those particulars with which in ourselves we are best satisfied. But if love and esteem were not produced by the same qualities as pride, according as these qualities are related to ourselves or others, this method of proceeding would be very absurd, nor could men expect a correspondence in the sentiments of every other person, with those themselves have entertained. It is true, few can form exact systems of the passions, or make reflections on their general nature and resemblances. But without such a progress in philosophy, we are not subject to many mistakes in this particular, but are sufficiently guided by common experience, as well as by a kind of *presentation*; which tells us what will operate on others, by what we feel immediately in ourselves. Since then the same qualities that produce pride or humility, cause love or hatred; all the arguments that have been employed to prove, that the causes of the former passions excite a pain or pleasure independent of the passion, will be applicable with equal evidence to the causes of the latter.

SECTION II *Experiments to confirm this system*

Upon duly weighing these arguments, no one will make any scruple to assent to that conclusion I draw from them, concerning the transition along related impressions and ideas, especially as it is a principle, in itself, so easy and natural, But that we may place this system beyond doubt both with regard to love and hatred, pride and humility, it will be proper to make some new experiments upon all these passions, as well as to recall a few of these observations, which I have formerly touched upon.

In order to make these experiments, let us suppose I am in company with a person, whom I formerly regarded without any sentiments either of friendship or enmity. Here I have the natural and ultimate object of all these four passions placed before me. Myself am the proper object of pride or humility; the other person of love or hatred.

Regard now with attention the nature of these passions, and their situation with respect to each other. It is evident here are four affections, placed, as it were, in a square or regular connection with, and distance from each other. The passions of pride and humility, as well as those of love and hatred, are connected together by the identity of their object, which to the first set of passions is self, to the second some other person. These two lines of communication or connection form two opposite sides of the square. Again, pride and love are agreeable passions; hatred and humility uneasy. This similitude of sensation betwixt pride and love, and that betwixt humility and hatred form a new connection, and may be considered as the other two sides of the square. Upon the whole, pride is connected with humility, love with hatred, by their objects or ideas: pride with love, humility with hatred, by their sensations or impressions.

I say then, that nothing can produce any of these passions without bearing it a double relation, *viz.* of ideas to the object of the passion, and of sensation to the passion itself. This we must prove by our experiments.

First experiment. To proceed with the greater order in these experiments, let us first suppose, that being placed in the situation above-mention'd, *viz.* in company with some other person, there is an object presented, that has no relation either of impressions or ideas to any of these passions. Thus suppose we regard together an ordinary stone, or other common object, belonging to neither of us, and causing of itself no emotion, or independent pain and pleasure. It is evident such an object will produce none of these four passions. Let us try it upon each of them successively. Let us apply it to love, to hatred, to humility, to pride; none of them ever arises in the smallest degree imaginable. Let us change the object, as oft as we please; provided still we choose one, that has neither of these two relations. Let us repeat the experiment in all the dispositions, of which the mind is susceptible. No object, in the vast variety of nature, will, in any disposition, produce any passion without these relations.

Second experiment. Since an object, that wants both these relations can ever produce any passion, let us bestow on it only one of these relations; and see what will follow. Thus suppose, I regard a stone or any common object, that belongs either to me or my companion, and by that means acquires a relation of ideas to the object of the passions: It is plain, that to consider the matter *a priori*, no emotion of any kind can reasonably be expected. For besides, that a relation of ideas operates secretly and calmly on the mind, it bestows an equal impulse towards the opposite passions of pride and humility, love and hatred, according as the object belongs to ourselves or others; which opposition of the passions must destroy both, and leave the mind perfectly free from any affection or emotion. This reasoning *a priori* is confirmed by experience. No trivial or vulgar object, that causes not a pain or pleasure, independent of the passion, will ever, by its property or other relations, either to ourselves or others, be able to produce the affections of pride or humility, love or hatred.

Third experiment. It is evident, therefore, that a relation of ideas is not able alone to give rise to these affections. Let us now remove this relation, and in its stead place a relation of impressions, by presenting an object, which is agreeable or disagreeable, but has no relation either to ourself or companion; and let us observe the consequences. To consider the matter first *a priori*, as in the preceding experiment; we may conclude, that the object will have a small, but an uncertain connection with these passions. For besides, that this relation is not a cold and imperceptible one, it has not the inconvenience of the relation of ideas, nor directs us with equal force to two contrary passions, which by their opposition destroy each other. But if we consider, on the other hand, that this transition from the sensation to the affection is not forwarded by any principle, that produces a transition of ideas; but, on the contrary, that though the one impression be easily transfused into the other, yet the change of objects is suppos'd contrary to all the principles, that cause a transition of that kind; we may from thence infer, that nothing will ever be a steady or durable cause of any passion, that is connected with the passion merely by a relation of impressions. What our reason would conclude from analogy, after balancing these arguments, would be, that an object, which produces pleasure or uneasiness, but has no manner of connection either with ourselves or others, may give such a turn to the disposition, as that it may naturally fall into pride or love, humility or hatred, and search for other objects, upon which, by a double relation, it can found these affections; but that an object, which has only one of these relations, though the most advantageous one, can never give rise to any constant and established passion.

Most fortunately all this reasoning is found to be exactly conformable to experience, and the phenomena of the passions. Suppose I were travelling with a companion through a country, to which we are both utter strangers; it is evident, that if the prospects be beautiful, the roads agreeable, and the inns commodious, this may put me into good humour both with myself and fellow-traveller. But as we suppose, that this country has no relation either to myself or friend, it can never be the immediate cause of pride or love; and therefore if I found not the passion on some other object, that bears either of us a closer relation, my emotions are rather to be considered as the overflowings of an elevate or humane disposition, than as an established passion. The case is the same where the object produces uneasiness.

Fourth experiment. Having found, that neither an object without any relation of ideas or impressions, nor an object, that has only one relation, can ever cause pride or humility, love or hatred; reason alone may convince us, without any farther experiment, that whatever has a double relation must necessarily excite these passions; since it is evident they must have some cause. But to leave as little room for doubt as possible, let us renew our experiments, and see whether the event in this case answers our expectation. I choose an object, such as virtue, that causes a separate satisfaction. On this object I bestow a relation to self; and find, that from this disposition of affairs, there immediately arises a passion. But what passion? That very one of pride, to which this object bears a double relation. Its idea is related to that of self, the object of the passion. The sensation it causes resembles the sensation of the passion. That I may be sure I am not mistaken in this experiment, I remove first one relation; then another; and find, that each removal destroys the passion, and leaves the object perfectly indifferent. But I am not content with this. I make a still farther trial; and instead of removing the relation, I only change it for one of a different kind. I suppose the virtue to belong to my companion, not to myself; and observe what follows from this alteration. I immediately perceive the affections to wheel about, and leaving pride, where there is only one relation, *viz.* of impressions, fall to the side of love, where they are attracted by a double relation of impressions and ideas. By repeating the same experiment, in changing anew the relation of ideas, I bring the affections back to pride; and by a new repetition I again place them at love or kindness. Being fully convinced of the influence of this relation, I try the effects of the other; and by changing virtue for vice, convert the pleasant impression, which arises from the former, into the disagreeable one, which proceeds from the latter. The effect still answers expectation. Vice, when placed on another, excites, by means of its double relations, the passion of hatred, instead of love, which for the same reason arises from virtue. To continue the experiment, I change anew the relation of ideas, and suppose the vice to belong to myself. What follows? What is usual. A subsequent change of the passion from hatred to humility. This humility I convert into pride by a new change of the impression; and find after all that I have completed the round, and have by these changes brought back the passion to that very situation, in which I first found it.

But to make the matter still more certain, I alter the object; and instead of vice and virtue, make the trial upon beauty and deformity, riches and poverty, power and servitude. Each of these objects runs the circle of the passions in the same manner, by a change of their relations; and in whatever order we proceed, whether through pride, love, hatred, humility, or through humility, hatred, love, pride, the experiment is not in the least diversified. Esteem and contempt, indeed, arise on some occasions instead of love and hatred; but these are at the bottom the same passions, only diversified by some causes, which we should explain afterwards.

Fifth experiment. To give greater authority to these experiments, let us change the situation of affairs as much as possible, and place the passions and objects in all the different positions, of which they are susceptible. Let us suppose, beside the relations above-mentioned, that the person, along with whom I make all these experiments, is closely connected with me either by blood or friendship. He is, we shall suppose, my son or brother, or is united to me by a long and familiar acquaintance. Let us next suppose, that the cause of the passion acquires a double relation of impressions and ideas to this person; and let us see what the effects are of all these complicated attractions and relations.

Before we consider what they are in fact, let us determine what they ought to be, conformable to my hypothesis. It is plain, that, according as the impression is either pleasant or uneasy, the passion of love or hatred must arise towards the person, who is thus connected to the cause of the impression by these double relations, which I have all along required. The virtue of a brother must make me love him; as his vice or infamy must excite the contrary passion. But to judge only from the situation of affairs, I should not expect, that the affections would rest there, and never transfuse themselves into any other impression. As there is here a person, who by means of a double relation is the object of my passion, the very same reasoning leads me to think the passion will be carried farther. The person has a relation of ideas to myself, according to the supposition; the passion, of which he is the object, by being either agreeable or uneasy, has a relation of impressions to pride or humility. It is evident, then, that one of these passions must arise from the love or hatred.

This is the reasoning I form in conformity to my hypothesis; and am pleased to find upon trial that everything answers exactly to my expectation. The virtue or vice of a son or brother not only excites love or hatred, but by a new transition, from similar causes, give rise to pride or humility. Nothing causes greater vanity than any shining quality in our relations; as nothing mortifies us more than their vice or infamy. This exact conformity of experience to our reasoning is a convincing proof of the solidity of that hypothesis, upon which we reason.

Sixth experiment. This evidence will be still augmented, if we reverse the experiment, and preserving still the same relations, begin only with a different passion. Suppose, that instead of the virtue or vice of a son or brother, which causes first love or hatred, and afterwards pride or humility, we place these good or bad qualities on ourselves, without any immediate connection with the person, who is related to us; experience shows us, that by this change of situation the whole chain is broke, and that the mind is not conveyed from one passion to another, as in the preceding instance. We never love or hate a son or brother for the virtue or vice we discern in ourselves; though it is evident the same qualities in him give us a very sensible pride or humility. The transition from pride or humility to love or hatred is not so natural as from love or hatred to pride or humility. This may at first sight be esteemed contrary to my hypothesis, since the relations of impressions and ideas are in both cases precisely the same. Pride and humility are impressions related to love and hatred. Myself am related to the person. It should, therefore, be expected, that like causes must produce like effects, and a perfect transition arise from the double relation, as in all other cases. This difficulty we may easily solve by the following reflections.

It is evident, that as we are at all times intimately conscious of ourselves, our sentiments and passions, their ideas must strike upon us with greater vivacity than the ideas of the sentiments and passions of any other person. But everything, that strikes upon us with vivacity, and appears in a full and strong light, forces itself, in a manner, into our consideration, and becomes present to the mind on the smallest hint and most trivial relation. For the same reason, when it is once present, it engages the attention, and keeps it from wandering to other objects, however strong may be their relation to our first object. The imagination passes easily from obscure to lively ideas, but with difficulty from lively to obscure. In the one case the relation is aided by another principle: in the other case, it is opposed by it.

Now I have observed, that those two faculties of the mind, the imagination and passions, assist each other in their operation, when their propensities are similar, and when they act upon the same object. The mind has always a propensity to pass from a passion to any other related to it; and this propensity is forwarded when the object of the one passion is related to that of the other. The two impulses concur with each other, and render the whole transition more smooth and easy. But if it should happen, that while the relation of ideas, strictly speaking, continues the same, its influence, in causing a transition of the imagination, should no longer take place, it is evident its influence on the passions must also cease, as being dependent entirely on that transition. This is the reason why pride or humility is not transfused into love or hatred with the same ease, that the latter passions are changed into the former. If a person be my brother I am his likewise. But though the relations be reciprocal, they have very different effects on the imagination. The passage is smooth and open from the consideration of any person related to us to that of ourself, of whom we are every moment conscious. But when the affections are once directed to ourself, the fancy passes not with the same facility from that object to any other person, how closely so ever connected with us. This easy or difficult transition of the imagination operates upon the passions, and facilitates or retards their transition; which is a clear proof, that these two faculties of the passions and imagination are connected together, and that the relations of ideas have an influence upon the affections. Besides innumerable experiments that prove this, we here find, that even when the relation remains; if by any particular circumstance its usual effect upon the fancy in producing an association or transition of ideas, is prevented; its usual effect upon the passions, in conveying us from one to another, is in like manner prevented.

Some may, perhaps, find a contradiction betwixt this phenomenon and that of sympathy, where the mind passes easily from the idea of ourselves to that of any other object related to us. But this difficulty will vanish, if we consider that in sympathy our own person is not the object of any passion, nor is there anything, that fixes our attention on ourselves; as in the present case, where we are supposed to be actuated with pride or humility. Ourself, independent of the perception of every other object, is in reality nothing; for which reason we must turn our view to external objects; and it is natural for us to consider with most attention such as lie contiguous to us, or resemble us. But when self is the object of a passion, it is not natural to quit the consideration of it, till the passion be exhausted; in which case the double relations of impressions and ideas can no longer operate.

Seventh experiment. To put this whole reasoning to a farther trial, let us make a new experiment; and as we have already seen the effects of related passions and ideas, let us here suppose an identity of passions along with a relation of ideas; and let us consider the effects of this new situation. It is evident a transition of the passions from the one object to the other is here in all reason to be expected; since the relation of ideas is supposed still to continue, and an identity of impressions must produce a stronger connection, than the most perfect resemblance, that can be imagined. If a double relation, therefore, of impressions and ideas is able to produce a transition from one to the other, much more an identity of impressions with a relation of ideas. Accordingly we find, that when we either love or hate any person, the passions seldom continue within their first bounds; but extend themselves towards all the contiguous objects, and comprehend the friends and relations of him we love or hate. Nothing is more natural than to bear a kindness to one brother on account of our friendship for another, without any farther examination of his character. A quarrel with one person gives us a hatred for the whole family, though entirely innocent of that, which displeases us. Instances of this kind are everywhere to be met with.

There is only one difficulty in this experiment, which it will be necessary to account for, before we proceed any farther. It is evident, that though all passions pass easily from one object to another related to it, yet this transition is made with greater facility, where the more considerable object is first presented, and the lesser follows it, than where this order is reversed, and the lesser takes the precedence. Thus it is more natural for us to love the son upon account of the father, than the father upon account of the son; the servant for the master, than the master for the servant; the subject for the prince, than the prince for the subject. In like manner we more readily contract a hatred against a whole family, where our first quarrel is with the head of it, than where we are displeased with a son, or servant, or some inferior member. In short, our passions, like other objects, descend with greater facility than they ascend.

That we may comprehend, wherein consists the difficulty of explaining this phenomenon, we must consider, that the very same reason, which determines the imagination to pass from remote to contiguous objects, with more facility than from contiguous to remote, causes it likewise to change with more ease, the less for the greater, than the greater for the less. Whatever has the greatest influence is most taken notice of; and whatever is most taken notice of, presents itself most readily to the imagination. We are more apt to overlook in any subject, what is trivial, than what appears of considerable moment; but especially if the latter takes the precedence, and first engages our attention. Thus if any accident makes us consider the *satellites* of *Jupiter*, our fancy is naturally determined to form the idea of that planet; but if we first reflect on the principal planet, it is more natural for us to overlook its attendants. The mention of the provinces of any empire conveys our thought to the seat of the empire; but the fancy returns not with the same facility to the consideration of the provinces. The idea of the servant makes us think of the master; that of the subject carries our view to the prince. But the same relation has not an equal influence in conveying us back again. And on this is founded that reproach of *Cornelia* to her sons, that they ought to be ashamed she should be more known by the title of the daughter of *Scipio*, than by that of the mother of the *Gracchi*. This was, in other words, exhorting them to render themselves as illustrious and famous as their grandfather, otherwise the imagination of the people, passing from her who was intermediate, and placed in an equal relation to both, would always leave them, and denominate her by what was more considerable and of greater moment. On the same principle is founded that common custom of making wives bear the name of their husbands, rather than husbands that of their wives; as also the ceremony of giving the precedency to those, whom we honour and respect. We might find many other instances to confirm this principle, were it not already sufficiently evident.

Now since the fancy finds the same facility in passing from the lesser to the greater, as from remote to contiguous, why does not this easy transition of ideas assist the transition of passions in the former case, as well as in the latter? The virtues of a friend or brother produce first love, and then pride; because in that case the imagination passes from remote to contiguous, according to its propensity. Our own virtues produce not first pride, and then love to a friend or brother; because the passage in that case would be from contiguous to remote, contrary to its propensity. But the love or hatred of an inferior causes not readily any passion to the superior, though that be the natural propensity of the imagination; while the love or hatred of a superior, causes a passion to the inferior, contrary to its propensity. In short, the same facility of transition operates not in the same manner upon superior and inferior as upon contiguous and remote. These two phenomena appear contradictory, and require some attention to be reconciled.

As the transition of ideas is here made contrary to the natural propensity of the imagination, that faculty must be overpowered by some stronger principle of another kind; and as there is nothing ever present to the mind but impressions and ideas, this principle must necessarily lie in the impressions. Now it has been observed, that impressions or passions are connected only by their resemblance, and that where any two passions place the mind in the same or in similar dispositions, it very naturally passes from the one to the other; as on the contrary, a repugnance in the dispositions produces a difficulty in the transition of the passions. But it is observable, that this repugnance may arise from a difference of degree as well as of kind; nor do we experience a greater difficulty in passing suddenly from a small degree of love to a small degree of hatred, than from a small to a great degree of either of these affections. A man, when calm or only moderately agitated, is so different, in every respect, from himself, when disturbed with a violent passion, that no two persons can be more unlike; nor is it easy to pass from the one extreme to the other, without a considerable interval betwixt them.

The difficulty is not less, if it be not rather greater, in passing from the strong passion to the weak, than in passing from the weak to the strong, provided the one passion upon its appearance destroys the other, and they do not both of them exist at once. But the case is entirely altered, when the passions unite together, and actuate the mind at the same time. A weak passion, when added to a strong, makes not so considerable change in the disposition, as a strong when added to a weak; for which reason there is a closer connection betwixt the great degree and the small, than betwixt the small degree and the great.

The degree of any passion depends upon the nature of its object; and an affection directed to a person, who is considerable in our eyes, fills and possesses the mind much more than one, which has for its object a person we esteem of less consequence. Here then the contradiction betwixt the propensities of the imagination and passion displays itself. When we turn our thought to a great and a small object, the imagination finds more facility in passing from the small to the great, than from the great to the small; but the affections find a greater difficulty; and as the affections are a more powerful principle than the imagination, no wonder they prevail over it, and draw the mind to their side. In spite of the difficulty of passing from the idea of great to that of little, a passion directed to the former, produces always a similar passion towards the latter; when the great and little are related together. The idea of the servant conveys our thought most readily to the master; but the hatred or love of the master produces with greater facility anger or good-will to the servant. The strongest passion in this case takes the precedence; and the addition of the weaker making no considerable change on the disposition, the passage is by that means rendered more easy and natural betwixt them.

As in the foregoing experiment we found, that a relation of ideas, which, by any particular circumstance, ceases to produce its usual effect of facilitating the transition of ideas, ceases likewise to operate on the passions; so in the present experiment we find the same property of the impressions. Two different degrees of the same passion are surely related together; but if the smaller be first present, it has little or no tendency to introduce the greater; and that because the addition of the great to the little, produces a more sensible alteration on the temper, than the addition of the little to the great. These phenomena, when duly weighed, will be found

3

convincing proofs of this hypothesis.

And these proofs will be confirmed, if we consider the manner in which the mind here reconciles the contradiction, I have observed betwixt the passions and the imagination. The fancy passes with more facility from the less to the greater, than from the greater to the less. But on the contrary a violent passion produces more easily a feeble, than that does a violent. In this opposition the passion in the end prevails over the imagination; but it is commonly by complying with it, and by seeking another quality, which may counterbalance that principle, from whence the opposition arises. When we love the father or master of a family, we little think of his children or servants. But when these are present with us, or when it lies any ways in our power to serve them, the nearness and contiguity in this case increases their magnitude, or at least removes that opposition, which the fancy makes to the transition of the affections. If the imagination finds a difficulty in passing from greater to less, it finds an equal facility in passing from remote to contiguous, which brings the matter to an equality, and leaves the way open from the one passion to the other.

Eighth experiment. I have observed that the transition from love or hatred to pride or humility, is more easy than from pride or humility to love or hatred; and that the difficulty, which the imagination finds in passing from contiguous to remote, is the cause why we scarce have any instance of the latter transition of the affections. I must, however, make one exception, *viz.* when the very cause of the pride and humility is placed in some other person. For in that case the imagination is necessitated to consider the person, nor can it possibly confine its view to ourselves. Thus nothing more readily produces kindness and affection to any person, than his approbation of our conduct and character, as on the other hand, nothing inspires us with a stronger hatred, than his blame or contempt. Here it is evident, that the original passion is pride or humility, whose object is self; and that this passion is transfused into love or hatred, whose object is some other person, notwithstanding the rule I have already established, *that the imagination passes with difficulty from contiguous to remote.* But the transition in this case is not made merely on account of the relation betwixt ourselves and the person; but because that very person is the real cause of our first passion, and of consequence is intimately connected with it. It is his approbation that produces pride; and disapprobation, humility. No wonder, then, the imagination returns back again attended with the related passions of love and hatred. This is not a contradiction, but an exception to the rule; and an exception that arises from the same reason with the rule itself.

Such an exception as this is, therefore, rather a confirmation of the rule. And indeed, if we consider all the eight experiments I have explained, we shall find that the same principle appears in all of them, and that it is by means of a transition arising from a double relation of impressions and ideas, pride and humility, love and hatred are produc'd. An object without a relation* or with but one,† never produces either of these passions; it is found that the passion always varies in conformity to the relation.‡ Nay we may observe, that where the relation, by any particular circumstances, has not its usual effect of producing a transition either of ideas or of impressions,§ it ceases to operate upon the passions, and gives rise neither to pride nor love, humility nor hatred. This rule we find still to hold good,‖ even under the appearance of its contrary; and as relation is frequently experienced to have no effect; which upon examination is found to proceed from some particular circumstance, that prevents the transition; so even in instances, where that circumstance, though present, prevents not the transition, it is found to arise from some other circumstance, which counterbalances it. Thus not only the variations resolve themselves into the general principle, but even the variations of these variations.

SECTION III *Difficulties solved*

After so many and such undeniable proofs drawn from daily experience and observation, it may seem superfluous to enter into a particular examination of all the causes of love and hatred. I shall, therefore, employ the sequel of this part,

---

* First experiment.
† Second and Third experiments.
‡ Fourth experiment.
§ Sixth experiment.
‖ Seventh and eighth experiments.

First, in removing some difficulties, concerning particular causes of these passions. *Secondly,* in examining the compound affections, which arise from the mixture of love and hatred with other emotions.[12]

Nothing is more evident, than that any person acquires our kindness, or is exposed to our ill-will, in proportion to the pleasure or uneasiness we receive from him, and that the passions keep pace exactly with the sensations in all their changes and variations. Whoever can find the means either by his services, his beauty, or his flattery, to render himself useful or agreeable to us, is sure of our affections; as on the other hand, whoever harms or displeases us never fails to excite our anger or hatred. When our own nation is at war with any other, we detest them under the character of cruel, perfidious, unjust and violent; but always esteem ourselves and allies equitable, moderate, and merciful. If the general of our enemies be successful, it is with difficulty we allow him the figure and character of a man. He is a sorcerer; he has a communication with demons; as is reported of *Oliver Cromwell* and the *Duke of Luxembourg;* he is bloody-minded, and takes a pleasure in death and destruction. But if the success be on our side, our commander has all the opposite good qualities, and is a pattern of virtue, as well as as of courage and conduct. His treachery we call policy; his cruelty is an evil inseparable from war. In short, every one of his faults we either endeavour to extenuate, or dignify it with the name of that virtue, which approaches it. It is evident the same method of thinking runs through common life.

There are some, who add another condition, and require not only that the pain and pleasure arise from the person, but likewise that it arise knowingly, and with a particular design and intention. A man, who wounds and harms us by accident, becomes not our enemy upon that account, nor do we think ourselves bound by any ties of gratitude to one, who does us any service after the same manner. By the intention we judge of the actions, and according as that is good or bad, they become causes of love or hatred.

But here we must make a distinction. If that quality in another, which pleases or displeases, be constant and inherent in his person and character, it will cause love or hatred independent of the intention. But otherwise a knowledge and design is requisite, in order to give rise to these passions. One that is disagreeable by his deformity or folly is the object of our aversion, though nothing be more certain, than that he has not the least intention of displeasing us by these qualities. But if the uneasiness proceed not from a quality, but an action, which is produced and annihilated in a moment, it is necessary, in order to produce some relation, and connect this action sufficiently with the person, that it be derived from a particular forethought and design. It is not enough, that the action arise from the person, and have him for its immediate cause and author. This relation alone is too feeble and inconstant to be a foundation for these passions. It reaches not the sensible and thinking part, and neither proceeds from anything *durable* in him, nor leaves anything behind it, but passes in a moment, and is as if it had never been. On the other hand, an intention shows certain qualities, which remaining after the action is performed, connect it with the person, and facilitate the transition of ideas from one to the other. We can never think of him without reflecting on these qualities, unless repentance and a change of life have produced an alteration in that respect; in which case the passion is likewise altered. This therefore is one reason, why an intention is requisite to excite either love or hatred.[13]

But we must farther consider, that an intention, besides its strengthening the relation of ideas, is often necessary to produce a relation of impressions, and give rise to pleasure and uneasiness. For it is observable, that the principal part of an injury is the contempt and hatred, which it shows in the person, that injures us; and without that, the mere harm gives us a less sensible uneasiness. In like manner, a good office is agreeable, chiefly because it flatters our vanity, and is a proof of the kindness and esteem of the person, who performs it. The removal of the intention, removes the mortification in the one case, and vanity in the other; and must of course cause a remarkable diminution in the passions of love and hatred.

I grant, that these effects of the removal of design, in diminishing the relations of impressions and ideas, are not entire, nor able to remove every degree of these relations. But then I ask, if the removal of design be able entirely to remove the passion of love and hatred? Experience, I am sure, informs us of the contrary, nor is there anything more certain, than that men often fall into a violent anger for injuries, which they themselves must own to be entirely involuntary and accidental. This emotion, indeed, cannot be of long continuance; but still is sufficient to show, that there is a natural connection betwixt uneasiness and anger, and that the relation of impressions will operate upon a very small relation of ideas. But when the violence of the impression is once a little abated, the defect of the relation begins to be better felt; and as the character of a person is no wise interested in such injuries as are casual and involuntary, it seldom happens that on their account, we entertain a lasting enmity.

To illustrate this doctrine by a parallel instance, we may observe, that not only the uneasiness, which proceeds from another by accident, has but little force to excite our passion, but also that which arises from an acknowledged necessity and duty. One that has a real design of harming us, proceeding not from hatred and ill-will, but from justice and equity, draws not upon him our anger, if we be in any degree reasonable; notwithstanding he is both the cause, and the knowing cause of our sufferings. Let us examine a little this phenomenon.

It is evident in the first place, that this circumstance is not decisive; and though it may be able to diminish the passions, it is seldom it can entirely remove them. How few criminals are there, who have no ill-will to the person, that accuses them, or to the judge, that condemns them, even though they be conscious of their own deserts? In like manner our antagonist in a law-suit, and our competitor for any office, are commonly regarded as our enemies, though we must acknowledge, if we would but reflect a moment, that their motive is entirely as justifiable as our own.

Besides we may consider, that when we receive harm from any person, we are apt to imagine him criminal, and it is with extreme difficulty we allow of his justice and innocence. This is a clear proof, that, independent of the opinion of iniquity, any harm or uneasiness has a natural tendency to excite our hatred, and that afterwards we seek for reasons upon which we may justify and establish the passion. Here the idea of injury produces not the passion, but arises from it.

Nor is it any wonder that passion should produce the opinion of injury; since otherwise it must suffer a considerable diminution, which all the passions avoid as much as possible. The removal of injury may remove the anger, without proving that the anger arises only from the injury. The harm and the justice are two contrary objects, of which the one has a tendency to produce hatred, and the other love; and it is according to their different degrees, and our particular turn of thinking, that either of the objects prevails, and excites its proper passion.

SECTION IV *Of the love of relations*

Having given a reason, why several actions, that cause a real pleasure or uneasiness, excite not any degree, or but a small one, of the passion of love or hatred towards the actors; it will be necessary to show, wherein consists the pleasure or uneasiness of many objects, which we find by experience to produce these passions.

According to the preceding system there is always required a double relation of impressions and ideas betwixt the cause and effect, in order to produce either love or hatred. But though this be universally true, it is remarkable that the passion of love may be excited by only one *relation* of a different kind *viz.* betwixt ourselves and the object; or more properly speaking, that this relation is always attended with both the others. Whoever is united to us by any connection is always sure of a share of our love, proportioned to the connection, without enquiring into his other qualities. Thus the relation of blood produces the strongest tie the mind is capable of in the love of parents to their children, and a lesser degree of the same affection, as the relation lessens. Nor has consanguinity alone this effect, but any other relation without exception. We love our countrymen, our neighbours, those of the same trade, profession, and even name with ourselves. Every one of these relations is esteemed some tie, and gives a title to a share of our affection.

There is another phenomenon, which is parallel to this, *viz.* that *acquaintance*, without any kind of relation, gives rise to love and kindness. When we have contracted a habitude and intimacy with any person; though in frequenting his company we have not been able to discover any very valuable quality, of which he is possessed; yet we cannot forbear preferring him to strangers, of whose superior merit we are fully convinced. These two phenomena of the effects of relation and acquaintance will give mutual light to each other, and may be both explained from the same principle.

Those, who take a pleasure in declaiming against human nature, have observed, that man is altogether insufficient to support himself; and that when you loosen all the holds, which he has of external objects, he immediately drops down into the deepest melancholy and despair. From this, say they, proceeds that continual search after amusement in gaming, in hunting, in business; by which we endeavour to forget ourselves, and excite our spirits from the languid state, into which they fall, when not sustained by some brisk and lively emotion. To this method of thinking I so far agree, that I own the mind to be insufficient, of itself, to its own entertainment, and that it naturally seeks after foreign objects, which may produce a lively sensation, and agitate the spirits. On the appearance of such an object it awakes, as it were, from a dream: the blood flows with a new tide; the heart is elevated; and the whole man acquires a vigour, which he cannot command in his solitary and calm moments. Hence company is naturally so rejoicing, as presenting the liveliest of all objects, *viz.* a rational and thinking being like ourselves, who communicates to us all the actions of his mind; makes us privy to his inmost sentiments and affections; and lets us see, in the very instant of their production, all the emotions, which are caused by any object. Every lively idea is agreeable, but especially that of a passion, because such an idea becomes a kind of passion, and gives a more sensible agitation to the mind, than any other image or conception.

This being once admitted, all the rest is easy. For as the company of strangers is agreeable to us for *a short time*, by enlivening our thought; so the company of our relations and acquaintance must be peculiarly agreeable, because it has this effect in a greater degree, and is of more *durable* influence. Whatever is related to us is conceived in a lively manner by the easy transition from ourselves to the related object. Custom also, or acquaintances facilitates the entrance, and strengthens the conception of any object. The first case is parallel to our reasonings from cause and effect; the second to education. And as reasoning and education concur only in producing a lively and strong idea of any object; so is this the only particular, which is common to relation and acquaintance. This must, therefore, be the influencing quality, by which they produce all their common effects; and love or kindness being one of these effects, it must be from the force and liveliness of conception, that the passion is derived. Such a conception is peculiarly agreeable, and makes us have an affectionate regard for everything, that produces it, when the proper object of kindness and goodwill.

It is obvious, that people associate together according to their particular tempers and dispositions, and that men of gay tempers naturally love the gay; as the serious bear an affection to the serious. This not only happens, where they remark this resemblance betwixt themselves and others, but also by the natural course of the disposition, and by a certain sympathy, which always arises betwixt similar characters. Where they remark the resemblance, it operates after the manner of a relation, by producing a connection of ideas. Where they do not remark it, it operates by some other principle; and if this latter principle be similar to the former, it must be received as a confimation of the foregoing reasoning.

The idea of ourselves is always intimately present to us, and conveys a sensible degree of vivacity to the idea of any other object, to which we are related. This lively idea changes by degrees into a real impression; these two kinds of perception being in a great measure the same, and differing only in their degrees of force and vivacity. But this change must be produced with the greater ease, that our natural temper gives us a propensity to the same impression, which we observe in others, and makes it arise upon any slight occasion. In that case resemblance converts the idea into an impression, not only by means of the relation, and by transfusing the original vivacity into the related idea; but also by presenting such materials as take fire from the least spark. And as in both cases a love or affection arises from the resemblance, we may learn that a sympathy with others is agreeable only by giving an emotion to the spirits, since an easy sympathy and correspondent emotions are alone common to *relation, acquaintance,* and *resemblance.*

The great propensity men have to pride may be considered as another similar phenomenon. It often happens, that after we have lived a considerable time in any city; however at first it might be disagreeable to us; yet as we become familiar with the objects, and contract an acquaintance, though merely with the streets and buildings, the aversion diminishes by degrees, and at last changes into the opposite passion. The mind finds a satisfaction and ease in the view of objects, to which it is accustomed, and naturally prefers them to others, which, though, perhaps, in themselves more valuable, are less known to it. By the same quality of the mind we are seduced into a good opinion of ourselves, and of all objects, that belong to us. They appear in a stronger light; are more agreeable; and consequently fitter subjects of pride and vanity, than any other.

It may not be amiss, in treating of the affection we bear our acquaintance and relations, to observe some pretty curious phenomena, which attend it. It is easy to remark in common life, that children esteem their relation to their mother to be weakened, in a great measure, by her second marriage, and no longer regard her with the same eye, as if she had continued in her state of widowhood. Nor does this happen only, when they have felt any inconveniencies from her second marriage, or when her husband is much her inferior; but even without any of these considerations, and merely because she has become part of another family. This also takes place with regard to the second marriage of a father; but in a much less degree; and it is certain the ties of blood are not so much loosened in the latter case as by the marriage of a mother. These two phenomena are remarkable in themselves, but much more so when compar'd.

In order to produce a perfect relation betwixt two objects, it is requisite, not only that the imagination be conveyed from one to the other by resemblance, contiguity or causation, but also that it return back from the second to the first with the same ease and facility. At first sight this may seem a necessary and unavoidable consequence. If one object resemble another, the latter object must necessarily resemble the former. If one object be the cause of another, the second object is effect to its cause. It is the same case with contiguity; and therefore the relation being always reciprocal, it may be thought, that the return of the imagination from the second to the first must also, in every case, be equally natural as its passage from the first to the second. But upon farther examination we shall easily discover our mistake. For supposing the second object, beside its reciprocal relation to the first, to have also a strong relation to a third object; in that case the thought, passing from the first object to the second, returns not back with the same facility, though the relation continues the same; but is readily carried on to the third object, by means of the new relation, which presents itself, and gives a new impulse to the imagination. This new relation, therefore, weakens the tie betwixt the first and second objects. The fancy is by its very nature wavering and inconstant; and considers always two objects as more strongly related together, where it finds the passage equally easy both in going and returning, than where the transition is easy only in one of these motions. The double motion is a kind of a double tie, and binds the objects together in the closest and most intimate manner.

The second marriage of a mother breaks not the relation of child and parent; and that relation suffices to convey my imagination from myself to her with the greatest ease and facility. But after the imagination is arrived at this point of view, it finds its object to be surrounded with so many other relations, which challenge its regard, that it knows not which to prefer, and is at a loss what new object to pitch upon. The ties of interest and duty bind her to another family, and prevent that return of the fancy from her to myself, which is necessary to support the union. The thought has no longer the vibration, requisite to set it perfectly at ease, and indulge its inclination to change. It goes with facility, but returns with difficulty; and by that interruption finds the relation much weakened from what it would be were the passage open and easy on both sides.

Now to give a reason, why this effect follows not in the same degree upon the second marriage of a father: we may reflect on what has been proved already, that though the imagination goes easily from the view of a lesser object to that of a greater, yet it returns not with the same facility from the greater to the less. When my imagination goes from myself to my father, it passes not so readily from him to his second wife, nor considers him as entering into a different family, but as continuing the head of that family, of which I am myself a part. His superiority prevents the easy transition of the thought from him to his spouse, but keeps the passage still open for a return to myself along the same relation of child and parent. He is not sunk in the new relation he acquires; so that the double motion or vibration of thought is still easy and natural. By this indulgence of the fancy in its inconstancy, the tie of child and parent still preserves its full force and influence.

A mother thinks not her tie to a son weakened, because it is shared with her husband; nor a son his with a parent, because it is shared with a brother. The third object is here related to the first, as well as to the second; so that the imagination goes and comes along all of them with the greatest facility.

Section V *Of our esteem for the rich and powerful*

Nothing has a greater tendency to give us an esteem for any person, than his power and riches; or a contempt, than his poverty and meanness. And as esteem and contempt are to be considered as species of love and hatred, it will be proper in this place to explain these phenomena.

Here it happens most fortunately, that the greatest difficulty is not to discover a principle capable of producing such an effect, but to choose the chief and predominant among several, that present themselves. The *satisfaction* we take in the riches of others, and the *esteem* we have for the possessors may be ascribed to three different causes. *First,* to the objects they possess; such as houses, gardens, equipages; which, being agreeable in themselves, necessarily produce a sentiment of pleasure in everyone, that either considers or surveys them. *Secondly,* to the expectation of advantage from the rich and powerful by our sharing their possessions. *Thirdly,* to sympathy, which makes us partake of the satisfaction of everyone, that approaches us. All these principles may concur in producing the present phenomenon. The question is, to which of them we ought principally to ascribe it.

It is certain, that the first principle, *viz.* the reflection on agreeable objects, has a greater influence, than what, at first sight, we may be apt to imagine. We seldom reflect on what is beautiful or ugly, agreeable or disagreeable, without an emotion of pleasure or uneasiness; and though these sensations appear not much in our common indolent way of thinking, it is easy, either in reading or conversation, to discover them. Men of wit always turn the discourse on subjects that are entertaining to the imagination; and poets never present any objects but such as are of the same nature. Mr *Philips* has chosen *cider* for the subject of an excellent poem. Beer wou'd not have been so proper, as being neither so agreeable to the taste nor eye. But he would certainly have preferred wine to either of them, could his native country have afforded him so agreeable a liquor. We may learn from thence, that everything, which is agreeable to the senses, is also in some measure agreeable to the fancy, and conveys to the thought an image of that satisfaction, which it gives by its real application to the bodily organs.

But though these reasons may induce us to comprehend this delicacy of the imagination among the causes of the respect, which we pay the rich and powerful, there are many other reasons, that may keep us from regarding it as the sole or principal. For as the ideas of pleasure can have an influence only by means of their vivacity, which makes them approach impressions, it is most natural those ideas should have that influence, which are favoured by most circumstances, and have a natural tendency to become strong and lively; such as our ideas of the passions and sensations of any human creature. Every human creature resembles ourselves, and by that means has an advantage above any other object, in operating on the imagination.

Besides, if we consider the nature of that faculty, and the great influence which all relations have upon it, we shall easily be persuaded, that however the ideas of the pleasant wines, music, or gardens, which the rich man enjoys, may become lively and agreeable, the fancy will not confine itself to them, but will carry its view to the related objects; and in particular, to the person, who possesses them. And this is the more natural, that the pleasant idea or image produces here a passion towards the person, by means of his relation to the object; so that it is unavoidable but he must enter into the original conception, since he makes the object of the derivative passion. But if he enters into the original conception, and is considered as enjoying these agreeable objects, it is *sympathy*, which is properly the cause of the affection; and the *third* principle is more powerful and universal than the *first*.

Add to this, that riches and power alone, even though unemployed, naturally cause esteem and respect; and consequently these passions arise not from the idea of any beautiful or agreeable objects. 'Tis true; money implies a kind of representation of such objects, by the power it affords of obtaining them; and for that reason may still be esteemed proper to convey those agreeable images, which may give rise to the passion. But as this prospect is very distant, it is more natural for us to take a contiguous object, *viz.* the satisfaction, which this power affords the person, who is possessed of it. And of this we shall be farther satisfied, if we consider, that riches represent the goods of life, only by means of the will; which employs them; and therefore imply in their very nature an idea of the person, and cannot be considered without a kind of sympathy with his sensations and enjoyments.

This we may confirm by a reflection, which to some will, perhaps, appear too subtle and refined. I have already observed, that power, as distinguished from its exercise, has either no meaning at all, or is nothing but a possibility or probability of existence; by which any object approaches to reality, and has a sensible influence on the mind. I have also observed, that this approach, by an illusion of the fancy, appears much greater, when we ourselves are possessed of the power, than when it is enjoy'd by another; and that in the former case the objects seem to touch upon the very verge of reality, and convey almost an equal satisfaction, as if actually in our possession. Now I assert, that where we esteem a person upon account of his riches, we must enter into this sentiment of the proprietor, and that without such a sympathy the idea of the agreeable objects, which they give him the power to produce, would have but a feeble influence upon us. An avaricious man is respected for his money, though he scarce is possest of a *power*; that is, there scarce is a *probability* or even *possibility* of his employing it in the acquisition of the pleasures and conveniences of life. To himself alone this power seems perfect and entire; and therefore we must receive his sentiments by sympathy, before we can have a strong intense idea of these enjoyments, or esteem him upon account of them.

Thus we have found, that the *first* principle, *viz. the agreeable idea of those objects, which riches afford the enjoyment of*; resolves itself in a great measure into the *third*, and becomes a *sympathy* with the person we esteem or love. Let us now examine the *second* principle, *viz. the agreeable expectation of advantage*, and see what force we may justly attribute to it.

It is obvious, that though riches and authority undoubtedly give their owner a power of doing us service, yet this power is not to be considered as on the same footing with that, which they afford him, of pleasing himself, and satisfying his own appetites. Self-love approaches the power and exercise very near each other in the latter case; but in order to produce a similar effect in the former, we must suppose a friendship and goodwill to be conjoined with the riches. Without that circumstance it is difficult to conceive on what we can found our hope of advantage from the riches of others, though there is nothing more certain, than that we naturally esteem and respect the rich, even before we discover in them any such favourable disposition towards us.

But I carry this farther, and observe, not only that we respect the rich and powerful, where they show no inclination to serve us, but also when we lie so much out of the sphere of their activity, that they cannot even be supposed to be endowed with that power. Prisoners of war are always treated with a respect suitable to their condition; and it is certain riches go very far towards fixing the condition of any person. If birth and quality enter for a share, this still affords us an argument of the same kind. For what is it we call a man of birth, but one who is descended from a long succession of rich and powerful ancestors, and who acquires our esteem by his relation to persons whom we esteem? His ancestors, therefore, though dead, are respected, in some measure, on account of their riches, and consequently without any kind of expectation.

But not to go so far as prisoners of war and the dead to find instances of this disinterested esteem for riches, let us observe with a little attention those phenomena that occur to us in common life and conversation. A man, who is himself of a competent fortune, upon coming into a company of strangers, naturally treats them with different degrees of respect and deference, as he is informed of their different fortunes and conditions; though it is impossible he can ever propose, and perhaps would not accept of any advantage from them. A traveller is always admitted into company, and meets with civility, in proportion as his train and equipage speak him a man of great or moderate fortune. In short, the different ranks of men are, in a great measure, regulated by riches, and that with regard to superiors as well as inferiors, strangers as well as acquaintance.

There is, indeed, an answer to these arguments, drawn from the influence of *general rules*. It may be pretended, that being accustomed to expect succour and protection from the rich and powerful, and to esteem them upon that account, we extend the same sentiments to those, who resemble them in their fortune, but from whom we can never hope for any advantage. The general rule still prevails, and by giving a bent to the imagination draws along the passion, in the same manner as if its proper object were real and existent.

But that this principle does not here take place, will easily appear, if we consider, that in order to establish a general rule, and extend it beyond its proper bounds, there is required a certain uniformity in our experience, and a great superiority of those instances, which are conformable to the rule, above the contrary. But here the case is quite otherwise. Of a hundred men of credit and fortune I meet with, there is not, perhaps, one from whom I can expect advantage; so that it is impossible any custom can ever prevail in the present case.

Upon the whole, there remains nothing, which can give us an esteem for power and riches, and a contempt for mean- ness and poverty, except the principle of *sympathy*, by which we enter into the sentiments of the rich and poor, and par- take of their pleasures and uneasiness. Riches give satisfaction to their possessor; and this satisfaction is conveyed to the beholder by the imagination, which produces an idea resembling the original impression in force and vivacity. This agreeable idea or impression is connected with love, which is an agreeable passion. It proceeds from a thinking conscious being, which is the very object of love. From this relation of impressions, and identity of ideas, the passion arises, according to my hypothesis.

The best method of reconciling us to this opinion is to take a general survey of the universe, and observe the force of sympathy through the whole animal creation, and the easy communication of sentiments from one thinking being to another. In all creatures, that prey not upon others, and are not agitated with violent passions, there appears a remarkable desire of company, which associates them together, without any advantages they can ever propose to reap from their union. This is still more conspicuous in man, as being the creature of the universe, who has the most ardent desire of society, and is fitted for it by the most advantages. We can form no wish, which has not a reference to society. A perfect solitude is, perhaps, the greatest punishment we can suffer. Every pleasure languishes when enjoyed apart from company, and every pain becomes more cruel and intolerable. Whatever other passions we may be actuated by; pride, ambition, avarice, curiosity, revenge or lust; the soul or animating principle of them all is sympathy; nor would they have any force, were we to abstract entirely from the thoughts and sentiments of others. Let all the powers and elements of nature conspire to serve and obey one man; let the sun rise and set at his command; the sea and rivers roll as he pleases, and the earth furnish spontaneously whatever may be useful or agreeable to him. He will still be miserable, till you give him some one person at least, with whom he may share his happiness, and whose esteem and friendship he may enjoy.

This conclusion from a general view of human nature, we may confirm by particular instances, wherein the force of sympathy is very remarkable. Most kinds of beauty are derived from this origin; and though our first object be some senseless inanimate piece of matter, it is seldom we rest there, and carry not our view to its influence on sensible and rational creatures. A man, who shows us any house or building, takes particular care among other things to point out the convenience of the apartments, the advantages of their situation, and the little room lost in the stairs, anti-chambers and passages; and indeed it is evident, the chief part of the beauty consists in these particulars. The observation of convenience gives pleasure, since convenience is a beauty. But after what manner does it give pleasure? It is certain our own interest is not in the least concern'd; and as this is a beauty of interest, not of form, so to speak, it must delight us merely by communication, and by our sympathizing with the proprietor of the lodging. We enter into his interest by the force of imagination, and feel the same satisfaction, that the objects naturally occasion in him.

This observation extends to tables, chairs, scritoires, chimneys, coaches, saddles, ploughs, and indeed to every work of art; it being an universal rule, that their beauty is chiefly derived from their utility, and from their fitness for that purpose, to which they are destined. But this is an advantage, that concerns only the owner, nor is there anything but sympathy, which can interest the spectator.

It is evident, that nothing renders a field more agreeable than its fertility, and that scarce any advantages of ornament or situation will be able to equal this beauty. It is the same case with particular trees and plants, as with the field on which they grow. I know not but a plain, overgrown with furze and broom, may be, in itself, as beautiful as a hill covered with vines or olive-trees; though it will never appear so to one, who is acquainted with the value of each. But this is a beauty merely of imagination, and has no foundation in what appears to the senses. Fertility and value have a plain reference to use; and that to riches, joy, and plenty; in which though we have no hope of partaking, yet we enter into them by the vivacity of the fancy, and share them, in some measure, with the proprietor.

There is no rule in painting more reasonable than that of balancing the figures, and placing them with the greatest exactness on their proper centre of gravity. A figure, which is not justly balanced, is disagreeable; and that because it conveys the ideas of its fall, of harm, and of pain; which ideas are painful, when by sympathy they acquire any degree of force and vivacity.

Add to this, that the principal part of personal beauty is an air of health and vigour, and such a construction of members as promises strength and activity. This idea of beauty cannot be accounted for but by sympathy.

In general we may remark, that the minds of men are mirrors to one another, not only because they reflect each other's emotions, but also because those rays of passions, sentiments and opinions, may be often reverberated, and may decay away by insensible degrees. Thus the pleasure, which a rich man receives from his possessions, being thrown upon the beholder, causes a pleasure and esteem; which sentiments again, being perceived and sympathized with, increase the pleasure of the possessor; and being once more reflected, become a new foundation for pleasure and esteem in the beholder. There is certainly an original satisfaction in riches derived from that power, which they bestow, of enjoying all the pleasures of life; and as this is their very nature and essence, it must be the first source of all the passions, which arise from them. One of the most considerable of these passions is that of love or esteem in others, which therefore proceeds from a sympathy with the pleasure of the possessor. But the possessor has also a secondary satisfaction in riches arising from the love and esteem he acquires by them, and this satisfaction is nothing but a second reflexion of that original pleasure, which proceeded from himself. This secondary satisfaction or vanity becomes one of the principal recommendations of riches, and is the chief reason, why we either desire them for ourselves, or esteem them in others. Here then is a third rebound of the original pleasure, after which it is difficult to distinguish the images and reflections, by reason of their faintness and confusion.[14]

SECTION VI *Of benevolence and anger*

Ideas may be compared to the extension and solidity of matter, and impressions, especially reflective ones, to colours, tastes, smells and other sensible qualities. Ideas never admit of a total union, but are endowed with a kind of impenetrability, by which they exclude each other, and are capable of forming a compound by their conjunction, not by their mixture. On the other hand, impressions and passions are susceptible of an entire union; and like colours, may be blended so perfectly together, that each of them may lose itself, and contribute only to vary that uniform impression, which arises from the whole. Some of the most curious phenomena of the human mind are derived from this property of the passions.

In examining those ingredients, which are capable of uniting with love and hatred, I begin to be sensible, in some measure, of a misfortune, that has attended every system of philosophy, with which the world has been yet acquainted. It is commonly found, that in accounting for the operations of nature by any particular hypothesis; among a number of experiments, that quadrate exactly with the principles we would endeavour to establish; there is always some phenomenon, which is more stubborn, and will not so easily bend to our purpose. We need not be surprised, that this should happen in natural philosophy. The essence and composition of external bodies are so obscure, that we must necessarily, in our reasonings, or rather conjectures concerning them, involve ourselves in contradictions and absurdities. But as the perceptions of the mind are perfectly known, and I have used all imaginable caution in forming conclusions concerning them, I have always hoped to keep clear of those contradictions, which have attended every other system. Accordingly the difficulty, which I have at present in my eye, is no-wise contrary to my system; but only departs a little from that simplicity, which has been hitherto its principal force and beauty.

The passions of love and hatred are always followed by, or rather conjoined with benevolence and anger. It is this conjunction, which chiefly distinguishes these affections from pride and humility. For pride and humility are pure emotions in the soul, unattended with any desire, and not immediately exciting us to action. But love and hatred are not completed within themselves, nor rest in that emotion, which they produce, but carry the mind to something farther. Love is always followed by a desire of the happiness of the person beloved, and an aversion to his misery; as hatred produces a desire of the misery and an aversion to the happiness of the person hated. So remarkable a difference betwixt these two sets of passions of pride and humility, love and hatred, which in so many other particulars correspond to each other, merits our attention.

The conjunction of this desire and aversion with love and hatred may be accounted for by two different hypotheses. The first is, that love and hatred have not only a *cause,* which excites them, *viz.* pleasure and pain; and an *object,* to which they are directed, *viz.* a person or thinking being; but likewise an *end,* which they endeavour to attain, *viz.* the happiness or misery of the person beloved or hated; all which views, mixing together, make only one passion. According to this system, love is nothing but the desire of happiness to another person, and hatred that of misery. The desire and aversion constitute the very nature of love and hatred. They are not only inseparable but the same.

But this is evidently contrary to experience. For though it is certain we never love any person without desiring his happiness, nor hate any without wishing his misery, yet these desires arise only upon the ideas of the happiness or misery of our friend or enemy being presented by the imagination, and are not absolutely essential to love and hatred. They are the most obvious and natural sentiments of these affections, but not the only ones. The passions may express themselves in a hundred ways, and may subsist a considerable time, without our reflecting on the happiness or misery of their objects; which clearly proves, that these desires are not the same with love and hatred, nor make any essential part of them.

We may, therefore, infer, that benevolence and anger are passions different from love and hatred, and only conjoined with them, by the original constitution of the mind. As nature has given to the body certain appetites and inclinations, which she increases, diminishes, or changes according to the situation of the fluids or solids; she has proceeded in the same manner with the mind. According as we are possessed with love or hatred, the correspondent desire of the happiness or misery of the person, who is the object of these passions, arises in the mind, and varies with each variation of these opposite passions. This order of things, abstractedly considered, is not necessary. Love and hatred might have been unattended with any such desires, or their particular connection might have been entirely reversed. If nature had so pleased, love might have had the same effect as hatred, and hatred as love. I see no contradiction in supposing a desire of producing misery annexed to love, and of happiness to hatred. If the sensation of the passion and desire be opposite, nature could have altered the sensation without altering the tendency of the desire and by that means made them compatible with each other.[15]

Section VII *Of compassion*

But though the desire of the happiness or misery of others, according to the love or hatred we bear them, be an arbitrary and original instinct implanted in our nature, we find it may be counterfeited on many occasions, and may arise from secondary principles. *Pity* is a concern for, and *malice* a joy in the misery of others, without any friendship or enmity to occasion this concern or joy. We pity even strangers, and such as are perfectly indifferent to us; and if our ill-will to another proceed from any harm or injury, it is not, properly speaking, malice, but revenge. But if we examine these affections of pity and malice we shall find them to be secondary ones, arising from original affections, which are varied by some particular turn of thought and imagination.

It will be easy to explain the passion of *pity*, from the precedent reasoning concerning *sympathy*. We have a lively idea of everything related to us. All human creatures are related to us by resemblance. Their persons, therefore, their interests, their passions, their pains and pleasures must strike upon us in a lively manner, and produce an emotion similar to the original one; since a lively idea is easily converted into an impression. If this be true in general, it must be more so of affliction and sorrow. These have always a stronger and more lasting influence than any pleasure or enjoyment.

A spectator of a tragedy passes through a long train of grief, terror, indignation, and other affections, which the poet represents in the persons he introduces. As many tragedies end happily, and no excellent one can be composed without some reverses of fortune, the spectator must sympathize with all these changes, and receive the fictitious joy as well as every other passion. Unless, therefore, it be asserted, that every distinct passion is communicated by a distinct original quality, and is not derived from the general principle of sympathy above explained, it must be allowed, that all of them arise from that principle. To except any one in particular must appear highly unreasonable. As they are all first present in the mind of one person, and afterwards appear in the mind of another; and as the manner of their appearance, first as an idea, then as an impression, is in every case the same, the transition must arise from the same principle. I am at least sure, that this method of reasoning would be considered as certain, either in natural philosophy or common life.

Add to this, that pity depends, in a great measure, on the contiguity, and even sight of the object; which is a proof, that it is derived from the imagination. Not to mention that women and children are most subject to pity, as being most guided by that faculty. The same infirmity, which makes them faint at the sight of a naked sword, though in the hands of their best friend, makes them pity extremely those, whom they find in any grief or affliction. Those philosophers, who derive this passion from I know not what subtle reflections on the instability of fortune, and our being liable to the same miseries we behold, will find this observation contrary to them among a great many others, which it were easy to produce.

There remains only to take notice of a pretty remarkable phenomenon of this passion; which is, that the communicated passion of sympathy sometimes acquires strength from the weakness of its original, and even arises by a transition from affections, which have no existence. Thus when a person obtains any honourable office, or inherits a great fortune, we are always the more rejoiced for his prosperity, the less sense he seems to have of it, and the greater equanimity and indifference he shows in its enjoyment. In like manner a man, who is not dejected by misfortunes, is the more lamented on account of his patience; and if that virtue extends so far as utterly to remove all sense of uneasiness, it still farther increases our compassion. When a person of merit falls into what is vulgarly esteemed a great misfortune, we form a notion of his condition; and carrying our fancy from the cause to the usual effect, first conceive a lively idea of his sorrow, and then feel an impression of it, entirely overlooking that greatness of mind, which elevates him above such emotions, or only considering it so far as to increase our admiration, love and tenderness for him. We find from experience, that such a degree of passion is usually connected with such a misfortune; and though there be an exception in the present case, yet the imagination is affected by the *general rule*, and makes us conceive a lively idea of the passion, or rather feel the passion itself, in the same manner, as if the person were really actuated by it. From the same principles we blush for the conduct of those, who behave themselves foolishly before us; and that though they show no sense of shame, nor seem in the least conscious of their folly. All this proceeds from sympathy; but it is of a partial kind, and views its objects only on one side, without considering the other, which has a contrary effect, and would entirely destroy that emotion, which arises from the first appearance.

We have also instances, wherein an indifference and insensibility under misfortune increases our concern for the misfortunate, even though the indifference proceed not from any virtue and magnanimity. It is an aggravation of a murder, that it was committed upon persons asleep and in perfect security; as historians readily observe of any infant prince, who is captive in the hands of his enemies, that he is more worthy of compassion the less sensible he is of his miserable condition. As we ourselves are here acquainted with the wretched situation of the person, it gives us a lively idea and sensation of sorrow, which is the passion that *generally* attends it; and this idea becomes still more lively, and the sensation more violent by a contrast with that security and indifference, which we observe in the person himself. A contrast of any kind never fails to affect the imagination, especially when presented by the subject; and it is on the imagination that pity entirely depends.*[16]

Section VIII *Of malice and envy*

We must now proceed to account for the passion of *malice*, which imitates the effects of hatred, as pity does those of love; and gives us a joy in the sufferings and miseries of others, without any offence or injury on their part.

So little are men governed by reason in their sentiments and opinions, that they always judge more of objects by comparison than from their intrinsic worth and value. When the mind considers, or is accustomed to, any degree of perfection, whatever falls short of it, though really estimable, has notwithstanding the same effect upon the passions, as what is defective and ill. This is an *original* quality of the soul, and similar to what we have everyday experience of in our bodies. Let a man heat one hand and cool the other; the same water will at the same time, seem both hot and cold, according to the disposition of the different organs. A small degree of any quality, succeeding a greater, produces the same sensation, as if less than it really is, and even sometimes as the opposite quality. Any gentle pain, that follows a violent one, seems as nothing, or rather becomes a pleasure; as on the other hand a violent pain, succeeding a gentle one, is doubly grievous and uneasy.

* To prevent all ambiguity, I must observe, that where I oppose the imagination to the memory, I mean in general the faculty that presents our fainter ideas. In all other places, and particularly when it is opposed to the understanding, I understand the same faculty, excluding only our demonstrative and probable reasonings.

This no one can doubt of with regard to our passions and sensations. But there may arise some difficulty with regard to our ideas and objects. When an object augments or diminishes to the eye or imagination from a comparison with others, the image and idea of the object are still the same, and are equally extended in the *retina*, and in the brain or organ of perception. The eyes refract the rays of light, and the optic nerves convey the images to the brain in the very same manner, whether a great or small object has preceded; nor does even the imagination alter the dimensions of its object on account of a comparison with others. The question then is, how from the same impression and the same idea we can form such different judgments concerning the same object, and at one time admire its bulk, and at another despise its littleness. This variation in our judgments must certainly proceed from a variation in some perception; but as the variation lies not in the immediate impression or idea of the object, it must lie in some other impression, that accompanies it.

In order to explain this matter, I shall just touch upon two principles, one of which shall be more fully explained in the progress of this treatise; the other has been already accounted for. I believe it may safely be established for a general maxim, that no object is presented to the senses, nor image formed in the fancy, but what is accompanied with some emotion or movement of spirits proportioned to it; and however custom may make us insensible of this sensation, and cause us to confound it with the object or idea, it will be easy, by careful and exact experiments, to separate and distinguish them. For to instance only in the cases of extension and number; it is evident, that any very bulky object, such as the ocean, an extended plain, a vast chain of mountains, a wide forest; or any very numerous collection of objects, such as an army, a fleet, a crowd, excite in the mind a sensible emotion; and that the admiration, which arises on the appearance of such objects, is one of the most lively pleasures, which human nature is capable of enjoying. Now as this admiration increases or diminishes by the increase or diminution of the objects, we may conclude, according to our foregoing* principles, that it is a compound effect, proceeding from the conjunction of the several effects, which

* Book I. Part III. sect. 15.

arise from each part of the cause. Every part, then, of extension, and every unit of number has a separate emotion attending it, when conceived by the mind; and though that emotion be not always agreeable, yet by its conjunction with others, and by its agitating the spirits to a just pitch, it contributes to the production of admiration, which is always agreeable. If this be allowed with respect to extension and number, we can make no difficulty with respect to virtue and vice, wit and folly, riches and poverty, happiness and misery, and other objects of that kind, which are always attended with an evident emotion.

The second principle I shall take notice of is that of our adherence to *general rules*; which has such a mighty influence on the actions and understanding, and is able to impose on the very senses. When an object is found by experience to be always accompanied with another; whenever the first object appears, though changed in very material circumstances; we naturally fly to the conception of the second, and form an idea of it in as lively and strong a manner, as if we had inferred its existence by the justest and most authentic conclusion of our understanding. Nothing can undeceive us, not even our senses, which, instead of correcting this false judgment, are often perverted by it, and seem to authorize its errors.

The conclusion I draw from these two principles, joined to the influence of comparison above-mentioned, is very short and decisive. Every object is attended with some emotion proportioned to it; a great object with a great emotion, a small object with a small emotion. A great *object*, therefore, succeeding a small one makes a great *emotion* succeed a small one. Now a great emotion succeeding a small one becomes still greater, and rises beyond its ordinary proportion. But as there is a certain degree of an emotion, which commonly attends every magnitude of an object; when the emotion increases, we naturally imagine that the object has likewise increased. The effect conveys our view to its usual cause, a certain degree of emotion to a certain magnitude of object; nor do we consider, that comparison may change the emotion without changing anything in the object. Those, who are acquainted with the metaphysical part of optics, and know how we transfer the judgments and conclusions of the understanding to the senses, will easily conceive this whole operation.

But leaving this new discovery of an impression, that secretly attends every idea; we must at least allow of that principle, from whence the discovery arose, *that objects appear greater or less by a comparison with others.* We have so many instances of this, that it is impossible we can dispute its veracity; and it is from this principle I derive the passions of malice and envy.

It is evident we must receive a greater or less satisfaction or uneasiness from reflecting on our own condition and circumstances, in proportion as they appear more or less fortunate or unhappy, in proportion to the degrees of riches, and power, and merit, and reputation, which we think ourselves possessed of. Now as we seldom judge of objects from their intrinsic value, but form our notions of them from a comparison with other objects; it follows, that according as we observe a greater or less share of happiness or misery in others, we must make an estimate of our own, and feel a consequent pain or pleasure. The misery of another gives us a more lively idea of our happiness, and his happiness of our misery. The former, therefore, produces delight; and the latter uneasiness.

Here then is a kind of pity reversed, or contrary sensations arising in the beholder, from those which are felt by the person, whom he considers. In general we may observe, that in all kinds of comparison an object makes us always receive from another, to which it is compared, a sensation contrary to what arises from itself in its direct and immediate survey. A small object makes a great one appear still greater. A great object makes a little one appear less. Deformity of itself produces uneasiness; but makes us receive new pleasure by its contrast with a beautiful object, whose beauty is augmented by it; as on the other hand, beauty, which of itself produces pleasure, makes us receive a new pain by the contrast with anything ugly, whose deformity it augments. The case, therefore, must be the same with happiness and misery. The direct survey of another's pleasure naturally gives us pleasure, and therefore produces pain when compared with our own. His plan, considered in itself, is painful to us, but augments the idea of our own happiness, and gives us pleasure.

Nor will it appear strange, that we may feel a reversed

sensation from the happiness and misery of others; since we find the same comparison may give us a kind of malice against ourselves, and make us rejoice for our pains, and grieve for our pleasures. Thus the prospect of past pain is agreeable, when we are satisfied with our present condition; as on the other hand our past pleasures give us uneasiness, when we enjoy nothing at present equal to them. The comparison being the same, as when we reflect on the sentiments of others, must be attended with the same effects.

Nay a person may extend this malice against himself, even to his present fortune, and carry it so far as designedly to seek affliction, and increase his pains and sorrows. This may happen upon two occasions. *First*, upon the distress and misfortune of a friend, or person dear to him. *Secondly*, upon the feeling any remorses for a crime, of which he has been guilty. It is from the principle of comparison that both these irregular appetites for evil arise. A person, who indulges himself in any pleasure, while his friend lies under affliction, feels the reflected uneasiness from his friend more sensibly by a comparison with the original pleasure, which he himself enjoys. This contrast, indeed, ought also to enliven the present pleasure. But as grief is here supposed to be the predominant passion, every addition falls to that side, and is swallowed up in it, without operating in the least upon the contrary affection. It is the same case with those penances, which men inflict on themselves for their past sins and failings. When a criminal reflects on the punishment he deserves, the idea of it is magnified by a comparison with his present ease and satisfaction; which forces him, in a manner, to seek uneasiness, in order to avoid so disagreeable a contrast.

This reasoning will account for the origin of *envy* as well as of malice. The only difference betwixt these passions lies in this, that envy is excited by some present enjoyment of another, which by comparison diminishes our idea of our own; whereas malice is the unprovoked desire of producing evil to another, in order to reap a pleasure from the comparison. The enjoyment, which is the object of envy, is commonly superior to our own. A superiority naturally seems to overshade us, and presents a disagreeable comparison. But even in the case of an inferiority, we still desire a greater distance, in order to augment still more the idea of ourself.

When this distance diminishes, the comparison is less to our advantage; and consequently gives us less pleasure, and is even disagreeable. Hence arises that species of envy, which men feel, when they perceive their inferiors approaching or overtaking them in the pursuit of glory or happiness. In this envy we may see the effects of comparison twice repeated. A man, who compares himself to his inferior, receives a pleasure from the comparison; and when the inferiority decreases by the elevation of the inferior, what should only have been a decrease of pleasure, becomes a real pain, by a new comparison with its preceding condition.

It is worthy of observation concerning that envy, which arises from a superiority in others, that it is not the great disproportion betwixt ourself and another, which produces it; but on the contrary, our proximity. A common soldier bears no such envy to his general as to his sergeant or corporal; nor does an eminent writer meet with so great jealousy in common hackney scribblers, as in authors, that more nearly approach him. It may, indeed, be thought, that the greater the disproportion is, the greater must be the uneasiness from the comparison. But we may consider on the other hand, that the great disproportion cuts off the relation, and either keeps us from comparing ourselves with what is remote from us, or diminishes the effects of the comparison. Resemblance and proximity always produce a relation of ideas; and where you destroy these ties, however other accidents may bring two ideas together; as they have no bond or connecting quality to join in the imagination; it is impossible they can remain long united, or have any considerable influence on each other.

I have observed in considering the nature of ambition, that the great feel a double pleasure in authority from the comparison of their own condition with that of their slaves; and that this comparison has a double influence, because it is natural, and presented by the subject. When the fancy, in the comparison of objects, passes not easily from the one object to the other, the action of the mind is, in a great measure, broke, and the fancy, in considering the second object, begins, as it were, upon a new footing. The impression, which attends every object, seems not greater in that case by succeeding a less of the same kind; but these two impressions are distinct, and produce their distinct effects, without any communication together. The want of relation in the ideas breaks the relation of the impressions, and by such a separation prevents their mutual operation and influence.

To confirm this we may observe, that the proximity in the degree of merit is not alone sufficient to give rise to envy, but must be assisted by other relations. A poet is not apt to envy a philosopher, or a poet of a different kind, of a different nation, or of a different age. All these differences prevent or weaken the comparison, and consequently the passion.

This too is the reason, why all objects appear great or little, merely by a comparison with those of the same species. A mountain neither magnifies nor diminishes a horse in our eyes; but when a *Flemish* and a *Welsh* horse are seen together, the one appears greater and the other less, than when viewed apart.

From the same principle we may account for that remark of historians, that any party in a civil war always choose to call in a foreign enemy at any hazard rather than submit to their fellow-citizens. *Guicciardin* applies this remark to the wars in *Italy*, where the relations betwixt the different states are, properly speaking, nothing but of name, language, and contiguity. Yet even these relations, when joined with superiority, by making the comparison more natural, make it likewise more grievous, and cause men to search for some other superiority, which may be attended with no relation, and by that means may have a less sensible influence on the imagination. The mind quickly perceives its several advantages and disadvantages; and finding its situation to be most uneasy, where superiority is conjoined with other relations, seeks its repose as much as possible, by their separation, and by breaking that association of ideas, which renders the comparison so much more natural and efficacious. When it cannot break the association, it feels a stronger desire to remove the superiority; and this is the reason why travellers are commonly so lavish of their praises to the *Chinese* and *Persians*, at the same time, that they depreciate those neighbouring nations, which may stand upon a foot of rivalship with their native country.

These examples from history and common experience are rich and curious; but we may find parallel ones in the arts, which are no less remarkable. Should an author compose a treatise, of which one part was serious and profound, another light and humorous, everyone would condemn so strange a mixture, and would accuse him of the neglect of all rules of art and criticism. These rules of art are founded on the qualities of human nature; and the quality of human nature, which requires a consistency in every performance, is that which renders the mind incapable of passing in a moment from one passion and disposition to a quite different one. Yet this makes us not blame Mr *Prior* for joining his *Alma* and his *Solomon* in the same volume; though that admirable poet has succeeded perfectly well in the gaiety of the one, as well as in the melancholy of the other. Even supposing the reader should peruse these two compositions without any interval, he would feel little or no difficulty in the change of passions. Why, but because he considers these performances as entirely different, and by this break in the ideas, breaks the progress of the affections, and hinders the one from influencing or contradicting the other?

An heroic and burlesque design, united in one picture, would be monstrous; though we place two pictures of so opposite a character in the same chamber, and even close by each other, without any scruple or difficulty.

In a word, no ideas can affect each other, either by comparison, or by the passions they separately produce, unless they be united together by some relation, which may cause an easy transition of the ideas, and consequently of the emotions or impressions, attending the ideas; and may preserve the one impression in the passage of the imagination to the object of the other. This principle is very remarkable, because it is analogous to what we have observed both concerning the *understanding* and the *passions*. Suppose two objects to be presented to me, which are not connected by any kind of relation. Suppose that each of these objects separately produces a passion; and that these two passions are in themselves contrary. We find from experience, that the want of relation in the objects or ideas hinders the natural contrariety of the passions, and that the break in the transition of the thought removes the affections from each other, and prevents their opposition. It is the same case with comparison; and from both these phenomena we may safely conclude, that the relation of ideas must forward the transition of impressions; since its absence alone is able to prevent it, and to separate what naturally should have operated upon each other. When the absence of an object or quality removes any usual or natural effect, we may certainly conclude that its presence contributes to the production of the effect.

SECTION IX *Of the mixture of benevolence and anger with compassion and malice*

Thus we have endeavoured to account for *pity* and *malice*. Both these affections arise from the imagination, according to the light, in which it places its object. When our fancy considers directly the sentiments of others, and enters deep into them, it makes us sensible of all the passions it surveys, but in a particular manner of grief or sorrow. On the contrary, when we compare the sentiments of others to our own, we feel a sensation directly opposite to the original one, *viz.* a joy from the grief of others, and a grief from their joy. But these are only the first foundations of the affections of pity and malice. Other passions are afterwards confounded with them. There is always a mixture of love or tenderness with pity, and of hatred or anger with malice. But it must be confessed, that this mixture seems at first sight to be contradictory to my system. For as pity is an uneasiness, and malice a joy, arising from the misery of others, pity should naturally, as in all other cases, produce hatred; and malice, love. This contradiction I endeavour to reconcile, after the following manner.

In order to cause a transition of passions, there is required a double relation of impressions and ideas, nor is one relation sufficient to produce this effect. But that we may understand the full force of this double relation, we must consider, that it is not the present sensation alone or momentary pain or pleasure, which determines the character of any passion, but the whole bent or tendency of it from the beginning to the end.[17] One impression may be related to another, not only when their sensations are resembling, as we have all along supposed in the preceding cases; but also when their impulses or directions are similar and correspondent. This cannot take place with regard to pride and humility; because these are only pure sensations, without any direction or tendency to action.[18] We are, therefore, to look for instances of this peculiar relation of impressions only in such affections, as are attended with a certain appetite or desire; such as those of love and hatred.

Benevolence or the appetite, which attends love, is a desire of the happiness of the person beloved, and an aversion to his misery; as anger or the appetite, which attends hatred, is a desire of the misery of the person hated, and an aversion to his happiness. A desire, therefore, of the happiness of another and aversion to his misery, are similar to benevolence; and a desire of his misery and aversion to his happiness are correspondent to anger. Now pity is a desire of happiness to another, and aversion to his misery; as malice is the contrary appetite. Pity, then, is related to benevolence; and malice to anger; and as benevolence has been already found to be connected with love, by a natural and original quality, and anger with hatred; it is by this chain the passions of pity and malice are connected with love and hatred.

This hypothesis is founded on sufficient experience. A man, who from any motives has entertained a resolution of performing an action, naturally runs into every other view or motive, which may fortify that resolution, and give it authority and influence on the mind. To confirm us in any design, we search for motives drawn from interest, from honour, from duty. What wonder, then, that pity and benevolence, malice, and anger, being the same desires arising from different principles, should so totally mix together as to be undistinguishable? As to the connection betwixt benevolence and love, anger and hatred, being *original* and primary, it admits of no difficulty.[19]

We may add to this another experiment, *viz.* that benevolence and anger, and consequently love and hatred, arise when our happiness or misery have any dependence on the happiness or misery of another person, without any farther relation. I doubt not but this experiment will appear so singular as to excuse us for stopping a moment to consider it.

Suppose, that two persons of the same trade should seek employment in a town, that is not able to maintain both, it is plain the success of one is perfectly incompatible with that of the other, and that whatever is for the interest of either is contrary to that of his rival, and so *vice versa*. Suppose again, that two merchants, though living in different parts of the world, should enter into co-partnership together, the advantage or loss of one becomes immediately the advantage or loss of his partner, and the same fortune necessarily attends both. Now it is evident, that in the first case, hatred always follows upon the contrariety of interests; as in the second, love arises from their union. Let us consider to what principle we can ascribe these passions.

It is plain they arise not from the double relations of impressions and ideas, if we regard only the present sensation. For taking the first case of rivalship; though the pleasure and advantage of an antagonist necessarily causes my pain and loss, yet to counterbalance this, his pain and loss causes my pleasure and advantage; and supposing him to be unsuccessful, I may by this means receive from him a superior degree of satisfaction. In the same manner the success of a partner rejoices me, but then his misfortunes afflict me in an equal proportion; and it is easy to imagine, that the latter sentiment may in many cases preponderate. But whether the fortune of a rival or partner be good or bad, I always hate the former and love the latter.

This love of a partner cannot proceed from the relation or connection betwixt us; in the same manner as I love a brother or countryman. A rival has almost as close a relation to me as a partner. For as the pleasure of the latter causes my pleasure, and his pain my pain; so the pleasure of the former causes my pain, and his pain my pleasure. The connection, then, of cause and effect is the same in both cases; and if in the one case, the cause and effect has a farther relation of resemblance, they have that of contrariety in the other; which, being also a species of resemblance, leaves the matter pretty equal.

The only explication, then, we can give of this phenomenon is derived from that principle of a parallel direction above mentioned. Our concern for our own interest gives us a pleasure in the pleasure, and a pain in the pain of a partner, after the same manner as by sympathy we feel a sensation correspondent to those, which appear in any person, who is present with us. On the other hand, the same concern for our interest makes us feel a pain in the pleasure, and a pleasure in the pain of a rival; and in short the same contrariety of sentiments as arises from comparison and malice. Since, therefore, a parallel direction of the affections, pro-

E

ceeding from interest, can give rise to benevolence or anger, no wonder the same parallel direction, derived from sympathy and from comparison, should have the same effect.

In general we may observe, that it is impossible to do good to others, from whatever motive, without feeling some touches of kindness and goodwill towards them; as the injuries we do, not only cause hatred in the person, who suffers them, but even in ourselves. These phenomena, indeed, may in part be accounted for from other principles.

But here there occurs a considerable objection, which it will be necessary to examine before we proceed any farther. I have endeavoured to prove, that power and riches, or poverty and meanness; which give rise to love or hatred, without producing any original pleasure or uneasiness; operate upon us by means of a secondary sensation derived from a sympathy with that pain or satisfaction, which they produce in the person, who possesses them. From a sympathy with his pleasure there arises love; from that with his uneasiness, hatred. But it is a maxim, which I have just now established, and which is absolutely necessary to the explication of the phenomena of pity and malice, 'That it is not the present sensation or momentary pain or pleasure, which determines the character of any passion, but the general bent or tendency of it from the beginning to the end.' For this reason, pity or a sympathy with pain produces love, and that because it interests us in the fortunes of others, good or bad, and gives us a secondary sensation correspondent to the primary; in which it has the same influence with love and benevolence. Since then this rule holds good in one case, why does it not prevail throughout, and why does sympathy in uneasiness ever produce any passion beside goodwill and kindness? Is it becoming a philosopher to alter his method of reasoning, and run from one principle to its contrary, according to the particular phenomenon, which he would explain?

I have mentioned two different causes, from which a transition of passion may arise, *viz.* a double relation of ideas and impressions, and what is similar to it, a conformity in the tendency and direction of any two desires, which arise from different principles. Now I assert, that when a sympathy with uneasiness is weak, it produces hatred or contempt by the former cause; when strong, it produces love or tenderness by the latter. This is the solution of the foregoing difficulty, which seems so urgent; and this is a principle founded on such evident arguments, that we ought to have established it, even though it were not necessary to the explication of any phenomenon.

It is certain, that sympathy is not always limited to the present moment, but that we often feel by communication the pains and pleasures of others, which are not in being, and which we only anticipate by the force of imagination. For supposing I saw a person perfectly unknown to me, who, while asleep in the fields, was in danger of being trod under foot by horses, I should immediately run to his assistance; and in this I should be actuated by the same principle of sympathy, which makes me concerned for the present sorrows of a stranger. The bare mention of this is sufficient. Sympathy being nothing but a lively idea converted into an impression, it is evident, that, in considering the future possible or probable condition of any person, we may enter into it with so vivid a conception as to make it our own concern; and by that means be sensible of pains and pleasures, which neither belong to ourselves, nor at the present instant have any real existence.

But however we may look forward to the future in sympathizing with any person, the extending of our sympathy depends in a great measure upon our sense of his present condition. It is a great effort of imagination, to form such lively ideas even of the present sentiments of others as to feel these very sentiments; but it is impossible we could extend this sympathy to the future, without being aided by some circumstance in the present, which strikes upon us in a lively manner. When the present misery of another has any strong influence upon me, the vivacity of the conception is not confined merely to its immediate object, but diffuses its influence over all the related ideas, and gives me a lively notion of all the circumstances of that person, whether past, present, or future; possible, probable or certain. By means of this lively notion I am interested in them; take part with them; and feel a sympathetic motion in my breast, conformable to whatever I imagine in his. If I diminish the vivacity of the first conception, I diminish that of the related ideas; as pipes can convey no more water than what arises at the fountain. By this diminution I destroy the future prospect, which is necessary to interest me perfectly in the fortune of another. I may feel the present impression, but carry my sympathy no farther, and never transfuse the force of the first conception into my ideas of the related objects. If it be another's misery, which is presented in his feeble manner, I receive it by communication, and am affected with all the passions related to it; but as I am not so much interested as to concern myself in his good fortune, as well as his bad, I never feel the extensive sympathy, nor the passions related to *it*.

Now in order to know what passions are related to these different kinds of sympathy, we must consider, that benevolence is an original pleasure arising from the pleasure of the person beloved, and a pain proceeding from his pain; from which correspondence of impressions there arises a subsequent desire of his pleasure, and aversion to his pain. In order, then, to make a passion run parallel with benevolence, it is requisite we should feel these double impressions, correspondent to those of the person, whom we consider; nor is any one of them alone sufficient for that purpose. When we sympathize only with one impression, and that a painful one, this sympathy is related to anger and to hatred, upon account of the uneasiness it conveys to us. But as the extensive or limited sympathy depends upon the force of the first sympathy; it follows, that the passion of love or hatred depends upon the same principle. A strong impression, when communicated, gives a double tendency of the passions; which is related to benevolence and love by a similarity of direction; however painful the first impression might have been. A weak impression, that is painful, is related to anger and hatred by the resemblance of sensations. Benevolence, therefore, arises from a great degree of misery, or any degree strongly sympathized with; hatred or contempt from a small degree, or one weakly sympathized with; which is the principle I intended to prove and explain.

Nor have we only our reason to trust to for this principle, but also experience. A certain degree of poverty produces contempt; but a degree beyond causes compassion and goodwill. We may undervalue a peasant or servant; but when the misery of a beggar appears very great, or is painted in very lively colours, we sympathize with him in his afflictions, and feel in our heart evident touches of pity and benevolence. The same object causes contrary passions according to its different degrees. The passions, therefore, must depend upon principles, that operate in such certain degrees, according to my hypothesis. The increase of the sympathy has evidently the same effect as the increase of the misery.

A barren or desolate country always seems ugly and disagreeable, and commonly inspires us with contempt for the inhabitants. This deformity, however, proceeds in a great measure from a sympathy with the inhabitants, as has been already observed; but it is only a weak one, and reaches no farther than the immediate sensation, which is disagreeable. The view of a city in ashes conveys benevolent sentiments; because we there enter so deep into the interests of the miserable inhabitants, as to wish for their prosperity, as well as feel their adversity.

But though the force of the impression generally produces pity and benevolence, it is certain, that by being carried too far it ceases to have that effect. This, perhaps, may be worth our notice. When the uneasiness is either small in itself, or remote from us, it engages not the imagination, nor is able to convey an equal concern for the future and contingent good, as for the present and real evil. Upon its acquiring greater force, we become so interested in the concerns of the person, as to be sensible both of his good and bad fortune; and from that complete sympathy there arises pity and benevolence. But it will easily be imagined, that where the present evil strikes with more than ordinary force, it may entirely engage our attention, and prevent that double sympathy, above-mentioned. Thus we find, that though everyone, but especially women, are apt to contract a kindness for criminals, who go to the scaffold, and readily imagine them to be uncommonly handsome and well-shaped; yet one, who is present at the cruel execution of the rack, feels no such tender emotions; but is in a manner overcome with horror, and has no leisure to temper this uneasy sensation by any opposite sympathy.

But the instance, which makes the most clearly for my hypothesis, is that wherein by a change of the objects we separate the double sympathy even from a middling degree of the passion; in which case we find, that pity, instead of producing love and tenderness as usual, always gives rise to the contrary affection. When we observe a person in misfortunes, we are affected with pity and love; but the author of that misfortune becomes the object of our strongest hatred, and is the more detested in proportion to the degree of our compassion. Now for what reason should the same passion of pity produce love to the person, who suffers the misfortune, and hatred to the person, who causes it; unless it be because in the latter case the author bears a relation only to the misfortune; whereas in considering the sufferer we carry our view on every side, and wish for his prosperity, as well as are sensible of his affliction?

I shall just observe, before I leave the present subject, that this phenomenon of the double sympathy, and its tendency to cause love, may contribute to the production of the kindness, which we naturally bear our relations and acquaintance. Custom and relation make us enter deeply into the sentiments of others; and whatever fortune we suppose to attend them, is rendered present to us by the imagination, and operates as if originally our own. We rejoice in their pleasures, and grieve for their sorrows, merely from the force of sympathy. Nothing that concerns them is indifferent to us; and as this correspondence of sentiments is the natural attendant of love, it readily produces that affection.

SECTION X *Of respect and contempt*

There now remains only to explain the passions of *respect* and *contempt*, along with the *amorous* affection, in order to understand all the passions which have any mixture of love or hatred. Let us begin with respect and contempt.

In considering the qualities and circumstances of others, we may either regard them as they really are in themselves; or may make a comparison betwixt them and our own qualities and circumstances; or may join these two methods of consideration. The good qualities of others, from the first point of view, produce love; from the second, humility; and from the third, respect; which is a mixture of these two passions. Their bad qualities, after the same manner, cause either hatred, or pride, or contempt, according to the light in which we survey them.

That there is a mixture of pride in contempt, and of humility in respect, is, I think, too evident, from their very feeling or appearance, to require any particular proof. That this mixture arises from a tacit comparison of the person contemned or respected with ourselves is no less evident. The same man may cause either respect, love, or contempt by his condition and talents, according as the person, who considers him, from his inferior becomes his equal or superior. In changing the point of view, though the object may remain the same, its proportion to ourselves entirely alters; which is the cause of an alteration in the passions. These passions, therefore, arise from our observing the proportion; that is, from a comparison.

I have already observed, that the mind has a much stronger propensity to pride than to humility, and have endeavoured, from the principles of human nature, to assign a cause for this phenomenon. Whether my reasoning be received or not, the phenomenon is undisputed, and appears in many instances. Among the rest, it is the reason why there is a much greater mixture of pride in contempt, than of humility in respect, and why we are more elevated with the view of one below us, than mortified with the presence of one above us. Contempt or scorn has so strong a tincture of pride, that there scarce is any other passion discernible; whereas in esteem or respect, love makes a more considerable ingredient than humility. The passion of vanity is so prompt, that it rouses at the least call; while humanity requires a stronger impulse to make it exert itself.

But here it may reasonably be asked, why this mixture takes place only in some cases, and appears not on every occasion. All those objects, which cause love, when placed on another person, are the causes of pride, when transferred to ourselves; and consequently ought to be causes of humility, as well as love, while they belong to others, and are only compared to those, which we ourselves possess. In like manner every quality, which, by being directly considered, produces hatred, ought always to give rise to pride by comparison, and by a mixture of these passions of hatred and pride ought to excite contempt or scorn. The difficulty then is, why any objects ever cause pure love or hatred, and produce not always the mixed passions of respect and contempt.

I have supposed all along, that the passions of love and pride, and those of humility and hatred are similar in their sensations, and that the two former are always agreeable, and the two latter painful. But though this be universally true, it is observable, that the two agreeable, as well as the two painful passions, have some differences, and even contrarieties, which distinguish them. Nothing invigorates and exalts the mind equally with pride and vanity; though at the same time love or tenderness is rather found to weaken and enfeeble it. The same difference is observable betwixt the uneasy passions. Anger and hatred bestow a new force on all our thoughts and actions; while humility and shame deject and discourage us. Of these qualities of the passions, it will be necessary to form a distinct idea. Let us remember, that pride and hatred invigorate the soul; and love and humility enfeeble it.

From this it follows, that tho' the conformity betwixt love and hatred in the agreeableness of their sensation makes them always be excited by the same objects, yet this other contrariety is the reason, why they are excited in very different degrees. Genius and learning are *pleasant* and *magnificent* objects, and by both these circumstances are adapted to pride and vanity; but have a relation to love by their pleasure only. Ignorance and simplicity are *disagreeable* and *mean*, which in the same manner gives them a double connection with humility, and a single one with hatred. We may, therefore, consider it as certain, that though the same object always produces love and pride, humility and hatred, according to its different situations, yet it seldom produces either the two former or the two latter passions in the same proportion.

It is here we must seek for a solution of the difficulty above-mentioned, why any object ever excites pure love or hatred, and does not always produce respect or contempt, by a mixture of humility or pride. No quality in another gives rise to humility by comparison, unless it would have produced pride by being placed in ourselves; and *vice versa* no object excites pride by comparison, unless it would have produced humility by the direct survey. This is evident, objects always produce by *comparison* a sensation directly contrary to their *original* one. Suppose, therefore, an object to be presented, which is peculiarly fitted to produce love, but imperfectly to excite pride; this object, belonging to another, gives rise directly to a great degree of love, but to a small one of humility by comparison; and consequently that latter passion is scarce felt in the compound, nor is able to convert the love into respect. This is the case with good nature, good humour, facility, generosity, beauty, and many other qualities.

These have a peculiar aptitude to produce love in others; but not so great a tendency to excite pride in ourselves; for which reason the view of them, as belonging to another person, produces pure love, with but a small mixture of humility and respect. It is easy to extend the same reasoning to the opposite passions.

Before we leave this subject, it may not be amiss to account for a pretty curious phenomenon, *viz.* why we commonly keep at a distance such as we contemn, and allow not our inferiors to approach too near even in place and situation. It has already been observed, that almost every kind of idea is attended with some emotion, even the ideas of number and extension, much more those of such objects as are esteemed of consequence in life, and fix our attention. It is not with entire indifference we can survey either a rich man or a poor one, but must feel some faint touches, at least, of respect in the former case, and of contempt in the latter. These two passions are contrary to each other; but in order to make this contrariety be felt, the objects must be someway related; otherwise the affections are totally separate and distinct, and never encounter. The relation takes place wherever the persons become contiguous; which is a general reason why we are uneasy at seeing such disproportioned objects, as a rich man and a poor one, a nobleman and a porter, in that situation.

This uneasiness, which is common to every spectator, must be more sensible to the superior; and that because the near approach of the inferior is regarded as a piece of ill-breeding, and shows that he is not sensible of the disproportion, and is no way affected by it. A sense of superiority in another breeds in all men an inclination to keep themselves at a distance from him, and determines them to redouble the marks of respect and reverence, when they are obliged to approach him; and where they do not observe that conduct, it is a proof they are not sensible of his superiority. From hence too it proceeds, that any great *difference* in the degrees of any quality is called a *distance* by a common metaphor, which, however trivial it may appear, is founded on natural principles of the imagination. A great difference inclines us to produce a distance. The ideas of distance and difference are, therefore, connected together. Connected ideas are readily taken for each other; and this is in general the source of the metaphor, as we shall have occasion to observe afterwards.

Section XI *Of the amorous passion, or love betwixt the sexes*

Of all the compound passions, which proceed from a mixture of love and hatred with other affections, no one better deserves our attention, than that love, which arises betwixt the sexes, as well on account of its force and violence, as those curious principles of philosophy, for which it affords us an uncontestable argument. It is plain, that this affection, in its most natural state, is derived from the conjunction of three different impressions or passions, *viz.* the pleasing sensation arising from beauty; the bodily appetite for generation; and a generous kindness or goodwill. The origin of kindness from beauty may be explained from the foregoing reasoning. The question is how the bodily appetite is excited by it.[20]

The appetite of generation, when confined to a certain degree, is evidently of the pleasant kind, and has a strong connection with all the agreeable emotions. Joy, mirth, vanity, and kindness are all incentives to this desire; as well as music, dancing, wine, and good cheer. On the other hand, sorrow, melancholy, poverty, humility are destructive of it. From this quality it is easily conceived why it should be connected with the sense of beauty.

But there is another principle that contributes to the same effect. I have observed that the parallel direction of the desires is a real relation, and no less than a resemblance in their sensation, produces a connection among them. That we may fully comprehend the extent of this relation, we must consider, that any principal desire may be attended with subordinate ones, which are connected with it, and to which if other desires are parallel, they are by that means related to the principal one. Thus hunger may oft be considered as the primary inclination of the soul, and the desire of approaching the meat as the secondary one; since it is absolutely necessary to the satisfying that appetite. If an object, therefore, by any separate qualities, inclines us to approach the meat, it naturally increases our appetite; as on the contrary, whatever inclines us to set our victuals at a distance, is contradictory to hunger, and diminishes our inclination to them. Now it is plain that beauty has the first effect, and deformity the second, which is the reason why the former gives us a keener appetite for our victuals, and the latter is sufficient to disgust us at the most savoury dish, that cookery has invented. All this is easily applicable to the appetite for generation.

From these two relations, *viz.* resemblance and a parallel desire, there arises such a connection betwixt the sense of beauty, the bodily appetite, and benevolence, that they become in a manner inseparable; and we find from experience, that it is indifferent which of them advances first; since any of them is almost sure to be attended with the related affections. One, who is inflamed with lust, feels at least a momentary kindness towards the object of it, and at the same time fancies her more beautiful than ordinary; as there are many, who begin with kindness and esteem for the wit and merit of the person, and advance from that to the other passions. But the most common species of love is that which first arises from beauty, and afterwards diffuses itself into kindness and into the bodily appetite. Kindness or esteem, and the appetite to generation, are too remote to unite easily together. The one is, perhaps, the most refined passion of the soul; the other the most gross and vulgar. The love of beauty is placed in a just medium betwixt them, and partakes of both their natures; from whence it proceeds, that it is so singularly fitted to produce both.

This account of love is not peculiar to my system, but is unavoidable on any hypothesis. The three affections, which compose this passion, are evidently distinct, and has each of them its distinct object. It is certain, therefore, that it is only by their relation they produce each other. But the relation of passions is not alone sufficient. It is likewise necessary, there shou'd be a relation of ideas. The beauty of one person never inspires us with love for another. This then is a sensible proof of the double relation of impressions and ideas. From one instance so evident as this we may form a judgment of the rest.

This may also serve in another view to illustrate what I have insisted on concerning the origin of pride and humility, love and hatred. I have observed, that though self be the object of the first set of passions, and some other person of the second, yet these objects cannot alone be the causes of the passions; as having each of them a relation to two contrary affections, which must from the very first moment destroy each other. Here then is the situation of the mind, as I have already described it. It has certain organs naturally fitted to produce a passion; that passion, when produced, naturally turns the view to a certain object. But this not being sufficient to produce the passion, there is required some other emotion, which by a double relation of impressions and ideas may set these principles in action, and bestow on them their first impulse. This situation is still more remarkable with regard to the appetite of generation. Sex is not only the object, but also the cause of the appetite. We not only turn our view to it, when actuated by that appetite; but the reflecting on it suffices to excite the appetite. But as this cause loses its force by too great frequency, it is necessary it should be quickened by some new impulse; and that impulse we find to arise from the *beauty* of the *person*; that is, from a double relation of impressions and ideas. Since this double relation is necessary where an affection has both a distinct cause, and object, how much more so, where it has only a distinct object, without any determinate cause?

Section XII *Of the love and hatred of animals*

But to pass from the passions of love and hatred, and from their mixtures and compositions, as they appear in man, to the same affections, as they display themselves in brutes; we may observe, not only that love and hatred are common to the whole sensitive creation, but likewise that their causes, as above-explained, are of so simple a nature, that they may easily be supposed to operate on mere animals. There is no force of reflection or penetration required. Everything is conducted by springs and principles, which are not peculiar to man, or any one species of animals. The conclusion from this is obvious in favour of the foregoing system.

Love in animals, has not for its only object animals of the same species, but extends itself farther, and comprehends almost every sensible and thinking being. A dog naturally loves a man above his own species, and very commonly meets with a return of affection.

As animals are but little susceptible either of the pleasures or pains of the imagination, they can judge of objects only by the sensible good or evil, which they produce, and from *that* must regulate their affections towards them. Accordingly we find, that by benefits or injuries we produce their love or hatred; and that by feeding and cherishing any animal, we quickly acquire his affections; as by beating and abusing him we never fail to draw on us his enmity and ill-will.

Love in beasts is not caused so much by relation, as in our species; and that because their thoughts are not so active as to trace relations, except in very obvious instances. Yet it is easy to remark, that on some occasions it has a considerable influence upon them. Thus acquaintance, which has the same effect as relation, always produces love in animals either to men or to each other. For the same reason any likeness among them is the source of affection. An ox confined to a park with horses, will naturally join their company, if I may so speak, but always leaves it to enjoy that of his own species, where he has the choice of both.

The affection of parents to their young proceeds from a peculiar instance in animals, as well as in our species.

It is evident, that *sympathy*, or the communication of passions, takes place among animals, no less than among men. Fear, anger, courage and other affections are frequently communicated from one animal to another, without their knowledge of that cause, which produced the original passion. Grief likewise is received by sympathy; and produces almost all the same consequences, and excites the same emotions as in our species. The howlings and lamentations of a dog produce a sensible concern in his fellows. And it is remarkable, that though almost all animals use in play the same member, and nearly the same action as in fighting; a lion, a tiger, a cat their paws; an ox his horns; a dog his teeth; a horse his heels. Yet they most carefully avoid harming their companion, even though they have nothing to fear from his resentment; which is an evident proof of the sense brutes have of each other's pain and pleasure.

Everyone has observed how much more dogs are animated when they hunt in a pack, than when they pursue their game apart; and it is evident this can proceed from nothing but from sympathy. It is also well known to hunters, that this effect follows in a greater degree, and even in too great a degree, where two packs, that are strangers to each other, are joined together. We might, perhaps, be at a loss to explain this phenomenon, if we had not experience of a similar in ourselves.

Envy and malice are passions very remarkable in animals. They are perhaps more common than pity; as requiring less effort of thought and imagination.

PART III *Of the Will and Direct Passions*

SECTION I *Of liberty and necessity*

We come now to explain the *direct* passions, or the impressions, which arise immediately from good or evil, from pain or pleasure. Of this kind are, *desire and aversion, grief and joy, hope and fear*.

Of all the immediate effects of pain and pleasure, there is none more remarkable than the *will*; and though, properly speaking, it be not comprehended among the passions, yet as the full understanding of its nature and properties, is necessary to the explanation of them, we shall here make it the subject of our enquiry. I desire it may be observed, that by the *will*, I mean nothing but *the internal impression we feel and are conscious of, when we knowingly give rise to any new motion of our body, or new perception of our mind.* This impression, like the preceding ones of pride and humility, love and hatred, it is impossible to define, and needless to describe any farther; for which reason we shall cut off all those definitions and distinctions, with which philosophers are wont to perplex rather than clear up this question; and entering at first upon the subject, shall examine that long disputed question concerning *liberty and necessity*; which occurs so naturally in treating of the will.[21]

It is universally acknowledged, that the operations of external bodies are necessary, and that in the communication of their motion, in their attraction, and mutual cohesion, there are not the least traces of indifference or liberty. Every object is determined by an absolute fate to a certain degree and direction of its motion, and can no more depart from that precise line, in which it moves, than it can convert itself into an angel, or spirit, or any other superior substance. The actions, therefore, of matter are to be regarded as instances of necessary actions; and whatever is in this respect on the same footing with matter, must be acknowledged to be necessary. That we may know whether this be the case with the actions of the mind, we shall begin with examining matter, and considering on what the idea of a necessity in its operations are founded, and why we conclude one body or action to be the infallible cause of another.

It has been observed already, that in no single instance the ultimate connection of any objects is discoverable, either by our senses or reason, and that we can never penetrate so far into the essence and construction of bodies, as to perceive the principle, on which their mutual influence depends. It is their constant union alone, with which we are acquainted; and it is from the constant union the necessity arises. If objects had not an uniform and regular conjunction with each other, we should never arrive at any idea of cause and effect; and even after all, the necessity, which enters into that idea, is nothing but a determination of the mind to pass from one object to its usual attendant, and infer the existence of one from that of the other. Here then are two particulars, which we are to consider as essential to necessity, *viz.* the constant *union* and the *inference* of the mind; and wherever we discover these we must acknowledge a necessity. As the actions of matter have no necessity, but what is derived from these circumstances, and it is not by any insight into the essence of bodies we discover their connection, the absence of this insight, while the union and inference remain, will never, in any case, remove the necessity. It is the observation of the union, which produces the inference; for which reason it might be thought sufficient, if we prove a constant union in the actions of the mind, in order to establish the inference, along with the necessity of these actions. But that I may bestow a greater force on my reasoning, I shall examine these particulars apart, and shall first prove from experience, that our actions have a constant union with our motives, tempers, and circumstances, before I consider the inferences we draw from it.

To this end a very slight and general view of the common course of human affairs will be sufficient. There is no light, in which we can take them, that does not confirm this principle. Whether we consider mankind according to the difference of sexes, ages, governments, conditions, or methods of education; the same uniformity and regular operation of natural principles are discernible. Like causes still produce like effects; in the same manner as in the mutual action of the elements and powers of nature.

There are different trees, which regularly produce fruit,

whose relish is different from each other; and this regularity will be admitted as an instance of necessity and causes in external bodies. But are the products of *Guienne* and of *Champagne* more regularly different than the sentiments, actions, and passions of the two sexes, of which the one are distinguished by their force and maturity, the other by their delicacy and softness?

Are the changes of our body from infancy to old age more regular and certain than those of our mind and conduct? And would a man be more ridiculous, who would expect that an infant of four years old will raise a weight of three hundred pound, than one, who from a person of the same age, would look for a philosophical reasoning, or a prudent and well-concerted action?

We must certainly allow, that the cohesion of the parts of matter arises from natural and necessary principles, whatever difficulty we may find in explaining them; and for a like reason we must allow, that human society is founded on like principles; and our reason in the latter case, is better than even that in the former; because we not only observe, that men *always* seek society, but can also explain the principles, on which this universal propensity is founded. For is it more certain, that two flat pieces of marble will unite together, than that two young savages of different sexes will copulate? Do the children arise from this copulation more uniformly, than does the parents' care for their safety and preservation? And after they have arrived at years of discretion by the care of their parents, are the inconveniencies attending their separation more certain than their foresight of these inconveniencies, and their care of avoiding them by a close union and confederacy?

The skin, pores, muscles, and nerves of a day-labourer are different from those of a man of quality; so are his sentiments, actions and manners. The different stations of life influence the whole fabric, external and internal; and these different stations arise necessarily, because uniformly, from the necessary and uniform principles of human nature. Men cannot live without society, and cannot be associated without government. Government makes a distinction of property, and establishes the different ranks of men. This produces industry, traffic, manufactures, law-suits, war, leagues, alliances, voyages, travels, cities, fleets, ports, and all those other actions and objects, which cause such a diversity, and at the same time maintain such an uniformity in human life.

Should a traveller, returning from a far country, tell us, that he had seen a climate in the fiftieth degree of northern latitude, where all the fruits ripen and come to perfection in the winter, and decay in the summer, after the same manner as in *England* they are produced and decay in the contrary seasons, he would find few so credulous as to believe him. I am apt to think a traveller would meet with as little credit, who should inform us of people exactly of the same character with those in *Plato's Republic* on the one hand, or those in *Hobbes's Leviathan* on the other. There is a general course of nature in human actions, as well as in the operations of the sun and the climate. There are also characters peculiar to different nations and particular persons, as well as common to mankind. The knowledge of these characters is founded on the observation of an uniformity in the actions, that flow from them; and this uniformity forms the very essence of necessity.

I can imagine only one way of eluding this argument, which is by denying that uniformity of human actions, on which it is founded. As long as actions have a constant union and connection with the situation and temper of the agent, however we may in words refuse to acknowledge the necessity, we really allow the thing. Now some may, perhaps, find a pretext to deny this regular union and connection. For what is more capricious than human actions? What more inconstant than the desires of man? And what creature departs more widely, not only from right reason, but from his own character and disposition? An hour, a moment is sufficient to make him change from one extreme to another, and overturn what cost the greatest pain and labour to establish. Necessity is regular and certain. Human conduct is irregular and uncertain. The one, therefore, proceeds not from the other.

To this I reply, that in judging of the actions of men we must proceed upon the same maxims, as when we reason concerning external objects. When any phenomena are constantly and invariably conjoined together, they acquire such a connection in the imagination, that it passes from one to the other, without any doubt or hesitation. But below this there are many inferior degrees of evidence and probability, nor does one single contrariety of experiment entirely destroy all our reasoning. The mind balances the contrary experiments, and deducting the inferior from the superior, proceeds with that degree of assurance or evidence, which remains. Even when these contrary experiments are entirely equal, we remove not the notion of causes and necessity; but supposing that the usual contrariety proceeds from the operation of contrary and concealed causes, we conclude, that the chance or indifference lies only in our judgment on account of our imperfect knowledge, not in the things themselves, which are in every case equally necessary, though to appearance not equally constant or certain. No union can be more constant and certain, than that of some actions with some motives and characters; and if in other cases the union is uncertain, it is no more than what happens in the operations of body, nor can we conclude anything from the one irregularity, which will not follow equally from the other.

It is commonly allowed that madmen have no liberty. But were we to judge by their actions, these have less regularity and constancy than the actions of wise men, and consequently are farther removed from necessity. Our way of thinking in this particular is, therefore, absolutely inconsistent; but is a natural consequence of these confused ideas and undefined terms, which we so commonly make use of in our reasonings, especially on the present subject.

We must now show, that as the *union* betwixt motives and actions has the same constancy, as that in any natural operations, so its influence on the understanding is also the same, in *determining* us to infer the existence of one from that of another. If this shall appear, there is no known circumstance, that enters into the connection and production of the actions of matter, that is not to be found in all the operations of the mind; and consequently we cannot, without a manifest absurdity, attribute necessity to the one, and refuse it to the other.

There is no philosopher, whose judgment is so riveted to this fantastical system of liberty, as not to acknowledge the force of *moral evidence*, and both in speculation and practice proceed upon it, as upon a reasonable foundation. Now moral evidence is nothing but a conclusion concerning the actions of men, derived from the consideration of their motives, temper and situation. Thus when we see certain characters or figures described upon paper, we infer that the persons who produced them, would affirm such facts, the death of *Cæsar*, the success of *Augustus*, the cruelty of *Nero*; and remembering many other concurrent testimonies, we conclude, that those facts were once really existent, and that so many men, without any interest, would never conspire to deceive us; especially since they must, in the attempt, expose themselves to the derision of all their contemporaries, when these facts were asserted to be recent and universally known. The same kind of reasoning runs through politics, war, commerce, economy, and indeed mixes itself so entirely in human life, that it is impossible to act or subsist a moment without having recourse to it. A prince, who imposes a tax upon his subjects, expects their compliance. A general, who conducts an army, makes account of a certain degree of courage. A merchant looks for fidelity and skill in his factor or super-cargo. A man, who gives orders for his dinner, doubts not of the obedience of his servants. In short, as nothing more nearly interests us than our own actions and those of others, the greatest part of our reasonings is employed in judgments concerning them. Now I assert, that whoever reasons after this manner, does *ipso facto* believe the actions of the will to arise from necessity, and that he knows not what he means, when he denies it.

All those objects, of which we call the one *cause* and the other *effect*, considered in themselves, are as distinct and separate from each other, as any two things in nature, nor can we ever, by the most accurate survey of them, infer the existence of the one from that of the other. It is only from experience and the observation of their constant union, that we are able to form this inference; and even after all, the inference is nothing but the effects of custom on the imagination. We must not here be content with saying, that the idea of cause and effect arises from objects constantly united; but must affirm, that it is the very same with the idea of these objects, and that the *necessary connection* is not discovered by a conclusion of the understanding, but is merely a perception of the mind. Wherever, therefore, we observe the same union, and wherever the union operates in the same manner upon the belief and opinion, we have the idea of causes and necessity, though perhaps we may avoid those expressions.

Motion in one body in all past instances, that have fallen under our observation, is followed upon impulse by motion in another. It is impossible for the mind to penetrate farther. From this constant union it *forms* the idea of cause and effect, and by its influence *feels* the necessity. As there is the same constancy, and the same influence in what we call moral evidence, I ask no more. What remains can only be a dispute of words.

And indeed, when we consider how aptly *natural* and *moral* evidence cement together, and form only one chain of argument betwixt them, we shall make no scruple to allow, that they are of the same nature, and derived from the same principles. A prisoner, who has neither money nor interest, discovers the impossibility of his escape, as well from the obstinacy of the goaler, as from the walls and bars with which he is surrounded; and in all attempts for his freedom chooses rather to work upon the stone and iron of the one, than upon the inflexible nature of the other. The same prisoner, when conducted to the scaffold, foresees his death as certainly from the constancy and fidelity of his guards as from the operation of the axe or wheel. His mind runs along a certain train of ideas: the refusal of the soldiers to consent to his escape, the action of the executioner; the separation of the head and body; bleeding, convulsive motions, and death. Here is a connected chain of natural causes and voluntary actions; but the mind feels no difference betwixt them in passing from one link to another; nor is less certain of the future event than if it were connected with the present impressions of the memory and senses by a train of causes cemented together by what we are pleased to call a *physical necessity*. The same experienced union has the same effect on the mind, whether the united objects be motives, volitions and actions; or figure and motion. We may change the names of things; but their nature and their operation on the understanding never change.

I dare be positive no one will ever endeavour to refute these reasonings otherwise than by altering my definitions, and assigning a different meaning to the terms of *cause, and effect, and necessity, and liberty, and chance.* According to my definitions, necessity makes an essential part of causation; and consequently liberty, by removing necessity, removes also causes, and is the very same thing with chance.

As chance is commonly thought to imply a contradiction, and is at least directly contrary to experience, there are always the same arguments against liberty or free-will. If anyone alters the definitions, I cannot pretend to argue with him, till I know the meaning he assigns to these terms.

SECTION II *The same subject continued*

I believe we may assign the three following reasons for the prevalence of the doctrine of liberty, however absurd it may be in one sense, and unintelligible in any other. First, after we have performed any action; though we confess we were influenced by particular views and motives; it is difficult for us to persuade ourselves we were governed by necessity, and that it was utterly impossible for us to have acted otherwise; the idea of necessity seeming to imply something of force, and violence, and constraint, of which we are not sensible. Few are capable of distinguishing betwixt the liberty of *spontaneity*, as it is called in the schools, and the liberty of *indifference*; betwixt that which is opposed to violence, and that which means a negation of necessity and causes. The first is even the most common sense of the word; and as it is only that species of liberty, which it concerns us to preserve, our thoughts have been principally turned towards it, and have almost universally confounded it with the other.[22]

Secondly, there is a *false sensation or experience* even of the liberty of indifference; which is regarded as an argument for its real existence. The necessity of any action, whether of matter or of the mind, is not properly a quality in the agent, but in any thinking or intelligent being, who may consider the action, and consists in the determination of his thought to infer its existence from some preceding objects; as liberty or chance, on the other hand, is nothing but the want of that determination, and a certain looseness, which we feel in passing or not passing from the idea of one to that of the other. Now we may observe, that though in reflecting on human actions we seldom feel such a looseness or indifference, yet it very commonly happens, that in performing the actions themselves we are sensible of something

like it; and as all related or resembling objects are readily
taken for each other, this has been employed as a demonstrative or even an intuitive proof of human liberty. We
feel that our actions are subject to our will on most occasions, and imagine we feel that the will itself is subject to
nothing; because when by a denial of it we are provoked
to try, we feel that it moves easily every way, and produces
an image of itself even on that side, on which it did not
settle. This image or faint motion, we persuade ourselves,
could have been completed into the thing itself; because,
should that be denied, we find, upon a second trial, that it
can. But these efforts are all in vain; and whatever capricious and irregular actions we may perform; as the desire
of showing our liberty is the sole motive of our actions; we
can never free ourselves from the bonds of necessity. We
may imagine we feel a liberty within ourselves; but a spectator can commonly infer our actions from our motives and
character; and even where he cannot, he concludes in general,
that he might, were he perfectly acquainted with every circumstance of our situation and temper, and the most secret
springs of our complexion and disposition. Now this is the
very essence of necessity, according to the foregoing doctrine.

A third reason why the doctrine of liberty has generally
been better received in the world, than its antagonist, proceeds from *religion*, which has been very unnecessarily interested in this question. There is no method of reasoning
more common, and yet none more blameable, than in philosophical debates to endeavour to refute any hypothesis by
a pretext of its dangerous consequences to religion and
morality. When any opinion leads us into absurdities, it is
certainly false; but it is not certain an opinion is false, because it is of dangerous consequence. Such topics, therefore,
ought entirely to be foreborne, as serving nothing to the discovery of truth, but only to make the person of an antagonist
odious. This I observe in general, without pretending to draw
any advantage from it. I submit myself frankly to an examination of this kind, and dare venture to affirm, that the
doctrine of necessity, according to my explication of it, is
not only innocent, but even advantageous to religion and
morality.

I define necessity two ways, conformable to the two
definitions of *cause*, of which it makes an essential part. I

place it either in the constant union and conjunction of like objects, or in the inference of the mind from the one to the other. Now necessity, in both these senses, has universally, though tacitly, in the schools, in the pulpit, and in common life, been allowed to belong to the will of man, and no one has ever pretended to deny, that we can draw inferences concerning human actions, and that those inferences are founded on the experienced union of like actions with like motives and circumstances. The only particular in which anyone can differ from me, is either, that perhaps he will refuse to call this necessity; but as long as the meaning is understood, I hope the word can do no harm; or that he will maintain there is something else in the operations of matter. Now whether it be so or not is of no consequence to religion, whatever it may be to natural philosophy. I may be mistaken in asserting, that we have no idea of any other connection in the actions of body, and shall be glad to be farther instructed on that head; but sure I am, I ascribe nothing to the actions of the mind, but what must readily be allowed of. Let no one, therefore, put an invidious construction on my words, by saying simply, that I assert the necessity of human actions, and place them on the same footing with the operations of senseless matter. I do not ascribe to the will that unintelligible necessity, which is supposed to lie in matter. But I ascribe to matter, that intelligible quality, call it necessity or not, which the most rigorous orthodoxy does or must allow to belong to the will. I change, therefore, nothing in the received systems, with regard to the will, but only with regard to material objects.

Nay I shall go farther, and assert, that this kind of necessity is so essential to religion and morality, that without it there must ensue an absolute subversion of both, and that every other supposition is entirely destructive to all laws both *divine* and *human*. It is indeed certain, that as all human laws are founded on rewards and punishments, it is supposed as a fundamental principle, that these motives have an influence on the mind, and both produce the good and prevent the evil actions. We may give to this influence what name we please; but as it is usually conjoined with the action, common sense requires it should be esteemed a cause, and be looked upon as an instance of that necessity, which I would establish.

This reasoning is equally solid, when applied to *divine* laws, so far as the deity is considered as a legislator, and is supposed to inflict punishment and bestow rewards with a design to produce obedience. But I also maintain, that even where he acts not in his magisterial capacity, but is regarded as the avenger of crimes merely on account of their odiousness and deformity, not only is it impossible, without the necessary connection of cause and effect in human actions, that punishments could be inflicted compatible with justice and moral equity; but also that it could ever enter into the thoughts of any reasonable being to inflict them. The constant and universal object of hatred or anger is a person or creature endowed with thought and consciousness; and when any criminal or injurious actions excite that passion, it is only by their relation to the person or connection with him. But according to the doctrine of liberty or chance, this connection is reduced to nothing, nor are men more accountable for those actions, which are designed and premeditated, than for such as are the most casual and accidental. Actions are by their very nature temporary and perishing; and where they proceed not from some cause in the characters and disposition of the person, who performed them, they infix not themselves upon him, and can neither redound to his honour, if good, nor infamy, if evil. The action itself may be blameable; it may be contrary to all the rules of morality and religion; but the person is not responsible for it; and as it proceeded from nothing in him, that is durable or constant, and leaves nothing of that nature behind it, it is impossible he can, upon its account, become the object of punishment or vengeance. According to the hypothesis of liberty, therefore, a man is as pure and untainted, after having committed the most horrid crimes, as at the first moment of his birth, nor is his character any way concerned in his actions; since they are not derived from it, and the wickedness of the one can never be used as a proof of the depravity of the other. It is only upon the principles of necessity, that a person acquires any merit or demerit from his actions, however the common opinion may incline to the contrary.

But so inconsistent are men with themselves, that though they often assert, that necessity utterly destroys all merit and demerit either towards mankind or superior powers, yet they continue still to reason upon these very principles of necessity in all their judgments concerning this matter. Men are not blamed for such evil actions as they perform ignorantly and casually, whatever may be their consequences. Why? But because the causes of these actions are only momentary, and terminate in them alone. Men are less blamed for such evil actions, as they perform hastily and unpremeditately, than for such as proceed from thought and deliberation. For what reason? But because a hasty temper, though a constant cause in the mind, operates only by intervals, and infects not the whole character. Again, repentance wipes off every crime, especially if attended with an evident reformation of life and manners. How is this to be accounted for? But by asserting that actions render a person criminal, merely as they are proofs of criminal passions or principles in the mind; and when by any alteration of these principles they cease to be just proofs, they likewise cease to be criminal. But according to the doctrine of *liberty* or *chance* they never were just proofs, and consequently never were criminal.

Here then I turn to my adversary, and desire him to free his own system from these odious consequences before he charge them upon others. Or if he rather chooses, that this question should be decided by fair arguments before philosophers, than by declamations before the people, let him return to what I have advanced to prove that liberty and chance are synonymous; and concerning the nature of moral evidence and regularity of human actions. Upon a review of these reasonings, I cannot doubt of an entire victory; and therefore having proved, that all actions of the will have particular causes, I proceed to explain what these causes are, and how they operate.

SECTION III *Of the influencing motives of the will*

Nothing is more usual in philosophy, and even in common life, than to talk of the combat of passion and reason, to give the preference to reason, and to assert that men are only so far virtuous as they conform themselves to its dictates. Every rational creature, it is said, is obliged to regulate his actions by reason; and if any other motive or principle challenge the direction of his conduct, he ought to oppose it, till it be entirely subdued, or at least brought to a conformity with that superior principle. On this method of thinking the greatest part of moral philosophy, ancient and modern, seems to be founded; nor is there an ampler field, as well for metaphysical arguments, as popular declamations, than this supposed pre-eminence of reason above passion. The eternity, invariableness, and divine origin of the former have been displayed to the best advantage; the blindness, unconstancy and deceitfulness of the latter have been as strongly insisted on. In order to show the fallacy of all this philosophy, I shall endeavour to prove *first*, that reason alone can never be a motive to any action of the will; and *secondly*, that it can never oppose passion in the direction of the will.

The understanding exerts itself after two different ways, as it judges from demonstration or probability; as it regards the abstract relations of our ideas, or those relations of objects, of which experience only gives us information. I believe it scarce will be asserted, that the first species of reasoning alone is ever the cause of any action. As its proper province is the world of ideas, and as the will always places us in that of realities, demonstration and volition seem, upon that account, to be totally removed, from each other. Mathematics, indeed, are useful in all mechanical operations, and arithmetic in almost every art and profession; but it is not of themselves they have any influence. Mechanics are the art of regulating the motions of bodies *to some designed end or purpose*; and the reason why we employ arithmetic in fixing the proportions of numbers, is only that we may discover the proportions of their influence and operation. A merchant is desirous of knowing the sum total of his accounts with any person. Why? But that he may learn what sum will have the same *effects* in paying his debt, and going to market, as all the particular articles taken together. Abstract or demonstrative reasoning, therefore, never influences any of our actions, but only as it directs our judgment concerning causes and effects; which leads us to the second operation of the understanding.

It is obvious, that when we have the prospect of pain or pleasure from any object, we feel a consequent emotion of aversion or propensity, and are carried to avoid or embrace what will give us this uneasiness or satisfaction. It is also obvious, that this emotion rests not here, but making us cast our view on every side, comprehends whatever objects are connected with its original one by the relation of cause and effect. Here then reasoning takes place to discover this relation; and according as our reasoning varies, our actions receive a subsequent variation. But it is evident in this case, that the impulse arises not from reason, but is only directed by it. It is from the prospect of pain or pleasure that the aversion or propensity arises towards any object; and these emotions extend themselves to the causes and effects of that object, as they are pointed out to us by reason and experience. It can never in the least concern us to know, that such objects are causes, and such others effects, if both the causes and effects be indifferent to us. Where the objects themselves do not affect us, their connection can never give them any influence; and it is plain, that as reason is nothing but the discovery of this connection, it cannot be by its means that the objects are able to affect us.

Since reason alone can never produce any action, or give rise to volition, I infer, that the same faculty is as incapable of preventing volition, or of disputing the preference with any passion or emotion. This consequence is necessary. It is impossible reason could have the latter effect of preventing volition, but by giving an impulse in a contrary direction to our passion; and that impulse, had it operated alone, would have been able to produce volition. Nothing can oppose or retard the impulse of passion, but a contrary impulse; and if this contrary impulse ever arises from reason, that latter faculty must have an original influence on the will, and must be able to cause, as well as hinder any act of volition. But if reason has no original influence, it is impossible it can withstand any principle, which has such an efficacy, or ever keep the mind in suspense a moment. Thus it appears, that the principle, which opposes our passion, cannot be the same with reason, and is only called so in an improper sense. We speak not strictly and philosophically when we talk of the combat of passion and of reason. Reason is, and ought only to be the slave of the passions, and can never pretend to any other office than to serve and obey them. As this opinion may appear somewhat extraordinary, it may not be improper to confirm it by some other considerations.

A passion is an original existence, or, if you will, modification of existence, and contains not any representative quality, which renders it a copy of any other existence or modification. When I am angry, I am actually possessed with the passion, and in that emotion have no more a reference to any other object, than when I am thirsty, or sick, or more than five foot high. It is impossible, therefore, that this passion can be opposed by, or be contradictory to truth and reason; since this contradiction consists in the disagreement of ideas, considered as copies, with those objects, which they represent.

What may at first occur on this head, is, that as nothing can be contrary to truth or reason, except what has a reference to it, and as the judgments of our understanding only have this reference, it must follow, that passions can be contrary to reason only so far as they are *accompanied* with some judgment or opinion. According to this principle, which is so obvious and natural, it is only in two senses, that any affection can be called unreasonable. First, when a passion, such as hope or fear, grief or joy, despair or security, is founded on the supposition of the existence of objects, which really do not exist. Secondly, when in exerting any passion in action, we choose means insufficient for the design'd end, and deceive ourselves in our judgment of causes and effects. Where a passion is neither founded on false suppositions, nor chooses means insufficient for the end, the understanding can neither justify nor condemn it. It is not contrary to reason to prefer the destruction of the whole world to the scratching of my finger. It is not contrary to reason for me to choose my total ruin, to prevent the least uneasiness of an *Indian* or person wholly unknown to me. It is as little contrary to reason to prefer even my own acknowledged lesser good to my greater, and have a more ardent affection for the former than the latter. A trivial good may, from certain circumstances, produce a desire superior to what arises from the greatest and most valuable enjoyment; nor is there anything more extraordinary in this, than in mechanics to see one pound weight raise up a hundred by the advantage of its situation. In short, a passion must be accompanied with some false judgment, in order to its being unreasonable; and even then it is not the passion, properly speaking, which is unreasonable, but the judgment.

The consequences are evident. Since a passion can never, in any sense, be called unreasonable, but when founded on a false supposition, or when it chooses means insufficient for the designed end, it is impossible, that reason and passion can ever oppose each other, or dispute for the government of the will and actions. The moment we perceive the falsehood of any supposition, or the insufficiency of any means our passions yield to our reason without any opposition. I may desire any fruit as of an excellent relish; but whenever you convince me of my mistake, my longing ceases. I may will the performance of certain actions as means of obtaining any desired good; but as my willing of these actions is only secondary, and founded on the supposition, that they are causes of the propos'd effect; as soon as I discover the falshood of that supposition, they must become indifferent to me.

It is natural for one, that does not examine objects with a strict philosophic eye, to imagine, that those actions of the mind are entirely the same, which produce not a different sensation, and are not immediately distinguishable to the feeling and perception. Reason, for instance, exerts itself without producing any sensible emotion; and except in the more sublime disquisitions of philosophy, or in the frivolous subtleties of the schools, scarce ever conveys any pleasure or uneasiness. Hence it proceeds, that every action of the mind, which operates with the same calmness and tranquility, is confounded with reason by all those, who judge of things from the first view and appearance. Now it is certain, there are certain calm desires and tendencies, which, though they be real passions, produce little emotion in the mind, and are more known by their effects than by the immediate feeling or sensation. These desires are of two kinds; either certain instincts originally implanted in our natures, such as benevolence and resentment, the love of life, and kindness to children; or the general appetite to good, and aversion to evil, considered merely as such. When any of these passions are calm, and cause no disorder in the soul, they are very readily taken for the determination of reason, and are supposed to proceed from the same faculty, with that, which judges of truth and falsehood. Their nature and principles have been supposed the same, because their sensations are not evidently different.

Beside these calm passions, which often determine the will, there are certain violent emotions of the same kind, which have likewise a great influence on that faculty. When

I receive any injury from another, I often feel a violent passion of resentment, which makes me desire his evil and punishment, independent of all considerations of pleasure and advantage to myself. When I am immediately threatened with any grievous ill, my fears, apprehensions, and aversions rise to a great height, and produce a sensible emotion.

The common error of metaphysicians has lain in ascribing the direction of the will entirely to one of these principles, and supposing the other to have no influence. Men often act knowingly against their interest; for which reason the view of the greatest possible good does not always influence them. Men often counteract a violent passion in prosecution of their interests and designs; it is not therefore the present uneasiness alone, which determines them. In general we may observe, that both these principles operate on the will; and where they are contrary, that either of them prevails, according to the *general* character or *present* disposition of the person. What we call strength of mind, implies the prevalence of the calm passions above the violent; though we may easily observe, there is no man so constantly possessed of this virtue, as never on any occasion to yield to the solicitations of passion and desire. From these variations of temper proceeds the great difficulty of deciding concerning the actions and resolutions of men, where there is any contrariety of motives and passions.

SECTION IV *Of the causes of the violent passions*

There is not in philosophy a subject of more nice speculation than this of the different *causes* and *effects* of the calm and violent passions. It is evident passions influence not the will in proportion to their violence, or the disorder they occasion in the temper; but on the contrary, that when a passion has once become a settled principle of action, and is the predominant inclination of the soul, it commonly produces no longer any sensible agitation. As repeated custom and its own force have made everything yield to it, it directs the actions and conduct without that opposition and emotion, which so naturally attend every momentary gust of passion. We must, therefore, distinguish betwixt a calm and a weak passion; betwixt a violent and a strong one. But notwithstanding this, it is certain, that when we would govern a man, and push him to any action, it will commonly be better policy to work upon the violent than the calm passions, and rather take him by his inclination, than what is vulgarly called his *reason*. We ought to place the object in such particular situations as are proper to increase the violence of the passion. For we may observe, that all depends upon the situation of the object, and that a variation in this particular will be able to change the calm and the violent passions into each other. Both these kinds of passions pursue good, and avoid evil; and both of them are increased or diminished by the increase or diminution of the good or evil. But herein lies the difference betwixt them; the same good, when near, will cause a violent passion, which, when remote, produces only a calm one. As this subject belongs very properly to the present question concerning the will, we shall here examine it to the bottom, and shall consider some of those circumstances and situations of objects, which render a passion either calm or violent.

It is a remarkable property of human nature, that any emotion, which attends a passion, is easily converted into it, though in their natures they be originally different from, and even contrary to each other. It is true; in order to make a perfect union among passions, there is always required a double relation of impressions and ideas; nor is one relation sufficient for that purpose. But though this be confirmed by undoubted experience, we must understand it with its proper limitations, and must regard the double relation, as requisite only to make one passion produce another. When two passions are already produced by their separate causes, and are both present in the mind, they readily mingle and unite, though they have but one relation, and sometimes without any. The predominant passion swallows up the inferior, and converts it into itself. The spirits, when once excited, easily receive a change in their direction; and it is natural to imagine this change will come from the prevailing affection. The connection is in many respects closer betwixt any two passions, than betwixt any passion and indifference.

When a person is once heartily in love, the little faults and caprice of his mistress, the jealousies and quarrels, to which that commerce is so subject; however unpleasant and related to anger and hatred; are yet found to give additional force to the prevailing passion. It is a common artifice of politicians, when they would affect any person very much by a matter of fact, of which they intend to inform him, first to excite his curiosity; delay as long as possible the satisfying it; and by that means raise his anxiety and impatience to the utmost, before they give him a full insight into the business. They know that his curiosity will precipitate him into the passion they design to raise, and assist the object in its influence on the mind. A soldier advancing to the battle, is naturally inspired with courage and confidence, when he thinks on his friends and fellow-soldiers; and is struck with fear and terror, when he reflects on the enemy. Whatever new emotion, therefore, proceeds from the former naturally increases the courage; as the same emotion, proceeding from the latter, augments the fear; by the relation of ideas, and the conversion of the inferior emotion into the predominant. Hence it is that in martial discipline, the uniformity and lustre of our habit, the regularity of our figures and motions, with all the pomp and majesty of war, encourage ourselves and allies; while the same objects in the enemy strike terror into us, though agreeable and beautiful in themselves.

Since passions, however independent, are naturally transfused into each other, if they are both present at the same time; it follows, that when good or evil is placed in such a situation, as to cause any particular emotion, beside its direct passion of desire or aversion, that latter passion must acquire new force and violence.

This happens, among other cases, whenever any object excites contrary passions. For it is observable that an opposition of passions commonly causes a new emotion in the spirits, and produces more disorder, than the concurrence of any two affections of equal force. This new emotion is easily converted into the predominant passion, and increases its violence, beyond the pitch it would have arrived at had it met with no opposition. Hence we naturally desire what is forbid, and take a pleasure in performing actions, merely because they are unlawful. The notion of duty, when opposite to the passions, is seldom able to overcome them; and when it fails of that effect, is apt rather to increase them, by producing an opposition in our motives and principles.

The same effect follows whether the opposition arises from internal motives or external obstacles. The passion commonly acquires new force and violence in both cases. The

F

efforts, which the mind makes to surmount the obstacle, excite the spirits and enliven the passion.

Uncertainty has the same influence as opposition. The agitation of the thought; the quick turns it makes from one view to another; the variety of passions, which succeed each other, according to the different views; all these produce an agitation in the mind, and transfuse themselves into the predominant passion.

There is not in my opinion any other natural cause, why security diminishes the passions, than because it removes that uncertainty, which increases them. The mind, when left to itself, immediately languishes; and in order to preserve its ardour, must be every moment supported by a new flow of passion. For the same reason, despair, though contrary to security, has a like influence.

It is certain nothing more powerfully animates any affection, than to conceal some part of its object by throwing it into a kind of shade, which at the same time that it shows enough to prepossess us in favour of the object, leaves still some work for the imagination. Besides that obscurity is always attended with a kind of uncertainty; the effort, which the fancy makes to complete the idea, rouses the spirits, and gives an additional force to the passion.

As despair and security, though contrary to each other, produce the same effect; so absence is observed to have contrary effects, and in different circumstances either increases or diminishes our affections. The *Duc de la Rochefoucault* has very well observed, that absence destroys weak passions, but increases strong; as the wind extinguishes a candle, but blows up a fire. Long absence naturally weakens our idea, and diminishes the passion; but where the idea is so strong and lively as to support itself, the uneasiness, arising from absence, increases the passion, and gives it new force and violence.

SECTION V *Of the effects of custom*

But nothing has a greater effect both to increase and diminish our passions, to convert pleasure into pain, and pain into pleasure, than custom and repetition. Custom has two *original* effects upon the mind, in bestowing a *facility* in the performance of any action or the conception of any object; and afterwards a *tendency or inclination* towards it; and from these we may account for all its other effects, however extraordinary.

When the soul applies itself to the performance of any action, or the conception of any object, to which it is not accustomed, there is a certain unpliableness in the faculties, and a difficulty of the spirit's moving in their new direction. As this difficulty excites the spirits, 'tis the source of wonder, surprise, and of all the emotions, which arise from novelty; and is in itself very agreeable, like everything, which enlivens the mind to a moderate degree. But though surprise be agreeable in itself, yet as it puts the spirits in agitation, it not only augments our agreeable affections, but also our painful, according to the foregoing principle, *that every emotion, which precedes or attends a passion, is easily converted into it.* Hence everything, that is new, is most affecting, and gives us either more pleasure or pain, than what, strictly speaking, naturally belongs to it. When it often returns upon us, the novelty wears off; the passions subside; the hurry of the spirits is over; and we survey the objects with greater tranquility.

By degrees the repetition produces a facility, which is another very powerful principle of the human mind, and an infallible source of pleasure, where the facility goes not beyond a certain degree. And here it is remarkable that the pleasure, which arises from a moderate facility, has not the same tendency with that which arises from novelty, to augment the painful, as well as the agreeable affections. The pleasure of facility does not so much consist in any ferment of the spirits, as in their orderly motion; which will sometimes be so powerful as even to convert pain into pleasure, and give us a relish in time for what at first was most harsh and disagreeable.

But again, as facility converts pain into pleasure, so it often converts pleasure into pain, when it is too great, and renders the actions of the mind so faint and languid, that they are no longer able to interest and support it. And indeed, scarce any other objects become disagreeable through custom; but such as are naturally attended with some emotion or affection, which is destroyed by the too frequent repetition. One can consider the clouds, and heavens, and trees, and stones, however frequently repeated, without ever feeling any aversion. But when the fair sex, or music, or good cheer, or anything, that naturally ought to be agreeable, becomes indifferent, it easily produces the opposite affection.

But custom not only gives a facility to perform any action, but likewise an inclination and tendency towards it, where it is not entirely disagreeable, and can never be the object of inclination. And this is the reason why custom increases all *active* habits, but diminishes *passive*, according to the observation of a late eminent philosopher. The facility takes off from the force of the passive habits by rendering the motion of the spirits faint and languid. But as in the active, the spirits are sufficiently supported of themselves, the tendency of the mind gives them new force, and bends them more strongly to the action.

Section VI *Of the influence of the imagination on the passions*

It is remarkable, that the imagination and affections have a close union together, and that nothing, which affects the former, can be entirely indifferent to the latter. Wherever our ideas of good or evil acquire a new vivacity, the passions become more violent; and keep pace with the imagination in all its variations. Whether this proceeds from the principle above-mentioned, *that any attendant emotion is easily converted into the predominant*, I shall not determine. It is sufficient for my present purpose, that we have many instances to confirm this influence of the imagination upon the passions.

Any pleasure, with which we are acquainted, affects us more than any other, which we own to be superior, but of whose nature we are wholly ignorant. Of the one we can form a particular and determinate idea; the other we conceive under the general notion of pleasure; and it is certain, that the more general and universal any of our ideas are, the less influence they have upon the imagination. A general idea, though it be nothing but a particular one considered in a certain view, is commonly more obscure; and that because no particular idea, by which we represent a general one, is ever fixed or determinate, but may easily be changed for other particular ones, which will serve equally in the representation.

There is a noted passage in the history of *Greece*, which may serve for our present purpose. *Themistocles* told the *Athenians*, that he had formed a design, which would be highly useful to the public, but which it was impossible for him to communicate to them without ruining the execution, since its success depended entirely on the secrecy with which it should be conducted. The *Athenians*, instead of granting him full power to act as he thought fitting, ordered him to communicate his design to *Aristides*, in whose prudence they had an entire confidence, and whose opinion they were resolved blindly to submit to. The design of *Themistocles* was secretly to set fire to the fleet of all the *Grecian* commonwealths, which was assembled in a neighbouring port, and which being once destroyed, would give the *Athenians* the empire of the sea without any rival. *Aristides* returned to the assembly, and told them, that nothing could be more advantageous than the design of *Themistocles*; but at the same time that nothing could be more unjust; upon which the people unanimously rejected the project.

A late celebrated historian* admires this passage of ancient history, as one of the most singular that is anywhere to be met with. *Here*, says he, *they are not philosophers, to whom it is easy in their schools to establish the finest maxims and most sublime rules of morality, who decide that interest ought never to prevail above justice. It is a whole people interested in the proposal, which is made to them, who consider it as of importance to the public good, and who notwithstanding reject it unanimously, and without hesitation, merely because it is contrary to justice.* For my part I see nothing so extraordinary in this proceeding of the *Athenians*. The same reasons, which render it so easy for philosophers to establish these sublime maxims, tend, in part, to diminish the merit of such a conduct in that people. Philosophers never balance betwixt profit and honesty, because their decisions are general, and neither their passions nor imaginations are interested in the objects. And though in the present case the advantage was immediate to the *Athenians*, yet as it was known only under the general notion of advantage, without being conceived by any particular idea, it must have had a less considerable influence on their imaginations, and have been a less

* Mons. *Rollin*.

violent temptation, than if they had been acquainted with all its circumstances; otherwise it is difficult to conceive, that a whole people, unjust and violent as men commonly are, should so unanimously have adhered to justice, and rejected any considerable advantage.

Any satisfaction, which we lately enjoyed, and of which the memory is fresh and recent, operates on the will with more violence, than another of which the traces are decayed, and almost obliterated. From whence does this proceed, but that the memory in the first case assists the fancy, and gives an additional force and vigour to its conceptions? The image of the past pleasure being strong and violent, bestows these qualities on the idea of the future pleasure, which is connected with it by the relation of resemblance.

A pleasure, which is suitable to the way of life, in which we are engaged, excites more our desires and appetites than another, which is foreign to it. This phenomenon may be explained from the same principle.

Nothing is more capable of infusing any passion into the mind, than eloquence, by which objects are represented in their strongest and most lively colours. We may of ourselves acknowledge, that such an object is valuable, and such another odious; but till an orator excites the imagination, and gives force to these ideas, they may have but a feeble influence either on the will or the affections.

But eloquence is not always necessary. The bare opinion of another, especially when enforced with passion, will cause an idea of good or evil to have an influence upon us, which would otherwise have been entirely neglected. This proceeds from the principle of sympathy or communication; and sympathy, as I have already observed, is nothing but the conversion of an idea into an impression by the force of imagination.

It is remarkable, that lively passions commonly attend a lively imagination. In this respect, as well as others, the force of the passion depends as much on the temper of the person, as the nature or situation of the object.

I have already observed, that belief is nothing but a lively idea related to a present impression. This vivacity is a requisite circumstance to the exciting all our passions, the calm as well as the violent; nor has a mere fiction of the imagination any considerable influence upon either of them.

It is too weak to take any hold of the mind, or be attended with emotion.

SECTION VII *Of contiguity, and distance in space and time*

There is an easy reason, why everything contiguous to us, either in space or time, should be conceived with a peculiar force and vivacity, and excel every other object, in its influence on the imagination. Ourself is intimately present to us, and whatever is related to self must partake of that quality. But where an object is so far removed as to have lost the advantage of this relation, why, as it is farther removed, its idea becomes still fainter and more obscure, would, perhaps, require a more particular examination.

It is obvious, that the imagination can never totally forget the points of space and time, in which we are existent; but receives such frequent advertisements of them from the passions and senses, that however it may turn its attention to foreign and remote objects, it is necessitated every moment to reflect on the present. It is also remarkable, that in the conception of those objects, which we regard as real and existent, we take them in their proper order and situation, and never leap from one object to another, which is distant from it, without running over, at least in a cursory manner, all those objects, which are interposed betwixt them. When we reflect, therefore, on any object distant from ourselves, we are obliged not only to reach it at first by passing through all the intermediate space betwixt ourselves and the object, but also to renew our progress every moment; being every moment recalled to the consideration of ourselves and our present situation. It is easily conceived, that this interruption must weaken the idea by breaking the action of the mind, and hindering the conception from being so intense and continued, as when we reflect on a nearer object. The *fewer* steps we make to arrive at the object, and the *smoother* the road is, this diminution of vivacity is less sensibly felt, but still may be observed more or less in proportion to the degrees of distance and difficulty.

Here then we are to consider two kinds of objects, the contiguous and remote; of which the former, by means of their relation to ourselves, approach an impression in force and vivacity; the latter by reason of the interruption in our manner of conceiving them, appear in a weaker and more imperfect light. This is their effect on the imagination. If my reasoning be just, they must have a proportionable effect on the will and passions. Contiguous objects must have an influence much superior to the distant and remote. Accordingly we find in common life, that men are principally concerned about those objects, which are not much removed either in space or time, enjoying the present, and leaving what is afar off to the care of chance and fortune. Talk to a man of his condition thirty years hence, and he will not regard you. Speak of what is to happen tomorrow, and he will lend you attention. The breaking of a mirror gives us more concern when at home, than the burning of a house, when abroad, and some hundred leagues distant.

But farther; though distance both in space and time has a considerable effect on the imagination, and by that means on the will and passions, yet the consequence of a removal in *space* are much inferior to those of a removal in *time*. Twenty years are certainly but a small distance of time in comparison of what history and even the memory of some may inform them of, and yet I doubt if a thousand leagues, or even the greatest distance of place this globe can admit of, will so remarkably weaken our ideas, and diminish our passions. A *West-India* merchant will tell you, that he is not without concern about what passes in *Jamaica*; though few extend their views so far into futurity, as to dread very remote accidents.

The cause of this phenomenon must evidently lie in the different properties of space and time. Without having recourse to metaphysics, anyone may easily observe, that space or extension consists of a number of co-existent parts disposed in a certain order, and capable of being at once present to the sight or feeling. On the contrary, time or succession, though it consists likewise of parts, never presents to us more than one at once; nor is it possible for any two of them ever to be co-existent. These qualities of the objects have a suitable effect on the imagination. The parts of extension being susceptible of an union to the senses, acquire an union in the fancy; and as the appearance of one part excludes not another, the transition or passage of the thought through the contiguous parts is by that means rendered more smooth and easy. On the other hand, the incompatibility of the parts of time in their real existence separates them in the imagination, and makes it more *difficult* for that faculty to trace any long succession or series of events. Every part must appear single and alone, nor can regularly have entrance into the fancy without banishing what is supposed to have been immediately precedent. By this means any distance in time causes a greater interruption in the thought than an equal distance in space, and consequently weakens more considerably the idea, and consequently the passions; which depend in a great measure, on the imagination, according to my system.

There is another phenomenon of a like nature with the foregoing, viz. *the superior effects of the same distance in futurity above that in the past.* This difference with respect to the will is easily accounted for. As none of our actions can alter the past, it is not strange it should never determine the will. But with respect to the passions the question is yet entire, and well worth the examining.

Besides the propensity to a gradual progression through the points of space and time, we have another peculiarity in our method of thinking, which concurs in producing this phenomenon. We always follow the succession of time in placing our ideas, and from the consideration of any object pass more easily to that, which follows immediately after it, than to that which went before it. We may learn this, among other instances, from the order, which is always observed in historical narrations. Nothing but an absolute necessity can oblige an historian to break the order of time, and in his *narration* give the precedence to an event, which was in *reality* posterior to another.

This will not easily be applied to the question in hand, if we reflect on what I have before observed, that the present situation of the person is always that of the imagination, and that it is from thence we proceed to the conception of any distant object. When the object is past, the progression of the thought in passing to it from the present is contrary to nature, as proceeding from one point of time, to that which is preceding, and from that to another preceding, in opposition to the natural course of the succession. On the other hand, when we turn our thought to a future object, our fancy flows along the stream of time, and arrives at the object by an order, which seems most natural, passing always from one point of time to that which is immediately posterior to it. This *easy* progression of ideas favours the imagination, and makes it conceive its object in a stronger and fuller light, than when we are continually opposed in our passage, and are obliged to overcome the difficulties arising from the natural propensity of the fancy. A small degree of distance in the past has, therefore, a greater effect, in interrupting and weakening the conception, than a much greater in the future. From this effect of it on the imagination is derived its influence on the will and passions.

There is another cause, which both contributes to the same effect, and proceeds from the same quality of the fancy, by which we are determined to trace the succession of time by a similar succession of ideas. When from the present instant we consider two points of time equally distant in the future and in the past, it is evident, that, abstractedly considered, their relation to the present is almost equal. For as the future will *sometime* be present, so the past was *once* present. If we could, therefore, remove this quality of the imagination, an equal distance in the past and in the future, would have a similar influence. Nor is this only true, when the fancy remains fixed, and from the present instant surveys the future and the past; but also when it changes its situation, and places us in different periods of time. For as on the one hand, in supposing ourselves existent in a point of time interposed betwixt the present instant and the future object, we find the future object approach to us, and the past retire, and become more distant; so on the other hand, in supposing ourselves existent in a point of time interposed betwixt the present and the past, the past approaches to us, and the future becomes more distant. But from the property of the fancy above-mentioned we rather choose to fix our thought on the point of time interposed betwixt the present and the future, than on that betwixt the present and the past. We advance, rather than retard our existence; and following what seems the natural succession of time, proceed from past to present, and from present to future. By which means we conceive the future as flowing every moment nearer us, and the past as retiring. An equal distance, therefore, in the past and in the future, has not the same effect on the imagination; and that because we consider the one as continually increasing, and the other as continually diminishing. The fancy anticipates the course of things, and surveys the object in that condition, to which it tends, as well as in that, which is regarded as the present.

SECTION VIII *The same subject continued*

Thus we have accounted for three phenomena, which seem pretty remarkable. Why distance weakens the conception and passion; why distance in time has a greater effect than that in space; and why distance in past time has still a greater effect than that in future. We must now consider three phenomena, which seem to be, in a manner, the reverse of these; why a very great distance increases our esteem and admiration for an object; why such a distance in time increases it more than that in space; and a distance in past time more than that in future. The curiousness of the subject will, I hope, excuse my dwelling on it for some time.

To begin with the first phenomenon, why a great distance increases our esteem and admiration for an object; it is evident that the mere view and contemplation of any greatness, whether successive or extended, enlarges the soul, and give it a sensible delight and pleasure. A wide plain, the ocean, eternity, a succession of several ages; all these are entertaining objects, and excel everything, however beautiful, which accompanies not its beauty with a suitable greatness. Now when any very distant object is presented to the imagination, we naturally reflect on the interposed distance, and by that means, conceiving something great and magnificent, receive the usual satisfaction. But as the fancy passes easily from one idea to another related to it, and transports to the second all the passions excited by the first, the admiration, which is directed to the distance, naturally diffuses itself over the distant object. Accordingly we find, that it is not necessary the object should be actually distant from us, in order to cause our admiration; but that it is sufficient, if, by the natural association of ideas, it conveys our view to any considerable distance. A great traveller, though in the same chamber, will pass for a very extraordinary person; as a *Greek* medal, even in our cabinet, is always esteemed a valuable curiosity. Here the object, by a natural transition, conveys our view to the distance; and the admiration, which arises from that distance, by another natural transition, returns back to the object.

But though every great distance produces an admiration for the distant object, a distance in time has a more considerable effect than that in space. Ancient busts and inscriptions are more valued than *Japan* tables; and not to mention the *Greeks* and *Romans*, it is certain we regard with more veneration the old *Chaldeans* and *Egyptians*, than the modern *Chinese* and *Persians*, and bestow more fruitless pains to clear up the history and chronology of the former, than it would cost us to make a voyage, and be certainly informed of the character, learning and government of the latter. I shall be obliged to make a digression in order to explain this phenomenon.

It is a quality very observable in human nature, that any opposition, which does not entirely discourage and intimidate us, has rather a contrary effect, and inspires us with a more than ordinary grandeur and magnanimity. In collecting our force to overcome the opposition, we invigorate the soul, and give it an elevation with which otherwise it would never have been acquainted. Compliance, by rendering our strength useless, makes us insensible of it; but opposition awakens and employs it.

This is also true in the inverse. Opposition not only enlarges the soul; but the soul, when full of courage and magnanimity, in a manner seeks opposition.

> *Spumantemque dari pecora inter inertia votis*
> *Optat aprum, aut fulvum descendere monte leonem.*

Whatever supports and fills the passions is agreeable to us; as on the contrary, what weakens and enfeebles them is uneasy. As opposition has the first effect, and facility the second, no wonder the mind, in certain dispositions, desires the former, and is averse to the latter.

These principles have an effect on the imagination as well as on the passions. To be convinced of this we need only consider the influence of *heights* and *depths* on that faculty. Any great elevation of place communicates a kind of pride or sublimity of imagination, and gives a fancied superiority over those that lie below; and, *vice versa*, a sublime and strong imagination conveys the idea of ascent and elevation. Hence it proceeds, that we associate, in a manner, the idea of whatever is good with that of height, and evil with lowness. Heaven is supposed to be above, and hell below. A noble genius is called an elevate and sublime one. *Atque udam spernit hūmūm fugiente penna.* On the contrary, a vulgar and trivial conception is styled indifferently low or mean. Prosperity is denominated ascent, and adversity descent. Kings and princes are supposed to be placed at the top of human affairs; as peasants and day-labourers are said to be in the lowest stations. These methods of thinking, and of expressing ourselves, are not of so little consequence as they may appear at first sight.

It is evident to common sense, as well as philosophy, that there is no natural nor essential difference betwixt high and low, and that this distinction arises only from the gravitation of matter, which produces a motion from the one to the other. The very same direction, which in this part of the globe is called *ascent*, is denominated *descent* in our antipodes; which can proceed from nothing but the contrary tendency of bodies. Now it is certain, that the tendency of bodies, continually operating upon our senses, must produce, from custom, a like tendency in the fancy, and that when we consider any object situated in an ascent, the idea of its weight gives us a propensity to transport it from the place in which it is situated, to the place immediately below it, and so on, till we come to the ground, which equally stops the body and our imagination. For a like reason we feel a difficulty in mounting, and pass not without a kind of reluctance from the inferior to that which is situated above it; as if our ideas acquired a kind of gravity from their objects. As a proof of this, do we not find, that the facility, which is so much studied in music and poetry, is called the fall or cadency of the harmony or period; the idea of facility communicating to us that of descent, in the same manner as descent produces a facility?

Since the imagination, therefore, in running from low to high, finds an opposition in its internal qualities and principles, and since the soul, when elevated with joy and courage, in a manner seeks opposition, and throws itself with alacrity into any scene of thought or action, where its courage meets with matter to nourish and employ it; it follows, that everything, which invigorates and enlivens the soul, whether by touching the passions or imagination, naturally conveys to the fancy this inclination for ascent, and determines it to run against the natural stream of its thoughts and conceptions. This aspiring progress of the imagination suits the present disposition of the mind; and the difficulty, instead of extinguishing its vigour and alacrity, has the contrary effect, of sustaining and increasing it. Virtue, genius, power, and riches are for this reason associated with height and sublimity; as poverty, slavery, and folly are conjoined with descent and lowness. Were the case the same with us as *Milton* represents it to be with the angels, to whom *descent is adverse*, and who *cannot sink without labour and compulsion*, this order of things would be entirely inverted; as appears hence, that the very nature of ascent and descent is derived from the difficulty and propensity, and consequently every one of their effects proceeds from that origin.

All this is easily applied to the present question, why a considerable distance in time produces a greater veneration for the distant objects than a like removal in space. The imagination moves with more difficulty in passing from one portion of time to another, than in a transition through the parts of space; and that because space or extension appears united to our senses, while time or succession is always broken and divided. This difficulty, when joined with a small distance, interrupts and weakens the fancy; but has a contrary effect in a great removal. The mind, elevated by the vastness of its object, is still farther elevated by the difficulty of the conception; and being obliged every moment to renew its efforts in the transition from one part of time to another, feels a more vigorous and sublime disposition, than in a transition through the parts of space, where the ideas flow along with easiness and facility. In this disposition, the imagination, passing, as is usual, from the consideration of the distance to the view of the distant objects, gives us a proportionable veneration for it; and this is the reason why all the relics of antiquity are so precious in our eyes, and appear more valuable than what is brought even from the remotest parts of the world.

The third phenomenon I have remarked will be a full confirmation of this. It is not every removal in time, which has the effect of producing veneration and esteem. We are not apt to imagine our posterity will excel us, or equal our ancestors. This phenomenon is the more remarkable, because any distance in futurity weakens not our ideas so much as an equal removal in the past. Though a removal in the past, when very great, increases our passions beyond a like removal in the future, yet a small removal has a greater influence in diminishing them.

In our common way of thinking we are placed in a kind of middle station betwixt the past and future; and as our imagination finds a kind of difficulty in running along the former, and a facility in following the course of the latter, the difficulty conveys the notion of ascent, and the facility of the contrary. Hence we imagine our ancestors to be, in a manner, mounted above us, and our posterity to lie below us. Our fancy arrives not at the one without effort, but easily reaches the other; which effort weakens the conception, where the distance is small; but enlarges and elevates the imagination, when attended with a suitable object. As on the other hand, the facility assists the fancy in a small removal, but takes off from its force when it contemplates any considerable distance.

It may not be improper, before we leave this subject of the will, to resume, in a few words, all that has been said concerning it, in order to set the whole more distinctly before the eyes of the reader. What we commonly understand by *passion* is a violent and sensible emotion of mind, when any good or evil is presented, or any object, which, by the original formation of our faculties, is fitted to excite an appetite. By *reason* we mean affections of the very same kind with the former; but such as operate more calmly, and cause no disorder in the temper; which tranquillity leads us into a mistake concerning them, and causes us to regard them as conclusions only of our intellectual faculties. Both the *causes* and *effects* of these violent and calm passions are pretty variable, and depend, in a great measure, on the peculiar temper and disposition of every individual. Generally speaking, the violent passions have a more powerful influence on the will; though it is often found, that the calm ones, when corroborated by reflection, and seconded by resolution, are able to controul them in their most furious movements. What makes this whole affair more uncertain, is, that a calm passion may easily be changed into a violent one, either by a change of temper, or of the circumstances and situation of the object, as by the borrowing of force from any attendant passion, by custom, or by exciting the imagination. Upon the whole, this struggle of passion and of reason, as it is called, diversifies human life, and makes men so different not only from each other, but also from themselves in different times. Philosophy can only account for a few of the greater and more sensible events of this war; but must leave all the smaller and more delicate revolutions, as dependent on principles too fine and minute for her comprehension.

SECTION IX *Of the direct passions*

It is easy to observe, that the passions, both direct and indirect, are founded on pain and pleasure, and that in order to produce an affection of any kind, it is only requisite to present some good or evil. Upon the removal of pain and pleasure there immediately follows a removal of love and hatred, pride and humility, desire and aversion, and of most of our reflective or secondary impressions.

The impressions, which arise from good and evil most naturally, and with the least preparation are the *direct* passions of desire and aversion, grief and joy, hope and fear, along with volition. The mind by an *original* instinct tends to unite itself with the good, and to avoid the evil, though they be conceived merely in idea, and be considered as to exist in any future period of time.

But supposing that there is an immediate impression of pain or pleasure, and *that* arising from an object related to ourselves or others, this does not prevent the propensity or aversion, with the consequent emotions, but by concurring with certain dormant principles of the human mind, excites the new impressions of pride or humility, love or hatred. That propensity, which unites us to the object, or separates us from it, still continues to operate, but in conjunction with the *indirect* passions, which arise from a double relation of impressions and ideas.

These indirect passions, being always agreeable or uneasy, give in their turn additional force to the direct passions, and increase our desire and aversion to the object. Thus a suit of fine clothes produces pleasure from their beauty; and this pleasure produces the direct passions, or the impressions of

18

volition and desire. Again, when these clothes are considered as belonging to ourself, the double relation conveys to us the sentiment of pride, which is an indirect passion; and the pleasure, which attends that passion, returns back to the direct affections, and gives new force to our desire or volition, joy or hope.

When good is certain or probable, it produces *joy*. When evil is in the same situation there arises *grief* or *sorrow*.

When either good or evil is uncertain, it gives rise to *fear* or *hope*, according to the degrees of uncertainty on the one side or the other.

Desire arises from good considered simply, and *aversion* is derived from evil. The *will* exerts itself, when either the good or the absence of the evil may be attained by any action of the mind or body.

Beside good and evil, or in other words, pain and pleasure, the direct passions frequently arise from a natural impulse or instinct, which is perfectly unaccountable. Of this kind is the desire of punishment to our enemies, and of happiness to our friends; hunger, lust, and a few other bodily appetites. These passions, properly speaking, produce good and evil, and proceed not from them, like the other affections.

None of the direct affections seem to merit our particular attention, except hope and fear, which we shall here endeavour to account for. It is evident that the very same event, which by its certainty would produce grief or joy, gives always rise to fear or hope, when only probable and uncertain. In order, therefore, to understand the reason why this circumstance makes such a considerable difference, we must reflect on what I have already advanced in the preceding book concerning the nature of probability.

Probability arises from an opposition of contrary chances or causes, by which the mind is not allowed to fix on either side, but is incessantly tossed from one to another, and at one moment is determined to consider an object as existent, and at another moment as the contrary. The imagination or understanding, call it which you please, fluctuates betwixt the opposite views; and though perhaps it may be oftener turned to the one side than the other, it is impossible for it, by reason of the opposition of causes or chances, to rest on either. The *pro* and *con* of the question alternately prevail; and the mind, surveying the object in its opposite principles, finds such a contrariety as utterly destroys all certainty and established opinion.

Suppose, then, that the object, concerning whose reality we are doubtful, is an object either of desire or aversion, it is evident, that, according as the mind turns itself to the one side or the other, it must feel a momentary impression of joy or sorrow. An object, whose existence we desire, gives satisfaction, when we reflect on those causes, which produce it; and for the same reason excites grief or uneasiness from the opposite consideration; so that as the understanding, in all probable questions, is divided betwixt the contrary points of view, the affections must in the same manner be divided betwixt opposite emotions.

Now if we consider the human mind, we shall find, that with regard to the passions, it is not of the nature of a wind-instrument of music, which in running over all the notes immediately loses the sound after the breath ceases; but rather resembles a string-instrument, where after each stroke the vibrations still retain some sound, which gradually and insensibly decays. The imagination is extreme quick and agile; but the passions are slow and restive; for which reason, when any object is presented, that affords a variety of views to the one, and emotions to the other; though the fancy may change its views with great celerity; each stroke will not produce a clear and distinct note of passion, but the one passion will always be mixed and confounded with the other. According as the probability inclines to good or evil, the passion of joy or sorrow predominates in the composition; because the nature of probability is to cast a superior number of views or chances on one side; or, which is the same thing, a superior number of returns of one passion; or since the dispersed passions are collected into one, a superior degree of that passion. That is, in other words, the grief and joy being intermingled with each other, by means of the contrary views of the imagination, produce by their union the passions of hope and fear.

Upon this head there may be started a very curious question concerning that contrariety of passions, which is our present subject. It is observable, that where the objects of contrary passions are presented at once, beside the increase of the predominant passion (which has been already explained, and commonly arises at their first shock or rencounter) it sometimes happens, that both the passions exist successively, and by short intervals; sometimes, that they destroy each other, and neither of them takes place; and sometimes that both of them remain united in the mind. It may, therefore, be asked, by what authority we can explain these variations, and to what general principle we can reduce them.

When the contrary passions arise from objects entirely different, they take place alternately, the want of relation in the ideas separating the impressions from each other, and preventing their opposition. Thus when a man is afflicted for the loss of a law-suit, and joyful for the birth of a son, the mind running from the agreeable to the calamitous object, with whatever celerity it may perform this motion, can scarcely temper the one affection with the other, and remain betwixt them in a state of indifference.

It more easily attains that calm situation, when the same event is of a mixed nature, and contains something adverse and something prosperous in its different circumstances. For in that case, both the passions, mingling with each other by means of the relation, become mutually destructive, and leave the mind in perfect tranquillity.

But suppose, in the third place, that the object is not a compound of good or evil, but is considered as probable or improbable in any degree; in that case I assert, that the contrary passions will both of them be present at once in the soul, and instead of destroying and tempering each other, will subsist together, and produce a third impression or affection by their union. Contrary passions are not capable of destroying each other, except when their contrary movements exactly rencounter, and are opposite in their direction, as well as in the sensation they produce. This exact rencounter depends upon the relations of those ideas, from which they are derived, and is more or less perfect, according to the degrees of the relation. In the case of probability the contrary chances are so far related, that they determine concerning the existence or non-existence of the same object. But this relation is far from being perfect; since some of the chances lie on the side of existence, and others on that of non-existence; which are objects altogether incompatible. It is impossible by one steady view to survey the opposite chances, and the events dependent on them; but it is necessary, that the imagination should run alternately from the one to the other. Each view of the imagination produces its peculiar passion, which decays away by degrees, and is followed by a sensible vibration after the stroke. The incompatibility of the views keeps the passions from shocking in a direct line, if that expression may be allowed; and yet their relation is sufficient to mingle their fainter emotions. It is after this manner that hope and fear arise from the different mixture of these opposite passions of grief and joy, and from their imperfect union and conjunction.

Upon the whole, contrary passions succeed each other alternately, when they arise from different objects; they mutually destroy each other, when they proceed from different parts of the same; and they subsist both of them, and mingle together, when they are derived from the contrary and incompatible chances or possibilities, on which any one object depends. The influence of the relations of ideas is plainly seen in this whole affair. If the objects of the contrary passions be totally different, the passions are like two opposite liquors in different bottles, which have no influence on each other. If the objects be intimately connected, the passions are like an *alkali* and an *acid*, which, being mingled, destroy each other. If the relation be more imperfect, and consists in the contradictory views of the same object, the passions are like oil and vinegar, which however mingled, never perfectly unite and incorporate.

As the hypothesis concerning hope and fear carries its own evidence along with it, we shall be the more concise in our proofs. A few strong arguments are better than many weak ones.

The passions of fear and hope may arise when the chances are equal on both sides, and no superiority can be discovered in the one above the other. Nay, in this situation the passions are rather the strongest, as the mind has then the least foundation to rest upon, and is tossed with the greatest uncertainty. Throw in a superior degree of probability to the side of grief, you immediately see that passion diffuse itself over the composition, and tincture it into fear. Increase the probability, and by that means the grief, the fear prevails still more and more, till at last it runs insensibly, as the joy continually diminishes, into pure grief. After you have brought it to this situation, diminish the grief, after the same manner that you increased it; by diminishing the probability on that side, and you'll see the passion clear every moment, till it changes insensibly into hope; which again runs, after the same manner, by slow degrees, into joy, as you increase that part of the composition by the increase of the probability. Are not these as plain proofs, that the passions of fear and hope are mixtures of grief and joy, as in optics 'tis a proof, that a coloured ray of the sun passing through a prism, is a composition of two others, when, as you diminish or encrease the quantity of either, you find it prevail proportionably more or less in the composition? I am sure neither natural nor moral philosophy admits of stronger proofs.

Probability is of two kinds, either when the object is really in itself uncertain, and to be determined by chance; or when, though the object be already certain, yet it is uncertain to our judgment, which finds a number of proofs on each side of the question. Both these kinds of probabilities cause fear and hope; which can only proceed from that property, in which they agree, *viz.* the uncertainty and fluctuation they bestow on the imagination by that contrariety of views, which is common to both.

It is a probable good or evil, that commonly produces hope or fear; because probability, being a wavering and unconstant method of surveying an object, causes naturally a like mixture and uncertainty of passion. But we may observe, that wherever from other causes this mixture can be produced, the passions of fear and hope will arise, even though there be no probability; which must be allowed to be a convincing proof of the present hypothesis.

We find that an evil, barely conceived as *possible*, does sometimes produce fear; especially if the evil be very great. A man cannot think of excessive pains and tortures without trembling, if he be in the least danger of suffering them. The smallness of the probability is compensated by the greatness of the evil; and the sensation is equally lively, as if the evil were more probable. One view or glimpse of the former, has the same effect as several of the latter.

But they are not only possible evils, that cause fear, but even some allowed to be *impossible*; as when we tremble on the brink of a precipice, though we know ourselves to be in perfect security, and have it in our choice whether we will advance a step farther. This proceeds from the immediate presence of the evil, which influences the imagination in the same manner as the certainty of it would do; but being encountered by the reflection on our security, is immediately retracted, and causes the same kind of passion, as when from a contrariety of chances contrary passions are produced.

Evils, that are *certain*, have sometimes the same effect in producing fear, as the possible or impossible. Thus a man in a strong prison well-guarded, without the least means of escape, trembles at the thought of the rack, to which he is sentenced. This happens only when the certain evil is terrible and confounding; in which case the mind continually rejects it with horror, while it continually presses in upon the thought. The evil is there fixed and established, but the mind cannot endure to fix upon it; from which fluctuation and uncertainty there arises a passion of much the same appearance with fear.

But it is not only where good or evil is uncertain, as to its *existence*, but also as to its *kind*, that fear or hope arises. Let one be told by a person, whose veracity he cannot doubt of, that one of his sons is suddenly killed, it is evident the passion this event would occasion, would not settle into pure grief, till he got certain information, which of his sons he had lost. Here there is an evil certain, but the kind of it uncertain; consequently the fear we feel on this occasion is without the least mixture of joy, and arises merely from the fluctuation of the fancy betwixt its objects. And though each side of the question produces here the same passion, yet that passion cannot settle, but receives from the imagination a tremulous and unsteady motion, resembling in its cause, as well as in its sensation, the mixture and contention of grief and joy.

From these principles we may account for a phenomenon in the passions, which at first sight seems very extraordinary, *viz.* that surprise is apt to change into fear, and everything that is unexpected affrights us. The most obvious conclusion from this is, that human nature is in general pusilanimous; since upon the sudden appearance of any object we immediately conclude it to be an evil, and without waiting till we can examine its nature, whether it be good or bad, are at first affected with fear. This I say is the most obvious conclusion; but upon farther examination we shall find that the phenomenon is otherwise to be accounted for. The suddenness and strangeness of an appearance naturally excite a commotion in the mind, like everything for which we are not prepared, and to which we are not accustomed. This commotion, again, naturally produces a curiosity or inquisitiveness, which being very violent, from the strong and sudden impulse of the object, becomes uneasy, and resembles in its fluctuation and uncertainty, the sensation of fear or the mixed passions of grief and joy. This image of fear naturally converts into the thing itself, and gives us a real apprehension of evil, as the mind always forms its judgments more from its present disposition than from the nature of its objects.

Thus all kinds of uncertainty have a strong connection with fear, even though they do not cause any opposition of passions by the opposite views and considerations they present to us. A person, who has left his friend in any malady, will feel more anxiety upon his account, than if he were present, though perhaps he is not only incapable of giving him assistance, but likewise of judging of the event of his sickness. In this case, though the principal object of the passion, *viz.* the life or death of his friend, be to him equally uncertain when present as when absent; yet there are a thousand little circumstances of his friend's situation and condition, the knowledge of which fixes the idea, and prevents that fluctuation and uncertainty so near allied to fear. Uncertainty is, indeed, in one respect as near allied to hope as to fear, since it makes an essential part in the composition of the former passion; but the reason, why it inclines not to that side, is, that uncertainty alone is uneasy, and has a relation of impressions to the uneasy passions.

It is thus our uncertainty concerning any minute circumstance relating to a person increases our apprehensions of his death or misfortune. *Horace* has remarked this phenomenon.

> *Ut assidens implumibus pullus avis*
> *Serpentium allapsus timet,*
> *Magis relictis; non, ut adsit, auxili*
> *Latura plus presentibus.*

But this principle of the connection of fear with uncertainty I carry farther, and observe that any doubt produces that passion, even though it presents nothing to us on any side but what is good and desirable. A virgin, on her bridal-night goes to bed full of fears and apprehensions, though she expects nothing but pleasure of the highest kind, and what she has long wished for. The newness and greatness of the event, the confusion of wishes and joys, so embarrass the mind, that it knows not on what passion to fix itself; from whence arises a fluttering or unsettledness of the spirits, which being, in some degree, uneasy, very naturally degenerates into fear.

Thus we still find, that whatever causes any fluctuation or mixture of passions, with any degree of uneasiness, always produces fear, or at least a passion so like it, that they are scarcely to be distinguished.

I have here confined myself to the examination of hope and fear in their most simple and natural situation, without considering all the variations they may receive from the mixture of different views and reflections. *Terror, consternation, astonishment, anxiety*, and other passions of that kind, are nothing but different species and degrees of fear. It is easy to imagine how a different situation of the object, or a different turn of thought, may change even the sensation of a passion; and this may in general account for all the particular subdivisions of the other affections, as well as of fear. Love may show itself in the shape of *tenderness, friendship, intimacy, esteem, goodwill*, and in many other appearances; which at the bottom are the same affections, and arise from the same causes, though with a small variation, which it is not necessary to give any particular account of. It is for this reason I have all along confined myself to the principal passion.

The same care of avoiding prolixity is the reason why I waive the examination of the will and direct passions, as they appear in animals; since nothing is more evident, than that they are of the same nature, and excited by the same causes as in human creatures. I leave this to the reader's own observation; desiring him at the same time to consider the additional force this bestows on the present system.

Section X *Of curiosity, or the love of truth*

But methinks we have been not a little inattentive to run over so many different parts of the human mind, and examine so many passions, without taking once into the consideration that love of truth, which was the first source of all our enquiries. It will therefore be proper, before we leave this subject, to bestow a few reflections on that passion and show its origin in human nature. It is an affection of so peculiar a kind, that it would have been impossible to have treated of it under any of those heads, which we have examined, without danger of obscurity and confusion.

Truth is of two kinds, consisting either in the discovery of the proportions of ideas, considered as such, or in the conformity of our ideas of objects to their real existence. It is certain, that the former species of truth, is not desired merely as truth, and that it is not the justness of our conclusions, which alone gives the pleasure. For these conclusions are equally just, when we discover the equality of two bodies by a pair of compasses, as when we learn it by a mathematical demonstration; and though in the one case the proofs be demonstrative, and in the other only sensible, yet generally speaking, the mind acquiesces with equal assurance in the one as in the other. And in an arithmetical operation, where both the truth and the assurance are of the same nature, as in the most profound algebraical problem, the pleasure is very inconsiderable, if rather it does not degenerate into pain; which is an evident proof, that the satisfaction, which we sometimes receive from the discovery of truth, proceeds not from it, merely as such, but only as endowed with certain qualities.

The first and most considerable circumstance requisite to render truth agreeable, is the genius and capacity, which is employed in its invention and discovery. What is easy and obvious is never valued; and even what is *in itself* difficult, if we come to the knowledge of it without difficulty, and without any stretch of thought or judgment, is but little regarded. We love to trace the demonstrations of mathematicians; but should receive small entertainment from a person, who should barely inform us of the proportions of lines and angles, though we reposed the utmost confidence both in his judgment and veracity. In this case it is sufficient to have ears to learn the truth. We never are obliged to fix our attention or exert our genius; which of all other exercises of the mind is the most pleasant and agreeable.

But though the exercise of genius be the principal source of that satisfaction we receive from the sciences, yet I doubt, if it be alone sufficient to give us any considerable enjoyment. The truth we discover must also be of some importance. It is easy to multiply algebraical problems to infinity, nor is there any end in the discovery of the proportions of conic sections; though few mathematicians take any pleasure in these researches, but turn their thoughts to what is more useful and important. Now the question is, after what manner this utility and importance operate upon us? The difficulty on this head arises from hence, that many philosophers have consumed their time, have destroyed their health, and neglected their fortune, in the search of such truths, as they esteemed important and useful to the world, though it appeared from their whole conduct and behaviour, that they were not endowed with any share of public spirit, nor had any concern for the interests of mankind. Were they convinced, that their discoveries were of no consequence, they would entirely lose all relish for their studies, and that though the consequences be entirely indifferent to them; which seems to be a contradiction.

To remove this contradiction, we must consider, that there are certain desires and inclinations, which go no farther than the imagination, and are rather the faint shadows and images of passions, than any real affections. Thus, suppose a man, who takes a survey of the fortifications of any city; considers their strength and advantages, natural or acquired; observes the disposition and contrivance of the bastions, ramparts, mines, and other military works; it is plain, that in proportion as all these are fitted to attain their ends, he will receive a suitable pleasure and satisfaction. This pleasure, as it arises from the utility, not the form of the objects, can be no other than a sympathy with the inhabitants, for whose security all this art is employed; though it is possible, that this person, as a stranger or an enemy, may in his heart have no kindness for them, or may even entertain a hatred against them.

It may indeed be objected, that such a remote sympathy is a very slight foundation for a passion, and that so much industry and application, as we frequently observe in philosophers, can never be derived from so inconsiderable an original. But here I return to what I have already remarked, that the pleasure of study consists chiefly in the action of the mind, and the exercise of the genius and understanding in the discovery or comprehension of any truth. If the importance of the truth be requisite to complete the pleasure, it is not on account of any considerable addition, which of itself it brings to our enjoyment, but only because it is, in some measure, requisite to fix our attention. When we are careless and inattentive, the same action of the understanding has no effect upon us, nor is able to convey any of that satisfaction, which arises from it, when we are in another disposition.

But beside the action of the mind, which is the principal foundation of the pleasure, there is likewise required a degree of success in the attainment of the end, or the discovery of that truth we examine. Upon this head I shall make a general remark, which may be useful on many occasions, *viz.* that where the mind pursues any end with passion; though that passion be not derived originally from the end, but merely from the action and pursuit; yet by the natural course of the affections, we acquire a concern for the end itself, and are uneasy under any disappointment we meet with in the pursuit of it. This proceeds from the relation and parallel direction of the passions above-mentioned.

To illustrate all this by a similar instance, I shall observe, that there cannot be two passions more nearly resembling each other, than those of hunting and philosophy, whatever disproportion may at first sight appear betwixt them. It is evident, that the pleasure of hunting consists in the action of the mind and body; the motion, the attention, the difficulty, and the uncertainty. It is evident likewise, that these actions must be attended with an idea of utility, in order to their having any effect upon us. A man of the greatest fortune, and the farthest removed from avarice, though he takes a pleasure in hunting after partridges and pheasants, feels no satisfaction in shooting crows and magpies; and that because he considers the first as fit for the table, and the other as entirely useless. Here it is certain, that the utility or importance of itself causes no real passion, but is only requisite to support the imagination; and the same person, who overlooks a ten times greater profit in any other subject, is pleased to bring home half a dozen woodcocks or plovers, after having employed several hours in hunting after them. To make the parallel betwixt hunting and philosophy more complete, we may observe, that though in both cases the end of our action may in itself be despised, yet in the heat of the action we acquire such an attention to this end, that we are very uneasy under any disappointments, and are sorry when we either miss our game, or fall into any error in our reasoning.

If we want another parallel to these affections, we may consider the passion of gaming, which affords a pleasure from the same principles as hunting and philosophy. It has been remarked, that the pleasure of gaming arises not from interest alone; since many leave a sure gain for this entertainment; neither is it derived from the game alone; since the same persons have no satisfaction, when they play for nothing; but proceeds from both these causes united, though separately they have no effect. It is here, as in certain chemical preparations, where the mixture of two clear and transparent liquids produces a third, which is opaque and coloured.

The interest, which we have in any game, engages our attention, without which we can have no enjoyment, either in that or in any other action. Our attention being once engaged, the difficulty, variety, and sudden reverses of fortune, still farther interest us; and it is from that concern our satisfaction arises. Human life is so tiresome a scene, and men generally are of such indolent dispositions, that whatever amuses them, though by a passion mixed with pain, does in the main give them a sensible pleasure. And this pleasure is here increased by the nature of the objects, which being sensible, and of a narrow compass, are entered into with facility, and are agreeable to the imagination.

The same theory, that accounts for the love of truth in mathematics and algebra, may be extended to morals, politics, natural philosophy, and other studies, where we consider not the abstract relations of ideas, but their real connections and existence. But beside the love of knowledge, which displays itself in the sciences, there is a certain curiosity implanted in human nature, which is a passion derived from a quite different principle. Some people have an insatiable desire of knowing the actions and circumstances of their neighbours, though their interest be no way concerned in them, and they must entirely depend on others for their information; in which case there is no room for study or application. Let us search for the reason of this phenomenon.

It has been proved at large, that the influence of belief is at once to enliven and infix any idea in the imagination, and prevent all kind of hesitation and uncertainty about it. Both these circumstances are advantageous. By the vivacity of the idea we interest the fancy, and produce, though in a lesser degree, the same pleasure, which arises from a moderate passion. As the vivacity of the idea gives pleasure, so its certainty prevents uneasiness, by fixing one particular idea in the mind, and keeping it from wavering in the choice of its objects. It is a quality of human nature, which is conspicuous on many occasions, and is common both to the mind and body, that too sudden and violent a change is unpleasant to us, and that however any objects may in themselves be indifferent, yet their alteration gives uneasiness. As it is the nature of doubt to cause a variation in the thought, and transport us suddenly from one idea to another, it must of consequence be the occasion of pain. This pain chiefly takes place, where interest, relation, or the greatness and novelty of any event interests us in it. It is not every matter of fact, of which we have a curiosity to be informed; neither are they such only as we have an interest to know. It is sufficient if the idea strikes on us with such force, and concerns us so nearly, as to give us an uneasiness in its instability and inconstancy. A stranger, when he arrives first at any town, may be entirely indifferent about knowing the history and adventures of the inhabitants; but as he becomes farther acquainted with them, and has lived any considerable time among them, he acquires the same curiosity as the natives. When we are reading the history of a nation, we may have an ardent desire of clearing up any doubt or difficulty, that occurs in it; but become careless in such researches, when the ideas of these events are, in a great measure, obliterated.

Book III *Of Morals*

PART I *Of Virtue and Vice in General*

SECTION I *Moral distinctions not derived from reason*

There is an inconvenience which attends all abstruse reasoning, that it may silence, without convincing an antagonist, and requires the same intense study to make us sensible of its force, that was at first requisite for its invention. When we leave our closet, and engage in the common affairs of life, its conclusions seem to vanish, like the phantoms of the night on the appearance of the morning; and it is difficult for us to retain even that conviction, which we had attained with difficulty. This is still more conspicuous in a long chain of reasoning, where we must preserve to the end the evidence of the first propositions, and where we often lose sight of all the most received maxims, either of philosophy or common life. I am not, however, without hopes, that the present system of philosophy will acquire new force as it advances; and that our reasonings concerning *morals* will corroborate whatever has been said concerning the *understanding* and the *passions*. Morality is a subject that interests us above all others; we fancy the peace of society to be at stake in every decision concerning it; and it is evident, that this concern must make our speculations appear more real and solid, than where the subject is, in a great measure, indifferent to us. What affects us, we conclude can never be a chimera; and as our passion is engaged on the one side or the other, we naturally think that the question lies within human comprehension; which, in other cases of this nature, we are apt to entertain some doubt of. Without this advantage I never should have ventured upon a third volume of such abstruse philosophy, in an age, wherein the greatest part of men seem agreed to convert reading into an amusement, and to reject everything that requires any considerable degree of attention to be comprehended.

It has been observed, that nothing is ever present to the mind but its perceptions; and that all the actions of seeing, hearing, judging, loving, hating, and thinking, fall under this denomination. The mind can never exert itself in any action, which we may not comprehend under the term of *perception*; and consequently that term is no less applicable to those judgments, by which we distinguish moral good and evil, than to every other operation of the mind. To approve of one character, to condemn another, are only so many different perceptions.

Now as perceptions resolve themselves into two kinds, *viz. impressions* and *ideas*, this distinction gives rise to a question, with which we shall open up our present enquiry concerning morals, *whether it is by means of our* ideas *or* impressions *we distinguish betwixt vice and virtue, and pronounce an action blameable or praiseworthy?* This will immediately cut off all loose discourses and declamations, and reduce us to something precise and exact on the present subject.

Those who affirm that virtue is nothing but a conformity to reason; that there are eternal fitnesses and unfitnesses of things, which are the same to every rational being that considers them; that the immutable measures of right and wrong impose an obligation, not only on human creatures, but also on the Deity himself; all these systems concur in the opinion, that morality, like truth, is discerned merely by ideas, and by their juxtaposition and comparison. In order, therefore, to judge of these systems, we need only consider, whether it be possible, from reason alone, to distinguish betwixt moral good and evil, or whether there must concur some other principles to enable us to make that distinction.

If morality had naturally no influence on human passions and actions, it were in vain to take such pains to inculcate it; and nothing would be more fruitless than that multitude of rules and precepts, with which all moralists abound. Philosophy is commonly divided into *speculative* and *practical*; and as morality is always comprehended under the latter division, it is supposed to influence our passions and actions, and to go beyond the calm and indolent judgments of the understanding. And this is confirmed by common experience, which informs us, that men are often governed by their duties, and are deterred from some actions by the opinion of injustice, and impelled to others by that of obligation.

Since morals, therefore, have an influence on the actions and affections, it follows, that they cannot be derived from reason; and that because reason alone, as we have already proved, can never have any such influence. Morals excite passions, and produce or prevent actions. Reason of itself is utterly impotent in this particular. The rules of morality, therefore, are not conclusions of our reason.

No one, I believe, will deny the justness of this inference; nor is there any other means of evading it, than by denying that principle, on which it is founded. As long as it is allowed, that reason has no influence on our passions and actions, it is in vain to pretend, that morality is discovered only by a deduction of reason. An active principle can never be founded on an inactive; and if reason · be inactive in itself, it must remain so in all its shapes and appearances, whether it exerts itself in natural or moral subjects, whether it considers the powers of external bodies, or the actions of rational beings.

It would be tedious to repeat all the arguments, by which I have proved, that reason is perfectly inert, and can never either prevent or produce any action or affection.* It will be easy to recollect what has been said upon that subject. I shall only recall on this occasion one of these arguments, which I shall endeavour to render still more conclusive, and more applicable to the present subject.

Reason is the discovery of truth or falsehood. Truth or falsehood consists in an agreement or disagreement either to the *real* relations of ideas, or to *real* existence and matter of fact.[23] Whatever, therefore, is not susceptible of this agreement or disagreement, is incapable of being true or false, and can never be an object of our reason. Now it is evident our passions, volitions, and actions, are not susceptible of any such agreement or disagreement; being original facts and realities, complete in themselves, and implying no reference to other passions, volitions, and actions. It is impossible, therefore, they can be pronounced either true or false, and be either contrary or conformable to reason.

This argument is of double advantage to our present purpose. For it proves *directly*, that actions do not derive their merit from a conformity to reason, nor their blame from a contrariety to it; and it proves the same truth more *indirectly*, by showing us, that as reason can never immediately prevent or produce any action by contradicting or

* Book II. Part III. sect. 3.

approving of it, it cannot be the source of moral good and evil, which are found to have that influence. Actions may be laudable or blameable; but they cannot be reasonable or unreasonable; laudable or blameable, therefore, are not the same with reasonable or unreasonable. The merit and demerit of actions frequently contradict, and sometimes control our natural propensities. But reason has no such influence. Moral distinctions, therefore, are not the offspring of reason. Reason is wholly inactive, and can never be the source of so active a principle as conscience, or a sense of morals.

But perhaps it may be said, that though no will or action can be immediately contradictory to reason, yet we may find such a contradiction in some of the attendants of the action, that is, in its causes or effects. The action may cause a judgment, or may be *obliquely* caused by one, when the judgment concurs with a passion; and by an abusive way of speaking, which philosophy will scarce allow of, the same contrariety may, upon that account, be ascribed to the action. How far this truth or falsehood may be the source of morals, it will now be proper to consider.

It has been observed, that reason, in a strict and philosophical sense, can have an influence on our conduct only after two ways; either when it excites a passion by informing us of the existence of something which is a proper object of it; or when it discovers the connection of causes and effects, so as to afford us means of exerting any passion. These are the only kinds of judgment, which can accompany our actions, or can be said to produce them in any manner; and it must be allowed, that these judgments may often be false and erroneous. A person may be affected with passion, by supposing a pain or pleasure to lie in an object, which has no tendency to produce either of these sensations, or which produces the contrary to what is imagined. A person may also take false measures for the attaining his end, and may retard, by his foolish conduct, instead of forwarding the execution of any project. These false judgments may be thought to affect the passions and actions, which are connected with them, and may be said to render them unreasonable, in a figurative and improper way of speaking. But though this be acknowledged, it is easy to observe, that these errors are so far from being the source of all immorality, that they are commonly very innocent, and draw no manner of guilt upon the person who is so unfortunate as to fall into them. They extend not beyond a mistake of *fact*, which moralists have not generally supposed criminal, as being perfectly involuntary. I am more to be lamented than blamed, if I am mistaken with regard to the influence of objects in producing pain or pleasure, or if I know not the proper means of satisfying my desires. No one can ever regard such errors as a defect in my moral character. A fruit, for instance, that is really disagreeable, appears to me at a distance, and thro' mistake I fancy it to be pleasant and delicious. Here is one error. I choose certain means of reaching this fruit, which are not proper for my end. Here is a second error; nor is there any third one, which can ever possibly enter into our reasonings concerning actions. I ask, therefore, if a man, in this situation, and guilty of these two errors, is to be regarded as vicious and criminal, however unavoidable they might have been; or if it be possible to imagine, that such errors are the sources of all immorality?

And here it may be proper to observe, that if moral distinctions be derived from the truth or falsehood of those judgments, they must take place wherever we form the judgments; nor will there be any difference, whether the question be concerning an apple or a kingdom, or whether the error be avoidable or unavoidable. For as the very essence of morality is supposed to consist in an agreement or disagreement to reason, the other circumstances are entirely arbitrary, and can never either bestow on any action the character of virtuous or vicious, or deprive it of that character. To which we may add, that this agreement or disagreement, not admitting of degrees, all virtues and vices would of course be equal.[24]

Should it be pretended, that though a mistake of *fact* be not criminal, yet a mistake of *right* often is; and that this may be the source of immorality: I would answer, that it is impossible such a mistake can ever be the original source of immorality, since it supposes a real right and wrong; that is, a real distinction in morals, independent of these judgments. A mistake, therefore, of right may become a species of immorality; but it is only a secondary one, and is founded on some other, antecedent to it.

As to those judgments which are the *effects* of our actions, and which, when false, give occasion to pronounce the actions contrary to truth and reason; we may observe, that our actions never cause any judgment, either true or false, in ourselves, and that it is only on others they have such an influence. It is certain, that an action, on many occasions, may give rise to false conclusions in others; and that a person, who through a window sees any lewd behaviour of mine with my neighbour's wife, may be so simple as to imagine she is certainly my own. In this respect my action resembles somewhat a lie or falsehood; only with this difference, which is material, that I perform not the action with any intention of giving rise to a false judgment in another, but merely to satisfy my lust and passion. It causes, however, a mistake and false judgment by accident; and the falsehood of its effects may be ascribed, by some odd figurative way of speaking, to the action itself. But still I can see no pretext of reason for asserting, that the tendency to cause such an error is the first spring or original source of all immorality.*

* One might think it were entirely superfluous to prove this, if a late author [Wollaston], who has had the good fortune to obtain some reputation, had not seriously affirmed, that such a falsehood is the foundation of all guilt and moral deformity.[25] That we may discover the fallacy of his hypothesis, we need only consider, that a false conclusion is drawn from an action, only by means of an obscurity of natural principles, which makes a cause be secretly interrupted in its operation, by contrary causes, and renders the connection betwixt two objects uncertain and variable. Now, as a like uncertainty and variety of causes take place, even in natural objects, and produce a like error in our judgment, if that tendency to produce error were the very essence of vice and immorality, it should follow, that even inanimate objects might be vicious and immoral.

It is in vain to urge, that inanimate objects act without liberty and choice. For as liberty and choice are not necessary to make an action produce in us an erroneous conclusion, they can be, in no respect, essential to morality; and I do not readily perceive, upon this system, how they can ever come to be regarded by it. If the tendency to cause error be the origin of immorality, that tendency and immorality would in every case be inseparable.

Add to this, that if I had used the precaution of shutting the windows, while I indulged myself in those liberties with my neighbour's wife, I should have been guilty of no immorality; and that because my action, being perfectly concealed, would have had no tendency to produce any false conclusion.

For the same reason, a thief, who steals in by a ladder at a window, and takes all imaginable care to cause no disturbance,

Thus upon the whole, it is impossible, that the distinction betwixt moral good and evil, can be made by reason; since that distinction has an influence upon our actions, of which reason alone is incapable. Reason and judgment may, indeed, be the mediate cause of an action, by prompting, or by directing a passion; but it is not pretended, that a judgment of this kind, either in its truth or falsehood, is attended with virtue or vice. And as to the judgments, which are caused by our judgments, they can still less bestow those moral qualities on the actions, which are their causes.

---

is in no respect criminal. For either he will not be perceived, or if he be, it is impossible he can produce any error, nor will any one, from these circumstances, take him to be other than what he really is.

It is well known, that those who are squint-sighted, do very readily cause mistakes in others, and that we imagine they salute or are talking to one person, while they address themselves to another. Are they therefore, upon that account, immoral?

Besides, we may easily observe, that in all those arguments there is an evident reasoning in a circle. A person who takes possession of *another*'s goods and uses them as his *own*, in a manner declares them to be his own; and this falsehood is the source of the immorality of injustice. But is property, or right, or obligation, intelligible, without an antecedent morality?

A man that is ungrateful to his benefactor, in a manner affirms, that he never received any favours from him. But in what manner? Is it because it is his duty to be grateful? But this supposes, that there is some antecedent rule of duty and morals. Is it because human nature is generally grateful, and makes us conclude, that a man who does any harm never received any favour from the person he harmed? But human nature is not so generally grateful, as to justify such a conclusion. Or if it were, is an exception to a general rule in every case criminal, for no other reason than because it is an exception?

But what may suffice entirely to destroy this whimsical system is, that it leaves us under the same difficulty to give a reason why truth is virtuous and falsehood vicious, as to account for the merit or turpitude of any other action. I shall allow, if you please, that all immorality is derived from this supposed falsehood in action, provided you can give me any plausible reason, why such a falsehood is immoral. If you consider rightly of the matter, you will find yourself in the same difficulty as at the beginning.[26]

This last argument is very conclusive; because, if there be not an evident merit or turpitude annexed to this species of truth or falsehood, it can never have any influence upon our actions. For, who ever thought of forbearing any action, because others might possibly draw false conclusions from it? Or, who ever performed any, that he might give rise to true conclusions?

But to be more particular, and to show, that those eternal immutable fitnesses and unfitnesses of things cannot be defended by sound philosophy, we may weigh the following considerations.

If the thought and understanding were alone capable of fixing the boundaries of right and wrong, the character of virtuous and vicious either must lie in some relations of objects, or must be a matter of fact, which is discovered by our reasoning. This consequence is evident. As the operations of human understanding divide themselves into two kinds, the comparing of ideas, and the inferring of matter of fact; were virtue discovered by the understanding; it must be an object of one of these operations, nor is there any third operation of the understanding, which can discover it. There has been an opinion very industriously propagated by certain philosophers, that morality is susceptible of demonstration; and though no one has ever been able to advance a single step in those demonstrations; yet it is taken for granted, that this science may be brought to an equal certainty with geometry or algebra. Upon this supposition, vice and virtue must consist in some relations; since it is allowed on all hands, that no matter of fact is capable of being demonstrated. Let us, therefore, begin with examining this hypothesis, and endeavour, if possible, to fix those moral qualities, which have been so long the objects of our fruitless researches. Point out distinctly the relations, which constitute morality or obligation, that we may know wherein they consist, and after what manner we must judge of them.

If you assert, that vice and virtue consist in relations susceptible of certainty and demonstration, you must confine yourself to those *four* relations, which alone admit of that degree of evidence; and in that case you run into absurdities, from which you will never be able to extricate yourself. For as you make the very essence of morality to lie in the relations, and as there is no one of these relations but what is applicable, not only to an irrational, but also to an inanimate object; it follows, that even such objects must be susceptible of merit or demerit. *Resemblance, contrariety, degrees in quality,* and *proportions in quantity and number*; all these relations belong as properly to matter, as to our actions, passions, and volitions. It is unquestionable, therefore, that morality lies not in any of these relations, nor the sense of it in their discovery.*

Should it be asserted, that the sense of morality consists in the discovery of some relation, distinct from these, and that our enumeration was not complete, when we comprehended all demonstrable relations under four general heads; to this I know not what to reply, till someone be so good as to point out to me this new relation. It is impossible to refute a system, which has never yet been explained. In such a manner of fighting in the dark, a man loses his blows in the air, and often places them where the enemy is not present.

I must, therefore, on this occasion, rest contented with requiring the two following conditions of anyone that would undertake to clear up this system. *First*, as moral good and evil being only to the actions of the mind, and are derived from our situation with regard to external objects, the relations, from which these moral distinctions arise, must lie only betwixt internal actions, and external objects, and must not be applicable either to internal actions, compared among themselves, or to external objects, when placed in opposition to other external objects. For as morality is supposed to attend certain relations, if these relations could belong to internal actions considered singly, it would follow, that we might be guilty of crimes in ourselves, and independent of our situation, with respect to the universe; and in like manner, if these moral relations could be applied to external objects, it would follow, that even inanimate beings would be

* As a proof, how confused our way of thinking on this subject commonly is, we may observe, that those who assert, that morality is demonstrable, do not say, that morality lies in the relations, and that the relations are distinguishable by reason. They only say, that reason can discover such an action, in such relations, to be virtuous, and such another vicious. It seems they thought it sufficient, if they could bring the word, 'Relation,' into the proposition, without troubling themselves whether it was to the purpose or not. But here, I think, is plain argument. Demonstrative reason discovers only relations. But that reason, according to this hypothesis, discovers also vice and virtue. These moral qualities, therefore, must be relations. When we blame any action, in any situation, the whole complicated object, of action and situation, must form certain relations, wherein the essence of vice consists. This hypothesis is not otherwise intelligible. For what does reason discover, when it pronounces any action vicious? Does it discover a relation or a matter of fact? These questions are decisive, and must not be eluded.[27]

susceptible of moral beauty and deformity. Now it seems difficult to imagine, that any relation can be discovered betwixt our passions, volitions and actions, compared to external objects, which relation might not belong either to these passions and volitions, or to these external objects, compared among *themselves*.[28]

But it will be still more difficult to fulfil the *second* condition, requisite to justify this system. According to the principles of those who maintain an abstract rational difference betwixt moral good and evil, and a natural fitness and unfitness of things, it is not only supposed, that these relations, being eternal and immutable, are the same, when considered by every rational creature, but their *effects* ars also supposed to be necessarily the same; and it is concluded they have no less, or rather a greater, influence in directing the will of the Deity, than in governing the rational and virtuous of our own species. These two particulars are evidently distinct. It is one thing to know virtue, and another to conform the will to it. In order, therefore, to prove, that the measures of right and wrong are eternal laws, *obligatory* on every rational mind, it is not sufficient to show the relations upon which they are founded; we must also point out the connection betwixt the relation and the will; and must prove that this connection is so necessary, that in every well-disposed mind, it must take place and have its influence; though the difference betwixt these minds be in other respects immense and infinite. Now besides what I have already proved, that even in human nature no relation can ever alone produce any action; besides this, I say, it has been shown, in treating of the understanding, that there is no connection of cause and effect, such as this is supposed to be, which is discoverable otherwise than by experience, and of which we can pretend to have any security by the simple consideration of the objects. All beings in the universe, considered in themselves, appear entirely loose and independent of each other. It is only by experience we learn their influence and connection; and this influence we ought never to extend beyond experience.

Thus it will be impossible to fulfil the *first* condition required to the system of eternal rational measures of right and wrong; because it is impossible to show those relations, upon which such a distinction may be founded; and it is as impossible to fulfil the *second* condition; because we cannot prove *a priori*, that these relations, if they really existed and were perceived, would be universally forcible and obligatory.

But to make these general reflections more clear and convincing, we may illustrate them by some particular instances, wherein this character of moral good or evil is the most universally acknowledged. Of all crimes that human creatures are capable of committing, the most horrid and unnatural is ingratitude, especially when it is committed against parents, and appears in the more flagrant instances of wounds and death. This is acknowledged by all mankind, philosophers as well as the people; the question only arises among philosophers, whether the guilt or moral deformity of this action be discovered by demonstrative reasoning, or be felt by an internal sense, and by means of some sentiment, which the reflecting on such an action naturally occasions. This question will soon be decided against the former opinion, if we can show the same relations in other objects without the notion of any guilt or iniquity attending them. Reason or science is nothing but the comparing of ideas, and the discovery of their relations; and if the same relations have different characters, it must evidently follow, that those characters are not discovered merely by reason. To put the affair, therefore, to this trial, let us choose an inanimate object, such as an oak or elm; and let us suppose, that by the dropping of its seed, it produces a sapling below it, which springing up by degrees, at last overtops and destroys the parent tree; I ask, if in this instance there be wanting any relation, which is discoverable in parricide or ingratitude? Is not the one tree the cause of the other's existence; and the latter the cause of the destruction of the former, in the same manner as when a child murders his parent? It is not sufficient to reply, that a choice or will is wanting. For in the case of parricide, a will does not give rise to any *different* relations, but is only the cause from which the action is derived; and consequently produces the *same* relations, that in the oak or elm arise from some other principles. It is a will or choice, that determines a man to kill his parent; and they are the laws of matter and motion, that determine a sapling to destroy the oak, from which it sprung. Here then the same relations have different causes; but still the relations are the same; and as their discovery is not in both cases attended with a notion of immorality, it follows, that the notion does not arise from such a discovery.

But to choose any instance, still more resembling; I would fain ask anyone, why incest in the human species is criminal, and why the very same action, and the same relations in animals have not the smallest moral turpitude and deformity? If it be answered, that this action is innocent in animals, because they have not reason sufficient to discover its turpitude; but that man, being endowed with the faculty, which *ought* to restrain him to his duty, the same action instantly becomes criminal to him; should this be said, I would reply, that this is evidently arguing in a circle. For before reason can perceive this turpitude, the turpitude must exist; and consequently is independent of the decisions of our reason, and is their object more properly than their effect. According to this system, then, every animal, that has sense, and appetite, and will; that is, every animal must be susceptible of all the same virtues and vices, for which we ascribe praise and blame to human creatures. All the difference is, that our superior reason may serve to discover the vice or virtue, and by that means may augment the blame or praise; but still this discovery supposes a separate being in these moral distinctions, and a being, which depends only on the will and appetite, and which, both in thought and reality, may be distinguished from the reason. Animals are susceptible of the same relations, with respect to each other, as the human species, and therefore would also be susceptible of the same morality, if the essence of morality consisted in these relations. Their want of a sufficient degree of reason may hinder them from perceiving the duties and obligations of morality, but can never hinder these duties from existing; since they must antecedently exist, in order to their being perceived. Reason must find them, and can never produce them. This argument deserves to be weighed, as being, in my opinion, entirely decisive.

Nor does this reasoning only prove, that morality consists not in any relations, that are the objects of science; but if examined, will prove with equal certainty, that it consists not in any *matter of fact*, which can be discovered by the understanding. This is the *second* part of our argument; and if it can be made evident, we may conclude, that morality is not an object of reason. But can there be any difficulty in proving, that vice and virtue are not matters of fact, whose existence we can infer by reason? Take any action allowed to be vicious: wilful murder, for instance. Examine it in all lights, and see if you can find that matter of fact, or real existence, which you call *vice*. In whichever way you take it, you find only certain passions, motives, volitions and thoughts. There is no other matter of fact in the case. The vice entirely escapes you, as long as you consider the object. You never can find it, till you turn your reflection into your own breast, and find a sentiment of disapprobation, which arises in you, towards this action. Here is a matter of fact; but it is the object of feeling, not of reason. It lies in yourself, not in the object. So that when you pronounce any action or character to be vicious, you mean nothing, but that from the constitution of your nature you have a feeling or sentiment of blame from the contemplation of it. Vice and virtue, therefore, may be compared to sounds, colours, heat and cold, which, according to modern philosophy, are not qualities in objects, but perceptions in the mind; and this discovery in morals, like that other in physics, is to be regarded as a considerable advancement of the speculative sciences; though, like that too, it has little or no influence on practice. Nothing can be more real, or concern us more, than our own sentiments of pleasure and uneasiness; and if these be favourable to virtue, and unfavourable to vice, no more can be requisite to the regulation of our conduct and behaviour.

I cannot forbear adding to these reasonings an observation, which may, perhaps, be found of some importance. In every system of morality, which I have hitherto met with, I have always remarked, that the author proceeds for some time in the ordinary way of reasoning, and establishes the being of a God, or makes observations concerning human affairs; when of a sudden I am surprised to find, that instead of the usual copulations of propositions, *is*, and *is not*, I meet with no proposition that is not connected with an *ought*, or an *ought not*. This change is imperceptible; but is, however, of the last consequence. For as this *ought*, or *ought not*, expresses some new relation or affirmation, it is necessary that it should be observed and explained; and at the same time that a reason should be given, for what seems altogether inconceivable, how this new relation can be a deduction from others, which are entirely different from it. But as authors do not commonly use this precaution, I shall presume to recommend it to the readers; and am persuaded, that this small attention would subvert all the vulgar systems of morality, and let us see, that the distinction of vice and virtue is not founded merely on the relations of objects, nor is perceived by reason.

SECTION II *Moral distinctions derived from a moral sense*

Thus the course of the argument leads us to conclude, that since vice and virtue are not discoverable merely by reason, or the comparison of ideas, it must be by means of some impression or sentiment they occasion, that we are able to mark the difference betwixt them. Our decisions concerning moral rectitude and depravity are evidently perceptions; and as all perceptions are either impressions or ideas, the exclusion of the one is a convincing argument for the other. Morality, therefore, is more properly felt than judged of; though this feeling or sentiment is commonly so soft and gentle, that we are apt to confound it with an idea, according to our common custom of taking all things for the same, which have any near resemblance to each other.[29]

The next question is, of what nature are these impressions, and after what manner do they operate upon us? Here we cannot remain long in suspense, but must pronounce the impression arising from virtue, to be agreeable, and that proceeding from vice to be uneasy. Every moment's experience must convince us of this. There is no spectacle so fair and beautiful as a noble and generous action; nor any which gives us more abhorrence than one that is cruel and treacherous. No enjoyment equals the satisfaction we receive from the company of those we love and esteem; as the greatest of all punishments is to be obliged to pass our lives with those we hate or contemn. A very play or romance may afford us instances of this pleasure, which virtue conveys to us; and pain, which arises from vice.

Now since the distinguishing impressions, by which moral good or evil is known, are nothing but *particular* pains or pleasures; it follows, that in all enquiries concerning these moral distinctions, it will be sufficient to show the principles, which make us feel a satisfaction or uneasiness from the survey of any character, in order to satisfy us why the character is laudable or blameable. An action, or sentiment, or character is virtuous or vicious; why? because its view causes a pleasure or uneasiness of a particular kind. In giving a reason, therefore, for the pleasure or uneasiness, we sufficiently explain the vice or virtue. To have the sense of virtue, is nothing but to *feel* a satisfaction of a particular kind from the contemplation of a character. The very *feeling* constitutes our praise or admiration. We go no farther; nor do we enquire into the cause of the satisfaction. We do not infer a character to be virtuous, because it pleases; but in feeling that it pleases after such a particular manner, we in effect feel that it is virtuous. The case is the same as in our judgments concerning all kinds of beauty, and tastes, and sensations. Our approbation is implied in the immediate pleasure they convey to us.

I have objected to the system, which establishes eternal rational measures of right and wrong, that it is impossible to show, in the actions of reasonable creatures, any relations, which are not found in external objects; and therefore, if morality always attended these relations, it were possible for inanimate matter to become virtuous or vicious. Now it may, in like manner, be objected to the present system, that if virtue and vice be determined by pleasure and pain, these qualities must, in every case, arise from the sensations; and consequently any object, whether animate or inanimate, rational or irrational, might become morally good or evil, provided it can excite a satisfaction or uneasiness. But though this objection seems to be the very same, it has by no means the same force, in the one case as in the other. For, *first*, it is evident, that under the term *pleasure*, we comprehend sensations, which are very different from each other, and which have only such a distant resemblance, as is requisite to make them be expressed by the same abstract term. A good composition of music and a bottle of good wine equally produce pleasure; and what is more, their goodness is determined merely by the pleasure. But shall we say upon that account, that the wine is harmonious, or the music of a good flavour? In like manner an inanimate object, and the character or sentiments of any person may, both of them, give satisfaction; but as the satisfaction is different, this keeps our sentiments concerning them from being confounded, and makes us ascribe virtue to the one, and not to the other. Nor is every sentiment of pleasure or pain, which arises from characters and actions, of that *peculiar* kind, which makes us praise or condemn. The good qualities of an enemy are hurtful to us; but may still command our esteem and respect. It is only when a character is considered in general, without reference to our particular interest, that it causes such a feeling or sentiment, as denominates it morally good or evil. It is true, those sentiments, from interest and morals, are apt to be confounded, and naturally run into one another. It seldom happens, that we do not think an enemy vicious, and can distinguish betwixt his opposition to our interest and real villainy or baseness. But this hinders not, but that the sentiments are, in themselves, distinct; and a man of temper and judgment may preserve himself from these illusions. In like manner, though it is certain a musical voice is nothing but one that naturally gives a *particular* kind of pleasure; yet it is difficult for a man to be sensible, that the voice of an enemy is agreeable, or to allow it to be musical. But a person of a fine ear, who has the command of himself, can separate these feelings, and give praise to what deserves it.[30]

Secondly, we may call to remembrance the preceding system of the passions, in order to remark a still more considerable difference among our pains and pleasures. Pride and humility, love and hatred are excited, when there is any thing presented to us, that both bears a relation to the object of the passion, and produces a separate sensation related to the sensation of the passion. Now virtue and vice are attended with these circumstances. They must necessarily be placed either in ourselves or others, and excite either pleasure or uneasiness; and therefore must give rise to one of these four passions; which clearly distinguishes them from the pleasure and pain arising from inanimate objects, that often bear no relation to us; and this is, perhaps, the most considerable effect that virtue and vice have upon the human mind.

It may now be asked *in general,* concerning this pain or pleasure, that distinguishes moral good and evil, *from what principles is it derived, and whence does it arise in the human mind?* To this I reply, *first,* that it is absurd to imagine, that in every particular instance, these sentiments are produced by an *original* quality and *primary* constitution. For as the number of our duties is, in a manner, infinite, it is im-

ossible that our original instincts should extend to each
f them, and from our very first infancy impress on the human
nind all that multitude of precepts, which are contained in
he completest system of ethics. Such a method of proceed-
ng is not conformable to the usual maxims, by which nature
s conducted, where a few principles produce all that variety
ve observe in the universe, and everything is carried on in
he easiest and most simple manner. It is necessary, there-
ore, to abridge those primary impulses, and find some more
eneral principles, upon which all our notions of morals are
ounded.[31]

But in the *second* place, should it be asked, whether we
ught to search for these principles in *nature*, or whether
ve must look for them in some other origin? I would reply,
hat our answer to this question depends upon the definition
f the word, nature, than which there is none more ambigu-
ous and equivocal. If *nature* be opposed to miracles, not only
he distinction betwixt vice and virtue is natural, but also
very event, which has ever happened in the world, *excepting
hose miracles, on which our religion is founded.*[32] In saying,
hen, that the sentiments of vice and virtue are natural in
his sense, we make no very extraordinary discovery.

But *nature* may also be opposed to rare and unusual; and
n this sense of the word, which is the common one, there
nay often arise disputes concerning what is natural or unnatural; and one may in general affirm, that we are not pos-
essed of any very precise standard, by which these disputes
an be decided. Frequent and rare depend upon the number
f examples we have observed; and as this number may
radually increase or diminish, it will be impossible to fix
ny exact boundaries betwixt them. We may only affirm on
his head, that if ever there was anything, which could be
all'd natural in this sense, the sentiments of morality cer-
ainly may; since there never was any nation of the world,
nor any single person in any nation, who was utterly deprived
f them, and who never, in any instance, showed the least
pprobation or dislike of manners. These sentiments are so
ooted in our constitution and temper, that without entirely
onfounding the human mind by disease or madness, it is
mpossible to extirpate and destroy them.

But *nature* may also be opposed to artifice, as well as to
vhat is rare and unusual; and in this sense it may be dis-

puted, whether the notions of virtue be natural or not. We
readily forget, that the designs, and projects, and views of
men are principles as necessary in their operation as heat and
cold, moist and dry; but taking them to be free and entirely
our own, it is usual for us to set them in opposition to the
other principles of nature. Should it, therefore, be demanded,
whether the sense of virtue be natural or artificial, I am of
opinion, that it is impossible for me at present to give any
precise answer to this question. Perhaps it will appear afterwards, that our sense of some virtues is artificial, and that of
others natural. The discussion of this question will be more
proper, when we enter upon an exact detail of each particular
vice and virtue.*

Meanwhile it may not be amiss to observe from these
definitions of *natural* and *unnatural*, that nothing can be more
unphilosophical than those systems, which assert, that virtue
is the same with what is natural, and vice with what is unnatural. For in the first sense of the word, Nature, as opposed
to miracles, both vice and virtue are equally natural; and in
the second sense, as opposed to what is unusual, perhaps
virtue will be found to be the most unnatural. At least it
must be owned, that heroic virtue, being as unusual, is as
little natural as the most brutal barbarity. As to the third
sense of the word, it is certain, that both vice and virtue are
equally artificial, and out of nature. For however it may be
disputed, whether the notion of a merit or demerit in certain
actions be natural or artificial, it is evident, that the actions
themselves are artificial, and are performed with a certain
design and intention; otherwise they could never be ranked
under any of these denominations. It is impossible, therefore,
that the character of natural and unnatural can ever, in any
sense, mark the boundaries of vice and virtue.[33]

Thus we are still brought back to our first position, that
virtue is distinguished by the pleasure, and vice by the pain,
that any action, sentiment or character gives us by the mere
view and contemplation. This decision is very commodious,
because it reduces us to this simple question, *why any action
or sentiment upon the general view or survey, gives a certain
satisfaction or uneasiness,* in order to show the origin of its

* In the following discourse *natural* is also opposed sometimes
to *civil*, sometimes to *moral*. The opposition will always discover
the sense, in which it is taken.

moral rectitude or depravity, without looking for any incomprehensible relations and qualities, which never did exist in nature, nor even in our imagination, by any clear and distinct conception. I flatter myself I have executed a great part of my present design by a state of the question, which appears to me so free from ambiguity and obscurity.

Part II *Of Justice and Injustice*

Section I *Justice, whether a natural or artificial virtue?*

I have already hinted, that our sense of every kind of virtue is not natural; but that there are some virtues, that produce pleasure and approbation by means of an artifice or contrivance, which arises from the circumstances and necessity of mankind. Of this kind I assert *justice* to be; and shall endeavour to defend this opinion by a short, and, I hope, convincing argument, before I examine the nature of the artifice, from which the sense of that virtue is derived.

It is evident, that when we praise any actions, we regard only the motives that produced them, and consider the actions as signs or indications of certain principles in the mind and temper. The external performance has no merit. We must look within to find the moral quality. This we cannot do directly; and therefore fix our attention on actions, as on external signs. But these actions are still considered as signs; and the ultimate object of our praise and approbation is the motive, that produced them.

After the same manner, when we require any action, or blame a person for not performing it, we always suppose, that one in that situation should be influenced by the proper motive of that action, and we esteem it vicious in him to be regardless of it. If we find, upon enquiry, that the virtuous motive was still powerful over his breast, though checked in its operation by some circumstances unknown to us, we retract our blame, and have the same esteem for him, as if he had actually performed the action, which we require of him.

It appears, therefore, that all virtuous actions derive their merit only from virtuous motives, and are considered merely as signs of those motives. From this principle I conclude, that the first virtuous motive, which bestows a merit on any action, can never be a regard to the virtue of that action, but must be some other natural motive or principle. To suppose, that the mere regard to the virtue of the action, may be the first motive, which produced the action, and rendered it virtuous, is to reason in a circle. Before we can have such a regard, the action must be really virtuous; and this virtue must be derived from some virtuous motive; and consequently the virtuous motive must be different from the regard to the virtue of the action. A virtuous motive is requisite to render an action virtuous. An action must be virtuous, before we can have a regard to its virtue. Some virtuous motive, therefore, must be antecedent to that regard.

Nor is this merely a metaphysical subtlety; but enters into all our reasonings in common life, though perhaps we may not be able to place it in such distinct philosophical terms. We blame a father for neglecting his child. Why? Because it shows a want of natural affection, which is the duty of every parent. Were not natural affection a duty, the care of children could not be a duty; and it were impossible we could have the duty in our eye in the attention we give to our offspring. In this case, therefore, all men suppose a motive to the action distinct from a sense of duty.

Here is a man, that does many benevolent actions; relieves the distressed, comforts the afflicted, and extends his bounty even to the greatest strangers. No character can be more amiable and virtuous. We regard these actions as proofs of the greatest humanity. This humanity bestows a merit on the actions. A regard to this merit is, therefore, a secondary consideration, and derived from the antecedent principle of humanity, which is meritorious and laudable.

In short, it may be established as an undoubted maxim, *that no action can be virtuous, or morally good, unless there be in human nature some motive to produce it, distinct from the sense of its morality.*[34]

But may not the sense of morality or duty produce an action, without any other motive? I answer, it may; but this is no objection to the present doctrine. When any virtuous motive or principle is common in human nature, a person, who feels his heart devoid of that motive, may hate himself upon that account, and may perform the action without the motive, from a certain sense of duty, in order to acquire by practice, that virtuous principle, or at least, to disguise to himself, as much as possible, his want of it. A man that really feels no gratitude in his temper, is still pleased to perform grateful actions, and thinks he has, by that means, fulfilled his duty. Actions are at first only considered as signs of motives, but it is usual, in this case, as in all others, to fix our attention on the signs, and neglect, in some measure, the thing signified. But though, on some occasions, a person may perform an action merely out of regard to its moral obligation, yet still this supposes in human nature some distinct principles, which are capable of producing the action, and whose moral beauty renders the action meritorious.

Now to apply all this to the present case; I suppose a person to have lent me a sum of money, on condition that it be restored in a few days; and also suppose, that after the expiration of the term agreed on, he demands the sum; I ask, *what reason or motive have I to restore the money?* It will, perhaps, be said, that my regard to justice, and abhorrence of villainy and knavery, are sufficient reasons for me, if I have the least grain of honesty, or sense of duty and obligation. And this answer, no doubt, is just and satisfactory to man in his civilized state, and when trained up according to a certain discipline and education. But in his rude and more *natural* condition, if you are pleased to call such a condition natural, this answer would be rejected as perfectly unintelligible and sophistical. For one in that situation wou'd immediately ask you, *wherein consists this honesty and justice, which you find in restoring a loan, and abstaining from the property of others?* It does not surely lie in the external action. It must, therefore be placed in the motive, from which the external action is derived. This motive can never be a regard to the honesty of the action. For it is a plain fallacy to say, that a virtuous motive is requisite to render an action honest, and at the same time that a regard to the honesty is the motive of the action. We can never have a regard to the virtue of an action, unless the action be antecedently virtuous. No action can be virtuous, but so far as it proceeds from a virtuous motive. A virtuous motive, therefore, must precede the regard to the virtue; and 'tis impossible, that the virtuous motive and the regard to the virtue can be the same.

It is requisite, then, to find some motive to acts of justice and honesty, distinct from our regard to the honesty; and in this lies the great difficulty. For should we say, that a concern for our private interest or reputation is the legitimate motive to all honest actions; it would follow, that wherever that concern ceases, honesty can no longer have place. But it is certain, that self-love, when it acts at its liberty, instead of engaging us to honest actions, is the source of all injustice and violence; nor can a man ever correct those vices, without correcting and restraining the *natural* movements of that appetite.

But should it be affirmed, that the reason or motive of such actions is the *regard to public interest*, to which nothing is more contrary than examples of injustice and dishonesty; should this be said, I would propose the three following considerations, as worthy of our attention. *First*, public interest is not naturally attached to the observation of the rules of justice; but is only connected with it, after an artificial convention for the establishment of these rules, as shall be shown more at large hereafter. *Secondly*, if we suppose, that the loan was secret, and that it is necessary for the interest of the person, that the money be restored in the same manner (as when the lender would conceal his riches) in that case the example ceases, and the public is no longer interested in the actions of the borrower; though I suppose there is no moralist, who will affirm, that the duty and obligation ceases. *Thirdly*, experience sufficiently proves, that men, in the ordinary conduct of life, look not so far as the public interest, when they pay their creditors, perform their promises, and abstain from theft, and robbery, and injustice of every kind. That is a motive too remote and too sublime to affect the generality of mankind, and operate with any force in actions so contrary to private interest as are frequently those of justice and common honesty.

In general, it may be affirmed, that there is no such passion in human minds, as the love of mankind, merely as such, independent of personal qualities, of services, or of relation to ourself. It is true, there is no human, and indeed no sensible, creature, whose happiness or misery does not, in some measure, affect us, when brought near to us, and represented in lively colours. But this proceeds merely from sympathy, and is no proof of such a universal affection to mankind, since this concern extends itself beyond our own species. An affection betwixt the sexes is a passion evidently implanted in human nature; and this passion not only appears in its peculiar symptoms, but also in inflaming every other principle of affection, and raising a stronger love from beauty, wit, kindness, than what would otherwise flow from them. Were there an universal love among all human creatures, it would appear after the same manner. Any degree of a good quality would cause a stronger affection than the same degree of a bad quality would cause hatred; contrary to what we find by experience. Men's tempers are different, and some have a propensity to the tender, and others to the rougher, affections, but in the main, we may affirm, that man in general, or human nature, is nothing but the object both of love and hatred, and requires some other cause, which by a double relation of impressions and ideas, may excite these passions. In vain would we endeavour to elude this hypothesis. There are no phenomena that point out any such kind affection to men, independent of their merit, and every other circumstance. We love company in general; but it is as we love any other amusement. An *Englishman* in *Italy* is a friend; a *Europæan* in *China*; and perhaps a man would be beloved as such, were we to meet him in the moon. But this proceeds only from the relation to ourselves; which in these cases gathers force by being confined to a few persons.

If public benevolence, therefore, or a regard to the interests of mankind, cannot be the original motive to justice, much less can *private benevolence*, or a *regard to the interests of the party concerned*, be this motive. For what if he be my enemy, and has given me just cause to hate him? What if he be a vicious man, and deserves the hatred of all mankind? What if he be a miser, and can make no use of what I would deprive him of? What if he be a profligate debauchee, and would rather receive harm than benefit from large possessions? What if I be in necessity, and have urgent motives to acquire something to my family? In all these cases, the original motive to justice would fail; and consequently the justice itself, and along with it all property, right, and obligation.

A rich man lies under a moral obligation to communicate to those in necessity a share of his superfluities. Were private benevolence the original motive to justice, a man would not be obliged to leave others in the possession of more than he is obliged to give them. At least the difference would be very inconsiderable. Men generally fix their affections more on what they are possessed of, than on what they never enjoyed; for this reason, it would be greater cruelty to dispossess a man of anything, than not to give it him. But who will assert, that this is the only foundation of justice?

Besides, we must consider, that the chief reason, why men attach themselves so much to their possessions is, that they consider them as their property, and as secured to them inviolably by the laws of society. But this is a secondary consideration, and dependent on the preceding notions of justice and property.

A man's property is supposed to be fenced against every mortal, in every possible case. But private benevolence is, and ought to be, weaker in some persons, than in others; and in many, or indeed in most persons, must absolutely fail. Private benevolence, therefore, is not the original motive of justice.

From all this it follows, that we have no real or universal motive for observing the laws of equality, but the very equity and merit of that observance; and as no action can be equitable or meritorious, where it cannot arise from some separate motive, there is here an evident sophistry and reasoning in a circle. Unless, therefore, we will allow, that nature has established a sophistry, and rendered it necessary and unavoidable, we must allow, that the sense of justice and injustice is not derived from nature, but arises artificially, though necessarily from education, and human conventions.

I shall add, as a corollary to this reasoning, that since no action can be laudable or blameable, without some motives or impelling passions, distinct from the sense of morals, these distinct passions must have a great influence on that sense. It is according to their general force in human nature, that we blame or praise. In judging of the beauty of animal bodies, we always carry in our eye the economy of a certain species; and where the limbs and features observe that proportion, which is common to the species, we pronounce them handsome and beautiful. In like manner we always consider the *natural* and *usual* force of the passions, when we determine concerning vice and virtue; and if the passions depart very much from the common measures on either side, they are always disapproved as vicious. A man naturally loves his children better than his nephews, his nephews better than his cousins, his cousins better than strangers, where everything else is equal. Hence arise our common measures of duty, in preferring the one to the other. Our sense of duty always follows the common and natural course of our passions.

To avoid giving offence, I must here observe, that when

I deny justice to be a natural virtue, I make use of the word, *natural*, only as opposed to *artificial*. In another sense of the word; as no principle of the human mind is more natural than a sense of virtue; so no virtue is more natural than justice. Mankind is an inventive species; and where an invention is obvious and absolutely necessary, it may as properly be said to be natural as anything that proceeds immediately from original principles, without the intervention of thought or reflection. Though the rules of justice be *artificial*, they are not *arbitrary*. Nor is the expression improper to call them *Laws of Nature*; if by natural we understand what is common to any species, or even if we confine it to mean what is inseparable from the species.

Section II *Of the origin of justice and property*

We now proceed to examine two questions, *viz. concerning the manner, in which the rules of justice are established by the artifice of men;* and *concerning the reasons, which determine us to attribute to the observance or neglect of these rules a moral beauty and deformity.* These questions will appear afterwards to be distinct. We shall begin with the former.

Of all the animals, with which this globe is peopled, there is none towards whom nature seems, at first sight, to have exercised more cruelty than towards man, in the numberless wants and necessities, with which she has loaded him, and in the slender means, which she affords to the relieving these necessities. In other creatures these two particulars generally compensate each other. If we consider the lion as a voracious and carnivorous animal, we shall easily discover him to be very necessitous; but if we turn our eye to his make and temper, his agility, his courage, his arms, and his force, we shall find, that his advantages hold proportion with his wants. The sheep and ox are deprived of all these advantages; but their appetites are moderate, and their food is of easy purchase. In man alone, this unnatural conjuction of infirmity, and of necessity, may be observed in its greatest perfection. Not only the food, which is required for his sustenance, flies his search and approach, or at least requires his labour to be produced, but he must be possessed of clothes and lodging, to defend him against the injuries of the weather; though to consider him only in himself, he is provided neither with arms, nor force, nor other natural abilities, which are in any degree answerable to so many necessities.

It is by society alone he is able to supply his defects, and raise himself up to an equality with his fellow-creatures, and even acquire a superiority above them. By society all his infirmities are compensated; and though in that situation his wants multiply every moment upon him, yet his abilities are still more augmented, and leave him in every respect more satisfied and happy, than it is possible for him, in his savage and solitary condition, ever to become. When every individual person labours apart, and only for himself, his force is too small to execute any considerable work; his labour being employed in supplying all his different necessities, he never attains a perfection in any particular art; and as his force and success are not at all times equal, the least failure in either of these particulars must be attended with inevitable ruin and misery. Society provides a remedy for these *three* inconveniences. By the conjunction of forces, our power is augmented; by the partition of employments, our ability increases; and by mutual succour we are less exposed to fortune and accidents. It is by this additional *force, ability,* and *security,* that society becomes advantageous.

But in order to form society, it is requisite not only that it be advantageous, but also that men be sensible of these advantages; and it is impossible, in their wild uncultivated state, that by study and reflection alone, they should ever be able to attain this knowledge. Most fortunately, therefore, there is conjoined to those necessities, whose remedies are remote and obscure, another necessity, which having a present and more obvious remedy, may justly be regarded as the first and original principle of human society. This necessity is no other than that natural appetite betwixt the sexes, which unites them together, and preserves their union, till a new tie takes place in their concern for their common offspring. This new concern becomes also a principle of union betwixt the parents and offspring, and forms a more numerous society; where the parents govern by the advantage of their superior strength and widsom, and at the same time are restrained in the exercise of their authority by that natural affection, which they bear their children. In a little time, custom and habit operating on the tender minds of the children, makes them sensible of the advantages, which they may reap from society, as well as fashions them by degrees for it, by rubbing off those rough corners and untoward affections, which prevent their coalition.

For it must be confessed, that however the circumstances of human nature may render an union necessary, and however those passions of lust and natural affection may seem to render it unavoidable; yet there are other particulars in our *natural temper*, and in our *outward circumstances*, which are very incommodious, and are even contrary to the requisite conjunction. Among the former, we may justly esteem our *selfishness* to be the most considerable. I am sensible, that, generally speaking, the representations of this quality have been carried much too far; and that the descriptions, which certain philosophers delight so much to form of mankind in this particular, are as wide of nature as any accounts of monsters, which we meet with in fables and romances. So far from thinking, that men have no affection for anything beyond themselves, I am of opinion, that though it be rare to meet with one, who loves any single person better than himself; yet it is as rare to meet with one, in whom all the kind affections, taken together, do not overbalance all the selfish. Consult common experience: do you not see, that though the whole expence of the family be generally under the direction of the master of it, yet there are few that do not bestow the largest part of their fortunes on the pleasures of their wives, and the education of their children, reserving the smallest portion for their own proper use and entertainment. This is what we may observe concerning such as have those endearing ties; and may presume, that the case would be the same with others, were they placed in a like situation.[35]

But though this generosity must be acknowledged to the honour of human nature, we may at the same time remark, that so noble an affection, instead of fitting men for large societies, is almost as contrary to them, as the most narrow selfishness. For while each person loves himself better than any other single person, and in his love to others bears the greatest affection to his relations and acquaintance, this must necessarily produce an opposition of passions, and a consequent opposition of actions; which cannot but be dangerous to the new-established union.

It is however worthwhile to remark, that this contrariety of passions would be attended with but small danger, did it not concur with a peculiarity in our *outward circumstances*, which affords it an opportunity of exerting itself. There are three different species of goods, which we are possessed of; the internal satisfaction of our minds, the external advantages of our body, and the enjoyment of such possessions as we have acquired by our industry and good fortune. We are perfectly secure in the enjoyment of the first. The second may be ravished from us, but can be of no advantage to him who deprives us of them. The last only are both exposed to the violence of others, and may be transferred without suffering any loss or alteration; while at the same time, there is not a sufficient quantity of them to supply everyone's desires and necessities. As the improvement, therefore, of these goods is the chief advantage of society, so the *instability* of their possession, along with the *scarcity*, is the chief impediment.

In vain should we expect to find, in *uncultivated nature*, a remedy to this inconvenience; or hope for any inartificial principle of the human mind, which might control those partial affections, and make us overcome the temptations arising from our circumstances. The idea of justice can never serve to this purpose, or be taken for a natural principle, capable of inspiring men with an equitable conduct towards each other. That virtue, as it is now understood, would never have been dreamed of among rude and savage men. For the notion of injury or injustice implies an immorality or vice committed against some other person; and as every immorality is derived from some defect or unsoundness of the passions, and as this defect must be judged of, in a great measure, from the ordinary course of nature in the constitution of the mind; it will be easy to know, whether we be guilty of any immorality, with regard to others, by considering the natural, and usual force of those several affections, which are directed towards them. Now it appears, that in the original frame of our mind, our strongest attention is confined to ourselves; our next is extended to our relations and acquaintance; and it is only the weakest which reaches to strangers and indifferent persons. This partiality, then, and unequal affection, must not only have an influence on our behaviour and conduct in society, but even on our ideas of vice and virtue; so as to make us regard any remarkable transgression of such a degree of partiality, either by too great an enlargement, or contraction of the affections, as vicious and immoral. This we may observe in our common judgments concerning actions, where we blame a person, who either centers all his affections in his family, or is so regardless of them, as, in any opposition of interest, to give the preference to a stranger, or mere chance acquaintance. From all which it follows, that our natural uncultivated ideas of morality, instead of providing a remedy for the partiality of our affections, do rather conform themselves to that partiality, and give it an additional force and influence.

The remedy, then, is not derived from nature, but from *artifice*; or more properly speaking, nature provides a remedy in the judgment and understanding, for what is irregular and incommodious in the affections. For when men, from their early education in society, have become sensible of the infinite advantages that result from it, and have besides acquired a new affection to company and conversation; and when they have observed, that the principal disturbance in society arises from those goods, which we call external, and from their looseness and easy transition from one person to another; they must seek for a remedy, by putting these goods, as far as possible, on the same footing with the fixed and constant advantages of the mind and body. This can be done after no other manner, than by a convention entered into by all the members of the society to bestow stability on the possession of those external goods, and leave everyone in the peaceable enjoyment of what he may acquire by his fortune and industry. By this means, every one knows what he may safely possess; and the passions are restrained in their partial and contradictory motions. Nor is such a restraint contrary to these passions; for if so, it could never be entered into, nor maintained; but it is only contrary to their heedless and impetuous movement. Instead of departing from our own interest, or from that of our nearest friends, by abstaining from the possessions of others, we cannot better consult both these interests, than by such a convention; because it is by that means we maintain society, which is so necessary to their wellbeing and subsistence, as well as to our own.[36]

This convention is not of the nature of a *promise*; for even promises themselves, as we shall see afterwards, arise from human conventions. It is only a general sense of common interest; which sense all the members of the society express to one another, and which induces them to regulate their conduct by certain rules. I observe, that it will be for my interest to leave another in the possession of his goods, *provided* he will act in the same manner with regard to me. He is sensible of a like interest in the regulation of his conduct. When this common sense of interest is mutually expressed, and is known to both, it produces a suitable resolution and behaviour. And this may properly enough be called a convention or agreement betwixt us, though without the interposition of a promise; since the actions of each of us have a reference to those of the other, and are performed upon the supposition, that something is to be performed on the other part. Two men, who pull the oars of a boat, do it by an agreement or convention, though they have never given promises to each other. Nor is the rule concerning the stability of possession the less derived from human conventions, that it arises gradually, and acquires force by a slow progression, and by our repeated experience of the inconveniences of transgressing it. On the contrary, this experience assures us still more, that the sense of interest has become common to all our fellows, and gives us a confidence of the future regularity of their conduct. And it is only on the expectation of this, that our moderation and abstinence are founded. In like manner are languages gradually established by human conventions without any promise. In like manner do gold and silver become the common measures of exchange, and are esteemed sufficient payment for what is of a hundred times their value.

After this convention, concerning abstinence from the possessions of others, is entered into, and everyone has acquired a stability in his possessions, there immediately arise the ideas of justice and injustice; as also those of *property, right*, and *obligation*. The latter are altogether unintelligible without first understanding the former. Our property is nothing but those goods, whose constant possession is established by the laws of society; that is, by the laws of justice. Those, therefore, who make use of the words *property*, or *right*, or *obligation*, before they have explained the origin of justice, or even make use of them in that explication, are guilty of a very gross fallacy, and can never reason upon any solid foundation. A man's property is some object related to him. This relation is not natural, but moral, and founded on justice. It is very preposterous, therefore, to imagine, that we can have any idea of property, without fully comprehending the nature of justice, and showing its origin in the artifice and contrivance of men. The origin of justice explains that of property. The same artifice gives rise to both. As our first and most natural sentiment of morals is founded on the nature of our passions, and gives the preference to ourselves and friends, above strangers; it is impossible there can be naturally any such thing as a fixed right or property, while the opposite passions of men impel them in contrary directions, and are not restrained by any convention or agreement.

No one can doubt, that the convention for the distinction of property, and for the stability of possession, is of all circumstances the most necessary to the establishment of human society, and that after the agreement for the fixing and observing of this rule, there remains little or nothing to be done towards settling a perfect harmony and concord. All the other passions, beside this of interest, are either easily restrained, or are not of such pernicious consequence, when indulged. *Vanity* is rather to be esteemed a social passion, and a bond of union among men. *Pity* and *love* are to be considered in the same light. And as to *envy* and *revenge*, though pernicious, they operate only by intervals, and are directed against particular persons, whom we consider as our superiors or enemies. This avidity alone, of acquiring goods and possessions for ourselves and our nearest friends, is insatiable, perpetual, universal, and directly destructive of society. There scarce is anyone, who is not actuated by it; and there is no one, who has not reason to fear from it, when it acts without any restraint, and gives way to its first and most natural movements. So that upon the whole, we are to esteem the difficulties in the establishment of society, to be greater or less, according to those we encounter in regulating and restraining this passion.

It is certain, that no affection of the human mind has both a sufficient force, and a proper direction to counterbalance the love of gain, and render men fit members of society, by making them abstain from the possessions of others. Benevolence to strangers is too weak for this purpose; and as to the other passions, they rather inflame this avidity, when we observe, that the larger our possessions are, the more ability we have of gratifying all our appetites. There is no passion, therefore, capable of controlling the interested affection, but the very affection itself, by an alteration of its direction. Now this alteration must necessarily take place upon the least reflection; since it is evident, that the passion is much better satisfied by its restraint, than by its liberty, and that in preserving society, we make much greater advances in the acquiring possessions, than in the solitary and forlorn condition, which must follow upon violence and an universal licence. The question, therefore, concerning the wickedness or goodness of human nature, enters not in the least into that other question concerning the origin of society; nor is there anything to be considered but the degrees of men's sagacity or folly. For whether the passion of self-interest be esteemed vicious or virtuous, it is all a case; since itself alone restrains it; so that if it be virtuous, men become social by their virtue; if vicious, their vice has the same effect.

Now as it is by establishing the rule for the stability of possession, that this passion restrains itself; if that rule be very abstruse, and of difficult invention; society must be esteemed, in a manner, accidental, and the effect of many ages. But if it be found, that nothing can be more simple and obvious than that rule; that every parent, in order to preserve peace among his children, must establish it; and that these first rudiments of justice must everyday be improved, as the society enlarges; if all this appear evident, as it certainly must, we may conclude, that it is utterly impossible for men to remain any considerable time in that savage condition, which precedes society; but that his very first state and situation may justly be esteemed social. This, however, hinders not, but that philosophers may, if they please, extend their reasoning to the supposed *state of nature*; provided they allow it to be a mere philosophical fiction, which never had, and never could have any reality. Human nature being composed of two principal parts, which are requisite in all its actions, the affections and understanding; it is certain, that the blind motions of the former, without the direction of the latter, incapacitate men for society; and it may be allowed us to consider separately the effects, that result from the separate operations of these two component parts of the mind. The same liberty may be permitted to moral, which is allowed to natural philosophers; and it is very usual with the latter to consider any motion as compounded and consisting of two parts separate from each other, though at the same time they acknowledge it to be in itself uncompounded and inseparable.

This *state of nature*, therefore, is to be regarded as a mere fiction, not unlike that of the *golden age*, which poets have invented; only with this difference, that the former is described as full of war, violence and injustice; whereas the latter is painted out to us, as the most charming and most peaceable condition, that can possibly be imagined. The seasons, in that first age of nature, were so temperate, if we may believe the poets, that there was no necessity for men to provide themselves with clothes and houses as a security against the violence of heat and cold. The rivers flowed with wine and milk; the oaks yielded honey; and nature spontaneously produced her greatest delicacies. Nor were these the chief advantages of that happy age. The storms and tempests were not alone removed from nature; but those more furious tempests were unknown to human breasts, which now cause such uproar, and engender such confusion. Avarice, ambition, cruelty, selfishness, were never heard of; cordial affection, compassion, sympathy, were the only movements, with which the human mind was yet acquainted. Even the distinction of *mine* and *thine* was banished from that happy race of mortals, and carried with them the very notions of property and obligation, justice and injustice.

This, no doubt, is to be regarded as an idle fiction; but yet deserves our attention, because nothing can more evidently show the origin of those virtues, which are the subjects of our present inquiry. I have already observed, that justice takes its rise from human conventions; and that these are intended as a remedy to some inconveniences, which proceed from the concurrence of certain *qualities* of the human mind with the *situation* of external objects. The qualities of the mind are *selfishness* and *limited generosity*; and the situation of external objects is their *easy change*, joined to their *scarcity* in comparison of the wants and desires of men. But however philosophers may have been bewildered in those speculations, poets have been guided more infallibly, by a certain taste or common instinct, which in most kinds of reasoning goes farther than any of that art and philosophy, with which we have been yet acquainted. They easily perceived, if every man had a tender regard for another, or if nature supplied abundantly all our wants and desires, that the jealousy of interest, which justice supposes, could no longer have place; nor would there be any occasion for those distinctions and limits of property and possession, which at present are in use among mankind. Increase to a sufficient degree the benevolence of men, or the bounty of nature, and you render justice useless, by supplying its place with much nobler virtues, and more valuable blessings. The selfishness of men is animated by the few possessions we have, in proportion to our wants, and it is to restrain this selfishness, that men have been obliged to separate themselves from the community, and to distinguish betwixt their own goods and those of others.

Nor need we have recourse to the fictions of poets to learn this; but, beside the reason of the thing, may discover the same truth by common experience and observation. It is easy to remark, that a cordial affection renders all things common among friends; and that married people in particular mutually lose their property, and are unacquainted with the *mine* and *thine*, which are so necessary, and yet cause such disturbance in human society. The same effect arises from any alteration in the circumstances of mankind; as when there is such a plenty of anything as satisfies all the desires of men; in which case the distinction of property is entirely lost, and everything remains in common. This we may observe with regard to air and water, though the most valuable of all external objects, and may easily conclude, that if men were supplied with everything in the same abundance, or if *everyone* had the same affection and tender regard for *everyone* as for himself; justice and injustice would be equally unknown among mankind.

Here then is a proposition, which, I think, may be regarded as certain, *that it is only from the selfishness and confined generosity of men, along with the scanty provision nature has made for his wants, that justice derives its origin.* If we look backward we shall find, that this proposition bestows an additional force on some of those observations, which we have already made on this subject.

First, we may conclude from it, that a regard to public interest, or a strong extensive benevolence, is not our first and original motive for the observation of the rules of justice; since it is allowed, that if men were endowed with such a benevolence, these rules would never have been dreamt of.

Secondly, we may conclude from the same principle, that the sense of justice is not founded on reason, or on the discovery of certain connections and relations of ideas, which are eternal, immutable, and universally obligatory. For since it is confessed, that such an alteration as that above-mentioned, in the temper and circumstances of mankind, would entirely alter our duties and obligations, it is necessary upon the common system, *that the sense of virtue is derived from reason*, to show the change which this must produce in the relations and ideas. But it is evident, that the only cause, why the extensive generosity of man, and the perfect abundance of everything, would destroy the very idea of justice, is because they render it useless; and that, on the other hand, his confined benevolence, and his necessitous condition, give rise to that virtue, only by making it requisite to the public interest and to that of every individual. It was therefore a concern for our own, and the public interest, which made us establish the laws of justice; and nothing can be more certain, than that it is not any relation of ideas, which gives us this concern, but our impressions and sentiments, without which everything in nature is perfectly indifferent to us, and can never in the least affect us. The sense of justice, therefore, is not founded on our ideas, but on our impressions.

Thirdly, we may farther confirm the foregoing proposition, *that those impressions, which give rise to this sense of justice, are not natural to the mind of man, but arise from artifice and human conventions*. For since any considerable alteration of temper and circumstances destroys equally justice and injustice; and since such an alteration has an effect only by changing our own and the public interest; it follows, that the first establishment of the rules of justice depends on these different interests. But if men pursued the public interest naturally, and with a hearty affection, they would never have dreamed of restraining each other by these rules; and if they pursued their own interest, without any precaution, they would run headlong into every kind of injustice and violence. These rules, therefore, are artificial, and seek their end in an oblique and indirect manner; nor is the interest, which gives rise to them, of a kind that could be pursued by the natural and inartificial passions of men.

To make this more evident, consider, that though the rules of justice are established merely by interest, their connection with interest is somewhat singular, and is different from what may be observed on other occasions. A single act of justice is frequently contrary to *public interest*; and were it to stand alone, without being followed by other acts, may, in itself, be very prejudicial to society. When a man of merit, of a beneficent disposition, restores a great fortune to a miser, or a seditious bigot, he has acted justly and laudably; but the public is a real sufferer. Nor is every single act of justice, considered apart, more conducive to private interest, than to public; and it is easily conceived how a man may impoverish himself by a signal instance of integrity, and have reason to wish, that with regard to that single act, the laws of justice were for a moment suspended in the universe. But however single acts of justice may be contrary, either to public or private interest, it is certain, that the whole plan or scheme is highly conducive, or indeed absolutely requisite, both to the support of society, and the wellbeing of every individual. It is impossible to separate the good from the ill. Property must be stable, and must be fixed by general rules. Though in one instance the public be a sufferer, this momentary ill is amply compensated by the steady prosecution of the rule, and by the peace and order, which it establishes in society. And even every individual person must find himself a gainer, on balancing the account; since, without justice, society must immediately dissolve, and everyone must fall into that savage and solitary condition, which is infinitely worse than the worst situation that can possibly be suppos'd in society.[37] When therefore men have had experience enough to observe, that whatever may be the consequence of any single act of justice, performed by a single person, yet the whole system of actions, concurred in by the whole society, is infinitely advantageous to the whole, and to every part; it is not long before justice and property take place. Every member of society is sensible of this interest; everyone expresses this sense to his fellows, along with the resolution he has taken of squaring his actions by it, on condition that others will do the same. No more is requisite to induce any one of them to perform an act of justice, who has the first opportunity. This becomes an example to others. And thus justice establishes itself by a kind of convention or agreement, that is, by a sense of interest, supposed to be common to all, and where every single act is performed in expectation that others are to perform the like. Without such a convention, no one would ever have dreamed, that there was such a virtue as justice, or have been induced to conform his actions to it. Taking any single act, my justice may be pernicious in every respect; and it is only upon the supposition, that others are to imitate my example, that I can be induced to embrace that virtue; since nothing but this combination can render justice advantageous, or afford me any motives to conform myself to its rules.

We come now to the *second* question we proposed, *viz, why we annex the idea of virtue to justice, and of vice to injustice.* This question will not detain us long after the principles, which we have already established. All we can say of it at present will be dispatched in a few words; and for farther satisfaction, the reader must wait till we come to the *third* part of this book. The *natural* obligation to justice, *viz.* interest, has been fully explained; but as the *moral* obligation, or the sentiment of right and wrong, it will first be requisite to examine the natural virtues, before we can give a full and satisfactory account of it.

After men have found by experience, that their selfishness and confined generosity, acting at their liberty, totally incapacitate them for society; and at the same time have observed, that society is necessary to the satisfaction of those very passions, they are naturally induced to lay themselves under the restraint of such rules, as may render their commerce more safe and commodious. To the imposition, then, and observance of these rules, both in general, and in every particular instance, they are at first induced only by a regard to interest; and this motive, on the first formation of society, is sufficiently strong and forcible. But when society has become numerous, and has increased to a tribe or nation, this interest is more remote; nor do men so readily perceive, that disorder and confusion follow upon every breach of these rules, as in a more narrow and contracted society. But though in our own actions we may frequently lose sight of that interest, which we have in maintaining order, and may follow a lesser and more present interest, we never fail to observe the prejudice we receive, either mediately or immediately, from the injustice of others; as not being in that case either blinded by passion, or biassed by any contrary temptation. Nay when the injustice is so distant from us, as no way to affect our interest, it still displeases us; because we consider it as prejudicial to human society, and pernicious to everyone that approaches the person guilty of it. We partake of their uneasiness by *sympathy;* and as everything, which gives uneasiness in human actions, upon the general survey, is called vice, and whatever produces satisfaction, in the same manner, is denominated virtue; this is the reason why the sense of moral good and evil follows upon justice and injustice. And though this sense, in the present case, be derived only from contemplating the actions of others, yet we fail not to extend it even to our own actions. The *general rule* reaches beyond those instances, from which it arose; while at the same time we naturally *sympathize* with others in the sentiments they entertain of us. *Thus self-interest is the original motive to the* establishment *of justice; but a* sympathy *with public interest is the source of the* moral approbation, *which attends that virtue.*

Though this progress of the sentiments be *natural,* and even necessary, it is certain, that it is here forwarded by the artifice of politicians, who, in order to govern men more easily, and preserve peace in human society, have endeavoured to produce an esteem for justice, and an abhorrence of injustice. This, no doubt, must have its effect; but nothing can be more evident, than that the matter has been carried too far by certain writers on morals, who seem to have employed their utmost efforts to extirpate all sense of virtue from among mankind. Any artifice of politicians may assist nature in the producing of those sentiments, which she suggests to us, and may even on some occasions, produce alone an approbation or esteem for any particular action; but it is impossible it should be the sole cause of the distinction we make betwixt vice and virtue. For if nature did not aid us in this particular, it would be in vain for politicians to talk of *honourable* or *dishonourable, praiseworthy* or *blameable.* These words would be perfectly unintelligible, and would no more have any idea annexed to them, than if they were of a tongue perfectly unknown to us. The utmost politicians can perform, is, to extend the natural sentiments beyond their original bounds; but still nature must furnish the materials, and give us some notion of moral distinctions.

As public praise and blame increase our esteem for justice; so private education and instruction contribute to the same effect. For as parents easily observe, that a man is the more useful, both to himself and others, the greater degree of probity and honour he is endowed with; and that those principles have greater force, when custom and education assist interest and reflection. For these reasons they are induced to inculcate on their children, from their earliest infancy, the principles of probity, and teach them to regard the observance of those rules, by which society is maintained, as worthy and honourable, and their violation as base and infamous. By this means the sentiments of honour may take root in their tender minds, and acquire such firmness and solidity, that they may fall little short of those principles, which are the most essential to our natures, and the most deeply radicated in our internal constitution.

What farther contributes to increase their solidity, is the interest of our reputation, after the opinion, *that a merit or demerit attends justice or injustice,* is once firmly established among mankind. There is nothing, which touches us more nearly than our reputation, and nothing on which our reputation more depends than our conduct, with relation to the property of others. For this reason, everyone, who has any regard to his character, or who intends to live on good terms with mankind, must fix an inviolable law to himself, never, by any temptation, to be induced to violate those principles, which are essential to a man of probity and honour.

I shall make only one observation before I leave this subject, *viz.* that though I assert, that in the *state of nature*, or that imaginary state, which precede society, there be neither justice nor injustice, yet I assert not, that it was allowable, in such a state, to violate the property of others. I only maintain, that there was no such thing as property; and consequently could be no such thing as justice or injustice. I shall have occasion to make a similar reflexion with regard to *promises*, when I come to treat of them; and I hope this reflection, when duly weighed, will suffice to remove all odium from the foregoing opinions, with regard to justice and injustice.

SECTION III *Of the rules, which determine property*

Though the establishment of the rule, concerning the stability of possession, be not only useful, but even absolutely necessary to human society, it can never serve to any purpose, while it remains in such general terms. Some method must be shown, by which we may distinguish what particular goods are to be assigned to each particular person, while the rest of mankind are excluded from their possession and enjoyment. Our next business, then, must be to discover the reasons which modify this general rule, and fit it to the common use and practice of the world.

It is obvious, that those reasons are not derived from any utility or advantage, which either the *particular* person or the public may reap from his enjoyment of any *particular* goods, beyond what would result from the possession of them by any other person. It were better, no doubt, that every one were possessed of what is most suitable to him, and proper for his use. But besides, that this relation of fitness may be common to several at once, it is liable to so many controversies, and men are so partial and passionate in judging of these controversies, that such a loose and uncertain rule would be absolutely incompatible with the peace of human society. The convention concerning the stability of possession is entered into, in order to cut off all occasions of discord and contention; and this end would never be attained, were we allowed to apply this rule differently in every particular case, according to every particular utility, which might be discovered in such an application. Justice, in her decisions, never regards the fitness or unfitness of objects to particular persons, but conducts herself by more extensive views. Whether a man be generous, or a miser, he is equally well received by her, and obtains with the same facility a decision in his favour, even for what is entirely useless to him.

It follows, therefore, that the general rule, *that possession must be stable*, is not applied by particular judgments, but by other general rules, which must extend to the whole society, and be inflexible either by spite or favour. To illustrate this, I propose the following instance. I first consider men in their savage and solitary condition; and suppose, that being sensible of the misery of that state, and foreseeing the advantages that would result from society, they seek each other's company, and make an offer of mutual protection and assistance. I also suppose, that they are endowed with such sagacity as immediately to perceive, that the chief impediment to this project of society and partnership lies in the avidity and selfishness of their natural temper; to remedy which, they enter into a convention for the stability of possession, and for mutual restraint and forbearance. I am sensible, that this method of proceeding is not altogether natural; but besides that I here only suppose those reflections to be formed at once, which in fact arise insensibly and by degrees; besides this, I say, it is very possible, that several persons, being by different accidents separated from the societies, to which they formerly belonged, may be obliged to form a new society among themselves; in which case they are entirely in the situation above-mentioned.

It is evident, then, that their first difficulty, in this situation, after the general convention for the establishment of society, and for the constancy of possession, is, how to separate their possessions, and assign to each his particular portion, which he must for the future inalterably enjoy. This difficulty will not detain them long; but it must immediately occur to them, as the most natural expedient, that everyone continue to enjoy what he is at present master of, and that property or constant possession be conjoined to the immediate possession. Such is the effect of custom, that it not only reconciles us to any thing we have long enjoyed, but even gives us an affection for it, and makes us prefer it to other objects, which may be more valuable, but are less known to us. What has long lain under our eye, and has often been employ'd to our advantage, *that* we are always the most unwilling to part with; but can easily live without possessions, which we never have enjoyed, and are not accustomed to. It is evident, therefore, that men would easily acquiesce in this expedient, *that everyone continue to enjoy what he is at present possessed of*; and this is the reason, why they would so naturally agree in preferring it.*

* No questions in philosophy are more difficult, than when a number of causes present themselves for the same phenomenon, to determine which is the principal and predominant. There seldom is any very precise argument to fix our choice, and men must be contented to be guided by a kind of taste or fancy,

But we may observe, that though the rule of the assignment of property to the present possessor be natural, and by that means useful, yet its utility extends not beyond the first formation of society; nor would anything be more pernicious, than the constant observance of it; by which restitution would be excluded, and every injustice would be authorized and rewarded. We must, therefore, seek for some other circumstance, that may give rise to property after society is once established; and of this kind, I find four most considerable, *viz.* occupation, prescription, accession, and succession.

---

arising from analogy, and a comparison of similar instances. Thus, in the present case, there are, no doubt, motives of public interest for most of the rules, which determine property; but still I suspect, that these rules are principally fixed by the imagination, or the more frivolous properties of our thought and conception. I shall continue to explain these causes, leaving it to the reader's choice, whether he will prefer those derived from public utility, or those derived from the imagination. We shall begin with the right of the present possessor.

It is a quality, which (*a*) I have already observed in human nature, that when two objects appear in a close relation to each other, the mind is apt to ascribe to them any additional relation, in order to complete the union; and this inclination is so strong, as often to make us run into errors (such as that of the conjunction of thought and matter) if we find that they can serve to that purpose. Many of our impressions are incapable of place or local position; and yet those very impressions we suppose to have a local conjunction with the impressions of sight and touch, merely because they are conjoined by causation, and are already united in the imagination. Since, therefore, we can feign a new relation, and even an absurd one, in order to complete any union, it will easily be imagined, that if there be any relations, which depend on the mind, it will readily conjoin them to any preceding relation, and unite, by a new bond, such objects as have already an union in the fancy. Thus for instance, we never fail, in our arrangement of bodies, to place those which are *resembling* in *contiguity* to each other, or at least in *correspondent* points of view; because we feel a satisfaction in joining the relation of contiguity to that of resemblance, or the resemblance of situation to that of qualities. And this is easily accounted for from the known properties of human nature. When the mind is determined to join certain objects, but undermined in its choice of the particular objects, it naturally turns its eye to such as are related together. They are already united in the mind; they present themselves at the same time to the conception; and instead of requiring any new reason for their conjunction, it would require a very powerful reason to make us overlook this natural affinity. This we shall have occa-

(*a*) *Book* I. *Part* IV. *sect.* 5.

We shall briefly examine each of these, beginning with *occupation*.

The possession of all external goods is changeable and uncertain; which is one of the most considerable impediments to the establishment of society, and is the reason why, by universal agreement, express or tacit, men restrain themselves by what we now call the rules of justice and equity. The misery of the condition, which precedes this restraint, is the cause why we submit to that remedy as quickly as possible; and this affords us an easy reason, why we annex the idea of property to the first possession, or to *occupation*. Men are unwilling to leave property in suspense, even for the shortest time, or open the least door to violence and disorder. To which we may add, that the first possession always engages the attention most; and did we neglect it, there would be no colour of reason for assigning property to any succeeding possession.*

There remains nothing, but to determine exactly, what is meant by possession; and this is not so easy as may at first sight be imagined. We are said to be in possession of any-

---

sion to explain more fully afterwards, when we come to treat of *beauty*. In the meantime, we may content ourselves with observing, that the same love of order and uniformity, which arranges the books in a library, and the chairs in a parlour, contribute to the formation of society, and to the well-being of mankind, by modifying the general rule concerning the stability of possession. And as property forms a relation betwixt a person and an object, it is natural to found it on some preceding relation; and as property is nothing but an constant possession, secured by the laws of society, it is natural to add it to the present possession, which is a relation that resembles it. For this also has its influence. If it be natural to conjoin all sorts of relations, it is more so, to conjoin such relations as are resembling, and are related together.

* Some philosophers account for the right of occupation, by saying, that everyone has a property in his own labour; and when he joins that labour to anything it gives him the property of the whole. But, (1) there are several kinds of occupation, where we cannot be said to join our labour to the object we acquire; as when we possess a meadow by grazing our cattle upon it. (2) This accounts for the matter by means of *accession*; which is taking a needless circuit. (3) We cannot be said to join our labour in anything but in a figurative sense. Properly speaking, we only make an alteration on it by our labour. This forms a relation betwixt us and the object; and thence arises the property, according to the preceding principles.

thing, not only when we immediately touch it, but also when we are so situated with respect to it, as to have it in our power to use it; and may move, alter, or destroy it, according to our present pleasure or advantage. This relation, then, is a species of cause and effect; and as property is nothing but a stable possession, derived from the rules of justice, or the conventions of men, it is to be considered as the same species of relation. But here we may observe, that as the power of using any object becomes more or less certain, according as the interruptions we may meet with are more or less probable; and as this probability may increase by insensible degrees; it is in many cases impossible to determine when possession begins or ends; nor is there any certain standard, by which we can decide such controversies. A wild boar, that falls into our snares, is deemed to be in our possession, if it be impossible for him to escape. But what do we mean by impossible? How do we separate this impossibility from an improbability? And how distinguish that exactly from a probability? Mark the precise limits of the one and the other, and show the standard, by which we may decide all disputes that may arise, and, as we find by experience, frequently do arise upon this subject.*

But such disputes may not only arise concerning the real

* If we seek a solution of these difficulties in reason and public interest, we never shall find satisfaction; and if we look for it in the imagination, it is evident, that the qualities, which operate upon that faculty, run so insensibly and gradually into each other, that it is impossible to give them any precise bounds of termination. The difficulties on this head must increase, when we consider, that our judgment alters very sensibly, according to the subject, and that the same power and proximity will be deemed possession in one case, which is not esteemed such in another. A person, who has hunted a hare to the last degree of weariness, would look upon it as an injustice for another to rush in before him, and seize his prey. But the same person, advancing to pluck an apple, that hangs within his reach, has no reason to complain, if another, more alert, passes him, and takes possession. What is the reason of this difference, but that immobility, not being natural to the hare, but the effect of industry, forms in that case a strong relation with the hunter, which is wanting in the other?

Here then it appears, that a certain and infallible power of enjoyment, without touch or some other sensible relation, often produces not property; and I farther observe, that a sensible relation, without any present power, is sometimes sufficient to give a title to any object. The sight of a thing is seldom a considerable relation, and is only regarded as such, when the object is hidden, or very obscure; in which case we find, that the view

existence of property and possession, but also concerning their extent; and these disputes are often susceptible of no decision, or can be decided by no other faculty than the imagination. A person who lands on the shore of a small island, that is desert and uncultivated, is deemed its possessor from the very first moment, and acquires the property of the

------

alone conveys a property; according to that maxim, *that even a whole continent belongs to the nation, which first discovered it.* 'Tis however remarkable, that both in the case of discovery and that of possession, the first discoverer and possessor must join to the relation an intention of rendering himself proprietor, otherwise the relation will not have its effect; and that because the connection in our fancy betwixt the property and the relation is not so great, but that it requires to be helped by such an intention.

From all these circumstances, it is easy to see how perplexed many questions may become concerning the acquisition of property by occupation; and the least effort of thought may present us with instances, which are not susceptible of any reasonable decision. If we prefer examples, which are real, to such as are feigned, we may consider the following one, which is to be met with in almost every writer, that has treated of the laws of nature. Two *Grecian* colonies, leaving their native country, in search of new seats, were informed that a city near them was deserted by its inhabitants. To know the truth of this report, they dispatch'd at once two messengers, one from each colony; who finding on their approach, that their information was true, began a race together with an intention to take possession of the city, each of them for his countrymen. One of these messengers, finding that he was not an equal match for the other, launched his spear at the gates of the city, and was so fortunate as to fix it there before the arrival of his companion. This produced a dispute betwixt the two colonies, which of them was the proprietor of the empty city; and this dispute still subsists among philosophers. For my part I find the dispute impossible to be decided, and that because the whole question hangs upon the fancy, which in this case is not possessed of any precise or determinate standard, upon which it can give sentence. To make this evident, let us consider, that if these two persons had been simply members of the colonies, and not messengers or deputies, their actions would not have been of any consequence; since in that case their relation to the colonies would have been but feeble and imperfect. Add to this, that nothing determined them to run to the gates rather than the walls, or any other part of the city, but that the gates, being the most obvious and remarkable part, satisfy the fancy best in taking them for the whole; as we find by the poets, who frequently draw their images and metaphors from them. Besides we may consider, that the touch or contact of the one messenger is not properly possession, no more than the piercing the gates with

whole; because the object is there bounded and circumscribed in the fancy, and at the same time is proportioned to the new possessor. The same person landing on a desert island, as large as *Great Britain*, extends his property no farther than his immediate possession; though a numerous colony are esteemed the proprietors of the whole from the instant of their debarkment.

But it often happens, that the title of first possession becomes obscure through time; and that it is impossible to determine many controversies, which may arise concerning it. In that case long possession or *prescription* naturally takes place, and gives a person a sufficient property in anything he enjoys. The nature of human society admits not of any great accuracy; nor can we always remount to the first origin of things, in order to determine their present condition. Any considerable space of time sets objects at such a distance, that they seem, in a manner, to lose their reality, and have as little influence on the mind, as if they never had been in being. A man's title, that is clear and certain at present, will seem obscure and doubtful fifty years hence, even though the facts, on which it is founded, should be proved with the greatest evidence and certainty. The same facts have not the same influence after so long an interval of time. And this may be received as a convincing argument for our preceding doctrine with regard to property and justice. Possession during a long tract of time conveys a title to any object. But as it is certain, that, however everything be produced in time, there is nothing real, that is produced by time; it follows, that property being produced by time, is not anything real in the objects, but is the offspring of the sentiments, on which alone time is found to have any influence.*

---

a spear; but only forms a relation; and there is a relation, in the other case, equally obvious, though not, perhaps, of equal force. Which of these relations, then, conveys a right and property, or whether any of them be sufficient for that effect, I leave to the decision of such as are wiser than myself.

* Present possession is plainly a relation betwixt a person and an object; but is not sufficient to counterbalance the relation of first possession, unless the former be long and uninterrupted; in which case the relation is increased on the side of the present possession, by the extent of time, and diminished on that of first possession, by the distance. This change in the relation produces a consequent change in the property.

We acquire the property of objects by *accession*, when they are connected in an intimate manner with objects that are already our property, and at the same time are inferior to them. Thus the fruits of our garden, the offspring of our cattle, and the work of our slaves, are all of them esteemed our property, even before possession. Where objects are connected together in the imagination, they are apt to be put on the same footing, and are commonly supposed to be endowed with the same qualities. We readily pass from one to the other, and make no difference in our judgments concerning them; especially if the latter be inferior to the former.*

* This source of property can never be explained but from the imaginations; and one may affirm, that the causes are here unmixed. We shall proceed to explain them more particularly, and illustrate them by examples from common life and experience.

It has been observed above, that the mind has a natural propensity to join relations, especially resembling ones, and finds a kind of fitness and uniformity in such an union. From this propensity are derived these laws of nature, *that upon the first formation of society, property always follows the present possession;* and afterwards, *that it arises from first or from long possession.* Now we may easily observe, that relation is not confined merely to one degree; but that from an object, that is related to us, we acquire a relation to every other object which is related to it, and so on, till the thought loses the chain by too long a progress. However the relation may weaken by each remove, it is not immediately destroyed; but frequently connects two objects by means of an intermediate one, which is related to both. And this principle is of such force as to give rise to the right of *accession,* and causes us to acquire the property not only of such objects as we are immediately possessed of, but also of such as are closely connected with them.

Suppose a *German,* a *Frenchman,* and a *Spaniard* to come into a room, where there are placed upon the table three bottles of wine, *Rhenish, Burgundy* and *Port;* and suppose they should fall a quarrelling about the division of them; a person, who was chosen for umpire, would naturally, to show his impartiality, give everyone the product of his own country; and this from a principle, which, in some measure, is the source of those laws of nature, that ascribe property to occupation, prescription and accession.

In all these cases, and particularly that of accession, there is first a *natural* union betwixt the idea of the person and that of the object, and afterwards a new and *moral* union produced by that right or property, which we ascribe to the person. But here there occurs a difficulty, which merits our attention, and may afford us an opportunity of putting to trial that singular method of reasoning, which has been employed on the present subject. I

The right of *succession* is a very natural one, from the presumed consent of the parent or near relation, and from the general interest of mankind, which requires, that men's

---

have already observed, that the imagination passes with greater facility from little to great, than from great to little, and that the transition of ideas is always easier and smoother in the former case than in the latter. Now as the right of accession arises from the easy transition of ideas, by which related objects are connected together, it should naturally be imagined, that the right of accession must increase in strength, in proportion as the transition of ideas is performed with greater facility. It may, therefore, be thought, that when we have acquired the property of any small object, we shall readily consider any great object related to it as an accession, and as belonging to the proprietor of the small one; hence the transition is in that case very easy from the small object to the great one, and should connect them together in the closest manner. But in fact the case is always found to be otherwise. The empire of *Great Britain* seems to draw along with it the dominion of the *Orkneys*, the *Hebrides*, the Isle of *Man*, and the Isle of *Wight;* but the authority over those lesser islands does not naturally imply any title to *Great Britain*. In short, a small object naturally follows a great one as its accession; but a great one is never supposed to belong to the proprietor of a small one related to it, merely on account of that property and relation. Yet in this latter case the transition of ideas is smoother from the proprietor to the small object, which is his property, and from the small object to the great one, than in the former case from the proprietor to the great object, and from the great one to the small. It may therefore be thought, that these phenomena are objections to the foregoing hypothesis, *that the ascribing of property to accession is nothing but an effect of the relations of ideas, and of the smooth transition of the imagination.*

It will be easy to solve this objection, if we consider the agility and unsteadiness of the imagination, with the different views, in which it is continually placing its objects. When we attribute to a person a property in two objects, we do not always pass from the person to one object, and from that to the other related to it. The objects being here to be considered as the property of the person, we are apt to join them together, and place them in the same light. Suppose, therefore, a great and a small object to be related together; if a person be strongly related to the great object, he will likewise be strongly related to both the objects, considered together, because he is related to the most considerable part. On the contrary, if he be only related to the small object, he will not be strongly related to both, considered together, since his relation lies only with the most trivial part, which is not apt to strike us in any great degree, when we consider the whole. And this is the reason, why small objects become accessions to great ones, and not great to small.

It is the general opinion of philosophers and civilians, that the

possessions should pass to those, who are dearest to them, in order to render them more industrious and frugal. Perhaps these causes are seconded by the influence of *relation*, or the

---

sea is incapable of becoming the property of any nation; and that because it is impossible to take possession of it, or form any such distinct relation with it, as may be the foundation of property. Where this reason ceases, property immediately takes place. Thus the most strenuous advocates for the liberty of the seas universally allow, that friths and bays naturally belong as an accession to the proprietors of the surrounding continent. These have properly no more bond or union with the land, than the *Pacific* ocean would have; but having an union in the fancy, and being at the same time *inferior*, they are of course regarded as an accession.

The property of rivers, by the laws of most nations, and by the natural turn of our thought, is attributed to the proprietors of their banks, excepting such vast rivers as the *Rhine* or the *Danube*, which seem too large to the imagination to follow as an accession the property of the neighbouring fields. Yet even these rivers are considered as the property of that nation, through whose dominions they run; the idea of a nation being of a suitable bulk to correspond with them, and bear them such a relation in the fancy.

The accessions, which are made to lands bordering upon rivers, follow the land, say the civilians, provided it be made by what they call *alluvion*, that is, insensibly and imperceptibly; which are circumstances that mightily assist the imagination in the conjunction. Where there is any considerable portion torn at once from one bank, and joined to another, it becomes not his property, whose land it falls on, till it unite with the land, and till the trees or plants have spread their roots into both. Before that, the imagination does not sufficiently join them.

There are other cases, which somewhat resemble this of accession, but which, at the bottom, are considerably different, and merit our attention. Of this kind is the conjunction of the properties of different persons, after such a manner as not to admit of *separation*. The question is, to whom the united mass must belong.

Where this conjunction is of such a nature as to admit of *division*, but not of *separation*, the decision is natural and easy. The whole mass must be supposed to be common betwixt the proprietors of the several parts, and afterwards must be divided according to the proportions of these parts. But here I cannot forbear taking notice of a remarkable subtlety of the *Roman* law, in distinguishing betwixt *confusion* and *commixtion*. Confusion is an union of two bodies, such as different liquors, where the parts become entirely undistinguishable. Commixtion is the blending of two bodies, such as two bushels of corn, where the parts remain separate in an obvious and visible manner. As in the latter case the imagination discovers not so entire an union as in

association of ideas, by which we are naturally directed to consider the son after the parent's decease, and ascribe to him a title to his father's possessions. Those goods must

---

the former, but is able to trace and preserve a distinct idea of the property of each; this is the reason, why the *civil* law, though it established an entire community in the case of *confusion*, and after that a proportional division, yet in the case of *commixtion*, supposes each of the proprietors to maintain a distinct right; however necessity may at last force them to submit to the same division.

Quod si frumentum Titii frumento tuo mistum fuerit: siquidem ex voluntate vestra, commune est: quia singula corpora, id est, singula grana, quæ cujusque propria fuerunt, ex consensu vestro communicata sunt. Quod si casu id mistum fuerit, vel Titius id miscuerit sine tua voluntate, non videtur id commune esse; quia singula corpora in sua substantia durant. Sed nec magis istis casibus commune sit frumentum quam grex intelligitur esse communis, si pecora Titii tuis pecoribus mista fuerint. Sed si ab alterutro vestrum totum id frumentum retineatur, in rem quidem actio pro modo frumenti cujusque competit. Arbitrio autem judicis, ut ipse æstimet quale cujusque frumentum fuerit. Inst. Lib. II. Tit. 1. § 28.

Where the properties of two persons are united after such a manner as neither admit to *division* nor *separation*, as when one builds a house on another's ground, in that case, the whole must belong to one of the proprietors; and here I assert, that it naturally is conceived to belong to the proprietor of the most considerable part. For however the compound object may have a relation to two different persons, and carry our view at once to both of them, yet as the most considerable part principally engages our attention, and by the strict union draws the inferior along it; for this reason, the whole bears a relation to the proprietor of that part, and is regarded as his property. The only difficulty is, what we shall be pleased to call the most considerable part, and most attractive to the imagination.

This quality depends on several different circumstances, which have little connection with each other. One part of a compound object may become more considerable than another, either because it is more constant and durable; because it is of greater value; because it is more obvious and remarkable; because it is of greater extent; or because its existence is more separate and independent. It will be easy to conceive, that, as these circumstances may be conjoined and opposed in all the different ways, and according to all the different degrees, which can be imagined, there will result many cases, where the reasons on both sides are so equally balanced, that it is impossible for us to give any satisfactory decision. Here then is the proper business of municipal laws, to fix what the principles of human nature have felt undetermined.

The superficies yields to the soil, says the civil law; the writing

become the property of somebody; but *of whom* is the question. Here it is evident the person's children naturally present themselves to the mind; and being already connected to those possessions by means of their deceased parent, we are apt to connect them still farther by the relation of property. Of this there are many parallel instances.*[38]

---

to the paper; the canvas to the picture. These decisions do not well agree together, and are a proof of the contrariety of those principles, from which they are derived.

But of all the questions of this kind the most curious is that, which for so many ages divided the disciples of *Proculus* and *Sabinus*. Suppose a person should make a cup from the metal of another, or a ship from his wood, and suppose the proprietor of the metal or wood should demand his goods, the question is, whether he acquires a title to the cup or ship. *Sabinus* maintained the affirmative, and asserted that the substance or matter is the foundation of all the qualities; that it is incorruptible and immortal, and therefore superior to the form, which is casual and dependent. On the other hand, *Proculus* observed, that the form is the most obvious and remarkable part, and that from it bodies are denominated of this or that particular species. To which he might have added, that the matter or substance is in most bodies so fluctuating and uncertain, that it is utterly impossible to trace it in all its changes. For my part, I know not from what principles such a controversy can be certainly determined. I shall therefore content myself with observing, that the decision of *Trebonion* seems to me pretty ingenious; that the cup belongs to the proprietor of the metal, because it can be brought back to its first form; but that the ship belongs to the author of its form for a contrary reason. But however ingenious this reason may seem, it plainly depends upon the fancy, which by the possibility of such a reduction, finds a closer connection and relation betwixt a cup and the proprietor of its metal, than betwixt a ship and the proprietor of its wood, where the substance is more fixed and unalterable.

* In examining the different titles to authority in government, we shall meet with many reasons to convince us, that the right of succession depends, in a great measure, on the imagination. Meanwhile I shall rest contented with observing one example, which belongs to the present subject. Suppose that a person die without children, and that a dispute arises among his relations concerning his inheritance; it is evident, that if his riches be deriv'd partly from his father, partly from his mother, the most natural way of determining such a dispute, is, to divide his possessions, and assign each part to the family, from whence it is derived. Now as the person is supposed to have been once the full and entire proprietor of those goods; I ask, what is it makes us find a certain equity and natural reason in this partition, except it be the imagination? His affection to these families does not

SECTION IV *Of the transference of property by consent*

However useful, or even necessary, the stability of possession may be to human society, it is attended with very considerable inconveniences. The relation of fitness or suitableness ought never to enter into consideration, in distributing the properties of mankind; but we must govern ourselves by rules, which are more general in their application, and more free from doubt and uncertainty. Of this kind is *present* possession upon the first establishment of society; and afterwards *occupation, prescription, accession,* and *succession.* As these depend very much on chance, they must frequently prove contradictory both to men's wants and desires; and persons and possessions must often be very ill adjusted. This is a grand inconvenience, which calls for a remedy. To apply one directly, and allow every man to seize by violence what he judges to be fit for him, would destroy society; and therefore the rules of justice seek some medium betwixt a rigid stability, and this changeable and uncertain adjustment. But there is no medium better than that obvious one, that possession and property should always be stable, except when the proprietor consents to bestow them on some other person. This rule can have no ill consequence, in occasioning wars and dissentions; since the proprietor's consent, who alone is concerned, is taken along in the alienation; and it may serve to many good purposes in adjusting property to persons. Different parts of the earth produce different commodities; and not only so, but different men both are by nature fitted for different employments, and attain to greater perfection in any one, when they confine themselves to it alone. All this requires a mutual exchange and commerce; for which reason the translation of property by consent is founded on a law of nature, as well as its stability without such a consent.

So far is determined by a plain utility and interest. But perhaps it is from more trivial reasons, that *delivery,* or a

---

depend upon his possessions; for which reason his consent can never be presumed precisely for such a partition. And as to the public interest, it seems not to be in the least concerned on the one side or the other.

sensible transference of the object is commonly required by civil laws, and also by the laws of nature, according to most authors, as a requisite circumstance in the translation of property. The property of an object, when taken for something real, without any reference to morality, or the sentiments of the mind, is a quality perfectly insensible, and even inconceivable; nor can we form any distinct notion, either of its stability or translation. This imperfection of our ideas is less sensibly felt with regard to its stability, as it engages less our attention, and is easily passed over by the mind, without any scrupulous examination. But as the translation of property from one person to another is a more remarkable event, the defect of our ideas becomes more sensible on that occasion, and obliges us to turn ourselves on every side in search of some remedy. Now as nothing more enlivens any idea than a present impression, and a relation betwixt that impression and the idea; it is natural for us to seek some false light from this quarter. In order to aid the imagination in conceiving the transference of property, we take the sensible object, and actually transfer its possession to the person, on whom we would bestow the property. The supposed resemblance of the actions, and the presence of this sensible delivery, deceive the mind, and make it fancy, that it conceives the mysterious transition of the property. And that this explication of the matter is just, appears hence, that men have invented a *symbolical* delivery, to satisfy the fancy, where the real one is impracticable. Thus the giving the keys of a granary is understood to be the delivery of the corn contained in it; the giving of stone and earth represents the delivery of a manor. This is a kind of superstitious practice in civil laws, and in the laws of nature, resembling the *Roman Catholic* superstitions in religion. As the *Roman Catholics* represent the inconceivable mysteries of the *Christian* religion, and render them more present to the mind, by a taper, or habit, or grimace, which is supposed to resemble them; so lawyers and moralists have run into like inventions for the same reason, and have endeavoured by those means to satisfy themselves concerning the transference of property by consent.

SECTION V *Of the obligation of promises*

That the rule of morality, which enjoins the performance of promises, is not *natural*, will sufficiently appear from these two propositions, which I proceed to prove, *viz. that a promise would not be intelligible, before human conventions had established it;* and *that even if it were intelligible, it would not be attended with any moral obligation.*

I say, *first*, that a promise is not intelligible naturally, nor antecedent to human conventions; and that a man, unacquainted with society, could never enter into any engagements with another, even though they could perceive each other's thoughts by intuition. If promises be natural and intelligible, there must be some act of the mind attending these words, *I promise*; and on this act of the mind must the obligation depend. Let us, therefore, run over all the faculties of the soul, and see which of them is exerted in our promises.

The act of the mind, expressed by a promise, is not a *resolution* to perform anything; for that alone never imposes any obligation. Nor is it a *desire* of such a performance; for we may bind ourselves without such a desire, or even with an aversion, declared and avowed. Neither is it the *willing* of that action, which we promise to perform; for a promise always regards some future time, and the will has an influence only on present actions. It follows, therefore, that since the act of the mind, which enters into a promise, and produces its obligation, is neither the resolving, desiring, nor willing any particular performance, it must necessarily be the *willing* of that *obligation*, which arises from the promise. Nor is this only a conclusion of philosophy; but is entirely conformable to our common ways of thinking and of expressing ourselves, when we say that we are bound by our own consent, and that the obligation arises from our mere will and pleasure. The only question, then, is, whether there be not a manifest absurdity in supposing this act of the mind, and such an absurdity as no man could fall into, whose ideas are not confounded with prejudice and the fallacious use of language.

All morality depends upon our sentiments; and when any action, or quality of the mind, pleases us *after a certain* *manner*, we say it is virtuous; and when the neglect, or non-performance of it, displeases us *after a like manner*, we say that we lie under an obligation to perform it.[39] A change of the obligation supposes a change of the sentiment; and a creation of a new obligation supposes some new sentiment to arise. But it is certain we can naturally no more change our own sentiments, than the motions of the heavens; nor by a single act of our will, that is, by a promise, render any action agreeable or disagreeable, moral or immoral; which, without that act, would have produc'd contrary impressions, or have been endowed with different qualities. It would be absurd, therefore, to will any new obligation, that is, any new sentiment of pain or pleasure; nor is it possible, that men could naturally fall into so gross an absurdity. A promise, therefore, is *naturally* something altogether unintelligible, nor is there any act of the mind belonging to it.*

But, *secondly*, if there was any act of the mind belonging to it, it could not *naturally* produce any obligation. This appears evidently from the foregoing reasoning. A promise creates a new obligation. A new obligation supposes new

---

* Were morality discoverable by reason, and not by sentiment, it would be still more evident, that promises could make no alteration upon it. Morality is supposed to consist in relation. Every new imposition of morality, therefore, must arise from some new relation of objects; and consequently the will could not produce *immediately* any change in morals, but could have that effect only by producing a change upon the objects. But as the moral obligation of a promise is the pure effect of the will, without the least change in any part of the universe; it follows, that promises have no *natural* obligation.

Should it be said, that this act of the will being in effect a new object, produces new relations and new duties; I wou'd answer, that this is a pure sophism, which may be detected by a very moderate share of accuracy and exactness. To will a new obligation, is to will a new relation of objects; and therefore, if this new relation of objects were formed by the volition itself, we should in effect will the volition; which is plainly absurd and impossible. The will has here no object to which it could tend; but must return upon itself *in infinitum*. The new obligation depends upon new relations. The new relations depend upon a new volition. The new volition has for object a new obligation, and consequently new relations, and consequently a new volition; which volition again has in view a new obligation, relation and volition, without any termination. It is impossible, therefore, we could ever will a new obligation; and consequently it is impossible the will could ever accompany a promise, or produce a new obligation of morality.

sentiments to arise. The will never creates new sentiments. There could not naturally, therefore, arise any obligation from a promise, even supposing the mind could fall into the absurdity of willing that obligation.

The same truth may be proved still more evidently by that reasoning, which proved justice in general to be an artificial virtue. No action can be required of us as our duty, unless there be implanted in human nature some actuating passion or motive, capable of producing the action. This motive cannot be the sense of duty. A sense of duty supposes an antecedent obligation; and where an action is not required by any natural passion, it cannot be required by any natural obligation; since it may be omitted without proving any defect or imperfection in the mind and temper, and consequently without any vice. Now it is evident we have no motive leading us to the performance of promises, distinct from a sense of duty. If we thought, that promises had no moral obligation, we never should feel any inclination to observe them. This is not the case with the natural virtues. Though there was no obligation to relieve the miserable, our humanity would lead us to it; and when we omit that duty, the immorality of the omission arises from its being a proof, that we want the natural sentiments of humanity. A father knows it to be his duty to take care of his children; but he has also a natural inclination to it. And if no human creature had that inclination, no one could lie under any such obligation. But as there is naturally no inclination to observe promises, distinct from a sense of their obligation; it follows, that fidelity is no natural virtue, and that promises have no force, antecedent to human conventions.

If anyone dissent from this, he must give a regular proof of these two propositions, *viz. that there is a peculiar act of the mind, annexed to promises;* and *that consequent to this act of the mind, there arises an inclination to perform, distinct from a sense of duty.* I presume, that it is impossible to prove either of these two points; and therefore I venture to conclude, that promises are human inventions, founded on the necessities and interests of society.

In order to discover these necessities and interests, we must consider the same qualities of human nature, which we have already found to give rise to the preceding laws of society. Men being naturally selfish, or endowed only with a confined generosity, they are not easily induced to perform any action for the interest of strangers, except with a view to some reciprocal advantage, which they had no hope of obtaining but by such a performance. Now as it frequently happens, that these mutual performances cannot be finished at the same instant, it is necessary, that one party be contented to remain in uncertainty, and depend upon the gratitude of the other for a return of kindness. But so much corruption is there among men, that, generally speaking, this becomes but a slender security; and as the benefactor is here supposed to bestow his favour with a view to self-interest, this both takes off from the obligation, and sets an example of selfishness, which is the true mother of ingratitude. Were we, therefore, to follow the natural course of our passions and inclinations, we should perform but few actions for the advantage of others, from disinterested views; because we are naturally very limited in our kindness and affection; and we should perform as few of that kind, out of a regard to interest; because we cannot depend upon their gratitude. Here then is the mutual commerce of good offices in a manner lost among mankind, and everyone reduced to his own skill and industry for his well being and subsistence. The invention of the law of nature, concerning the *stability* of possession, has already rendered men tolerable to each other; that of the *transference* of property and possession by consent has begun to render them mutually advantageous; but still these laws of nature, however strictly observed, are not sufficient to render them so serviceable to each other, as by nature they are fitted to become. Though possession be *stable*, men may often reap but small advantage from it, while they are possessed of a greater quantity of any species of goods than they have occasion for, and at the same time suffer by the want of others. The *transference* of property, which is the proper remedy for this inconvenience, cannot remedy it entirely; because it can only take place with regard to such objects as are *present* and *individual*, but not to such as are *absent* or *general*. One cannot transfer the property of a particular house, twenty leagues distant; because the consent cannot be attended with delivery, which is a requisite circumstance. Neither can one transfer the property of ten bushels of corn, or five hogsheads of wine, by the mere expression and consent; because these are only general terms, and have no direct relation to any particular heap of corn, or barrels of wine. Besides, the commerce of mankind is not confined to the barter of commodities, but may extend to services and actions, which we may exchange to our mutual interest and advantage. Your corn is ripe today; mine will be so tomorrow. It is profitable for us both, that I should labour with you today, and that you should aid me tomorrow. I have no kindness for you, and know you have as little for me: I will not, therefore, take any pains upon your account; and should I labour with you upon my own account, in expectation of a return, I know I should be disappointed, and that I should in vain depend upon your gratitude. Here then I leave you to labour alone; you treat me in the same manner. The seasons change; and both of us lose our harvests for want of mutual confidence and security.

All this is the effect of the natural and inherent principles and passions of human nature; and as these passions and principles are inalterable, it may be thought, that our conduct, which depends on them, must be so too, and that it would be in vain, either for moralists or politicians, to tamper with us, or attempt to change the usual course of our actions, with a view to public interest. And indeed, did the success of their designs depend upon their success in correcting the selfishness and ingratitude of men, they would never make any progress, unless aided by omnipotence, which is alone able to new-mould the human mind, and change its character in such fundamental articles. All they can pretend to, is, to give a new direction to those natural passions, and teach us that we can better satisfy our appetites in an oblique and artificial manner, than by their headlong and impetuous motion. Hence I learn to do a service to another, without bearing him any real kindness; because I forsee, that he will return my service, in expectation of another of the same kind, and in order to maintain the same correspondence of good offices with me or with others. And accordingly, after I have served him, and he is in possession of the advantage arising from my action, he is induced to perform his part, as foreseeing the consequences of his refusal.

But though this self-interested commerce of men begins to take place, and to predominate in society, it does not entirely abolish the more generous and noble intercourse of friendship and good offices. I may still do services to such persons as I love, and am more particularly acquainted with, without any prospect of advantage; and they may make me a return in the same manner, without any view but that of recompensing my past services. In order, therefore, to distinguish those two different sorts of commerce, the interested and the disinterested, there is a *certain form of words* invented for the former, by which we bind ourselves to the performance of any action. This form of words constitutes what we call a *promise*, which is the sanction of the interested commerce of mankind. When a man says *he promises anything*, he in effect expresses a *resolution* of performing it; and along with that, by making use of this *form of words*, subjects himself to the penalty of never being trusted again in case of failure. A resolution is the natural act of the mind, which promises express; but were there no more than a resolution in the case, promises would only declare our former motives, and would not create any new motive or obligation. They are the conventions of men, which create a new motive, when experience has taught us, that human affairs would be conducted much more for mutual advantage, were there certain *symbols* or *signs* instituted, by which we might give each other security of our conduct in any particular incident. After these signs are instituted, whoever uses them is immediately bound by his interest to execute his engagements, and must never expect to be trusted any more, if he refuse to perform what he promised.

Nor is that knowledge, which is requisite to make mankind sensible of this interest in the *institution* and *observance* of promises, to be esteemed superior to the capacity of human nature, however savage and uncultivated. There needs but a very little practice of the world, to make us perceive all these consequences and advantages. The shortest experience of society discovers them to every mortal; and when each individual perceives the same sense of interest in all his fellows, he immediately performs his part of any contract, as being assured, that they will not be wanting in theirs. All of them, by concert, enter into a scheme of actions, calculated for common benefit, and agree to be true to their word; nor is there anything requisite to form this concert or convention, but that everyone have a sense of interest in the faithful fulfilling of engagements, and express that sense to other members of the society. This immediately causes that interest to operate upon them; and interest is the *first* obligation to the performance of promises.

Afterwards a sentiment of morals concurs with interest, and becomes a new obligation upon mankind. This sentiment of morality, in the performance of promises, arises from the same principles as that in the abstinence from the property of others. *Public interest, education,* and *the artifices of politicians,* have the same effect in both cases. The difficulties, that occur to us, in supposing a moral obligation to attend promises, we either surmount or elude. For instance; the expression of a resolution is not commonly supposed to be obligatory; and we cannot readily conceive how the making use of a certain form of words should be able to cause any material difference. Here, therefore, we *feign* a new act of the mind, which we call the *willing* an obligation; and on this we suppose the morality to depend. But we have proved already, that there is no such act of the mind, and consequently that promises impose no natural obligation.

To confirm this, we may subjoin some other reflections concerning that will, which is supposed to enter into a promise, and to cause its obligation. It is evident, that the will alone is never supposed to cause the obligation, but must be expressed by words or signs, in order to impose a tye upon any man. The expression being once brought in as subservient to the will, soon becomes the principal part of the promise; nor will a man be less bound by his word, though he secretly give a different direction to his intention, and withhold himself both from a resolution, and from willing an obligation. But though the expression makes on most occasions the whole of the promise, yet it does not always so; and one, who should make use of any expression, of which he knows not the meaning, and which he uses without any intention of binding himself, would not certainly be bound by it. Nay, though he knows its meaning, yet if he uses it in jest only, and with such signs as show evidently he has no serious intention of binding himself, he would not lie under any obligation of performance; but it is necessary, that the words be a perfect expression of the will, without any contrary signs. Nay, even this we must not carry so far as to imagine, that one, whom, by our quickness of understanding, we conjecture, from certain signs, to have an intention of deceiving us, is not bound by his expression or verbal promise, if we accept of it; but must limit this conclusion to those cases, where the signs are of a different kind from those of deceit. All these contradictions are easily accounted for, if the obligation of promises be merely a human invention for the convenience of society; but will never be explained, if it be something *real* and *natural*, arising from any action of the mind or body.

I shall farther observe, that since every new promise imposes a new obligation of morality on the person who promises, and since this new obligation arises from his will; it is one of the most mysterious and incomprehensible operations that can possibly be imagined, and may even be compared to *transubstantiation*, or *holy orders*,* where a certain form of words, along with a certain intention, changes entirely the nature of an external object, and even of a human creature. But though these mysteries be so far alike, it is very remarkable, that they differ widely in other particulars, and that this difference may be regarded as a strong proof of the difference of their origins. As the obligation of promises is an invention for the interest of society, it is warped into as many different forms as that interest requires, and even runs into direct contradictions, rather than lose sight of its object. But as those other monstrous doctrines are merely priestly inventions, and have no public interest in view, they are less disturbed in their progress by new obstacles; and it must be owned, that, after the first absurdity, they follow more directly the current of reason and good sense. Theologians clearly perceived, that the external form of words, being mere sound, require an intention to make them have any efficacy; and that this intention being once considered as a requisite circumstance, its absence must equally prevent the effect, whether avowed or concealed, whether sincere or deceitful. Accordingly they have commonly determined, that the intention of the priest makes the sacrament, and that when he secretly withdraws his intention, he is highly criminal in himself; but still destroys the baptism, or communion, or holy orders. The terrible con-

---

* I mean so far, as holy orders are supposed to produce the *indelible character*. In other respects they are only a legal qualification.

sequences of this doctrine were not able to hinder its taking place; as the inconvenience of a similar doctrine, with regard to promises, have prevented that doctrine from establishing itself. Men are always more concerned about the present life than the future; and are apt to think the smallest evil, which regards the former, more important than the greatest, which regards the latter.

We may draw the same conclusion, concerning the origin of promises, from the *force*, which is supposed to invalidate all contracts, and to free us from their obligation. Such a principle is a proof, that promises have no natural obligation, and are mere artificial contrivances for the convenience and advantage of society. If we consider aright of the matter, force is not essentially different from any other motive of hope or fear, which may induce us to engage our word, and lay ourselves under any obligation. A man, dangerously wounded, who promises a competent sum to a surgeon to cure him, would certainly be bound to performance; though the case be not so much different from that of one, who promises a sum to a robber, as to produce so great a difference in our sentiments of morality, if these sentiments were not built entirely on public interest and convenience.

SECTION VI *Some farther reflections concerning justice and injustice*

We have now run over the three fundamental laws of nature, *that of the stability of possession, of its transference by consent,* and *of the performance of promises.* It is on the strict observance of those three laws, that the peace and security of human society entirely depend; nor is there any possibility of establishing a good correspondence among men, where these are neglected. Society is absolutely necessary for the wellbeing of men; and these are as necessary to the support of society. Whatever restraint they may impose on the passions of men, they are the real offspring of those passions, and are only a more artful and more refined way of satisfying them. Nothing is more vigilant and inventive than our passions; and nothing is more obvious, than the convention for the observance of these rules. Nature has, therefore, trusted this affair entirely to the conduct of men, and has not placed in the mind any peculiar original principles, to determine us to a set of actions, into which the other principles of our frame and constitution were sufficient to lead us. And to convince us the more fully of this truth, we may here stop a moment, and from a review of the preceding reasonings may draw some new arguments, to prove that those laws, however necessary, are entirely artificial, and of human invention; and consequently that justice is an artificial, and not a natural virtue.

I. The first argument I shall make use of is derived from the vulgar definition of justice. Justice is commonly defined to be *a constant and perpetual will of giving everyone his due*. In this definition it is supposed, that there are such things as right and property, independent of justice, and antecedent to it; and that they would have subsisted, though men had never dreamed of practising such a virtue. I have already observed, in a cursory manner, the fallacy of this opinion, and shall here continue to open up a little more distinctly my sentiments on that subject.

I shall begin with observing, that this quality, which we call *property*, is like many of the imaginary qualities of the *peripatetic* philosophy, and vanishes upon a more accurate inspection into the subject, when considered apart from our moral sentiments. It is evident property does not consist in any of the sensible qualities of the object. For these may continue invariably the same, while the property changes. Property, therefore, must consist in some relation of the object. But it is not in its relation with regard to other external and inanimate objects. For these may also continue invariably the same, while the property changes. This quality, therefore, consists in the relations of objects to intelligent and rational beings. But it is not the external and corporeal relation, which forms the essence of property. For that relation may be the same betwixt inanimate objects, or with regard to brute creatures; though in those cases it forms no property. It is, therefore, in some internal relation, that the property consists; that is, in some influence, which the external relations of the object have on the mind and actions. Thus the external relation, which we call *occupation* or first possession, is not of itself imagined to be the property of the object, but only to cause its property. Now it is evident, this external relation causes nothing in external objects, and has only an influence on the mind, by giving us a sense of duty in abstaining from that object, and in restoring it to the first possessor. These actions are properly what we call *justice*; and consequently it is on that virtue that the nature of property depends, and not the virtue on the property.

If anyone, therefore, would assert, that justice is a natural virtue, and injustice a natural vice, he must assert, that abstracting from the notions of *property*, and *right* and *obligation*, a certain conduct and train of actions, in certain external relations of objects, has naturally a moral beauty or deformity, and causes an original pleasure or uneasiness. Thus the restoring a man's goods to him is considered as virtuous, not because nature has annexed a certain sentiment of pleasure to such a conduct, with regard to the property of others, but because she has annex'd that sentiment to such a conduct, with regard to those external objects, of which others have had the first or long possession, or which they have received by the consent of those, who have had first or long possession. If nature has given us no such sentiment, there is not, naturally, nor antecedent to human conventions, any such thing as property. Now, though it seems sufficiently evident, in this dry and accurate consideration of the present subject, that nature has annexed no pleasure or sentiment of approbation to such a conduct; yet that I may leave as little room for doubt as possible, I shall subjoin a few more arguments to confirm my opinion.

First, if nature had given us a pleasure of this kind, it would have been as evident and discernible as on every other occasion; nor should we have found any difficulty to perceive, that the consideration of such actions, in such a situation, gives a certain pleasure and sentiment of approbation. We should not have been obliged to have recourse to notions of property in the definition of justice, and at the same time make use of the notions of justice in the definition of property. This deceitful method of reasoning is a plain proof, that there are contained in the subject some obscurities and difficulties, which we are not able to surmount, and which we desire to evade by this artifice.

Secondly, those rules, by which properties, rights, and obligations are determined, have in them no marks of a natural origin, but many of artifice and contrivance. They are too numerous to have proceeded from nature; they are changeable by human laws; and have all of them a direct and evident tendency to public good, and the support of civil society. This last circumstance is remarkable upon two accounts. *First*, because, though the cause of the establishment of these laws had been a *regard* for the public good, as much as the public good is their natural tendency, they would still have been artificial, as being purposely contrived and directed to a certain end. *Secondly*, because, if men had been endowed with such a strong regard for public good, they would never have restrained themselves by these rules; so that the laws of justice arise from natural principles in a manner still more oblique and artificial. It is self-love which is their real origin; and as the self-love of one person is naturally contrary to that of another, these several interested passions are obliged to adjust themselves after such a manner as to concur in some system of conduct and behaviour. This system, therefore, comprehending the interest of each individual, is of course advantageous to the public; though it be not intended for that purpose by the inventors.

II. In the second place we may observe, that all kinds of vice and virtue run insensibly into each other, and may approach by such imperceptible degrees as will make it very difficult, if not absolutely impossible, to determine when the one ends, and the other begins; and from this observation we may derive a new argument for the foregoing principle. For whatever may be the case, with regard to all kinds of vice and virtue, it is certain, that rights, and obligations, and property, admit of no such insensible gradation, but that a man either has a full and perfect property, or none at all; and is either entirely obliged to perform any action, or lies under no manner of obligation. However civil laws may talk of a perfect *dominion*, and of an imperfect, it is easy to observe, that this arises from a fiction, which has no foundation in reason, and can never enter into our notions of natural justice and equity. A man that hires a horse, though but for a day, has as full a right to make use of it for that time, as he whom we call its proprietor has to make use of it any other day; and it is evident, that however the use may be bounded in time or degree, the right itself is not susceptible of any such gradation, but is absolute and entire, so far as it extends. Accordingly we may observe, that this right both arises and perishes in an instant; and that a man entirely acquires the property of any object by occupation, or the consent of the proprietor; and loses it by his own consent; without any of that insensible gradation, which is remarkable in other qualities and relations. Since, therefore, this is the case with regard to property, and rights, and obligations, I ask, how it stands with regard to justice and injustice? After whatever manner you answer this question, you run into inextricable difficulties. If you reply, that justice and injustice admit of degree, and run insensibly into each other, you expressly contradict the foregoing position, that obligation and property are not susceptible of such a gradation. These depend entirely upon justice and injustice, and follow them in all their variations. Where the justice is entire, the property is also entire; where the justice is imperfect, the property must also be imperfect. And *vice versa*, if the property admit of no such variations, they must also be incompatible with justice. If you assent, therefore, to this last proposition, and assert, that justice and injustice are not susceptible of degrees, you in effect assert, that they are not *naturally* either vicious or virtuous; since vice and virtue, moral good and evil, and indeed all *natural* qualities, run insensibly into each other, and are, on many occasions, undistinguishable.

And here it may be worth while to observe, that though abstract reasoning, and the general maxims of philosophy and law establish this position, *that property, and right, and obligation admit not of degrees*, yet in our common and negligent way of thinking, we find great difficulty to entertain that opinion, and do even *secretly* embrace the contrary principle. An object must either be in the possession of one person or another. An action must either be performed or not. The necessity there is of choosing one side in these dilemmas, and the impossibility there often is of finding any just medium, oblige us, when we reflect on the matter, to acknowledge, that all property and obligations are entire. But on the other hand, when we consider the origin of property and obligation, and find that they depend on public utility, and sometimes on the propensities of the imagination, which are seldom entire on any side; we are naturally inclined to imagine, that these moral relations admit of an insensible gradation. Hence it is, that in references, where the consent of the parties leave the referees entire masters of the subject, they commonly discover so much equity and justice on both sides, as induces them to strike a medium, and divide the difference betwixt the parties. Civil judges, who have not this liberty, but are obliged to give a decisive sentence on some one side, are often at a loss how to determine, and are necessitated to proceed on the most frivolous reasons in the world. Half rights and obligations, which seem so natural in common life, are perfect absurdities in their tribunal; for which reason they are often obliged to take half arguments for whole ones, in order to terminate the affair one way or other.

III. The third argument of this kind I shall make use of may be explained thus. If we consider the ordinary course of human actions, we shall find, that the mind restrains not itself by any general and universal rules; but acts on most occasions as it is determined by its present motives and inclination. As each action is a particular individual event, it must proceed from particular principles, and from our immediate situation within ourselves, and with respect to the rest of the universe. If on some occasions we extend our motives beyond those very circumstances, which gave rise to them, and form something like *general rules* for our conduct, it is easy to observe, that these rules are not perfectly inflexible, but allow of many exceptions. Since, therefore, this is the ordinary course of human actions, we may conclude, that the laws of justice, being universal and perfectly inflexible, can never be derived from nature, nor be the immediate offspring of any natural motive or inclination. No action can be either morally good or evil, unless there be some natural passion or motive to impel us to it, or deter us from it; and it is evident, that the morality must be susceptible of all the same variations, which are natural to the passion. Here are two persons, who dispute for an estate; of whom one is rich, a fool, and a batchelor; the other poor, a man of sense, and has a numerous family. The first is my enemy; the second my friend. Whether I be actuated in this affair by a view to public or private interest, by friendship or enmity, I must be induced to do my utmost to procure the estate to the latter. Nor would any consideration of the right and property of the persons be able to restrain me, were I actuated only by natural motives, without any combination or convention with others. For as all property depends on morality; and as all morality depends on the ordinary course of our passions and actions; and as these again are only directed by particular motives; it is evident, such a partial conduct must be suitable to the strictest morality, and could never be a violation of property. Were men, therefore, to take the liberty of acting with regard to the laws of society, as they do in every other affair, they would conduct themselves, on most occasions, by particular judgments, and would take into consideration the characters and circumstances of the persons, as well as the general nature of the question. But it is easy to observe, that this would produce an infinite confusion in human society, and that the avidity and partiality of men would quickly bring disorder into the world, if not restrained by some general and inflexible principles. It was, therefore, with a view to this inconvenience, that men have established those principles, and have agreed to restrain themselves by general rules, which are unchangeable by spite and favour, and by particular views of private or public interest. These rules, then, are artificially invented for a certain purpose, and are contrary to the common principles of human nature, which accommodate themselves to circumstances, and have no stated invariable method of operation.

Nor do I perceive how I can easily be mistaken in this matter. I see evidently, that when any man imposes on himself general inflexible rules in his conduct with others, he considers certain objects as their property, which he supposes to be sacred and inviolable. But no proposition can be more evident, than that property is perfectly unintelligible without first supposing justice and injustice; and that these virtues and vices are as unintelligible, unless we have motives, independent of the morality, to impel us to just actions, and deter us from unjust ones. Let those motives, therefore, be what they will, they must accommodate themselves to circumstances, and must admit of all the variations, which human affairs, in their incessant revolutions, are susceptible of. They are consequently a very improper foundation for such rigid inflexible rules as the laws of [justice?]; and it is evident these laws can only be derived from human conventions, when men have perceived the disorders that result from following their natural and variable principles.

Upon the whole, then, we are to consider this distinction betwixt justice and injustice, as having two different foundations, *viz.* that of *interest*, when men observe, that it is impossible to live in society without restraining themselves by certain rules; and that of *morality*, when this interest is once observed, and men receive a pleasure from the view of such actions as tend to the peace of society, and an uneasiness from such as are contrary to it. It is the voluntary convention and artifice of men, which makes the first interest take place; and therefore those laws of justice are so far to be considered as *artificial*. After that interest is once established and acknowledged, the sense of morality in the observance of these rules follows *naturally*, and of itself; though it is certain, that it is also augmented by a new *artifice*, and that the public instructions of politicians, and the private education of parents, contribute to the giving us a sense of honour and duty in the strict regulation of our actions with regard to the properties of others.

Section VII *Of the origin of government*

Nothing is more certain, than that men are, in a great measure, governed by interest, and that even when they extend their concern beyond themselves, it is not to any great distance; nor is it usual for them, in common life, to look farther than their nearest friends and acquaintance. It is no less certain, that it is impossible for men to consult their interest in so effectual a manner, as by an universal and inflexible observance of the rules of justice, by which alone they can preserve society, and keep themselves from falling into that wretched and savage condition, which is commonly represented as the *state of nature*. And as this interest, which all men have in the upholding of society, and the observation of the rules of justice, is great, so is it palpable and evident, even to the most rude and uncultivated of the human race; and it is almost impossible for anyone, who has had experience of society, to be mistaken in this particular. Since, therefore, men are so sincerely attached to their interest, and their interest is so much concerned in the observance of justice, and this interest is so certain and avow'd; it may be asked, how any disorder can ever arise in society, and what principle there is in human nature so *powerful* as to overcome so strong a passion, or so *violent* as to obscure so clear a knowledge?

It has been observed, in treating of the passions, that men

are mightily governed by the imagination, and proportion their affections more to the light, under which any object appears to them, than to its real and intrinsic value. What strikes upon them with a strong and lively idea commonly prevails above what lies in a more obscure light; and it must be a great superiority of value, that is able to compensate this advantage. Now as everything, that is contiguous to us, either in space or time, strikes upon us with such an idea, it has a proportional effect on the will and passions, and commonly operates with more force than any object, that lies in a more distant and obscure light. Though we may be fully convinced, that the latter object excels the former, we are not able to regulate our actions by this judgment; but yield to the solicitations of our passions, which always plead in favour of whatever is near and contiguous.

This is the reason why men so often act in contradiction to their known interest; and in particular why they prefer any trivial advantage, that is present, to the maintenance of order in society, which so much depends on the observance of justice. The consequences of every breach of equity seem to lie very remote, and are not able to counter balance any immediate advantage, that may be reaped from it. They are, however, nevertheless real for being remote; and as all men are, in some degree, subject to the same weakness, it necessarily happens, that the violations of equity must become very frequent in society, and the commerce of men, by that means, be rendered very dangerous and uncertain. You have the same propension, that I have, in favour of what is contiguous above what is remote. You are, therefore, naturally carried to commit acts of injustice as well as me. Your example both pushes me forward in this way by imitation, and also affords me a new reason for any breach of equity, by showing me, that I should be the cully of my integrity, if I alone should impose on myself a severe restraint amidst the licentiousness of others.

This quality, therefore, of human nature, not only is very dangerous to society, but also seems, on a cursory view, to be incapable of any remedy. The remedy can only come from the consent of men; and if men be incapable of themselves to prefer remote to contiguous, they will never consent to anything, which would oblige them to such a choice, and contradict, in so sensible a manner, their natural principles and propensities. Whoever chooses the means, chooses also the end; and if it be impossible for us to prefer what is remote, it is equally impossible for us to submit to any necessity, which would oblige us to such a method of acting.

But here it is observable, that this infirmity of human nature becomes a remedy to itself, and that we provide against our negligence about remote objects, merely because we are naturally inclined to that negligence. When we consider any objects at a distance, all their minute distinctions vanish, and we always give the preference to whatever is in itself preferable, without considering its situation and circumstances. This gives rise to what in an improper sense we call *reason*, which is a principle, that is often contradictory to those propensities that display themselves upon the approach of the object. In reflecting on any action, which I am to perform a twelve-month hence, I always resolve to prefer the greater good, whether at that time it will be more contiguous or remote; nor does any difference in that particular make a difference in my present intentions and resolutions. My distance from the final determination makes all those minute differences vanish, nor am I affected by anything, but the general and more discernable qualities of good and evil. But on my nearer approach, those circumstances, which I at first overlooked, begin to appear, and have an influence on my conduct and affections. A new inclination to the present good springs up, and makes it difficult for me to adhere inflexibly to my first purpose and resolution. This natural infirmity I may very much regret, and I may endeavour, by all possible means, to free myself from it. I may have recourse to study and reflection within myself; to the advice of friends; to frequent meditation, and repeated resolution; and having experienced how ineffectual all there are, I may embrace with pleasure any other expedient, by which I may impose a restraint upon myself, and guard against this weakness.

The only difficulty, therefore, is to find out this expedient, by which men cure their natural weakness, and lay themselves under the necessity of observing the laws of justice and equity, notwithstanding their violent propension to prefer contiguous to remote. It is evident such a remedy can never be effectual without correcting this propensity; and as it is impossible to change or correct anything material in our nature, the utmost we can do is to change our circumstances and situation, and render the observance of the laws of justice our nearest interest, and their violation our most remote. But this being impracticable with respect to all mankind, it can only take place with respect to a few, whom we thus immediately interest in the execution of justice. These are the persons, whom we call magistrates, kings and their ministers, our governors and rulers, who being indifferent persons to the greatest part of the state, have no interest, or but a remote one, in any act of injustice; and being satisfied with their present condition, and with their part in society, have an immediate interest in every execution of justice, which is so necessary to the upholding of society. Here then is the origin of civil government and society. Men are not able radically to cure, either in themselves or others, that narrowness of soul, which makes them prefer the present to the remote. They cannot change their natures. All they can do is to change their situation, and render the observance of justice the immediate interest of some particular persons, and its violation their more remote. These persons, then, are not only induced to observe those rules in their own conduct, but also to constrain others to a like regularity, and inforce the dictates of equity through the whole society. And if it be necessary, they may also interest others more immediately in the execution of justice, and create a number of officers, civil and military, to assist them in their government.

But this execution of justice, though the principal, is not the only advantage of government. As violent passion hinders men from seeing distinctly the interest they have in an equitable behaviour towards others; so it hinders them from seeing that equity itself, and gives them a remarkable partiality in their own favours. This inconvenience is corrected in the same manner as that above-mentioned. The same persons, who execute the laws of justice, will also decide all controversies concerning them; and being indifferent to the greatest part of the society, will decide them more equitably than everyone would in his own case.

By means of these two advantages, in the *execution* and *decision* of justice, men acquire a security against each others' weakness and passion, as well as against their own, and under the shelter of their governors, begin to taste at ease the sweets of society and mutual assistance. But government extends farther its beneficial influence; and not contented to protect men in those conventions they make for their mutual interest, it often obliges them to make such conventions, and forces them to seek their own advantage, by a concurrence in some common end or purpose. There is no quality in human nature, which causes more fatal errors in our conduct, than that which leads us to prefer whatever is present to the distant and remote, and makes us desire objects more according to their situation than their intrinsic value. Two neighbours may agree to drain a meadow, which they possess in common; because it is easy for them to know each others mind; and each must perceive, that the immediate consequence of his failing in his part, is the abandoning the whole project. But it is very difficult, and indeed impossible, that a thousand persons should agree in any such action; it being difficult for them to concert so complicated a design, and still more difficult for them to execute it; while each seeks a pretext to free himself of the trouble and expense, and would lay the whole burden on others. Political society easily remedies both these inconveniences. Magistrates find an immediate interest in the interest of any considerable part of their subjects. They need consult nobody but themselves to form any scheme for the promoting of that interest. And as the failure of any one piece in the execution is connected, though not immediately, with the failure of the whole, they prevent that failure, because they find no interest in it, either immediate or remote. Thus bridges are built; harbours opened; ramparts raised; canals formed; fleets equipped; and armies disciplined; everywhere, by the care of government, which, though composed of men subject to all human infirmities, becomes, by one of the finest and most subtle inventions imaginable, a composition, which is, in some measure, exempted from all these infirmities.

Section VIII *Of the source of allegiance*

Though government be an invention very advantageous, and even in some circumstances absolutely necessary to mankind; it is not necessary in all circumstances, nor is it impossible for men to preserve society for some time, without having recourse to such an invention. Men, it is true, are always much inclined to prefer present interest to distant and remote; nor is it easy for them to resist the temptation of any advantage, that they may immediately enjoy, in apprehension of an evil, that lies at a distance from them; but still this weakness is less conspicuous, where the possessions, and the pleasures of life are few, and of little value, as they always are in the infancy of society. An *Indian* is but little tempted to dispossess another of his hut, or to steal his bow, as being already provided of the same advantages; and as to any superior fortune, which may attend one above another in hunting and fishing, it is only casual and temporary, and will have but small tendency to disturb society. And so far am I from thinking with some philosophers, that men are utterly incapable of society without government, that I assert the first rudiments of government to arise from quarrels, not among men of the same society, but among those of different societies. A less degree of riches will suffice to this latter effect, than is requisite for the former. Men fear nothing from public war and violence but the resistance they meet with, which, because they share it in common, seems less terrible; and because it comes from strangers, seems less pernicious in its consequences, than when they are expos'd singly against one whose commerce is advantageous to them, and without whose society it is impossible they can subsist. Now foreign war to a society without government necessarily produces civil war. Throw any considerable goods among men, they instantly fall a-quarrelling, while each strives to get possession of what pleases him, without regard to the consequences. In a foreign war the most considerable of all goods, life and limbs, are at stake; and as everyone shuns dangerous ports, seizes the best arms, seeks excuse for the slightest wounds, the laws, which may be well enough observed, while men were calm, can now no longer take place, when they are in such commotion.

This we find verified in the *American* tribes, where men live in concord and amity among themselves without any established government; and never pay submission to any of their fellows, except in time of war, when their captain enjoys a shadow of authority, which he loses after their return from the field, and the establishment of peace with the neighbouring tribes. This authority, however, instructs them in the advantages of government, and teaches them to have recourse to it, when either by the pillage of war, by commerce, or by any fortuitous inventions, their riches and possessions have become so considerable as to make them forget, on every emergence, the interest they have in the preservation of peace and justice. Hence we may give a plausible reason, among others, why all governments are at first monarchical, without any mixture and variety; and why republics arise only from the abuses of monarchy and despotic power. Camps are the true mothers of cities; and as war cannot be administered, by reason of the suddenness of every exigency, without some authority in a single person, the same kind of authority naturally takes place in that civil government, which succeeds the military. And this reason I take to be more natural, than the common one derived from patriarchal government, or the authority of a father, which is said first to take place in one family, and to accustom the members of it to the government of a single person. The state of society without government is one of the most natural states of men, and must subsist with the conjunction of many families, and long after the first generation. Nothing but an increase of riches and possessions could oblige men to quit it; and so barbarous and uninstructed are all societies on their first formation, that many years must elapse before these can increase to such a degree, as to disturb men in the enjoyment of peace and concord.

But though it be possible for men to maintain a small uncultivated society without government, it is impossible they should maintain a society of any kind without justice, and the observance of those three fundamental laws concerning the stability of possession, its translation by consent, and the performance of promises. These are, therefore, antecedent to government, and are supposed to impose an obligation before the duty of allegiance to civil magistrates has once been thought of. Nay, I shall go farther, and assert, that government, *upon its first establishment*, would naturally be supposed to derive its obligation from those laws of nature, and, in particular, from that concerning the performance of promises. When men have once perceived the necessity of government to maintain peace, and execute justice, they would naturally assemble together, would choose magistrates, determine their power, and *promise* them obedience. As a promise is supposed to be a bond or security already in use, and attended with a moral obligation, it is to be considered as the original sanction of government, and as the source of the first obligation to obedience. This reasoning appears so natural, that it has become the foundation of our fashionable system of politics, and is in a manner the creed of a party amongst us, who pride themselves, with reason, on the soundness of their philosophy, and their liberty of thought. *All men*, say they, *are born free and equal; government and superiority can only be established by consent; the consent of men, in establishing government, imposes on them a new obligation, unknown to the laws of nature. Men, therefore, are bound to obey their magistrates, only because they promise it; and if they had not given their word, either expressly or tacitly, to preserve allegiance, it would never have become a part of their moral duty.*[40] This conclusion, however, when carried so far as to comprehend government in all its ages and situations, is entirely erroneous; and I maintain, that though the duty of allegiance be at first grafted on the obligation of promises, and be for some time supported by that obligation, yet it quickly takes root of itself, and has an original obligation and authority, independent of all contracts. This is a principle of moment, which we must examine with care and attention, before we proceed any farther.

It is reasonable for those philosophers, who assert justice to be a natural virtue, and antecedent to human conventions, to resolve all civil allegiance into the obligation of a promise, and assert that it is our own consent alone, which binds us to any submission to magistracy. For as all government is plainly an invention of men, and the origin of most governments is known in history, it is necessary to mount higher, in order to find the source of our political duties, if we would assert them to have any *natural* obligation of morality. These philosophers, therefore, quickly observe, that society is as ancient as the human species, and those three fundamental laws of nature as ancient as society; so that taking advantage of the antiquity, and obscure origin of these laws, they first deny them to be artificial and voluntary inventions of men, and then seek to engraft on them those other duties, which are more plainly artificial. But being once undeceived in this particular, and having found that *natural*, as well as *civil* justice, derives its origin from human conventions, we shall quickly perceive, how fruitless it is to resolve the one into the other, and seek, in the laws of nature, a stronger foundation for our political duties than interest, and human conventions; while these laws themselves are built on the very same foundation. On whichever side we turn this subject, we shall find, that these two kinds of duty are exactly on the same footing, and have the same source both of their *first invention* and *moral obligation*. They are contrived to remedy like inconveniences, and acquire their moral sanction in the same manner, from their remedying those inconveniences. These are two points, which we shall endeavour to prove as distinctly as possible.

We have already shown, that men *invented* the three fundamental laws of nature, when they observed the necessity of society to their mutual subsistence, and found, that it was impossible to maintain any correspondence together, without some restraint on their natural appetites. The same self-love, therefore, which renders men so incommodious to each other, taking a new and more convenient direction, produces the rules of justice, and is the *first* motive of their observance. But when men have observed, that though the rules of justice be sufficient to maintain any society, yet 'tis impossible for them, of themselves, to observe those rules, in large and polished societies; they establish government, as a new invention to attain their ends, and preserve the old, or procure new advantages, by a more strict execution of justice. So far, therefore, our *civil* duties are connected with our *natural*, that the former are invented chiefly for the sake of the latter; and that the principal object of government is to constrain men to observe the laws of nature. In this respect, however, that law of nature, concerning the performance of promises, is only comprised along with the rest; and its exact observance is to be considered as an effect of the institution of government, and not the obedience to government as an effect of the obligation of a promise. Though the object of our civil duties be the enforcing of our natural, yet the *first*** motive of the invention, as well as performance of both, is nothing but self-interest; and since there is a separate interest in the obedience to government, from that in the performance of promises, we must also allow of a separate obligation. To

* First in time, not in dignity or force.

obey the civil magistrate is requisite to preserve order and concord in society. To perform promises is requisite to beget mutual trust and confidence in the common offices of life. The ends, as well as the means, are perfectly distinct; nor is the one subordinate to the other.

To make this more evident, let us consider, that men will often bind themselves by promises to the performance of what it would have been their interest to perform, independent of these promises; as when they would give others a fuller security, by super-adding a new obligation of interest to that which they formerly lay under. The interest in the performance of promises, besides its moral obligation, is general, avowed, and of the last consequence in life. Other interests may be more particular and doubtful; and we are apt to entertain a greater suspicion, that men may indulge their humour, or passion, in acting contrary to them. Here, therefore, promises come naturally in play, and are often required for fuller satisfaction and security. But supposing those other interests to be as general and avowed as the interest in the performance of a promise, they will be regarded as on the same footing, and men will begin to repose the same confidence in them. Now this is exactly the case with regard to our civil duties, or obedience to the magistrate; without which no government could subsist, nor any peace or order be maintained in large societies, where there are so many possessions on the one hand, and so many wants, real or imaginary, on the other. Our civil duties, therefore, must soon detach themselves from our promises, and acquire a separate force and influence. The interest in both is of the very same kind; it is general, avowed, and prevails in all times and places. There is, then, no pretext of reason for founding the one upon the other; while each of them has a foundation peculiar to itself. We might as well resolve the obligation to abstain from the possessions of others, into the obligation of a promise, as that of allegiance. The interests are not more distinct in the one case than the other. A regard to property is not more necessary to natural society, than obedience is to civil society or government; nor is the former society more necessary to the being of mankind, than the latter to their wellbeing and happiness. In short, if the performance of promises be advantageous, so is obedience to government; if the former interest be general, so is the latter; if the one interest be obvious and avowed, so is the other. And as these two rules are founded on like obligations of interest, each of them must have a peculiar authority, independent of the other.

But it is not only the *natural* obligations of interest, which are distinct in promises and allegiance; but also the *moral* obligations of honour and conscience. Nor does the merit or demerit of the one depend in the least upon that of the other. And indeed, if we consider the close connection there is betwixt the natural and moral obligations, we shall find this conclusion to be entirely unavoidable. Our interest is always engaged on the side of obedience to magistracy; and there is nothing but a great present advantage, that can lead us to rebellion, by making us overlook the remote interest, which we have in the preserving of peace and order in society. But though a present interest may thus blind us with regard to our own actions, it takes not place with regard to those of others; nor hinders them from appearing in their true colours, as highly prejudicial to public interest, and to our own in particular. This naturally gives us an uneasiness, in considering such seditious and disloyal actions, and makes us attach to them the idea of vice and moral deformity. It is the same principle, which causes us to disapprove of all kinds of private injustice, and in particular of the breach of promises. We blame all treachery and breach of faith; because we consider, that the freedom and extent of human commerce depend entirely on a fidelity with regard to promises. We blame all disloyalty to magistrates; because we perceive, that the execution of justice, in the stability of possession, its translation by consent, and the performance of promises, is impossible, without submission to government. As there are here two interests entirely distinct from each other, they must give rise to two moral obligations, equally separate and independant. Though there was no such thing as a promise in the world, government would still be necessary in all large and civilized societies; and if promises had only their own proper obligation, without the separate sanction of government, they would have but little efficacy in such societies. This separates the boundaries of our public and private duties, and shows that the latter are more dependent on the former, than the former on the latter. *Education*, and *the artifice of politicians*, concur to bestow a farther morality on loyalty, and to brand all rebellion with a greater degree of guilt and infamy. Nor is it a wonder, that politicians should be very industrious in inculating such notions, where their interest is so particularly concerned.

Lest those arguments should not appear entirely conclusive (as I think they are) I shall have recourse to authority, and shall prove, from the universal consent of mankind, that the obligation of submission to government is not derived from any promise of the subjects. Nor need anyone wonder, that though I have all along endeavoured to establish my system on pure reason, and have scarce ever cited the judgment even of philosophers or historians on any article, I should now appeal to popular authority, and oppose the sentiments of the rabble to any philosophical reasoning. For it must be observed, that the opinions of men, in this case, carry with them a peculiar authority, and are, in a great measure, infallible. The distinction of moral good and evil is founded on the pleasure or pain, which results from the view of any sentiment, or character; and as that pleasure or pain cannot be unknown to the person who feels it, it follows, that there is just so much vice or virtue in any character, as every one places in it, and that it is impossible in this particular we can ever be mistaken.* And though our judgments concerning the *origin* of any vice or virtue, be not so certain as those concerning their *degrees*; yet, since the question in this case regards not any philosophical origin of an obligation, but a plain matter of fact, it is not easily conceived how we can fall into an error. A man, who acknowledges himself to be bound to another, for a certain sum, must certainly know whether it be by his own bond, or that of his father; whether it be of his mere goodwill, or for money lent him; and under what conditions, and for what purposes he has bound himself. In like manner, it being certain, that there is a moral obligation to submit to government, because everyone thinks so; it must be as certain, that this obligation arises not from a promise; since

* This proposition must hold strictly true, with regard to every quality, that is determined merely by sentiment. In what sense we can talk either of a *right* or a *wrong* taste in morals, eloquence, or beauty, shall be considered afterwards. In the meantime, it may be observed, that there is such an uniformity in the *general* sentiments of mankind, as to render such questions of but small importance.

no one, whose judgment has not been led astray by too strict adherence to a system of philosophy, has ever yet dreamed of ascribing it to that origin. Neither magistrates nor subjects have formed this idea of our civil duties.

We find, that magistrates are so far from deriving their authority, and the obligation to obedience in their subjects, from the foundation of a promise or original contract, that they conceal, as far as possible, from their people, especially from the vulgar, that they have origin from thence. Were this the sanction of government, our rulers would never receive it tacitly, which is the utmost that can be pretended; since what is given tacitly and insensibly can never have such influence on mankind, as what is performed expressly and openly. A tacit promise is, where the will is signified by other more diffuse signs than those of speech; but a will there must certainly be in the case, and that can never escape the person's notice, who exerted it, however silent or tacit. But were you to ask the far greatest part of the nation, whether they had ever consented to the authority of their rulers, or promised to obey them, they would be inclined to think very strangely of you; and would certainly reply, that the affair depended not on their consent, but that they were born to such an obedience. In consequence of this opinion, we frequently see them imagine such persons to be their natural rulers, as are at that time deprived of all power and authority, and whom no man, however foolish, would voluntarily choose; and this merely because they are in that line, which ruled before, and in that degree of it, which used to succeed; though perhaps in so distant a period, that scarce any man alive could ever have given any promise of obedience. Has a government, then, no authority over such as these, because they never consented to it, and would esteem the very attempt of such a free choice a piece of arrogance and impiety? We find by experience, that it punishes them very freely for what it calls treason and rebellion, which, it seems, according to this system, reduces itself to common injustice. If you say, that by dwelling in its dominions, they in effect consented to the established government; I answer, that this can only be, where they think the affair depends on their choice, which few or none, beside those philosophers, have ever yet imagined. It never was pleaded as an excuse for a rebel, that the first act he performed, after he came to years of discretion, was to levy war against the sovereign of the state; and that while he was a child he could not bind himself by his own consent, and having become a man, showed plainly, by the first act he performed, that he had no design to impose on himself any obligation to obedience. We find, on the contrary, that civil laws punish this crime at the same age as any other, which is criminal, of itself, without our consent; that is, when the person is come to the full use of reason; whereas to this crime they ought in justice to allow some intermediate time, in which a tacit consent at least might be supposed. To which we may add, that a man living under an absolute government, would owe it no allegiance; since, by its very nature, it depends not on consent. But as that is as *natural* and *common* a government as any, it must certainly occasion some obligation; and it is plain from experience, that men, who are subjected to it, do always think so. This is a clear proof, that we do not commonly esteem our allegiance to be derived from our consent or promise; and a farther proof is, that when our promise is upon any account expressly engaged, we always distinguish exactly betwixt the two obligations, and believe the one to add more force to the other, than in a repetition of the same promise. Where no promise is given, a man looks not on his faith as broken in private matters, upon account of rebellion; but keeps those two duties of honour and allegiance perfectly distinct and separate. As the uniting of them was thought by these philosophers a very subtle invention, this is a convincing proof, that it is not a true one; since no man can either give a promise, or be restrained by its sanction and obligation unknown to himself.

Section IX *Of the measures of allegiance*

Those political writers, who have had recourse to a promise, or original contract, as the source of our allegiance to government, intended to establish a principle, which is perfectly just and reasonable; though the reasoning, upon which they endeavoured to establish it, was fallacious and sophistical. They would prove, that our submission to government admits of exceptions, and that an egregious tyranny in the rulers is sufficient to free the subjects from all ties of allegiance. Since men enter into society, say they, and submit themselves to government, by their free and voluntary consent, they must have in view certain advantages, which they propose to reap from it, and for which they are contented to resign their native liberty. There is, therefore, something mutual engaged on the part of the magistrate, *viz.* protection and security; and it is only by the hopes he affords of these advantages, that he can ever persuade men to submit to him. But when instead of protection and security, they meet with tyranny and oppression, they are freed from their promises, (as happens in all conditional contracts) and return to that state of liberty, which preceded the institution of government. Men would never be so foolish as to enter into such engagements as should turn entirely to the advantage of others, without any view of bettering their own condition. Whoever proposes to draw any profits from our submission, must engage himself, either expressly or tacitly, to make us reap some advantage from his authority; nor ought he to expect, that without the performance of his part we will ever continue in obedience.

I repeat it; this conclusion is just, though the principles be erroneous; and I flatter myself, that I can establish the same conclusion on more reasonable principles. I shall not take such a compass, in establishing our political duties, as to assert, that men perceive the advantages of government; that they institute government with a view to those advantages; that this institution requires a promise of obedience; which imposes a moral obligation to a certain degree, but being conditional, ceases to be binding, whenever the other contracting party performs not his part of the engagement. I perceive, that a promise itself arises entirely from human conventions, and is invented with a view to a certain interest. I seek, therefore, some such interest more immediately connected with government, and which may be at once the original motive to its institution, and the source of our obedience to it. This interest I find to consist in the security and protection, which we enjoy in political society, and which we can never attain, when perfectly free and independent. As interest, therefore, is the immediate sanction of government, the one can have no longer being than the other; and whenever the civil magistrate carries his oppression so far as to render his authority perfectly intolerable, we are no longer bound to submit to it. The cause ceases; the effect must cease also.

So far the conclusion is immediate and direct, concerning the *natural* obligation which we have to allegiance. As to the *moral* obligation, we may observe, that the maxim would here be false, that *when the cause ceases, the effect must cease also*. For there is a principle of human nature, which we have frequently taken notice of, that men are mightily addicted to *general rules*, and that we often carry our maxims beyond those reasons, which first induced us to establish them. Where cases are similar in many circumstances, we are apt to put them on the same footing, without considering, that they differ in the most material circumstances, and that the resemblance is more apparent than real. It may, therefore, be thought, that in the case of allegiance our moral obligation of duty will not cease, even though the natural obligation of interest, which is its cause, has ceased; and that men may be bound by *conscience* to submit to a tyrannical government against their own and the public interest. And indeed, to the force of this argument I so far submit, as to acknowledge, that general rules commonly extend beyond the principles, on which they are founded; and that we seldom make any exception to them, unless that exception have the qualities of a general rule, and be founded on very numerous and common instances. Now this I assert to be entirely the present case. When men submit to the authority of others, it is to procure themselves some security against the wickedness and injustice of men, who are perpetually carried, by their unruly passions, and by their present and immediate interest, to the violation of all the laws of society. But as this imperfection is inherent in human nature, we know that it must attend men in all their states and conditions; and that those, whom we choose for rulers, do not immediately become of a superior nature to the rest of mankind, upon account of their superior power and authority. What we expect from them depends not on a change of their nature but of their situation, when they acquire a more immediate interest in the preservation of order and the execution of justice. But besides that this interest is only more immediate in the execution of justice among their subjects; besides this, I say, we may often expect, from the irregularity of human nature, that they will neglect even this immediate interest, and be transported by their passions into all the excesses of cruelty and ambition. Our general knowledge of human nature, our observation of the past history of mankind, our experience of present times; all these causes must induce us to open the door to exceptions, and must make us conclude, that we may resist the more violent effects of supreme power, without any crime or injustice.

Accordingly we may observe, that this is both the general practice and principle of mankind, and that no nation, that could find any remedy, ever yet suffered the cruel ravages of a tyrant, or were blam'd for their resistance. Those who took up arms against *Dionysius* or *Nero*, or *Philip the second*, have the favour of every reader in the perusal of their history; and nothing but the most violent perversion of common sense can ever lead us to condemn them. It is certain, therefore, that in all our notions of morals we never entertain such an absurdity as that of passive obedience, but make allowances for resistance in the more flagrant instances of tyranny and oppression. The general opinion of mankind has some authority in all cases; but in this of morals it is perfectly infallible. Nor is it less infallible, because men cannot distinctly explain the principles, on which it is founded. Few persons can carry on this train of reasoning: 'Government is a mere human invention for the interest of society. Where the tyranny of the governor removes this interest, it also removes the natural obligation to obedience. The moral obligation is founded on the natural, and therefore must cease where *that* ceases; especially where the subject is such as makes us foresee very many occasions wherein the natural obligation may cease, and causes us to form a kind of general rule for the regulation of our conduct in such occurrences.' But though this train of reasoning be too subtle for the vulgar, it is certain, that all men have an implicit notion of it, and are sensible, that they owe obedience to government merely on account of the public interest; and at the same time, that human nature is so subject to frailties and passions, as may easily pervert this institution, and change their governors into tyrants and public enemies. If the sense of common interest were not our original motive to obedience, I would fain ask, what other principle is there in human nature capable of subduing the natural ambition of men, and forcing them to such a submission? Imitation and custom are not sufficient. For the question still recurs, what motive first produces those instances of submission, which we imitate, and that train of actions, which produces the custom? There evidently is no other principle than common interest; and if interest first produces obedience to government, the obligation to obedience must cease, whenever the interest ceases, in any great degree, and in a considerable number of instances.

SECTION X *Of the objects of allegiance*

But though, on some occasions, it may be justifiable, both in sound politics and morality, to resist supreme power, it is certain, that in the ordinary course of human affairs nothing can be more pernicious and criminal; and that besides the convulsions, which always attend revolutions, such a practice tends directly to the subversion of all government, and the causing an universal anarchy and confusion among mankind. As numerous and civilized societies cannot subsist without government, so government is entirely useless without an exact obedience. We ought always to weigh the advantages, which we reap from authority, against the disadvantages; and by this means we shall become more scrupulous of putting in practice the doctrine of resistance. The common rule requires submission; and it is only in cases of grievous tyranny and oppression, that the exception can take place.

Since then such a blind submission is commonly due to magistracy, the next question is, *to whom it is due, and whom we are to regard as our lawful magistrates?* In order to answer this question, let us recollect what we have already established concerning the origin of government and political society. When men have once experienced the impossibility of preserving any steady order in society, while everyone is his own master, and violates or observes the laws of society, according to his present interest or pleasure, they naturally run into the invention of government, and put it out of their own power, as far as possible, to transgress the laws of society. Government, therefore, arises from the voluntary convention of men; and it is evident, that the same convention, which establishes government, will also determine the persons who are to govern, and will remove all doubt and ambiguity in this particular. And the voluntary consent of men must here have the greater efficacy, that the authority of the magistrate does *at first* stand upon the foundation of a promise of the subjects, by which they bind themselves to obedience; as in every other contract or engagement. The same promise, then, which binds them to obedience, ties them down to a particular person, and makes him the object of their allegiance.

But when government has been established on this footing for some considerable time, and the separate interest, which we have in submission, has produced a separate sentiment of morality, the case is entirely altered, and a promise is no longer able to determine the particular magistrate; since it is no longer considered as the foundation of government. We naturally suppose ourselves born to submission; and imagine, that such particular persons have a right to command, as we on our part are bound to obey. These notions of right and obligation are derived from nothing but the *advantage* we reap from government, which gives us a repugnance to practise resistance ourselves, and makes us displeased with any instance of it in others. But here it is remarkable, that in this new state of affairs, the original sanction of government, which is *interest*, is not admitted to determine the persons, whom we are to obey, as the original sanction did at first, when affairs were on the footing of a *promise*. A *promise* fixes and determines the persons, without any uncertainty; but it is evident, that if men were to regulate their conduct in this particular, by the view of a peculiar *interest*, either public or private, they would involve themselves in endless confusion, and would render all government, in a great measure, ineffectual. The private interest of everyone is different; and though the public interest in itself be always one and the same, yet it becomes the source of as great dissentions, by reason of the different opinions of particular persons concerning it. The same interest, therefore, which causes us to submit to magistracy, makes us renounce itself in the choice of our magistrates, and binds us down to a certain form of government, and to particular persons, without allowing us to aspire to the utmost perfection in either. The case is here the same as in that law of nature concerning the stability of possession. It is highly advantageous, and even absolutely necessary to society, that possession should be stable; and this leads us to the establishment of such a rule; but we find, that were we to follow the same advantage, in assigning particular possessions to particular persons, we should disappoint our end, and perpetuate the confusion, which that rule is intended to prevent. We must, therefore, proceed by general rules, and regulate ourselves by general interests, in modifying the law of nature concerning the stability of possession. Nor need we fear, that our attachment to this law will diminish upon account of the seeming frivolousness of those interests, by which it is determined. The impulse of the mind is derived from a very strong interest; and those other more minute interests serve only to direct the motion, without adding anything to it, or diminishing from it. It is the same case with government. Nothing is more advantageous to society than such an invention; and this interest is sufficient to make us embrace it with ardour and alacrity; though we are obliged afterwards to regulate and direct our devotion to government by several considerations, which are not of the same importance, and to choose our magistrates without having in view any particular advantage from the choice.

The *first* of those principles I shall take notice of, as a foundation of the right of magistracy, is that which gives authority to all the most established governments of the world without exception; I mean, *long possession* in any one form of government, or succession of princes. It is certain, that if we remount to the first origin of every nation, we shall find, that there scarce is any race of kings, or form of a commonwealth, that is not primarily founded on usurpation and rebellion, and whose title is not at first worse than doubtful and uncertain. Time alone gives solidity to their right; and operating gradually on the minds of men, reconciles them to any authority, and makes it seem just and reasonable. Nothing causes any sentiment to have a greater influence upon us than custom, or turns our imagination more strongly to any object. When we have been long accustomed to obey any set of men, that general instinct or tendency, which we have to suppose a moral obligation attending loyalty, takes easily this direction, and chooses that set of men for its objects. It is interest which gives the general instinct; but it is custom which gives the particular direction.

And here it is observable, that the same length of time has a different influence on our sentiments of morality, according to its different influence on the mind. We naturally judge of everything by comparison; and since in considering the fate of kingdoms and republics, we embrace a long extent of time, a small duration has not in this case a like influence on our sentiments, as when we consider any other object. One thinks he acquires a right to a horse, or a suit of clothes, in a very short time; but a century is scarce sufficient to establish any new government, or remove all scruples in the minds of the subjects concerning it. Add to this, that a shorter period of time will suffice to give a prince a title to any additional power he may usurp, than will serve to fix his right, where the whole is an usurpation. The kings of *France* have not been possessed of absolute power for above two reigns; and yet nothing will appear more extravagant to *Frenchmen* than to talk of their liberties. If we consider what has been said concerning *accession*, we shall easily account for this phenomenon.

When there is no form of government established by *long* possession, the *present* possession is sufficient to supply its place, and may be regarded as the *second* source of all public authority. Right to authority is nothing but the constant possession of authority, maintained by the laws of society and the interests of mankind; and nothing can be more natural than to join this constant possession to the present one, according to the principles above-mentioned. If the same principles did not take place with regard to the property of private persons, it was because these principles were counter-balanced by very strong considerations of interest; when we observed, that all restitution would by that means be prevented, and every violence be authorized and protected. And though the same motives may seem to have force, with regard to public authority, yet they are opposed by a contrary interest; which consists in the preservation of peace, and the avoiding of all changes, which, however they may be easily produced in private affairs, are unavoidably attended with bloodshed and confusion, where the public is interested.

Anyone, who finding the impossibility of accounting for the right of the present possessor, by any received system of ethics, should resolve to deny absolutely that right, and assert, that it is not authorized, by morality, would be justly thought to maintain a very extravagant paradox, and to shock the common sense and judgment of mankind. No maxim is more conformable, both to prudence and morals, than to submit quietly to the government, which we find established in the country where we happen to live, without inquiring too curiously into its origin and first establishment. Few governments will bear being examined so rigorously. How many kingdoms are there at present in the world, and how many more do we find in history, whose governors have no better foundation for their authority than that of present possession? To confine ourselves to the *Roman* and *Grecian* empire; is it not evident, that the long succession of emperors, from the dissolution of the *Roman* liberty, to the final extinction of that empire by the *Turks*, could not so much as pretend to any other title to the empire? The election of the senate was a mere form, which always followed the choice of the legions; and these were almost always divided in the different provinces, and nothing but the sword was able to terminate the difference. It was by the sword, therefore, that every emperor acquired, as well as defended his right; and we must either say, that all the known world, for so many ages, had no government, and owed no allegiance to anyone, or must allow, that the right of the stronger, in public affairs, is to be received as legitimate, and authorized by morality, when not opposed by any other title.

The right of *conquest* may be considered as a *third* source of the title of sovereigns. This right resembles very much that of present possession; but has rather a superior force, being seconded by the notions of glory and honour, which we ascribe to *conquerors*, instead of the sentiments of hatred and detestation, which attend *usurpers*. Men naturally favour those they love; and therefore are more apt to ascribe a right to successful violence, betwixt one sovereign and another, than to the successful rebellion of a subject against his sovereign.*

When neither long possession, nor present possession, nor conquest take place, as when the first sovereign, who founded any monarchy, dies; in that case, the right of *succession* naturally prevails in their stead, and men are commonly

* It is not here asserted, that *present possession* or *conquest* are sufficient to give a title against *long possession* and *positive laws*; but only that they have some force, and will be able to cast the balance where the titles are otherwise equal, and will even be sufficient *sometimes* to sanctify the weaker title. What degree of force they have is difficult to determine. I believe all moderate men will allow, that they have great force in all disputes concerning the rights of princes.

induced to place the son of their late monarch on the throne, and suppose him to inherit his father's authority. The presumed consent of the father, the imitation of the succession to private families, the interest, which the state has in choosing the person, who is most powerful, and has the most numerous followers; all these reasons lead men to prefer the son of their late monarch to any other person.*

These reasons have some weight; but I am persuaded, that to one, who considers impartially of the matter, it will appear, that there concur some principles of the imagination, along with those views of interest. The royal authority seems to be connected with the young prince even in his father's life-time, by the natural transition of the thought; and still more after his death; so that nothing is more natural than to complete this union by a new relation, and by putting him actually in possession of what seems so naturally to belong to him.

To confirm this we may weigh the following phenomena, which are pretty curious in their kind. In elective monarchies the right of succession has no place by the laws and settled custom; and yet its influence is so natural, that it is impossible entirely to exclude it from the imagination, and render the subjects indifferent to the son of their deceased monarch. Hence in some governments of this kind, the choice commonly falls on one or other of the royal family; and in some governments they are all excluded. Those contrary phenomena proceed from the same principle. Where the royal family is excluded, it is from a refinement in politics, which makes people sensible of their propensity to choose a sovereign in that family, and gives them a jealousy of their liberty, lest their new monarch, aided by this propensity, should establish his family, and destroy the freedom of elections for the future.

The history of *Artaxerxes*, and the younger *Cyrus*, may furnish us with some reflections to the same purpose. *Cyrus* pretended a right to the throne above his elder brother, because he was born after his father's accession. I do not pretend, that this reason was valid. I would only infer from

---

* To prevent mistakes I must observe that this case of succession is not the same with that of hereditary monarchies, where custom has fixed the right of succession. These depend upon the principles of long possession above-explained.

it, that he would never have made use of such a pretext, were it not for the qualities of the imagination-above-mentioned, by which we are naturally inclined to unite by a new relation whatever objects we find already united. *Artaxerxes* had an advantage above his brother, as being the eldest son, and the first in succession; but *Cyrus* was more closely related to the royal authority, as being begot after his father was invested with it.

Should it here be pretended, that the view of convenience may be the source of all the right of succession, and that men gladly take advantage of any rule, by which they can fix the successor of their late sovereign, and prevent that anarchy and confusion, which attends all new elections; to this I would answer, that I readily allow, that this motive may contribute something to the effect; but at the same time I assert, that without another principle, it is impossible such a motive should take place. This interest of a nation requires, that the succession to the crown should be fixed one way or other; but it is the same thing to its interest in what way it be fixed; so that if the relation of blood had not an effect independent of public interest, it would never have been regarded, without a positive law; and it would have been impossible, that so many positive laws of different nations could ever have concurred precisely in the same views and intentions.

This leads us to consider the *fifth* source of authority, *viz.* *positive laws*; when the legislature establishes a certain form of government and succession of princes. At first sight it may be thought, that this must resolve into some of the preceding titles of authority. The legislative power, whence the positive law is derived, must either be established by original contract, long possession, present possession, conquest, or succession; and consequently the positive law must derive its force from some of those principles. But here it is remarkable, that though a positive law can only derive its force from these principles, yet it acquires not all the force of the principle from whence it is derived, but loses considerably in the transition; as it is natural to imagine. For instance; a government is established for many centuries on a certain system of laws, forms, and methods of succession. The legislative power, established by this long succession, changes all on a sudden the whole system of government, and introduces a new constitution in its stead. I believe few of the subjects will think themselves bound to comply with this alteration, unless it have an evident tendency to the public good; but will think themselves still at liberty to return to the ancient government. Hence the notion of *fundamental laws*; which are supposed to be inalterable by the will of the sovereign; and of this nature the *Salic* law is understood to to be in *France*. How far these fundamental laws extend is not determined in any government; nor is it possible it ever should. There is such an insensible gradation from the most material laws to the most trivial, and from the most ancient laws to the most modern, that it will be impossible to set bounds to the legislative power, and determine how far it may innovate in the principles of government. That is the work more of imagination and passion than of reason.

Whoever considers the history of the several nations of the world; their revolutions, conquests, increase, and diminution; the manner in which their particular governments are established, and the successive right transmitted from one person to another, will soon learn to treat very lightly all disputes concerning the rights of princes, and will be convinced, that a strict adherence to any general rules, and the rigid loyalty to particular persons and families, on which some people set so high a value, are virtues that hold less of reason, than of bigotry and superstition. In this particular, the study of history confirms the reasonings of true philosophy; which, showing us the original qualities of human nature, teaches us to regard the controversies in politics as incapable of any decision in most cases, and as entirely subordinate to the interests of peace and liberty. Where the public good does not evidently demand a change; it is certain, that the concurrence of all those titles, *original contract, long possession, present possession, succession,* and *positive laws,* forms the strongest title to sovereignty, and is justly regarded as sacred and inviolable. But when these titles are mingled and opposed in different degrees, they often occasion perplexity; and are less capable of solution from the arguments of lawyers and philosophers, than from the swords of the soldiery. Who shall tell me, for instance, whether *Germanicus,* or *Drusus,* ought to have succeeded *Tiberius,* had he died while they were both alive, without naming any of them for his successor? Ought the right of adoption to be received as equivalent to that of blood in a nation, where it had the same effect in private families, and had already, in two instances, taken place in the public? Ought *Germanicus* to be esteemed the eldest son, because he was born before *Drusus*; or the younger, because he was adopted after the birth of his brother? Ought the right of the elder to be regarded in a nation where the eldest brother had no advantage in the succession to private families? Ought the *Roman* empire at that time to be esteemed hereditary, because of two examples; or ought it, even so early, to be regarded as belonging to the stronger, or the present possessor, as being founded on so recent an usurpation? Upon whatever principles we may pretend to answer these and such like questions, I am afraid we shall never be able to satisfy an impartial inquirer, who adopts no party in political controversies, and will be satisfied with nothing but sound reason and philosophy.

But here an *English* reader will be apt to inquire concerning that famous *revolution*, which has had such a happy influence on our constitution, and has been attended with such mighty consequences. We have already remarked, that in the case of enormous tyranny and oppression, it is lawful to take arms even against supreme power; and that as government is a mere human invention for mutual advantage and security, it no longer imposes any obligation, either natural or moral, when once it ceases to have that tendency. But though this *general* principle be authorized by common sense, and the practice of all ages, it is certainly impossible for the laws, or even for philosophy, to establish any *particular* rules, by which we may know when resistance is lawful; and decide all controversies, which may arise on that subject. This may not only happen with regard to supreme power; but it is possible, even in some constitutions, where the legislative authority is not lodged in one person, that there may be a magistrate so eminent and powerful, as to oblige the laws to keep silence in this particular. Nor would this silence be an effect only of their *respect*, but also of their *prudence*; since it is certain, that in the vast variety of circumstances, which occur in all governments, an exercise of power, in so great a magistrate, may at one time be beneficial to the public, which at another time would be pernicious and tyrannical. But notwithstanding this silence of the laws in limited monarchies, it is certain, that the people still retain the right of resistance; since it is impossible, even in the most despotic governments, to deprive them of it. The same necessity of self-preservation, and the same motive of public good, give them the same liberty in the one case as in the other. And we may farther observe, that in such mixed governments, the cases, wherein resistance is lawful, must occur much oftener, and greater indulgence be given to the subjects to defend themselves by force of arms, than in arbitrary governments. Not only where the chief magistrate enters into measures, in themselves, extremely pernicious to the public, but even when he would encroach on the other parts of the constitution, and extend his power beyond the legal bounds, it is allowable to resist and dethrone him; though such resistance and violence may, in the general tenor of the laws, be deemed unlawful and rebellious. For besides that nothing is more essential to public interest, than the preservation of public liberty; it is evident, that if such a mixed government be once supposed to be established, every part or member of the constitution must have a right of self-defence, and of maintaining its ancient bounds against the encroachment of every other authority. As matters would have been created in vain, were it deprived of a power of resistance, without which no part of it could preserve a distinct existence, and the whole might be crowded up into a single point: So it is a gross absurdity to suppose, in any government, a right without a remedy, or allow, that the supreme power is shared with the people, without allowing, that it is lawful for them to defend their share against every invader. Those, therefore, who would seem to respect our free government, and yet deny the right of resistance, have renounced all pretensions to common sense, and do not merit a serious answer.

It does not belong to my present purpose to show, that these general principles are applicable to the late *revolution*; and that all the rights and privileges, which ought to be sacred to a free nation, were at that time threatened with the utmost danger. I am better pleased to leave this controverted subject, if it really admits of controversy; and to indulge myself in some philosophical reflections, which naturally arise from that important event.

First, we may observe, that should the *lords* and *commons* in our constitution, without any reason from public interest, either depose the king in being, or after his death exclude the prince, who, by laws and settled custom, ought to succeed, no one would esteem their proceedings legal, or think themselves bound to comply with them. But should the king, by his unjust practices, or his attempts for a tyrannical and despotic power, justly forfeit his legal, it then *not only becomes morally lawful and suitable to the nature of political society to dethrone him; but what is more, we are apt likewise to think, that the remaining members of the constitution acquire a right of excluding his next heir, and of choosing whom they please for his successor. This is founded on a very singular quality of our thought and imagination. When a king forfeits his authority, his heir ought naturally to remain in the same situation, as if the king were removed by death; unless by mixing himself in the tyranny, he forfeit it for himself. But though this may seem reasonable, we easily comply with the contrary opinion. The deposition of a king, in such a government as ours, is certainly an act beyond all common authority, and an illegal assuming a power for public good, which, in the ordinary course of government, can belong to no member of the constitution. When the public good is so great and so evident as to justify the action, the commendable use of this licence causes us naturally to attribute to the *parliament* a right of using farther licences; and the ancient bounds of the laws being once transgressed with approbation, we are not apt to be so strict in confining ourselves precisely within their limits. The mind naturally runs on with any train of action, which it has begun; nor do we commonly make any scruple concerning our duty, after the first action of any kind, which we perform. Thus at the *revolution*, no one who thought the deposition of the father justifiable, esteemed themselves to be confined to his infant son; though had that unhappy monarch died innocent at that time, and had his son, by any accident, been conveyed beyond seas, there is no doubt but a regency would have been appointed till he should come to age, and could be restored to his dominions. As the slightest properties of the imagination have an effect on the judgments of the people, it shows the wisdom of the laws and of the parliament to take advantage of such properties, and to choose the magistrates either in or out of a line, according as the vulgar will most naturally attribute authority and right to them.

Secondly, though the accession of the *Prince* of *Orange* to the throne might at first give occasion to many disputes, and his title be contested, it ought not now to appear doubtful, but must have acquired a sufficient authority from those three princes, who have succeeded him upon the same title. Nothing is more usual, though nothing may, at first sight, appear more unreasonable, than this way of thinking. Princes often *seem* to acquire a right from their successors, as well as from their ancestors; and a king, who during his lifetime might justly be deemed an usurper, will be regarded by posterity as a lawful prince, because he has had the good fortune to settle his family on the throne, and entirely change the ancient form of government. *Julius Cæsar* is regarded as the first *Roman* emperor; while *Sylla* and *Marius*, whose titles were really the same as his, are treated as tyrants and usurpers. Time and custom give authority to all forms of government, and all successions of princes; and that power, which at first was founded only on injustice and violence, becomes in time legal and obligatory. Nor does the mind rest there; but returning back upon its footsteps, transfers to their predecessors and ancestors that right, which it naturally ascribes to the posterity, as being related together, and united in the imagination. The present *king* of *France* makes *Hugh Capet* a more lawful prince than *Cromwell*; as the established liberty of the *Dutch* is no inconsiderable apology for their obstinate resistance to *Philip* the Second.

Section XI *Of the laws of nations*

When civil government has been established over the greatest part of mankind, and different societies have been formed contiguous to each other, there arises a new set of duties among the neighbouring states, suitable to the nature of that commerce, which they carry on with each other. Political writers tell us, that in every kind of intercourse, a body politic is to be considered as one person; and indeed this assertion is so far just, that different nations, as well as private persons, require mutual assistance; at the same time that their selfishness and ambition are perpetual sources of war and discord. But though nations in this particular resemble individuals, yet as they are very different in other respects, no wonder they regulate themselves by different maxims, and give rise to a new set of rules, which we call *the laws of nations*. Under this head we may comprise the sacredness of the persons of ambassadors, the declaration of war, the abstaining from poisoned arms, with other duties of that kind, which are evidently calculated for the commerce, that is peculiar to different societies.

But though these rules be super-added to the laws of nature, the former do not entirely abolish the latter; and one may safely affirm, that the three fundamental rules of justice, the stability of possession, its transference by consent, and the performance of promises, are duties of princes, as well as of subjects. The same interest produces the same effect in both cases. Where possession has no stability, there must be perpetual war. Where property is not transferred by consent, there can be no commerce. Where promises are not observed, there can be no leagues nor alliances. The advantages, therefore, of peace, commerce, and mutual succour, make us extend to different kingdoms the same notions of justice, which take place among individuals.

There is a maxim very current in the world, which few politicians are willing to avow, but which has been authorized by the practice of all ages, *that there is a system of morals calculated for princes, much more free than that which ought to govern private persons*. It is evident this is not to be understood of the lesser *extent* of public duties and obligations; nor will anyone be so extravagant as to assert, that the most solemn treaties ought to have no force among princes. For as princes do actually form treaties among themselves, they must propose some advantage from the execution of them; and the prospect of such advantage for the future must engage them to perform their part, and must establish that law of nature. The meaning, therefore, of this political maxim is, that though the morality of princes has the same *extent*, yet it has not the same *force* as that of private persons, and may lawfully be transgressed from a more trivial motive. However shocking such a proposition may appear to certain philosophers, it will be easy to defend it upon those principles, by which we have accounted for the origin of justice and equity.

When men have found by experience, that it is impossible to subsist without society, and that it is impossible to maintain society, while they give free course to their appetites; so urgent an interest quickly restrains their actions, and imposes an obligation to observe those rules, which we call *the laws of justice*. This obligation of interest rests not here; but by the necessary course of the passions and sentiments, gives rise to the moral obligation of duty; while we approve of such actions as tend to the peace of society, and disapprove of such as tend to its disturbance. The same *natural* obligation of interest takes place among independent kingdoms, and gives to the same *morality*; so that no one of ever so corrupt morals will approve of a prince, who voluntarily, and of his own accord, breaks his word, or violates any treaty. But here we may observe, that though the intercourse of different states be advantageous, and even sometimes necessary, yet it is not so necessary nor advantageous as that among individuals, without which it is utterly impossible for human nature ever to subsist. Since, therefore, the *natural* obligation to justice, among different states, is not so strong as among individuals, the *moral* obligation, which arises from it, must partake of its weakness; and we must necessarily give a greater indulgence to a prince or minister, who deceives another; than to a private gentleman, who breaks his word of honour.

Should it be asked, *what proportion these two species of morality bear to each other?* I would answer, that this is a question, to which we can never give any precise answer; nor is it possible to reduce to numbers the proportion, which we ought to fix betwixt them. One may safely affirm, that this proportion finds itself, without any art or study of men; as we may observe on many other occasions. The practice of the world goes farther in teaching us the degrees of our duty, than the most subtle philosophy, which was ever yet invented. And this may serve as a convincing proof, that all men have an implicit notion of the foundation of those moral rules concerning natural and civil justice, and are sensible, that they arise merely from human conventions, and from the interest, which we have in the preservation of peace and order. For otherwise the diminution of the interest would never produce a relaxation of the morality, and reconcile us more easily to any transgression of justice among princes and republics, than in the private commerce of one subject with another.

SECTION XII *Of chastity and modesty*

If any difficulty attend this system concerning the laws of nature and nations, it will be with regard to the universal approbation or blame, which follows their observance or transgression, and which some may not think sufficiently explained from the general interests of society. To remove, as far as possible, all scruples of this kind, I shall here consider another set of duties, *viz.* the *modesty* and *chastity* which belong to the fair sex; and I doubt not but these virtues will be found to be still more conspicuous instances of the operation of those principles, which I have insisted on.

There are some philosophers, who attack the female virtues with great vehemence, and fancy they have gone very far in detecting popular errors, when they can show, that there is no foundation in nature for all that exterior modesty, which we require in the expressions, and dress, and behaviour of the fair sex. I believe I may spare myself the trouble of insisting on so obvious a subject, and may proceed, without farther preparation, to examine after what manner such notions arise from education, from the voluntary conventions of men, and from the interest of society.

Whoever considers the length and feebleness of human infancy, with the concern which both sexes naturally have for their offspring, will easily perceive, that there must be an union of male and female for the education of the young, and that this union must be of considerable duration. But in order to induce the men to impose on themselves this restraint, and undergo cheerfully all the fatigues and expenses, to which it subjects them, they must believe, that the children are their own, and that their natural instinct is not directed to a wrong object, when they give loose to love and tenderness. Now if we examine the structure of the human body, we shall find, that this security is very difficult to be attained on our part; and that since, in the copulation of the sexes, the principle of generation goes from the man to the woman, an error may easily take place on the side of the former, though it be utterly impossible with regard to the latter. From this trivial and anatomical observation is derived that vast difference betwixt the education and duties of the two sexes.

Were a philosopher to examine the matter *a priori*, he would reason after the following manner. Men are induced to labour for the maintenance and education of their children, by the persuasion that they are really their own; and therefore it is reasonable, and even necessary, to give them some security in this particular. This security cannot consist entirely in the imposing of severe punishments on any transgressions of conjugal fidelity on the part of the wife; since these public punishments cannot be inflicted without legal proof, which it is difficult to meet with in this subject. What restraint, therefore, shall we impose on women, in order to counterbalance so strong a temptation as they have to infidelity? There seems to be no restraint possible, but in the punishment of bad fame or reputation; a punishment, which has a mighty influence on the human mind, and at the same time is inflicted by the world upon surmises, and conjectures, and proofs, that would never be received in any court of judicature. In order, therefore, to impose a due restraint on the female sex, we must attach a peculiar degree of shame to their infidelity, above what arises merely from its injustice, and must bestow proportionable praises on their chastity.

But though this be a very strong motive to fidelity, our philosopher would quickly discover, that it would not alone be sufficient to that purpose. All human creatures, especially of the female sex, are apt to overlook remote motives in favour of any present temptation; the temptation is here the strongest imaginable; its approaches are insensible and seducing; and a woman easily finds, or flatters herself she shall find, certain means of securing her reputation, and preventing all the pernicious consequences of her pleasures. It is necessary, therefore, that, besides the infamy attending such licences, there should be some preceding backwardness or dread, which may prevent their first approaches, and may give the female sex a repugnance to all expressions, and postures, and liberties, that have an immediate relation to that enjoyment.

Such would be the reasonings of our speculative philosopher; but I am persuaded, that if he had not a perfect knowledge of human nature, he would be apt to regard them as mere chimerical speculations, and would consider the infamy attending infidelity, and backwardness to all its approaches, as principles that were rather to be wished than hoped for in the world. For what means, would he say, of persuading mankind, that the transgressions of conjugal duty are more infamous than any other kind of injustice, when it is evident they are more excusable, upon account of the greatness of the temptation? And what possibility of giving a backwardness to the approaches of a pleasure, to which nature has inspired so strong a propensity; and a propensity that it is absolutely necessary in the end to comply with, for the support of the species?

But speculative reasonings, which cost so much pains to philosophers, are often formed by the world naturally, and without reflection; as difficulties, which seem unsurmountable in theory, are easily got over in practice. Those, who have an interest in the fidelity of women, naturally disapprove of their infidelity, and all the approaches to it. Those, who have no interest, are carried along with the stream. Education takes possession of the ductile minds of the fair sex in their infancy. And when a general rule of this kind is once established, men are apt to extend it beyond those principles, from which it first arose. Thus batchelors, however debauched, cannot choose but be shocked with any instance of lewdness or impudence in women. And though all these maxims have a plain reference to generation, yet women past child-bearing have no more privilege in this respect, than those who are in the flower of their youth and beauty. Men have undoubtedly an implicit notion, that all those ideas of modesty and decency have a regard to generation; since they impose not the same laws, *with the same force*, on the male sex, where that reason takes not place. The exception is there obvious and extensive, and founded on a remarkable difference, which produces a clear separation and disjunction of ideas. But as the case is not the same with regard to the different ages of women, for this reason, though men know, that these notions are founded on the public interest, yet the general rule carries us beyond the original principle, and makes us extend the notions of modesty over the whole sex, from their earliest infancy to their extremest old-age and infirmity.

Courage, which is the point of honour among men, derives

its merit, in a great measure, from artifice, as well as the chastity of women; though it has also some foundation in nature, as we shall see afterwards.

As to the obligations which the male sex lie under, with regard to chastity, we may observe, that according to the general notions of the world, they bear nearly the same proportion of the obligations of women, as the obligations of the law of nations do to those of the law of nature. It is contrary to the interest of civil society, that men should have an *entire* liberty of indulging their appetites in venereal enjoyment; but as this interest is weaker than in the case of the female sex, the moral obligation, arising from it, must be proportionably weaker. And to prove this we need only appeal to the practice and sentiments of all nations and ages.

PART III *Of the Other Virtues and Vices*

SECTION I *Of the origin of the natural virtues and vices*

We come to the examination of such virtues and vices as are entirely natural, and have no dependence on the artifice and contrivance of men. The examination of these will conclude this system of morals.

The chief spring or actuating principle of the human mind is pleasure or pain; and when these sensations are removed, both from our thought and feeling, we are, in a great measure, incapable of passion or action, of desire or volition. The most immediate effects of pleasure and pain are the propense and averse motions of the mind; which are diversified into volition, into desire and aversion, grief and joy, hope and fear, according as the pleasure or pain changes its situation, and becomes probable or improbable, certain or uncertain, or is considered as out of our power for the present moment. But when along with this, the objects, that cause pleasure or pain, acquire a relation to ourselves or others; they still continue to excite desire and aversion, grief; and joy; but cause, at the same time, the indirect passions of pride or humility, love or hatred, which in this case have a double relation of impressions and ideas to the pain or pleasure.

We have already observed, that moral distinctions depend entirely on certain peculiar sentiments of pain and pleasure, and that whatever mental quality in ourselves or others gives us a satisfaction, by the survey or reflection, is of course virtuous; as everything of this nature, that gives uneasiness, is vicious. Now since every quality in ourselves or others, which gives pleasure, always causes pride or love; as every one, that produces uneasiness, excites humility or hatred; it follows, that these two particulars are to be considered as equivalent, with regard to our mental qualities, *virtue* and the power of producing love or pride, *vice* and the power of producing humility or hatred. In every case, therefore, we must judge of the one by the other; and may pronounce any *quality* of the mind virtuous, which causes love or pride; and any one vicious, which causes hatred or humility.

If any *action* be either virtuous or vicious, it is only as a sign of some quality or character. It must depend upon durable principles of the mind, which extend over the whole conduct, and enter into the personal character. Actions themselves, not proceeding from any constant principle, have no influence on love or hatred, pride or humility; and consequently are never considered in morality.[41]

This reflection is self-evident, and deserves to be attended to, as being of the utmost importance in the present subject. We are never to consider any single action in our enquiries concerning the origin of morals; but only the quality or character from which the action proceeded. These alone are *durable* enough to affect our sentiments concerning the person. Actions are, indeed, better indications of a character than words, or even wishes and sentiments; but it is only so far as they are such indications, that they are attended with love or hatred, praise or blame.

To discover the true origin of morals, and of that love or hatred, which arises from mental qualities, we must take the matter pretty deep, and compare some principles, which have been already examined and explained.

We may begin with considering anew the nature and force of *sympathy*. The minds of all men are similar in their feelings and operations, nor can anyone be actuated by any affection, of which all others are not, in some degree, susceptible. As in strings equally wound up, the motion of one communicates itself to the rest; so all the affections readily pass from one person to another, and beget correspondent movements in every human creature. When I see the *effects* of passion in the voice and gesture of any person, my mind immediately passes from these effects to their causes, and forms such a lively idea of the passion, as is presently converted into the passion itself. In like manner, when I perceive the *causes* of any emotion, my mind is conveyed to the effects, and is actuated with a like emotion. Were I present at any of the more terrible operations of surgery, it is certain, that even before it begun, the preparation of the instruments, the laying of the bandages in order, the heating of the irons, with all the signs of anxiety and concern in the patients and assistants, would have a great effect upon my mind, and excite the strongest sentiments of pity and terror. No passion of another discovers itself immediately to the mind. We are only sensible of its causes or effects. From *these* we infer the passion; and consequently *these* give rise to our sympathy.

Our sense of beauty depends very much on this principle; and where any object has a tendency to produce pleasure in its possessor, it is always regarded as beautiful; as every object, that has a tendency to produce pain, is disagreeable and deformed. Thus the conveniency of a house, the fertility of a field, the strength of a horse, the capacity, security, and swift-sailing of a vessel, form the principal beauty of these several objects. Here the object, which is denominated beautiful, pleases only by its tendency to produce a certain effect. That effect is the pleasure or advantage of some other person. Now the pleasure of a stranger, for whom we have no friendship, pleases us only by sympathy. To this principle, therefore, is owing the beauty, which we find in everything that is useful. How considerable a part this is of beauty will easily appear upon reflection. Wherever an object has a tendency to produce pleasure in the possessor, or in other words, is the proper *cause* of pleasure, it is sure to please the spectator, by a delicate sympathy with the possessor. Most of the works of art are esteemed beautiful, in proportion to their fitness for the use of man, and even many of the productions of nature derive their beauty from that source. Handsome and beautiful, on most occasions, is not an absolute but a relative quality, and pleases us by nothing but its tendency to produce an end that is agreeable.*

The same principle produces, in many instances, our sentiments of morals, as well as those of beauty. No virtue is more esteemed than justice, and no vice more detested than injustice; nor are there any qualities, which go farther to fixing the character, either as amiable or odious. Now justice is a moral virtue, merely because it has that tendency to the good of mankind; and, indeed, is nothing but an artificial invention to that purpose. The same may be said of allegiance, of the laws of nations, of modesty, and of good-manners. All these are mere human contrivances for the

* Decentior equus cujus astricta sunt ilia; sed idem velocior. Pulcher aspectu sit athleta, cujus lacertos exercitatio expressit; idem certamini paratior. Nunquam vero *species* ab *utilitate* dividitur. Sed hoc quidem discernere, modici judicii est. *Quinct.* lib. 8.

interest of society. And since there is a very strong sentiment of morals, which in all nations, and all ages, has attended them, we must allow, that the reflecting on the tendency of characters and mental qualities, is sufficient to give us the sentiments of approbation and blame. Now as the means to an end can only be agreeable, where the end is agreeable; and as the good of society, where our own interest is not concerned, or that of our friends, pleases only by sympathy; it follows, that sympathy is the source of the esteem, which we pay to all the artificial virtues.

Thus it appears, *that* sympathy is a very powerful principle in human nature, *that* it has a great influence on our taste of beauty, and *that* it produces our sentiment of morals in all the artificial virtues. From thence we may presume, that it also gives rise to many of the other virtues; and that qualities acquire our approbation, because of their tendency to the good of mankind. This presumption must become a certainty, when we find that most of those qualities, which we *naturally* approve of, have actually that tendency, and render a man a proper member of society; while the qualities, which we *naturally* disapprove of, have a contrary tendency, and render any intercourse with the person dangerous or disagreeable. For having found, that such tendencies have force enough to produce the strongest sentiment of morals, we can never reasonably, in these cases, look for any other cause of approbation or blame; it being an inviolable maxim in philosophy, that where any particular cause is sufficient for an effect, we ought to rest satisfied with it, and ought not to multiply causes without necessity. We have happily attained experiments in the artificial virtues, where the tendency of qualities to the good of society, is the *sole* cause of our approbation, without any suspicion of the concurrence of another principle. From thence we learn the force of that principle. And where that principle may take place, and the quality approved of is really beneficial to society, a true philosopher will never require any other principle to account for the strongest approbation and esteem.

That many of the natural virtues have this tendency to the good of society, no one can doubt of. Meekness, beneficence, charity, generosity, clemency, moderation, equity, bear the greatest figure among the moral qualities, and are commonly denominated the *social* virtues, to mark their tendency to the good of society. This goes so far, that some philosophers have represented all moral distinctions as the effect of artifice and education, when skilful politicians endeavoured to restrain the turbulent passions of men, and make them operate to the public good, by the notions of honour and shame. This system, however, is not consistent with experience. For, *first*, there are other virtues and vices besides those which have this tendency to the public advantage and loss. *Secondly*, had not men a natural sentiment of approbation and blame, it could never be excited by politicians; nor would the words *laudable* and *praiseworthy*, *blameable* and *odious*, be any more intelligible, than if they were a language perfectly unknown to us, as we have already observed. But though this system be erroneous, it may teach us, that moral distinctions arise, in a great measure, from the tendency of qualities and characters to the interests of society, and that it is our concern for that interest, which makes us approve or disapprove of them. Now we have no such extensive concern for society but from sympathy; and consequently it is that principle, which takes us so far out of ourselves, as to give us the same pleasure or uneasiness in the characters of others, as if they had a tendency to our own advantage or loss.

The only difference betwixt the natural virtues and justice lies in this, that the good, which results from the former, arises from every single act, and is the object of some natural passion; whereas a single act of justice, considered in itself, may often be contrary to the public good; and it is only the concurrence of mankind, in a general scheme or system of action, which is advantageous. When I relieve persons in distress, my natural humanity is my motive; and so far as my succour extends, so have I promoted the happiness of my fellow-creatures. But if we examine all the questions, that come before any tribunal of justice, we shall find, that, considering each case apart, it would as often be an instance of humanity to decide contrary to the laws of justice as conformable to them. Judges take from a poor man to give to a rich; they bestow on the dissolute the labour of the industrious; and put into the hands of the vicious the means of harming both themselves and others. The whole scheme, however, of law and justice is advantageous to the society; and it was with a view to this advantage, that men, by their voluntary conventions, established it. After it is once established by these conventions, it is *naturally* attended with a strong sentiment of morals; which can proceed from nothing but our sympathy with the interests of society. We need no other explication of that esteem, which attends such of the natural virtues, as have a tendency to the public good.

I must farther add, that there are several circumstances, which render this hypothesis much more probable with regard to the natural than the artificial virtues. It is certain, that the imagination is more affected by what is particular, than by what is general; and that the sentiments are always moved with difficulty, where their objects are, in any degree, loose and undetermined; now every particular act of justice is not beneficial to society, but the whole scheme or system; and it may not, perhaps, be any individual person, for whom we are concerned, who receives benefit from justice, but the whole society alike. On the contrary, every particular act of generosity, or relief of the industrious and indigent, is beneficial; and is beneficial to a particular person, who is not underserving of it. It is more natural, therefore, to think, that the tendencies of the latter virtue will affect our sentiments, and command our approbation, than those of the former; and therefore, since we find, that the approbation of the former arises from their tendencies, we may ascribe, with better reason, the same cause to the approbation of the latter. In any number of similar effects, if a cause can be discovered for one, we ought to extend that cause to all the other effects, which can be accounted for by it; but much more, if these other effects be attended with peculiar circumstances, which facilitate the operation of that cause.

Before I proceed farther, I must observe two remarkable circumstances in this affair, which may seem objections to the present system. The first may be thus explained. When any quality, or character, has a tendency to the good of mankind, we are pleased with it, and approve of it; because it presents the lively idea of pleasure; which idea affects us by sympathy, and is itself a kind of pleasure. But as this sympathy is very variable, it may be thought, that our sentiments of morals must admit of all the same variations. We sympathize more with persons contiguous to us, than with persons remote from us; with our acquaintance, than with strangers; with our countrymen, than with foreigners. But notwithstanding this variation of our sympathy, we give the same approbation to the same moral qualities in *China* as in *England*. They appear equally virtuous, and recommend themselves equally to the esteem of a judicious spectator. The sympathy varies without a variation in our esteem. Our esteem, therefore, proceeds not from sympathy.

To this I answer: the approbation of moral qualities most certainly is not derived from reason, or any comparison of ideas; but proceeds entirely from a moral taste, and from certain sentiments of pleasure or disgust, which arise upon the contemplation and view of particular qualities or characters. Now it is evident, that those sentiments, whence-ever they are derived, must vary according to the distance or contiguity of the objects; nor can I feel the same lively pleasure from the virtues of a person, who lived in *Greece* two thousand years ago, that I feel from the virtues of a familiar friend and acquaintance. Yet I do not say, that I esteem the one more than the other; and therefore, if the variation of the sentiment, without a variation of the esteem, be an objection, it must have equal force against every other system, as against that of sympathy. But to consider the matter aright, it has no force at all; and it is the easiest matter in the world to account for it. Our situation, with regard both to persons and things, is in continual fluctuation; and a man, that lies at a distance from us, may, in a little time, become a familiar acquaintance. Besides, every particular man has a peculiar position with regard to others; and it is impossible we could ever converse together on any reasonable terms, were each of us to consider characters and persons, only as they appear from his peculiar point of view. In order, therefore, to prevent those continual *contradictions*, and arrive at a more *stable* judgment of things, we fix on some *steady* and *general* points of view; and always, in our thoughts, place ourselves in them, whatever may be our present situation. In like manner, external beauty is determined merely by pleasure; and it is evident, a beautiful countenance cannot give so much pleasure, when seen at the distance of twenty paces, as when it is brought nearer us. We say not, however, that it appears to us less beautiful; because we know what effect it will have in such a position, and by that reflection we correct its momentary appearance.

In general, all sentiments of blame or praise are variable, according to our situation of nearness or remoteness, with regard to the person blamed or praised, and according to the present disposition of our mind. But these variations we regard not in our general decisions, but still apply the terms expressive of our liking or dislike, in the same manner, as if we remained in one point of view. Experience soon teaches us this method of correcting our sentiments, or at least, of correcting our language, where the sentiments are more stubborn and inalterable. Our servant, if diligent and faithful, may excite stronger sentiments of love and kindness than *Marcus Brutus,* as represented in history; but we say not upon that account, that the former character is more laudable than the latter. We know, that were we to approach equally near to that renowned patriot, he would command a much higher degree of affection and admiration. Such corrections are common with regard to all the senses; and indeed it were impossible we could ever make use of language, or communicate our sentiments to one another, did we not correct the momentary appearances of things, and overlook our present situation.

It is therefore from the influence of characters and qualities, upon those who have an intercourse with any person, that we blame or praise him. We consider not whether the persons, affected by the qualities, be our acquaintance or strangers, countrymen or foreigners. Nay, we overlook our own interest in those general judgments; and blame not a man for opposing us in any of our pretensions, when his own interest is particularly concerned. We make allowance for a certain degree of selfishness in men; because we know it to be inseparable from human nature, and inherent in our frame and constitution. By this reflection we correct those sentiments of blame, which so naturally arise upon any opposition.

But however the general principle of our blame or praise may be corrected by those other principles, it is certain, they are not altogether efficacious, nor do our passions often correspond entirely to the present theory. It is seldom men heartily love what lies at a distance from them, and what no way redounds to their particular benefit; as it is no less rare to meet with persons, who can pardon another any opposition he makes to their interest, however justifiable that opposition may be by the general rules of morality. Here we are contented with saying, that reason requires such an impartial conduct, but that it is seldom we can bring ourselves to it, and that our passions do not readily follow the determination of our judgment. This language will be easily understood, if we consider what we formerly said concerning that *reason*, which is able to oppose our passion; and which we have found to be nothing but a general calm determination of the passions, founded on some distant view or reflection. When we form our judgments of persons, merely from the tendency of their characters to our own benefit, or to that of our friends, we find so many contradictions to our sentiments in society and conversation, and such an uncertainty from the incessant changes of our situation, that we seek some other standard of merit and demerit, which may not admit of so great variation. Being thus loosened from our first station, we cannot afterwards fix ourselves so commodiously by any means as by a sympathy with those, who have any commerce with the person we consider. This is far from being as lively as when our own interest is concerned, or that of our particular friends; nor has it such an influence on our love and hatred. But being equally comfortable to our calm and general principles, it is said to have an equal authority over our reason, and to command our judgment and opinion. We blame equally a bad action, which we read of in history, with one performed in our neighbourhood the other day; the meaning of which is, that we know from reflection, that the former action would excite as strong sentiments of disapprobation as the latter, were it placed in the same position.

I now proceed to the *second* remarkable circumstance, which I proposed to take notice of. Where a person is possessed of a character, that in its natural tendency is beneficial to society, we esteem him virtuous, and are delighted with the view of his character, even though particular accidents prevent its operation, and incapacitate him from being serviceable to his friends and country. Virtue in rags is still virtue; and the love, which it procures, attends a man into a dungeon or desart, where the virtue can no longer be exerted in action, and is lost to all the world. Now this may be esteemed an objection to the present system. Sympathy interests us in the good of mankind; and if sympathy were the source of our esteem for virtue, that sentiment of approbation could only take place, where the virtue actually attained its end, and was beneficial to mankind. Where it fails of its end, it is only an imperfect means; and therefore can never acquire any merit from that end. The goodness of an end can bestow a merit on such means alone as are complete, and actually produce the end.

To this we may reply, that where any object, in all its parts, is fitted to attain any agreeable end, it naturally gives us pleasure, and is esteemed beautiful, even though some external circumstances be wanting to render it altogether effectual. It is sufficient if everything be complete in the object itself. A house, that is contrived with great judgment for all the commodities of life, pleases us upon that account; though perhaps we are sensible, that no one will ever dwell in it. A fertile soil, and a happy climate, delight us by a reflexion on the happiness which they would afford the inhabitants, though at present the country be desert and uninhabited. A man, whose limbs and shape promise strength and activity, is esteemed handsome, though condemned to perpetual imprisonment. The imagination has a set of passions belonging to it, upon which our sentiments of beauty much depend. These passions are moved by degrees of liveliness and strength, which are inferior to *belief*, and independent of the real existence of their objects. Where a character is, in every respect, fitted to be beneficial to society, the imagination passes easily from the cause to the effect, without considering that there are still some circumstances wanting to render the cause a complete one. *General rules* create a species of probability, which sometimes influences the judgment, and always the imagination.

It is true, when the cause is complete, and a good disposition is attended with good fortune, which renders it really beneficial to society, it gives a stronger pleasure to the spectator, and is attended with a more lively sympathy. We are more affected by it; and yet we do not say that it is more virtuous, or that we esteem it more. We know, that an alteration of fortune may render the benevolent disposition entirely impotent; and therefore we separate, as much as possible, the fortune from the disposition. The case is the same, as when we correct the different sentiments of virtue, which proceed from its different distances from ourselves. The passions do not always follow our corrections; but these corrections serve sufficiently to regulate our abstract notions, and are alone regarded, when we pronounce in general concerning the degrees of vice and virtue.

It is observed by critics, that all words or sentences, which are difficult to the pronunciation, are disagreeable to the ear. There is no difference, whether a man hear them pronounced, or read them silently to himself. When I run over a book with my eye, I imagine I hear it all; and also, by the force of imagination, enter into the uneasiness, which the delivery of it would give the speaker. The uneasiness is not real; but as such a composition of words has a natural tendency to produce it, this is sufficient to affect the mind with a painful sentiment, and render the discourse harsh and disagreeable. It is a similar case, where any real quality is, by accidental circumstances, rendered impotent, and is deprived of its natural influence on society.

Upon these principles we may easily remove any contradiction, which may appear to be betwixt the *extensive sympathy*, on which our sentiments of virtue depend, and that *limited generosity* which I have frequently observed to be natural to men, and which justice and property suppose, according to the precedent reasoning. My sympathy with another may give me the sentiment of pain and disapprobation, when any object is presented, that has a tendency to give him uneasiness; though I may not be willing to sacrifice anything of my own interest, or cross any of my passions, for his satisfaction. A house may displease me by being ill-contrived for the convenience of the owner; and yet I may refuse to give a shilling towards the rebuilding of it. Sentiments must touch the heart, to make them control our passions. But they need not extend beyond the imagination, to make them influence our taste. When a building seems clumsy and tottering to the eye, it is ugly and disagreeable; though we be fully assured of the solidity of the workmanship. It is a kind of fear, which causes this sentiment of disapprobation; but the passion is not the same with that which we feel, when obliged to stand under a wall, that we really think tottering and insecure. The *seeming tendencies* of objects affect the mind; and the emotions they excite are of a like species with those, which proceed from the *real consequences* of objects, but their feeling is different. Nay, these emotions are so different in their feeling, that they may often be contrary, without destroying each other; as when the fortifications of a city belonging to an enemy are esteemed beautiful upon account of their strength, though we could wish that they were entirely destroyed. The imagination adheres to the *general* views of things, and distinguishes the feelings they produce, from those which arise from our particular and momentary situation.[42]

If we examine the panegyrics that are commonly made of great men, we shall find, that most of the qualities, which are attributed to them, may be divided into two kinds, *viz.* such as make them perform their part in society; and such as render them serviceable to themselves, and enable them to promote their own interest. Their *prudence, temperance, frugality, industry, assiduity, enterprise, dexterity,* are celebrated, as well as their *generosity* and *humanity*. If we ever give an indulgence to any quality, that disables a man from making a figure in life, it is to that of *indolence*, which is not supposed to deprive one of his parts and capacity, but only suspends their exercise; and that without any inconvenience to the person himself, since it is in some measure, from his own choice. Yet indolence is always allowed to be a fault, and a very great one, if extreme; nor do a man's friends ever acknowledge him to be subject to it, in order to save his character in more material articles. He could make a figure, say they, if he pleased to give application; his understanding is sound, his conception quick, and his memory tenacious; but he hates business, and is indifferent about his fortune. And this a man sometimes may make even a subject of vanity; though with the air of confessing a fault; because he may think, that this incapacity for business implies much more noble qualities; such as a philosophical spirit, a fine taste, a delicate wit, or a relish for pleasure and society. But take any other case : suppose a quality, that without being an indication of any other good qualities, incapacitates a man *always* for business, and is destructive to his interest; such as a blundering understanding, and a wrong judgment of everything in life; inconstancy and irresolution; or a want of address in the management of men and business. These are all allowed to be imperfections in a character; and many men would rather acknowledge the greatest crimes, than have it suspected, that they are, in any degree, subject to them.

It is very happy, in our philosophical researches, when

we find the same phenomenon diversified by a variety of circumstances; and by discovering what is common among them, can the better assure ourselves of the truth of any hypothesis we may make use of to explain it. Were nothing esteemed virtue but what were beneficial to society, I am persuaded, that the foregoing explication of the moral sense ought still to be received, and that upon sufficient evidence; but this evidence must grow upon us, when we find other kinds of virtue, which will not admit of any explication except from that hypothesis. Here is a man, who is not remarkably defective in his social qualities; but what principally recommends him is his dexterity in business, by which he has extricated himself from the greatest difficulties, and conducted the most delicate affairs with a singular address and prudence. I find an esteem for him immediately to arise in me; his company is a satisfaction to me; and before I have any farther acquaintance with him, I would rather do him a service than another, whose character is in every other respect equal, but is deficient in that particular. In this case, the qualities that please me are all considered as useful to the person, and as having a tendency to promote his interest and satisfaction. They are only regarded as means to an end, and please me in proportion to their fitness for that end. The end, therefore, must be agreeable to me. But what makes the end agreeable? The person is a stranger; I am no way interested in him, nor lie under any obligation to him; his happiness concerns not me, farther than the happiness of every human, and indeed of every sensible creature; that is, it affects me only by sympathy. From that principle, whenever I discover his happiness and good, whether in its causes or effects, I enter so deeply into it, that it gives me a sensible emotion. The appearance of qualities, that have a *tendency* to promote it, have an agreeable effect upon my imagination, and command my love and esteem.

This theory may serve to explain, why the same qualities, in all cases, produce both pride and love, humility and hatred; and the same man is always virtuous or vicious, accomplished or despicable to others, who is so to himself. A person, in whom we discover any passion or habit, which originally is only incommodious to himself, becomes always disagreeable to us, merely on its account; as on the other hand, one whose character is only dangerous and disagreeable to others, can never be satisfied with himself, as long as he is sensible of that disadvantage. Nor is this observable only with regard to characters and manners, but may be remarked even in the most minute circumstances. A violent cough in another gives us uneasiness; though in itself it does not in the least affect us. A man will be mortified, if you tell him he has a stinking breath; though it is evidently no annoyance to himself. Our fancy easily changes its situation; and either surveying ourselves as we appear to others, or considering others as they feel themselves, we enter, by that means, into sentiments, which no way belong to us, and in which nothing but sympathy is able to interest us. And this sympathy we sometimes carry so far, as even to be displeased with a quality commodious to us, merely because it displeases others, and makes us disagreeable in their eyes; though perhaps we never can have any interest in rendering ourselves agreeable to them.

There have been many systems of morality advanced by philosophers in all ages; but if they are strictly examined, they may be reduced to two, which alone merit our attention. Moral good and evil are certainly distinguished by our *sentiments*, not by *reason*; but these sentiments may arise either from the mere species or appearance of characters and passions, or from reflections on their tendency to the happiness of mankind, and of particular persons. My opinion is, that both these causes are intermixed in our judgments of morals; after the same manner as they are in our decisions concerning most kinds of external beauty; though I am also of opinion, that reflections on the tendencies of actions have by far the greatest influence, and determine all the great lines of our duty. There are, however, instances, in cases of less moment, wherein this immediate taste or sentiment produces our approbation. Wit, and a certain easy and disengaged behaviour, are qualities *immediately agreeable* to others, and command their love and esteem. Some of these qualities produce satisfaction in others by particular *original* principles of human nature, which cannot be accounted for; others may be resolved into principles, which are more general. This will best appear upon a particular enquiry.

As some qualities acquire their merit from their being *immediately agreeable* to others, without any tendency to public interest; so some are denominated virtuous from their being *immediately agreeable* to the person himself, who possesses them. Each of the passions and operations of the mind has a particular feeling, which must be either agreeable or disagreeable. The first is virtuous, the second vicious. This particular feeling constitutes the very nature of the passion; and therefore needs not be accounted for.

But however directly the distinction of vice and virtue may seem to flow from the immediate pleasure or uneasiness, which particular qualities cause to ourselves or others; it is easy to observe, that it has also a considerable dependence on the principle of *sympathy* so often insisted on. We approve of a person, who is possessed of qualities *immediately agreeable* to those, with whom he has any commerce; though perhaps we ourselves never reaped any pleasure from them. We also approve of one, who is possessed of qualities, that are *immediately agreeable* to himself; though they be of no service to any mortal. To account for this we must have recourse to the foregoing principles.[43]

Thus, to take a general review of the present hypothesis: every quality of the mind is denominated virtuous, which gives pleasure by the mere survey; as every quality, which produces pain, is called vicious. This pleasure and this pain may arise from four different sources. For we reap a pleasure from the view of a character, which is naturally fitted to be useful to others, or to the person himself, or which is agreeable to others, or to the person himself. One may, perhaps, be surprised, that amidst all these interests and pleasures, we should forget our own, which touch us so nearly on every other occasion. But we shall easily satisfy ourselves on this head, when we consider, that every particular person's pleasure and interest being different, it is impossible men could ever agree in their sentiments and judgments, unless they chose some common point of view, from which they might survey their object, and which might cause it to appear the same to all of them. Now, in judging of characters, the only interest or pleasure, which appears the same to every spectator, is that of the person himself, whose character is examined; or that of persons, who have a connection with him. And though such interests and pleasures touch us more faintly than our own, yet being more constant and universal, they counterbalance the latter even in practice, and are alone admitted in speculation as the standard of virtue and morality. They alone produce that particular feeling or sentiment, on which moral distinctions depend.

As to the good or ill desert of virtue or vice, it is an evident consequence of the sentiments of pleasure or uneasiness. These sentiments produce love or hatred; and love or hatred, by the original constitution of human passion, is attended with benevolence or anger; that is, with a desire of making happy the person we love, and miserable the person we hate. We have treated of this more fully on another occasion.

Section II *Of greatness of mind*

It may now be proper to illustrate this general system of morals, by applying it to particular instances of virtue and vice, and showing how their merit or demerit arises from the four sources here explained. We shall begin with examining the passions of *pride* and *humility*, and shall consider the vice or virtue that lies in their excesses or just proportion. An excessive pride or overweaning conceit of ourselves is always esteemed vicious, and is universally hated; as modesty, or a just sense of our weakness, is esteemed virtuous, and procures the goodwill of everyone. Of the four sources of moral distinctions, this is to be ascribed to the *third*; *viz*. the immediate agreeableness and disagreeableness of a quality to others, without any reflections on the tendency of that quality.

In order to prove this, we must have recourse to two principles, which are very conspicuous in human nature. The *first* of these is the *sympathy*, and communication of sentiments and passions above-mentioned. So close and intimate is the correspondence of human souls, that no sooner any person approaches me, than he diffuses on me all his opinions, and draws along my judgment in a greater or lesser degree. And though, on many occasions, my sympathy with him goes not so far as entirely to change my sentiments, and way of thinking; yet it seldom is so weak as not to disturb the easy course of my thought, and give an authority to that opinion, which is recommended to me by his assent and approbation. Nor is it any way material upon what subject he and I employ our thoughts. Whether we judge of an indifferent person, or of my own character, my sympathy gives equal force to his decision; and even his sentiments of his own merit make me consider him in the same light, in which he regards himself.

This principle of sympathy is of so powerful and insinuating a nature, that it enters into most of our sentiments and passions, and often takes place under the appearance of its contrary. For it is remarkable, that when a person opposes me in anything, which I am strongly bent upon, and rouses up my passion by contradiction, I have always a degree of sympathy with him, nor does my commotion proceed from any other origin. We may here observe an evident conflict or rencounter of opposite principles and passions. On the one side there is that passion or sentiment, which is natural to me; and it is observable, that the stronger this passion is, the greater is the commotion. There must also be some passion or sentiment on the other side; and this passion can proceed from nothing but sympathy. The sentiments of others can never affect us, but by becoming, in some measure, our own; in which case they operate upon us, by opposing and increasing our passions, in the very same manner, as if they had been originally derived from our own temper and disposition. While they remain concealed in the minds of others, they can never have any influence upon us; and even when they are known, if they went no farther than the imagination, or conception; that faculty is so accustomed to objects of every different kind, that a mere idea, though contrary to our sentiments and inclinations, would never alone be able to affect us.

The *second* principle I shall take notice of is that of *comparison*, or the variation of our judgments concerning objects, according to the proportion they bear to those with which we compare them. We judge more of objects by comparison, than by their intrinsic worth and value; and regard every thing as mean, when set in opposition to what is superior of the same kind. But no comparison is more obvious than that with ourselves; and hence it is that on all occasions it takes place, and mixes with most of our passions. This kind of comparison is directly contrary to sympathy in its operation, as we have observed in treating of *compassion* and *malice.**
In all kinds of comparison an object makes us always receive from another, to which it is compared, a sensation contrary to what arises from itself in its direct and immediate

* Book II. Part II. sect. 8.

*survey. The direct survey of another's pleasure naturally
gives us pleasure; and therefore produces pain, when compared with our own. His pain, considered in itself, is painful;
but augments the idea of our own happiness, and gives us
pleasure.*

Since then those principles of sympathy, and a comparison
with ourselves, are directly contrary, it may be worthwhile
to consider, what general rules can be formed, beside the
particular temper of the person, for the prevalence of the one
or the other. Suppose I am now in safety at land, and would
willingly reap some pleasure from this consideration; I
must think on the miserable condition of those who are at
sea in a storm, and must endeavour to render this idea as
strong and lively as possible, in order to make me more
sensible of my own happiness. But whatever pains I may
take, the comparison will never have an equal efficacy, as
if I were really on the shore,* and saw a ship at a distance,
tossed by a tempest, and in danger every moment of perishing
on a rock or sand-bank. But suppose this idea to become
still more lively. Suppose the ship to be driven so near me,
that I can perceive distinctly the horror, painted on the
countenance of the seamen and passengers, hear their lament-
able cries, see the dearest friends give their last adieu, or
embrace with a resolution to perish in each others arms; no
man has so savage a heart as to reap any pleasure from such
a spectacle, or withstand the motions of the tenderest compassion and sympathy. It is evident, therefore, there is a
medium in this case; and that if the idea be too faint, it has
no influence by comparison; and on the other hand, if it
be too strong, it operates on us entirely by sympathy, which
is the contrary to comparison. Sympathy being the conversion of an idea into an impression, demands a greater
force and vivacity in the idea than is requisite to comparison.

All this is easily applied to the present subject. We sink
very much in our own eyes, when in the presence of a great
man, or one of a superior genius; and this humility makes
a considerable ingredient in that *respect*, which we pay our

* Suave mari magno turbantibus æquora ventis
  E terra magnum alterius spectare laborem;
  Non quia vexari quenquam est jucunda voluptas,
  Sed quibus ipse malis careas quia cernere sauv' est.

  Lucret.

superiors, according to our foregoing reasonings on that passion.* Sometimes even envy and hatred arise from the comparison; but in the greatest part of men, it rests at respect and esteem. As sympathy has such a powerful influence on the human mind, it causes pride to have, in some measure, the same effect as merit; and by making us enter into those elevated sentiments, which the proud man entertains of himself, presents that comparison, which is so mortifying and disagreeable. Our judgment does not entirely accompany him in the flattering conceit, in which he pleases himself; but still is so shaken as to receive the idea it presents, and to give it an influence above the loose conceptions of the imagination. A man, who, in an idle humour, would form a notion of a person of a merit very much superior to his own, would not be mortified by that fiction. But when a man, whom we are really persuaded to be of inferior merit, is presented to us; if we observe in him any extraordinary degree of pride and self-conceit; the firm persuasion he has of his own merit, takes hold of the imagination, and diminishes us in our own eyes, in the same manner, as if he were really possessed of all the good qualities which he so liberally attributes to himself. Our idea is here precisely in that medium, which is requisite to make it operate on us by comparison. Were it accompanied with belief, and did the person appear to have the same merit, which he assumes to himself, it would have a contrary effect, and would operate on us by sympathy. The influence of that principle would then be superior to that of comparison, contrary to what happens where the person's merit seems below his pretensions.

The necessary consequence of these principles is, that pride, or an overweaning conceit of ourselves, must be vicious; since it causes uneasiness in all men, and presents them every moment with a disagreeable comparison. It is a trite observation in philosophy, and even in common life and conversation, that it is our own pride, which makes us so much displeased with the pride of other people; and that vanity becomes insupportable to us merely because we are vain. The gay naturally associate themselves with the gay, and the amorous with the amorous; but the proud never can endure the proud, and rather seek the company of those who are of an opposite disposition. As we are, all of us,

* Book II. Part II. sect. 10.

proud in some degree, pride is universally blamed and condemned by all mankind; as having a natural tendency to
cause uneasiness in others by means of comparison. And this
effect must follow the more naturally, that those, who have
an ill-grounded conceit of themselves, are for ever making
those comparisons, nor have they any other method of
supporting their vanity. A man of sense and merit is pleased
with himself, independent of all foreign considerations; but a
fool must always find some person, that is more foolish, in
order to keep himself in good humour with his own parts
and understanding.

But though an overweening conceit of our own merit be
vicious and disagreeable, nothing can be more laudable, than
to have a value for ourselves, where we really have qualities
that are valuable. The utility and advantage of any quality to
ourselves is a source of virtue, as well as its agreeableness to
others; and it is certain, that nothing is more useful to us
in the conduct of life, than a due degree of pride, which
makes us sensible of our own merit, and gives us a confidence
and assurance in all our projects and enterprises. Whatever
capacity anyone may be endowed with, it is entirely useless
to him, if he be not acquainted with it, and form not designs
suitable to it. It is requisite on all occasions to know our
own force; and were it allowable to err on either side, it would
be more advantageous to overrate our merit, than to form
ideas of it, below its just standard. Fortune commonly
favours the bold and enterprising; and nothing inspires us
with more boldness than a good opinion of ourselves.

Add to this, that though pride, or self-applause, be sometimes disagreeable to others, it is always agreeable to ourselves; as on the other hand, modesty, though it give pleasure
to every one, who observes it, produces often uneasiness in the
person endowed with it. Now it has been observed, that our
own sensations determine the vice and virtue of any quality,
as well as those sensations, which it may excite in others.

Thus self-satisfaction and vanity may not only be allowable, but requisite in a character. It is, however, certain, that
good-breeding and decency require that we should avoid all
signs and expressions, which tend directly to show that
passion. We have, all of us, a wonderful partiality for ourselves, and were we always to give vent to our sentiments

in this particular, we should mutually cause the greatest indignation in each other, not only by the immediate presence of so disagreeable a subject of comparison, but also by the contrariety of our judgments. In like manner, therefore, as we establish the *laws of nature*, in order to secure property in society, and prevent the opposition of self-interest; we establish the *rules of good-breeding*, in order to prevent the opposition of men's pride, and render conversation agreeable and inoffensive. Nothing is more disagreeable than a man's overweening conceit of himself; everyone almost has a strong propensity to this vice; no one can well distinguish *in himself* betwixt the vice and virtue, or be certain, that his esteem of his own merit is well-founded. For these reasons, all direct expressions of this passion are condemned; nor do we make any exception to this rule in favour of men of sense and merit. They are not allowed to do themselves justice openly, in words, no more than other people; and even if they show a reserve and secret doubt in doing themselves justice in their own thoughts, they will be more applauded. That impertinent, and almost universal propensity of men, to over-value themselves, has given us such a *prejudice* against self-applause, that we are apt to condemn it, by a *general rule*, wherever we meet with it; and it is with some difficulty we give a privilege to men of sense, even in their most secret thoughts. At least, it must be owned, that some disguise in this particular is absolutely requisite; and that if we harbour pride in our breasts, we must carry a fair outside, and have the appearance of modesty and mutual deference in all our conduct and behaviour. We must, on every occasion, be ready to prefer others to ourselves; to treat them with a kind of deference, even though they be our equals; to seem always the lowest and least in the company, where we are not very much distinguished above them; and if we observe these rules in our conduct, men will have more indulgence for our secret sentiments, when we discover them in an oblique manner.

I believe no one, who has any practice of the world, and can penetrate into the inward sentiments of men, will assert, that the humility, which good-breeding and decency require of us, goes beyond the outside, or that a thorough sincerity in this particular is esteemed a real part of our duty. On the contrary, we may observe, that a genuine and hearty pride, or self-esteem, if well concealed and well founded, is essential to the character of a man of honour, and that there is no quality of the mind, which is more indispensibly requisite to procure the esteem and approbation of mankind. There are certain deferences and mutual submissions, which custom requires of the different ranks of men towards each other; and whoever exceeds in this particular, if through interest, is accused of meanness; if through ignorance, of simplicity. It is necessary, therefore, to know our rank and station in the world, whether it be fixed by our birth, fortune, employments, talents or reputation. It is necessary to feel the sentiment and passion of pride in conformity to it, and to regulate our actions accordingly. And should it be said, that prudence may suffice to regulate our actions in this particular, without any real pride, I would observe, that here the object of prudence is to conform our actions to the general usage and custom; and that it is impossible those tacit airs of superiority should ever have been established and authorized by custom, unless men were generally proud, and unless that passion were generally approved, when well-grounded.

If we pass from common life and conversation to history, this reasoning acquires new force, when we observe, that all those great actions and sentiments, which have become the admiration of mankind, are founded on nothing but pride and self-esteem. *Go*, says *Alexander* the Great to his soldiers, when they refused to follow him to the *Indies*, *go tell your countrymen, that you left Alexander completing the conquest of the world.* This passage was always particularly admired by the prince of *Condé*, as we learn from *St. Evremond.* 'Alexander,' said that prince, 'abandoned by his soldiers, among barbarians, not yet fully subdued, felt in himself such a dignity and right of empire, that he could not believe it possible anyone could refuse to obey him. Whether in *Europe* or in *Asia*, among *Greeks* or *Persians*, all was indifferent to him; wherever he found men, he fancied he had found subjects.'

In general we may observe, that whatever we call *heroic virtue*, and admire under the character of greatness and elevation of mind, is either nothing but a steady and well-established pride and self-esteem, or partakes largely of that passion. Courage, intrepidity, ambition, love of glory, magnanimity, and all the other shining virtues of that kind, have plainly a strong mixture of self-esteem in them, and derive a great part of their merit from that origin. Accordingly we find, that many religious declaimers decry those virtues as purely pagan and natural, and represent to us the excellency of the *Christian* religion, which places humility in the rank of virtues, and corrects the judgment of the world, and even of philosophers, who so generally admire all the efforts of pride and ambition. Whether this virtue of humility has been rightly understood, I shall not pretend to determine. I am content with the concession, that the world naturally esteems a well-regulated pride, which secretly animates our conduct, without breaking out into such indecent expressions of vanity, as may offend the vanity of others.

The merit of pride or self-esteem is derived from two circumstances, *viz.* its utility and its agreeableness to ourselves; by which it capacitates us for business, and, at the same time, gives us an immediate satisfaction. When it goes beyond its just bounds, it loses the first advantage, and even becomes prejudicial; which is the reason why we condemn an extravagant pride and ambition, however regulated by the decorums of good-breeding and politeness. But as such a passion is still agreeable, and conveys an elevated and sublime sensation to the person, who is actuated by it, the sympathy with that satisfaction diminishes considerably the blame, which naturally attends its dangerous influence on his conduct and behaviour. Accordingly we may observe, that an excessive courage and magnanimity, especially when it displays itself under the frowns of fortune, contributes, in a great measure, to the character of a hero, and will render a person the admiration of posterity; at the same time, that it ruins his affairs, and leads him into dangers and difficulties, with which otherwise he would never have been acquainted.

Heroism, or military glory, is much admired by the generality of mankind. They consider it as the most sublime kind of merit. Men of cool reflection are not so sanguine in their praises of it. The infinite confusions and disorder, which it has caused in the world, diminish much of its merit in their eyes. When they would oppose the popular notions on this head, they always paint out the evils, which this supposed virtue has produced in human society; the subversion of empires, the devastation of provinces, the sack of cities. As long as these are present to us, we are more inclined to hate than admire the ambition of heroes. But when we fix our view on the person himself, who is the author of all this mischief, there is something so dazzling in his character, the mere contemplation of it so elevates the mind, that we cannot refuse it our admiration. The pain, which we receive from its tendency to the prejudice of society, is over-powered by a stronger and more immediate sympathy.

Thus our explication of the merit or demerit, which attends the degrees of pride or self-esteem, may serve as a strong argument for the preceding hypothesis, by showing the effects of those principles above explained in all the variations of our judgments concerning that passion. Nor will this reasoning be advantageous to us only by showing, that the distinction of vice and virtue arises from the *four* principles of the *advantage* and of the *pleasure* of the *person himself*, and of *others*; but may also afford us a strong proof of some under-parts of that hypothesis.

No one, who duly considers of this matter, will make any scruple of allowing, that any piece of ill-breeding, or any expression of pride and haughtiness, is displeasing to us, merely because it shocks our own pride, and leads us by sympathy into a comparison, which causes the disagreeable passion of humility. Now as an insolence of this kind is blamed even in a person who has always been civil to ourselves in particular; nay, in one, whose name is only known to us in history; it follows, that our disapprobation proceeds from a sympathy with others, and from the reflection, that such a character is highly displeasing and odious to everyone, who converses or has any intercourse with the person possessed of it. We sympathize with those people in their uneasiness; and as their uneasiness proceeds in part from a sympathy with the person who insults them, we may here observe a double rebound of the sympathy; which is a principle very similar to what we have observed on another occasion.*

SECTION III *Of goodness and benevolence*

Having thus explained the origin of that praise and approbation, which attends everything we call *great* in human

* Book II. Part II. sect. 5.

affections; we now proceed to give an account of their *goodness*, and show whence its merit is derived.

When experience has once given us a competent knowledge of human affairs, and has taught us the proportion they bear to human passion, we perceive, that the generosity of men is very limited, and that it seldom extends beyond their friends and family, or, at most, beyond their native country. Being thus acquainted with the nature of man, we expect not any impossibilities from him; but confine our view to that narrow circle, in which any person moves, in order to form a judgment of his moral character. When the natural tendency of his passions leads him to be serviceable and useful within his sphere, we approve of his character, and love his person, by a sympathy with the sentiments of those, who have a more particular connection with him. We are quickly obliged to forget our own interest in our judgments of this kind, by reason of the perpetual contradictions, we meet with in society and conversation, from persons that are not placed in the same situation, and have not the same interest with ourselves. The only point of view, in which our sentiments concur with those of others, is, when we consider the tendency of any passion to the advantage or harm of those, who have any immediate connection or intercourse with the person possessed of it. And though this advantage or harm be often very remote from ourselves, yet sometimes it is very near us, and interests us strongly by sympathy. This concern we readily extend to other cases, that are resembling; and when these are very remote, our sympathy is proportionably weaker, and our praise or blame fainter and more doubtful. The case is here the same as in our judgments concerning external bodies. All objects seem to diminish by their distance; but though the appearance of objects to our senses be the original standard, by which we judge of them, yet we do not say, that they actually diminish by the distance; but correcting the appearance by reflection, arrive at a more constant and established judgment concerning them. In like manner, though sympathy be much fainter than our concern for ourselves, and a sympathy with persons remote from us much fainter than that with persons near and contiguous; yet we neglect all these differences in our calm judgments concerning the characters of men. Besides, that we ourselves often change our situation in this particular, we every day meet with persons, who are in a different situation from ourselves, and who could never converse with us on any reasonable terms, were we to remain constantly in that situation and point of view, which is peculiar to us. The intercourse of sentiments, therefore, in society and conversation, makes us form some general inalterable standard, by which we may approve or disapprove of characters and manners. And though the *heart* does not always take part with those general notions, or regulate its love and hatred by them, yet are they sufficient for discourse, and serve all our purposes in company, in the pulpit, on the theatre, and in the schools.

From these principles we may easily account for that merit, which is commonly ascribed to *generosity, humanity, compassion, gratitude, friendship, fidelity, zeal, disinterestedness, liberality,* and all those other qualities, which form the character of good and benevolent. A propensity to the tender passions makes a man agreeable and useful in all the parts of life; and gives a just direction to all his other qualities, which otherwise may become prejudicial to society. Courage and ambition, when not regulated by benevolence, are fit only to make a tyrant and public robber. It is the same case with judgment and capacity, and all the qualities of that kind. They are indifferent in themselves to the interests of society, and have a tendency to the good or ill of mankind, according as they are directed by these other passions.

As love is *immediately agreeable* to the person, who is actuated by it, and hatred *immediately disagreeable*; this may also be a considerable reason, why we praise all the passions that partake of the former, and blame all those that have any considerable share of the latter. It is certain we are infinitely touched with a tender sentiment, as well as with a great one. The tears naturally start in our eyes at the conception of it; nor can we forbear giving a loose to the same tenderness towards the person who exerts it. All this seems to me a proof, that our approbation has, in those cases, an origin different from the prospect of utility and advantage, either to ourselves or others. To which we may add, that men naturally, without reflection, approve of that character, which is most like their own. The man of a mild disposition and tender affections, in forming a notion of the most perfect virtue, mixes in it more of benevolence and humanity, than the man of courage and enterprise, who naturally looks upon a certain elevation of mind as the most accomplished character. This must evidently proceed from an *immediate* sympathy, which men have with characters similar to their own. They enter with more warmth into such sentiments, and feel more sensibly the pleasure, which arises from them.

It is remarkable, that nothing touches a man of humanity more than any instance of extraordinary delicacy in love or friendship, where a person is attentive to the smallest concerns of his friends, and is willing to sacrifice to them the most considerable interest of his own. Such delicacies have little influence on society; because they make us regard the greatest trifles; but they are the more engaging, the more minute the concern is, and are a proof of the highest merit in anyone, who is capable of them. The passions are so contagious, that they pass with the greatest facility from one person to another, and produce correspondent movements in all human breasts. Where friendship appears in very signal instances, my heart catches the same passion, and is warmed by those warm sentiments, that display themselves before me. Such agreeable movements must give me an affection to every one that excites them. This is the case with everything that is agreeable in any person. The transition from pleasure to love is easy; but the transition must here be still more easy; since the agreeable sentiment, which is excited by sympathy, is love itself; and there is nothing required but to change the object.

Hence the peculiar merit of benevolence in all its shapes and appearances. Hence even its weaknesses are virtuous and amiable; and a person, whose grief upon the loss of a friend were excessive, would be esteemed upon that account. His tenderness bestows a merit, as it does a pleasure, on his melancholy.

We are not, however, to imagine, that all the angry passions are vicious, though they are disagreeable. There is a certain indulgence due to human nature in this respect. Anger and hatred are passions inherent in our very frame and constitution. The want of them, on some occasions, may even be a proof of weakness and imbecility. And where they appear only in a low degree, we not only excuse them because they are natural; but even bestow our applauses on them, because they are inferior to what appears in the greatest part of mankind.

Where these angry passions rise up to cruelty, they form the most detested of all vices. All the pity and concern which we have for the miserable sufferers by this vice, turns against the person guilty of it, and produces a stronger hatred than we are sensible of on any other occasion.

Even when the vice of inhumanity rises not to this extreme degree, our sentiments concerning it are very much influenced by reflections on the harm that results from it. And we may observe in general, that if we can find any quality in a person, which renders him incommodious to those, who live and converse with him, we always allow it to be a fault or blemish, without any farther examination. On the other hand, when we enumerate the good qualities of any person, we always mention those parts of his character, which render him a safe companion, an easy friend, a gentle master, an agreeable husband, or an indulgent father. We consider him with all his relations in society; and love or hate him, according as he affects those, who have any immediate intercourse with him. And it is a most certain rule, that if there be no relation of life, in which I could not wish to stand to a particular person, his character must so far be allowed to be perfect. If he be as little wanting to himself as to others, his character is entirely perfect. This is the ultimate test of merit and virtue.

SECTION IV *Of natural abilities*

No distinction is more usual in all systems of ethics, than that betwixt *natural abilities* and *moral virtues*; where the former are placed on the same footing with bodily endowments, and are supposed to have no merit or moral worth annexed to them. Whoever considers the matter accurately, will find, that a dispute upon this head would be merely a dispute of words, and that though these qualities are not altogether of the same kind, yet they agree in the most material circumstances. They are both of them equally mental qualities; and both of them equally produce pleasure; and have of course an equal tendency to procure the love and esteem of mankind. There are few, who are not as jealous of their character, with regard to sense and knowledge, as to honour and courage; and much more than with regard to temperance and sobriety. Men are even afraid of passing for good-natured lest *that* should be taken for want of understanding; and often boast of more debauches than they have been really engaged in, to give themselves airs of fire and spirit. In short, the figure a man makes in the world, the reception he meets with in company, the esteem paid him by his acquaintance; all these advantages depend almost as much upon his good sense and judgment, as upon any other part of his character. Let a man have the best intentions in the world, and be the farthest from all injustice and violence, he will never be able to make himself be much regarded, without a moderate share, at least, of parts and understanding. Since then natural abilities, though, perhaps, inferior, yet are on the same footing, both as to their causes and effects, with those qualities which we call moral virtues, why should we make any distinction betwixt them?

Though we refuse to natural abilities the title of virtues, we must allow, that they procure the love and esteem of mankind; that they give a new lustre to the other virtues; and that a man possessed of them is much more entitled to our goodwill and services, than one entirely void of them. It may, indeed, be pretended, that the sentiment of approbation, which those qualities produce, besides its being *inferior*, is also somewhat *different* from that, which attends the other virtues. But this, in my opinion, is not a sufficient reason for excluding them from the catalogue of virtues. Each of the virtues, even benevolence, justice, gratitude, integrity, excites a different sentiment or feeling in the spectator. The characters of *Cæsar* and *Cato*, as drawn by *Sallust*, are both of them virtuous, in the strictest sense of the word; but in a different way; nor are the sentiments entirely the same, which arise from them. The one produces love; the other esteem; the one is amiable; the other awful; we could wish to meet with the one character in a friend; the other character we would be ambitious of in ourselves. In like manner, the approbation, which attends natural abilities, may be somewhat different to the feeling from that, which arises from the other virtues, without making them entirely of a different species. And indeed we may observe, that the natural abilities, no more than the other virtues, produce not, all of them, the same kind of approbation. Good sense and genius beget esteem;

wit and humour excite love.*

Those, who represent the distinction betwixt natural abilities and moral virtues as very material, may say, that the former are entirely involuntary, and have therefore no merit attending them, as having no dependence on liberty and free-will. But to this I answer, *first*, that many of those qualities, which all moralists, especially the ancients, comprehend under the title of moral virtues, are equally involuntary and necessary, with the qualities of the judgment and imagination. Of this nature are constancy, fortitude, magnanimity; and, in short, all the qualities which form the *great* man. I might say the same, in some degree, of the others; it being almost impossible for the mind to change its character in any considerable article, or cure itself of a passionate or splenetic temper, when they are natural to it. The greater degree there is of these blameable qualities, the more vicious they become, and yet they are the less voluntary. *Secondly*, I would have anyone give me a reason, why virtue and vice may not be involuntary, as well as beauty and deformity. These moral distinctions arise from the natural distinctions of pain and pleasure; and when we receive those feelings from the general consideration of any quality or character, we denominate it vicious or virtuous. Now I believe no one will assert, that a quality can never produce pleasure or pain to the person who considers it, unless it be perfectly voluntary in the person who possesses it. *Thirdly*, as to free-will, we have shown that it has no place with regard to the actions, no more than the qualities of men. It is not a just consequence, that what is voluntary is free. Our actions are more voluntary than our judgments; but we have not more liberty in the one than in the other.

But though this distinction[44] betwixt voluntary and involuntary be not sufficient to justify the distinction betwixt natural abilities and moral virtues, yet the former distinction will

---

* Love and esteem are at the bottom the same passions, and arise from like causes. The qualities, that produce both, are agreeable, and give pleasure. But where this pleasure is severe and serious; or where its object is great, and makes a strong impression; or where it produces any degree of humility and awe; in all these cases, the passion, which arises from the pleasure, is more properly denominated esteem than love. Benevolence attends both; but is connected with love in a more eminent degree.

afford us a plausible reason, why moralists have invented the latter. Men have observed, that though natural abilities and moral qualities be in the main on the same footing, there is, however, this difference betwixt them, that the former are almost invariable by any art or industry; while the latter, or at least, the actions, that proceed from them, may be changed by the motives of rewards and punishments, praise and blame. Hence legislators, and divines, and moralists, have principally applied themselves to the regulating these voluntary actions, and have endeavoured to produce additional motives for being virtuous in that particular. They knew, that to punish a man for folly, or exhort him to be prudent and sagacious, would have but little effect; though the same punishments and exhortations, with regard to justice and injustice, might have a considerable influence. But as men, in common life and conversation, do not carry those ends in view, but naturally praise or blame whatever pleases or displeases them, they do not seem much to regard this distinction, but consider prudence under the character of virtue as well as benevolence, and penetration as well as justice. Nay, we find, that all moralists, whose judgment is not perverted by a strict adherence to a system, enter into the same way of thinking; and that the ancient moralists in particular made no scruple of placing prudence at the head of the cardinal virtues. There is a sentiment of esteem and approbation, which may be excited, in some degree, by any faculty of the mind, in its perfect state and condition; and to account for this sentiment is the business of *Philosophers*. It belongs to *Grammarians* to examine what qualities are entitled to the denomination of *virtue;* nor will they find, upon trial, that this is so easy a task, as at first sight they may be apt to imagine.

The principal reason why natural abilities are esteemed, is because of their tendency to be useful to the person, who is possessed of them. It is impossible to execute any design with success, where it is not conducted with prudence and discretion; nor will the goodness of our intentions alone suffice to procure us a happy issue to our enterprises. Men are superior to beasts principally by the superiority of their reason; and they are the degrees of the same faculty, which set such an infinite difference betwixt one man and another. All the advantages of art are owing to human reason; and where fortune is not very capricious, the most considerable part of these advantages must fall to the share of the prudent and sagacious.

When it is asked, whether a quick or a slow apprehension be most valuable? whether one, that at first view penetrates into a subject, but can perform nothing upon study; or a contrary character, which must work out everything by dint of application? whether a clear head, or a copious invention? whether a profound genius, or a sure judgment? in short, what character, or peculiar understanding, is more excellent than another? It is evident we can answer none of these questions, without considering which of those qualities capacitates a man best for the world, and carries him farthest in any of his undertakings.

There are many other qualities of the mind, whose merit is derived from the same origin. *Industry, perseverance, patience, activity, vigilance, application, constancy*, with other virtues of that kind, which it will be easy to recollect, are esteemed valuable upon no other account, than their advantage in the conduct of life. It is the same case with *temperance, frugality, economy, resolution*; as on the other hand, *prodigality, luxury, irresolution, uncertainty*, are vicious, merely because they draw ruin upon us, and incapacitate us for business and action.

As wisdom and good-sense are valued, because they are *useful* to the person possessed of them; so *wit* and *eloquence* are valued, because they are *immediately agreeable* to others. On the other hand, *good humour* is loved and esteemed, because it is *immediately agreeable* to the person himself. It is evident, that the conversation of a man of wit is very satisfactory; as a cheerful good-humoured companion diffuses a joy over the whole company, from a sympathy with his gaiety. These qualities, therefore, being agreeable, they naturally beget love and esteem, and answer to all the characters of virtue.

It is difficult to tell, on many occasions, what it is that renders one man's conversation so agreeable and entertaining, and another's so insipid and distasteful. As conversation is a transcript of the mind as well as books, the same qualities, which render the one valuable, must give us an esteem for the other. This we shall consider afterwards. In the meantime it may be affirmed in general, that all the merit a man may derive from his conversation (which, no doubt, may be very considerable) arises from nothing but the pleasure it conveys to those who are present.

In this view, *cleanliness* is also to be regarded as a virtue; since it naturally renders us agreeable to others, and is a very considerable source of love and affection. No one will deny, that a negligence in this particular is a fault; and as faults are nothing but smaller vices, and this fault can have no other origin than the uneasy sensation, which it excites in others, we may in this instance, seemingly so trivial, clearly discover the origin of the moral distinction of vice and virtue in other instances.

Besides all those qualities, which render a person lovely or valuable, there is also a certain *je-ne-sais-quoi* of agreeable and handsome, that concurs to the same effect. In this case, as well as in that of wit and eloquence, we must have recourse to a certain sense, which acts without reflection, and regards not the tendencies of qualities and characters. Some moralists account for all the sentiments of virtue by this sense. Their hypothesis is very plausible. Nothing but a particular enquiry can give the preference to any other hypothesis. When we find, that almost all the virtues have such particular tendencies; and also find, that these tendencies are sufficient alone to give a strong sentiment of approbation; we cannot doubt, after this, that qualities are approved of, in proportion to the advantage, which results from them.

The *decorum* or *indecorum* of a quality, with regard to the age, or character, or station, contributes also to its praise or blame. This decorum depends, in a great measure, upon experience. It is usual to see men lose their levity, as they advance in years. Such a degree of gravity, therefore, and such years, are connected together in our thoughts. When we observe them separated in any person's character, this imposes a kind of violence on our imagination, and is disagreeable.

That faculty of the soul, which, of all others, is of the least consequence to the character, and has the least virtue or vice in its several degrees, at the same time, that it admits of a great variety of degrees, is the *memory*. Unless it rise up to the stupendous height as to surprise us, or sink so low as, in some measure, to affect the judgment, we commonly take no notice of its variations, nor ever mention them to the praise or dispraise of any person. It is so far from being a virtue to have a good memory, that men generally affect to complain of a bad one; and endeavouring to persuade the world, that what they say is entirely of their own invention sacrifice it to the praise of genius and judgment. Yet to consider the matter abstractedly, it would be difficult to give a reason, why the faculty of recalling past ideas with truth and clearness, should not have as much merit in it, as the faculty of placing our present ideas in such an order, as to form true propositions and opinions. The reason of the difference certainly must be, that the memory is exerted without any sensation of pleasure or pain; and in all its middling degrees serves almost equally well in business and affairs. But the least variations in the judgment are sensibly felt in their consequences; while at the same time that faculty is never exerted in any eminent degree, without an extraordinary delight and satisfaction. The sympathy with this utility and pleasure bestows a merit on the understanding; and the absence of it makes us consider the memory as a faculty very indifferent to blame or praise.

Before I leave this subject of *natural abilities*, I must observe, that, perhaps, one source of the esteem and affection which attends them, is derived from the *importance* and *weight*, which they bestow on the person possessed of them. He becomes of greater consequence in life. His resolution and actions affect a greater number of his fellow-creatures Both his friendship and enmity are of moment. And it is easy to observe, that whoever is elevated, after this manner above the rest of mankind, must excite in us the sentiment of esteem and approbation. Whatever is important engages our attention, fixes our thought, and is contemplated with satisfaction. The histories of kingdoms are more interesting than domestic stories; the histories of great empires more than those of small cities and principalities; and the histories of wars and revolutions more than those of peace and order We sympathize with the persons that suffer, in all the various sentiments which belong to their fortunes. The mind is occupied by the multitude of the objects, and by the strong passions, that display themselves. And this occupation o agitation of the mind is commonly agreeable and amusing The same theory accounts for the esteem and regard we pay to men of extraordinary parts and abilities. The good and ill of multitudes are connected with their actions. Whatever they undertake is important, and challenges our attention. Nothing is to be overlooked and despised, that regards them. And where any person can excite these sentiments, he soon acquires our esteem; unless other circumstances of his character render him odious and disagreeable.

SECTION V *Some farther reflections concerning the natural virtues*

It has been observed, in treating of the passions, that pride and humility, love and hatred, are excited by any advantages or disadvantages of the *mind, body,* or *fortune;* and that these advantages or disadvantages have that effect, by producing a separate impression of pain or pleasure. The pain or pleasure, which arises from the general survey or view of any action or quality of the *mind,* constitutes its vice or virtue, and gives rise to our approbation or blame, which is nothing but a fainter and more imperceptible love or hatred. We have assigned four different sources of this pain and pleasure; and in order to justify more fully that hypothesis, it may here be proper to observe, that the advantages or disadvantages of the *body* and of *fortune,* produce a pain or pleasure from the very same principles. The tendency of any object to be *useful* to the person possessed of it, or to others; to convey *pleasure* to him or to others; all these circumstances convey an immediate pleasure to the person, who considers the object, and command his love and approbation.

To begin with the advantages of the *body;* we may observe a phenomenon, which might appear somewhat trivial and ludicrous, if anything could be trivial, which fortified a conclusion of such importance, or ludicrous, which was employed in a philosophical reasoning. It is a general remark, that those we call good *women's men,* who have either signalized themselves by their amorous exploits, or whose make of body promises any extraordinary vigour of that kind, are well received by the fair sex, and naturally engage the affections even of those, whose virtue prevents any design of ever giving employment to those talents. Here it is evident, that the ability of such a person to give enjoyment, is the real source of that love and esteem he meets with among the females; at the same time that the women, who love and esteem him, have no prospect of receiving that enjoyment themselves, and can only be affected by means of their sympathy with one, that has a commerce of love with him. This instance is singular, and merits our attention.

Another source of the pleasure we receive from considering bodily advantages, is their utility to the person himself, who is possessed of them. It is certain, that a considerable part of the beauty of men, as well as of other animals, consists in such a conformation of members, as we find by experience to be attended with strength and agility, and to capacitate the creature for any action or exercise. Broad shoulders, a lank belly, firm joints, taper legs; all these are beautiful in our species, because they are signs of force and vigour, which being advantages we naturally sympathize with, they convey to the beholder a share of that satisfaction they produce in the possessor.

So far as to the *utility*, which may attend any quality of the body. As to the immediate *pleasure*, it is certain, that an air of health, as well as of strength and agility, makes a considerable part of beauty; and that a sickly air in another is always disagreeable, upon account of that idea of pain and uneasiness, which it conveys to us. On the other hand, we are pleased with the regularity of our own features, though it be neither useful to ourselves nor others; and it is necessary for us, in some measure, to set ourselves at a distance, to make it convey to us any satisfaction. We commonly consider ourselves as we appear in the eyes of others, and sympathize with the advantageous sentiments they entertain with regard to us.

How far the advantages of *fortune* produce esteem and approbation from the same principles, we may satisfy ourselves by reflecting on our precedent reasoning on that subject. We have observed, that our approbation of those, who are possessed of the advantages of fortune, may be ascrib'd to three different causes. *First*, to that immediate pleasure, which a rich man gives us, by the view of the beautiful clothes, equipage, gardens, or houses, which he possesses. *Secondly*, to the advantage, which we hope to reap from him by his generosity and liberality. *Thirdly*, to the pleasure and advantage, which he himself reaps from his possessions, and which produce an agreeable sympathy in us. Whether we ascribe our esteem of the rich and great to one or all of these causes, we may clearly see the traces of those principles, which give rise to the sense of vice and virtue. I believe most people, at first sight, will be inclined to ascribe our esteem of the rich to self-interest, and the prospect of advantage. But as it is certain, that our esteem or deference extends beyond any prospect of advantage to ourselves, it is evident, that that sentiment must proceed from a sympathy with those, who are dependent on the person we esteem and respect, and who have an immediate connection with him. We consider him as a person capable of contributing to the happiness or enjoyment of his fellow-creatures, whose sentiments, with regard to him, we naturally embrace. And this consideration will serve to justify my hypothesis in preferring the *third* principle to the other two, and ascribing our esteem of the rich to a sympathy with the pleasure and advantage, which they themselves receive from their possessions. For as even the other two principles cannot operate to a due extent, or account for all the phenomena, without having recourse to a sympathy of one kind or other; it is much more natural to choose that sympathy, which is immediate and direct, than that which is remote and indirect. To which we may add, that where the riches or power are very great, and render the person considerable and important in the world, the esteem attending them, may, in part, be ascribed to another source, distinct from these three, *viz.* their interesting the mind by a prospect of the multitude, and importance of their consequences; though, in order to account for the operation of this principle, we must also have recourse to *sympathy*; as we have observed in the preceding section.

It may not be amiss, on this occasion, to remark the flexibility of our sentiments, and the several changes they so readily receive from the objects, with which they are conjoined. All the sentiments of approbation, which attend any particular species of objects, have a great resemblance to each other, though derived from different sources; and, on the other hand, those sentiments, when directed to different objects, are different to the feeling, though derived from the same source. Thus the beauty of all visible objects causes a pleasure pretty much the same, though it be sometimes derived from the mere *species* and appearance of the objects; sometimes from sympathy, and an idea of their utility. In like manner, whenever we survey the actions and characters of men, without any particular interest in them, the pleasure, or pain, which arises from the survey (with some minute differences) is, in the main, of the same kind, though perhaps there be a great diversity in the causes, from which it is derived. On the other hand, a convenient house, and a virtuous character, cause not the same feeling of approbation; even though the source of our approbation be the same, and flow from sympathy and an idea of their utility. There is something very inexplicable in this variation of our feelings; but it is what we have experience of with regard to all our passions and sentiments.

Section VI *Conclusion of this book*

Thus upon the whole I am hopeful, that nothing is wanting to an accurate proof of this system of ethics. We are certain, that sympathy is a very powerful principle in human nature. We are also certain, that it has a great influence on our sense of beauty, when we regard external objects, as well as when we judge of morals. We find, that it has force sufficient to give us the strongest sentiments of approbation, when it operates alone, without the concurrence of any other principle; as in the cases of justice, allegiance, chastity, and good-manners. We may observe, that all the circumstances requisite for its operation are found in most of the virtues; which have, for the most part, a tendency to the good of society, or to that of the person possessed of them. If we compare all these circumstances, we shall not doubt, that sympathy is the chief source of moral distinctions; especially when we reflect, that no objection can be raised against this hypothesis in one case, which will not extend to all cases. Justice is certainly approved of for no other reason, than because it has a tendency to the public good; and the public good is indifferent to us, except so far as sympathy interests us in it. We may presume the like with regard to all the other virtues, which have a like tendency to the public good. They must derive all their merit from our sympathy with those, who reap any advantage from them; as the virtues, which have a tendency to the good of the person possessed of them, derive their merit from our sympathy with him.

Most people will readily allow, that the useful qualities of the mind are virtuous, because of their utility. This way of thinking is so natural, and occurs on so many occasions, that few will make any scruple of admitting it. Now this being once admitted, the force of sympathy must necessarily be acknowledged. Virtue is consider'd as means to an end. Means to an end are only valued so far as the end is valued. But the happiness of strangers affects us by sympathy alone. To that principle, therefore, we are to ascribe the sentiment of approbation, which arises from the survey of all those virtues, that are useful to society, or to the person possessed of them. These form the most considerable part of morality.

Were it proper in such a subject to bribe the readers assent, or employ anything but solid argument, we are here abundantly supplied with topics to engage the affections. All lovers of virtue (and such we all are in speculation, however we may degenerate in practice) must certainly be pleased to see moral distinction derived from so noble a source, which gives us a just notion both of the *generosity* and *capacity* of human nature. It requires but very little knowledge of human affairs to perceive, that a sense of morals is a principle inherent in the soul, and one of the most powerful that enters into the composition. But this sense must certainly acquire new force, when reflecting on itself, it approves of those principles, from whence it is derived, and finds nothing but what is great and good in its rise and origin. Those who resolve the sense of morals into original instincts of the human mind, may defend the cause of virtue with sufficient authority; but want the advantage, which those possess, who account for that sense by an extensive sympathy with mankind. According to their system, not only virtue must be approved of, but also the sense of virtue; and not only that sense, but also the principles, from whence it is derived. So that nothing is presented on any side, but what is laudable and good.

This observation may be extended to justice, and the other virtues of that kind. Though justice be artificial, the sense of its morality is natural. It is the combination of men, in a system of conduct, which renders any act of justice beneficial to society. But when once it has that tendency, we *naturally* approve of it; and if we did not so, it is impossible any combination or convention could ever produce that sentiment.

Most of the inventions of men are subject to change.

They depend upon humour and caprice. They have a vogue for a time, and then sink into oblivion. It may, perhaps, be apprehended, that if justice were allowed to be a human invention, it must be placed on the same footing. But the cases are widely different. The interest, on which justice is founded, is the greatest imaginable, and extends to all times and places. It cannot possibly be served by any other invention. It is obvious, and discovers itself on the very first formation of society. All these causes render the rules of justice steadfast and immutable; at least, as immutable as human nature. And if they were founded on original instincts, could they have any greater stability?

The same system may help us to form a just notion of the *happiness*, as well as of the *dignity* of virtue, and may interest every principle of our nature in the embracing and cherishing that noble quality. Who indeed does not feel an accession of alacrity in his pursuits of knowledge and ability of every kind, when he considers, that besides the advantage, which immediately result from these acquisitions, they also give him a new lustre in the eyes of mankind, and are universally attended with esteem and approbation? And who can think any advantages of fortune a sufficient compensation for the least breach of the *social* virtues, when he considers, that not only his character with regard to others, but also his peace and inward satisfaction entirely depend upon his strict observance of them; and that a mind will never be able to bear its own survey, that has been wanting in its part to mankind and society? But I forbear insisting on this subject. Such reflections require a work apart, very different from the genius of the present. The anatomist ought never to emulate the painter; nor in his accurate dissections and portraitures of the smaller parts of the human body, pretend to give his figures any graceful and engaging attitude or expression. There is even something hideous, or at least minute in the views of things, which he presents; and it is necessary the objects should be set more at a distance, and be more cover'd up from sight, to make them engaging to the eye and imagination. An anatomist, however, is admirably fitted to give advice to a painter; and it is even impracticable to excel in the latter art, without the assistance of the former. We must have an exact knowledge of the parts, their situation and connection, before we can design with any elegance or correctness. And thus the most abstract speculations concerning human nature, however cold and unentertaining, become subservient to *practical morality*; and may render this latter science more correct in its precepts, and more persuasive in its exhortations.

Editor's Notes

Book II

Part I *Of Pride and Humility*

1. Hume tends to think of the passions as simple impressions, unanalysable inner experiences. He describes them as indefinable and this leads him to conceive of his task as the description of the conditions that give rise to the passions. He neither provides an analysis of the nature of the passions, nor does he analyse the meaning of terms standing for passions.

For a discussion of Hume's views on the passions, see in particular P. S. Árdal, *Passion and Value in Hume's Treatise*, Chapters 1 and 2; P. L. Gardiner, 'Hume's Theory of the Passions'; Anthony Kenny, *Action, Emotion and Will* (Routledge, 1963), Chapter 1; John B. Stewart, *The Moral and Political Philosophy of David Hume*, Chapter 3; and E. Rotwein, *David Hume's Writings on Economics*, the introduction.

2. Hume tends to think of the relation between passions in mechanical terms. Pride and humility are related in such a way that producing an equal degree of each leaves the mind calm and indifferent. It is not easy to see how this is possible if the passions are simple impressions. Does the fact that the mind is in a complete equilibrium and calm not entail that neither passion is aroused; although one may produce the conditions that normally do arouse each of them? Hume's somewhat strange way of writing about these phenomena may be due to the fact that he had in mind an analogy with the opposition of forces. When two equal forces pull in opposite directions the forces are present and yet the object upon which the forces are exerted remains immobile, in an equilibrium. The reader of Book II of the *Treatise* should constantly keep in mind the fact that Hume was adapting conceptions from mechanics to the explanation of the emotions.

3. It seems puzzling to talk of the similarity as the relation of association between impressions. Hume seems, however, to think that it is simply an empirical fact about human

nature that one impression tends to be followed by a re-sembling one. It is not being claimed that this is because we have *noticed* the similarity.

See Kemp Smith, *The Philosophy of David Hume*, p. 161 and Chapter XII. Also Passmore, *Hume's Intentions*, Chapter VI.

4. The Green and Grose edition gives the reference as the *Spectator*, No. 412.

5. Hume writes as if pride causes us to think of ourselves and that this is the sense in which pride has self as its object. But to be proud *is* a form of self-valuing. It is absurd to suggest that a change in human nature could have resulted in pride always having another as its object. It misdescribes the situation to contend that we think of ourselves *when we are already proud*. It is an essential part of pride to be a form of self-valuing. Hume's account of the passions as simple impressions makes it difficult for him to give a satisfactory account of the relation between pride and its object; he here describes a conceptual relation as if it were a causal one.

Hume's causal account of the passions sometimes reveals conceptual insights. This is not least true of his account of pride. One can understand why this is so if one thinks of the conceptual account as revealing the necessary conditions for pride; the conditions without which whatever I feel could not be pride. A causal account would have to state the sufficient conditions and also the necessary conditions unless you presume that there may be a multiplicity of alternative causes. Throughout his treatment of the passions Hume appears to assume that a change in the causal conditions would lead to a change in the resulting passion. He can thus be presumed to state what he takes to be the necessary conditions for the various passions and this helps to explain why certain conceptual lessons can be learnt from his causal account.

6. Hume's account of judgment of beauty is entirely parallel to his account of moral judgment. In each case the judgment consists in a special kind of passion or emotion. Do not be misled by the fact that he sometimes writes as if the beauty literally *is* in the eye of the beholder. It is rather that there is no such quality as beauty; we call things beautiful because of our emotional response to them. Similarly it is misleading of Hume to describe beauty as the power of

producing pleasure. It is this power that makes us call the object beautiful because it pleases us; the word beauty does not name the power. It is of course wrong to suggest that beauty for Hume *is* an emotion in the soul like surprise. (For a discussion of the reasons why Hume should write in a way that has misled many of his commentators, see *Passion and Value*, Chapter 9.)

7. The argument of the preceding section makes explicit reference to Hume's discussion of causality and power in Book I and his discussion of the will in Sections I and II of Part III of Book II. It is always extremely important to have in mind Hume's account of causality in one's attempt to understand what he means by saying that there is no distinction between power and the exercise of it. Hume thinks that the performance of an individual action shows that the power to do something else was absent, otherwise our action is wholly due to chance and cannot be a responsible human action. But prior to the action one may not have been able to assert more than a possible or a probable occurrence of it. This leads one to talk of the man possibly or probably doing the deed, this judgment being based upon our prior experience. If we think that a person does not have decisive motives for doing something we may then say that he has the power to refrain from doing it. This notion of power is entirely to be cashed in terms of the notions of possibility and probability. To say after the event that a man had the power to act otherwise than he did is strictly philosophically incorrect but it may refer to the fact that prior to the event there was no way of making anything more than a probability judgment about its occurrence. Of course the man could have acted differently if his character had been different, or if the considerations or motives that led him to act had not been what they were. But to say that he could have acted differently, even though both these factors had been the same, is either to say that there is an element of complete caprice in the action or it is a way of saying that there were no external circumstances preventing it. Whereas freedom from external *compulsion* is obviously a necessary condition for responsibility it would be absurd to suggest that one is responsible only when one acts completely capriciously. It is true that, in one sense, a capricious action may be taken to be an irresponsible action and thus to show some defect in

an agent's character. But in the sense in which the word is here used a completely capricious action is one which cannot be taken to indicate any particular characteristic in the agent. If 'free' is equated with 'capricious,' in this sense, then our free actions are precisely those we are not to be held responsible for.

8. This section, in spite of its heading, is more important because of its discussion of the nature of sympathy. It is to be read together with the further elucidation of this principle in Book II, Part II, Section V, curiously entitled *Of our esteem for the rich and powerful.* Both these discussions and other references to sympathy in Book II must be kept in mind when Hume, in Book III, Part III, attempts to explain the precise way in which we can come to have moral emotions. The principle of sympathy explains the communication of passions and is not itself a passion. For an explanation of the way it works and some of the modifications Hume has to introduce to the account of its operation see note 14 to Book II, Part II, Section V.

9. The gait of a swan or a peacock resembles that of a proud man. If, as Hume suggests, these birds are proud of their beauty, then they must have discovered this beauty. Is this not rather implausible? The peacock does not have to have seen its image in water or a mirror before it starts to strut; it naturally has a proud gait. Consider also how unlikely the account becomes, if one thinks of pride as a simple impression and takes seriously the account of its origin in accordance with the double association of impressions and ideas.

Hume does not think animals are capable of the artificial virtues. This is because they cannot understand contracts and conventions. Presumably they are incapable of approval and disapproval because they cannot adopt a self-forgetful, objective point of view. But, it seems animals could enter the moral sphere in two ways. (1) They can have some form of at least some natural virtues and vices, such as kindness and cruelty, and (2) we must take them into account in considering the moral quality of *our* actions because animals are capable of feeling pains and pleasures. I consider it likely that Hume maintains that we feel differently about what we might loosely call 'moral' qualities in animals and that our praise and condemnation (love and hatred) of them would thus be different. The difference would primarily be in what must be generally described as the lack of understanding in animals. (For an interesting discussion related to this topic, see Knut Erik Tranöy, *The Journal of Philosophy*, 1959.)

PART II *Of Love and Hatred*

10. 'Pride', 'humility', 'love' and 'hatred' stand for the four possible biased ways of valuing. This is why Hume has to rule out self-love and self-hatred. The terms he has chosen for self-valuing are pride and humility. He really has no right to refuse to class self-love with love on the ground that it differs from the tender emotions we have towards a mistress; for Hume himself distinguishes between love as an indirect, but simple passion, and love between the sexes, which is a complex emotion. (See Book II, Part III, Section XI.)

11. Notice that the object of love and hatred is described as some thinking person. We could presumably only have these emotions directed towards animals in so far as they resemble us in this respect. This would help to explain why, for the most part, we do not attribute morality to animals. Hume's general account of thought and experience, including evaluation, tends to diminish the gap between animals and men; at least he does not consider it an absolute difference in kind, however large the gap may in fact be. (See note 9.)

Compare Hume's position with that of Immanuel Kant in his *Foundation of the Metaphysic of Morals* and the chapter 'Duties towards Animals and Spirits' in his *Lectures on Ethics*, Harper Torchbooks, New York, 1963.

12. In what sense can simple impressions mix? Are the compound affections still simple impressions? It would seem (see note 1) that the answer to the second question must be in the affirmative.

13. It is not at all clear what it is that is permanent behind an intentional action. Hume clearly shows here that he realized that a person may change his character without ceasing to be responsible for his actions. He thinks, however, that it would be unreasonable to hate a person on account of his actions unless they somehow showed him to be hateful. We must remember that he thinks all moral evalua-

tion is of people or other conscious agents. Actions are immoral only as showing immoral tendencies in agents.

14. The reference to mirrors and echoes suggests that sympathy presupposes that there exists a real emotion or thought to be communicated. Hume soon finds that he has to modify this view and in the end it is sympathy as operating through the imagination that proves crucial for his account of evaluation.

See note 42, Árdal, *Passion and Value*, Chapter 6, and Bernard Wand, 'A Note on Sympathy in Hume's Moral Theory.'

15. Nowhere does Hume more explicitly reveal the difficulty involved in treating the passions as simple impressions, contingently related to each other. Is it compatible with our concepts of love and hatred to suppose that we always want to hurt the people we love and show kindness to those whom we hate? If the passions are all purely contingently connected with behaviour it seems we should have to say that this is also true of the passions that constitute approval and disapproval. Is it possible that *disapproval* of persecution could, through a change in human nature, come to be associated with consistently furthering its ends?

16. Hume here draws attention to features of sympathy that are not clearly consistent with the conception of it as a principle of communication. How can the absence of concern in the object of sympathy increase the sympathy?

17. This is the closest Hume comes to treating dispositional characteristics as essential elements of certain passions. It is not entirely clear that he can do this and retain the view that the passions are simple impressions. Of course he can maintain that no passion is purely dispositional, that each passion involves a tendency to have special feelings. The contrast Hume draws between the passions that are pure sensations and those that involve a direction and tendency to action suggests a more adequate view than the one he seems to espouse in his earlier discussion of love and hatred. (See note 15.)

18. Is Hume right to suggest that pride and humility are pure sensations and that they do not essentially involve any tendency to action?

19. Hume clearly distinguishes between pity, sympathy, love and benevolence. Notice how he explains the meaning

of each term. This terminological precision is not much in evidence in the second *Enquiry*.

20. Here is a passion that consists in a conjunction of elements and is consequently not just a simple impression. This passion is definable in the sense that an account can be given of the way in which the three elements that constitute it are related. Each of the three passions that go to make up 'the amorous passion' may be a simple impression in Hume's eyes but it must be said that, at this point, the notion of each passion as a simple impression already has been shown to be partly inadequate. (See notes 15 and 17.)

PART III *Of the Will and Direct Passions*

21. It is of the utmost importance to pay attention to the fact that Hume seems to think that we know from immediate experience what the will is. It is an impression and in ordinary speech we describe the situation where the will is involved as 'knowingly giving rise to' thoughts and actions. Thus when I raise my arm I have an impression of the will. When it is raised by another, or I find it automatically rising, the impression of the will is missing. But to be aware of the impression of the will is not to know the cause of one's behaviour. To discover a cause is to discover irregularities and to be determined to beliefs on the basis of these observations. Hume's view must be kept in mind in all attempts to understand his views about liberty and necessity, although one may want to insist that there is room for the concept of agent causality (see items on freedom and determinism in the bibliography) in dealing with the nature of action. It remains true that for Hume it makes no sense to talk of immediate awareness of the cause of an action, although this view may be open to criticism and Hume's views about the nature of causality may be found indefensible.

22. I do not think the liberty of spontaneity is an entirely negative concept for we should presumably have an impression of the will when we act freely in this sense, though that impression does not guarantee the freedom. Hume says far too little about the liberty of spontaneity.

Book III

PART I *Of Virtue and Vice in General*

23. Hume here repeats the assertion that reason is the discovery of truth or falsehood and makes it clear that he is denying that moral assessments are true or false at all; he is not denying only that they are necessary truths.

24. This paragraph and the previous one are intelligible if one takes Hume to be arguing against the thesis that truth and falsity (conformity with reason and disagreement with reason) are the ultimate source of, and explanation of, moral good and evil. The paragraph that follows plainly shows that this thesis is a reductivist one. Hume could not use this argument against those who believe there is a non-natural unique moral quality rightness intuited by a rational moral faculty. He clearly supposes that if you have to admit such a unique quality of rightness then you have destroyed the rationalist thesis that reason is the foundation of morality. So long as one thinks that Hume has exclusively in mind an intuitionist theory, similar to the views of such modern writers as Ross, Prichard and Carritt, then this paragraph would be absurd, for they do believe that there is 'a real right and wrong' independent of the judgment that actions are right or wrong.

25. The 'late author' Hume is referring to is William Wollaston whose *The Religion of Nature Delineated* was extremely widely read and won the author considerable respect. It was first published for private circulation in 1722 and reprinted in 1724; it sold 10,000 copies within a few years and by 1750 it had gone into seven editions. Hume does not seem to have thought that Wollaston's fame was merited but Francis Hutcheson refers to him with respect.

See Leslie Stephen's *History of English Thought in the Eighteenth Century* for an interesting and entertaining account of Wollaston and his work.

It is not entirely clear that Hume here correctly states Wollaston's position. Wollaston did not maintain that actions were wrong because they led people to have false opinions. His was the more radical claim that actions, as well as statements, could be true or false and that the immorality of actions consisted in their falsehood. Hume, however, maintains that the assertion, that an action is false, must be a figurative way of speaking. But Wollaston meant it literally and Hume may have thought of himself as stating an intelligible theory, meaning to suggest that Wollaston's view, as stated by Wollaston himself, was strictly absurd.

Hume's line of thought may have been as follows: to make love to your neighbour's wife is, according to Wollaston, to assert falsely that she is your wife. You are not asserting this to yourself for you know perfectly well that the woman is not your wife. You cannot be asserting it to her; she might not be at all pleased if she interpreted your action in that way. If you have drawn the blinds then it seems absurd to suggest that you are in your action making to anyone the assertion in the falsity of which the immorality is supposed to consist. Are we then to conclude that adultery, in private, is not immoral?

26. This paragraph contains the most powerful point against Wollaston. We need the morality of truth and immorality of falsehood demonstrated. It was only because moral laws were thought of as laws of nature that moral actions like true propositions could be thought of as fitting nature and this as true. Hume here correctly states Wollaston's view: He thought that the immorality of actions consisted in their falsehood.

27. Hume claims to have shown in Book I that the relations he lists are the only relations discoverable between ideas. He here points out a serious lack of clarity in the views of people like Clarke. Morality, they claim, is discoverable by reason and this, it appears, amounts to seeing the eternal relations of things based upon their nature. The analogy with mathematics was stressed. Here from knowledge of certain relations you deduce other relations. If virtue and vice are discoverable by reason it would thus seem that they must *consist in* relations. That however is not the view they present us with: We are told that reason *discovers* that certain actions are right or wrong *given that the agent is placed in certain relations*. It is not explained why this insight must be attributed to the same faculty as the one that demonstrates truths based upon the necessary relations between ideas. The fact that actions are moral or immoral because agents are in

certain relations is insufficient to justify the claim that to discover moral qualities is to discover relations. Hume's argument is clearly a good one if you grant that demonstrative reason only discovers relations; it has persuasive force if this is not presupposed, for it must then be shown by his opponents that there is justification for attributing moral and mathematical insights to the same faculty.

28. Virtues are qualities of mind. If morality depends upon relations moral relations must relate actions of the mind to the situation in which the person finds himself. Hume does not seem to be on very safe ground in suggesting that it is *absurd* to maintain that there are relations that can hold only between internal actions and external situation. He is, however, right to insist that an explication of this peculiar relation is needed. Thus the relation must not only hold between terms in the world, for consider what happens in moral thinking. In coming to a decision as to whether an action would be the right one, you are considering the relations between an actual situation and a number of *possible actions*. Only one of these would be the relation of moral rightness and no adequate account is offered of the way in which this relation is picked out.

29. Notice that Hume, in this paragraph, claims to have shown in the previous section that our moral decisions are not thoughts (ideas) and therefore must be impressions. Moral decisions are emotional reactions and not thoughts that can be true or false. In insisting that morality is 'more properly felt than judged of' he is not merely denying that moral judgments are analytic: they are not judgments and therefore neither judgments of the relation between ideas nor judgments concerning matters of fact.

30. The above paragraph is of supreme importance. It makes it clear that the emotions that constitute evaluations of different kinds of things (e.g. wine, music, persons) vary. This is to be expected because the causal conditions are different. Similarly there is a difference between a personal reaction (e.g. your reaction to a man as your enemy) and that evaluation which presupposes an objective point of view (no particular interests are given precedence). This whole issue is taken up again and discussed at length in Part III of Book III.

31. Hume tries to explain how the usual emotions come

to arise; he does not postulate a special moral sense (faculty) fitted to the *discovery* of virtue. It is more appropriate to describe his theory as a moral sentiment theory than as a moral sense theory.

32. The italicized qualification is clearly ironical.

33. Hume is here clearly rejecting all those theories which think of value as an essential aspect of nature. He is throwing overboard the whole tradition of European thought which claims that the universe, as God's creation or the realization of Platonic forms must somehow be valuable.

See A. O. Lovejoy, *The Great Chain of Being*, Harvard University Press, Cambridge, Massachusetts, 1936, for a learned account of this tradition and the tracing of it to its source in Plato's *Timaeus* as well as in certain theological ideas, prevalent in the Christian tradition.

PART II *Of Justice and Injustice*

34. An action, considered externally, as a mere change in the world, has no merit. A man is not entitled to our love (approval) simply because he does something that benefits mankind. It is only when we look upon the action as issuing from some tendency (motive) in the agent that we think of as entitling him to our approval that he and his action come to have merit. A meritorious motive is thus a necessary condition for an action being meritorious. Regard for the merit of the action thus presupposes a meritorious motive from which it arises; for you can have no regard for the merit unless the merit is there and this arises from the quality of the motive.

There is no known natural motive that can explain the just man's adherence to the complicated behaviour we call just. To make this behaviour intelligible one must not refer to the motive of duty; that would make the account circular for the reasons given above. The problem is thus at least threefold: (1) How can one make the origin of justice intelligible by referring in the explanation to natural motive only? (2) How can one explain our approval of the just man? and (3) How can one explain the general adherence to just behaviour in spite of frequent conflicts with man's strongest motives, such as self-interest and confined benevolence?

35. Here Hume makes the important point that one must not only show that society is advantageous but also how men may have come to discover its advantages. This is where 'the natural appetite betwixt the sexes' comes in.

36. Hume here seems to be maintaining that the convention is entered into by all the members of society and that we have a sufficient natural motive for strictly adhering to the rules of justice. Notice how Hume here clearly distinguishes between the convention and a promise—the mutual agreement, based on self-interest, may suffice in a small society, whereas the motive of duty is necessary to account for adherence to justice in a bigger society.

37. The consequence of the abolition of justice here mentioned could hardly be thought to follow from an individual act of injustice and would thus not furnish a very strong motive for sticking to justice on each and every occasion.

38. Hume's emphasis upon the effect of the fancy in determining what establishes property rights and the rules governing transference of property is both interesting and original. It has great persuasive force against those who believe that there is an intuitive faculty for discovering what is or is not just or that there is a special sense of justice. The long footnotes must on no account be omitted.

39. Notice that Hume talks of the experiences as the occasion or cause of the use of the evaluative expressions. It is incorrect to maintain that 'Hume's official view' is that '... the meanings of words are ideas, ideas again being identified with mental images' (A. Flew, *Hume's Philosophy of Belief*). Highly illuminating about Hume's theory of meaning is Richard I. Aaron, *The Theory of Universals*, Chapter IV. It further complicates Hume's views about meaning that, in this chapter, he anticipates Austin's insight that 'I promise' is a performance, and not a statement about a mental act. See Farhang Zabeeh, *Hume: Precursor of Modern Empiricism*, pp. 63–4.

40. For a full appreciation of the position Hume is attacking, read Locke's *Second Treatise of Government*. Hume's criticisms of the concepts of social contract and consent are of major importance. Refer to the bibliography for works concerned with Hume's political theory.

PART III *Of the Other Virtues and Vices*

41. This part of the *Treatise* contains the clearest statements of the importance of the indirect passions for Hume's account of evaluation. Notice particularly how treating approval and disapproval as a species of love, hatred, pride and humility helps to explain Hume's emphatically stated view that the object of *moral* evaluation is always human character. Actions can only be assessed morally if they can be seen to have been 'caused' by some quality in an agent. See in particular the first paragraph of Book III, Part III, Section V.

42. It is most important to pay close attention to what Hume says in this part of the *Treatise* about the modifications that have to be made to the account of sympathy as a principle of communication of passions. Hume never satisfactorily explains how his account of sympathy helps to explain the *concern* for the interests of our fellow-man that morality seems to demand. The reader must pay close attention to the function Hume attributes to the imagination and the account Hume gives of objectivity in moral 'judgments.' See Árdal, *Passion and Value*, Chapter 6.

43. Qualities of mind or character may be useful to the person himself or others, immediately agreeable to the person himself or to others. Hume is here classifying the sources of value in human qualities, and the same virtue may derive its value from more than one source e.g. benevolence is immediately agreeable to the person himself, immediately agreeable to others and also useful to others.

44. This paragraph makes it clear that Hume recognizes a ground for the distinction between virtues and talents. It may be found instructive to compare Hume's view with P. H. Nowell-Smith's *Ethics*, Chapter 20, p. 306.

Bibliography

Principal Works

(Other than *A Treatise of Human Nature*)

Essays, Moral and Political (1741–2).
Three Essays ('Of Natural Character,' 'The Original Contract,' 'Passive Obedience'), (1748).
Inquiry concerning Human Understanding (1748), and *Inquiry concerning the Principles of Morals* (1751) (*Hume's Enquiries*, ed. L. A. Selby-Bigge, 1894).
Political Discourses (1752).
Four Dissertations ('The Natural History of Religion,' 'The Passions,' 'Tragedy,' 'The Standard of Taste') (1757).
Two Essays ('On Suicide' and the 'Immortality of the Soul') (1777).
Autobiography (1777).
Dialogues Concerning Natural Religion. (Published after his death.)
History of England (1754–62).

(All the above, except *History of England*, appear in *The Philosophical Works of Hume*, eds. T. H. Green and T. H. Grose, Longmans, Green, London, 1895.)

Correspondence

A Letter From a Gentleman to His Friends in Edinburgh, eds. E. C. Mossner and J. V. Price, Edinburgh University Press, 1967.
The Letters of David Hume, ed. J. Y. T. Greig, Oxford University Press, 1932.
New Letters of David Hume, eds. R. Klibansky and E. C. Mossner, Oxford University Press, 1954.

Articles

In addition to critical articles the bibliography includes a number of modern articles about the topics dealt with by Hume.

The following collections are referred to in this section of the bibliography by indicating the editor only:

CHAPPELL, V. C. (ed.), *Hume: A Collection of Critical Essays*, Anchor Books, New York, 1966.

BEROFSKY, B. (ed.), *Freewill and Determination*, Harper & Row, New York, 1966.

FOOT, P. (ed.), *Theories of Ethics*, Oxford University Press, London, 1967.

HUDSON, W. D. (ed.), *The Is/Ought Question*, Macmillan, London, 1969.

ANSCOMBE, G. E. M., 'Modern Moral Philosophy,' *Philosophy*, XXXIII (1958), pp. 1–19. Also in W. D. Hudson (ed.).

ÁRDAL, PÁLL S., 'The Account of the Nature of Moral Evaluation in Hume's Treatise,' *Philosophy*, XXXIX (1964), pp. 341–5.

' "And That's a Promise," ' *The Philosophical Quarterly*, XVIII (1968), pp. 225–37.

ATKINSON, R. F., 'Hume on "Is" and "Ought": A Reply to Mr. MacIntyre,' *The Philosophical Review*, LXX (1961), pp. 231–8. Also in Chappell (ed.) and Hudson (ed.).

AUSTIN, J. L., 'Performative Utterances,' in J. L. Austin, *Philosophical Papers*, Oxford University Press, Oxford, 1961.

'Ifs and Cans,' *Proceedings of the British Academy*, XLII (1956) and J. L. Austin, *Philosophical Papers*, Oxford University Press, Oxford, 1961. And in Berofsky (ed.).

AYER, A. J., 'On the Analysis of Moral Judgments,' *Horizon* (London), XX (1949), pp. 171–82. And in A. J. Ayer, *Philosophical Essays*, Macmillan, London, 1963 (Paper).

BARNES, W. H. F., 'Ethics Without Propositions,' *Proceedings of the Aristotelian Society, Supplementary Volume*, XXII (1948).

BAXTER, IAN F. G., 'David Hume and Justice,' *Revue Internationale de Philosophie*, XIII (1959), pp. 112–31.

BLACK, MAX, 'The Gap between "Is" and "Should," ' *The Philosophical Review*, LXXIII (1964), pp. 165–81. Also in Hudson (ed.).

BRADLEY, M. C., 'A note on Mr. MacIntyre's *Determinism*,' *Mind*, LXVIII (1959), pp. 521–6. And in Berofsky (ed.).

BRANDT, RICHARD B., 'An Emotional Theory of the Judgment of Moral Worth,' *Ethics*, LII (1941–42), pp. 41–79.

BROAD, C. D., 'Some Reflection on Moral Sense Theories in Ethics,' *Proceedings of the Aristotelian Society*, XLV (1944–5). This was inspired by his reading of Price's 'Review.' It does contain some discussion of Hume.

CAMPBELL, C. A., 'Is "Freewill" a Pseudo-Problem?', *Mind*, LX (1951), pp. 441–65. And in Berofsky (ed.).

'The Psychology of Effort and Will,' *Proceedings of the Aristotelian Society*, XL (1939–40). And in Berofsky (ed.).

CAPALDI, NICHOLAS, 'Hume's Rejection of "Ought" as a

Moral Category,' *The Journal of Philosophy*, LXIII (1966), pp. 126–37.

COHEN, MENDEL F., 'Motives, Causal Necessity and Moral Accountability,' *Australasian Journal of Philosophy*, XLII (1964), pp. 322–34.

DAY, JOHN, 'Hume on Justice and Allegiance,' *Philosophy*, XL (1965), pp. 35–56.

DAVIDSON, DONALD, 'Action, Reasons, and Causes,' *The Journal of Philosophy*, LX (1963), pp. 685–700. And in Berofsky (ed.).

DIETL, PAUL, 'Hume on the Passions,' *Philosophy and Phenomenological Research*, XXVIII (1967–8), pp. 554–66.

DIGGS, B. J., 'Rules and Utilitarianism,' *The American Philosophical Quarterly*, I (1964), pp. 32–44.

DUCASSE, C. J., 'The Nature and Function of Theory in Ethics,' *Ethics*, LI (1940–1), pp. 22–37.

DURRANT, R. G., 'Promising,' *Australasian Journal of Philosophy*, XLI (1963), pp. 44–56.

EWING, A. C. and WARNOCK, M., 'The Justification of Emotions,' *Proceedings of the Aristotelian Society Supplementary Volume*, XXXI (1957). Mrs. Warnock's paper contains a discussion of Hume.

FLEW, A. G. N., 'Hume's Check,' *The Philosophical Quarterly*, IX (1959), pp. 1–18.
' "Not Proven"—At Most,' in Chappell (ed.).
'On the Interpretation of Hume,' *Philosophy*, XXXVIII (1963), pp. 178–82. Also in Chappell (ed.) and Hudson (ed.).
'On not deriving "ought" from "is",' *Analysis*, 25 (1964–5), pp. 25–32. Also in Hudson (ed.).

FOOT, MRS. PHILIPPA R., 'Hume on Moral Judgment,' in *David Hume. A Symposium*, (ed. D. F. Pears), Macmillan, London, 1963.
'Moral Beliefs,' *Proceedings of the Aristotelian Society*, LIX (1958–9). Also in Foot (ed.) and Hudson (ed.).
'Goodness and Choice,' *Proceedings of the Aristotelian Society, Supplementary Volume*, XXXV (1961). Also in Hudson (ed.).
'Free Will as Involving Determinism,' *The Philosophical Review*, LXVI (1957), pp. 439–50. And in Berofsky (ed.).

GARDINER, P. L., 'Hume's Theory of the Passions,' in *David Hume. A Symposium*, (ed. D. F. Pears), Macmillan, London, 1963.

GLOSSOP, RONALD J., 'The Nature of Hume's Ethics,' *Philosophy and Phenomenological Research*, XXVII (1966–7), pp. 527–36.

GOSLING, J. D., 'Emotion and Object,' *Philosophical Review*, LXXIV (1965), pp. 486–503.

HANLY, KENNETH, 'Zimmerman's "Is-is": A schizophrenic

monism,' *Mind*, LXXIII (1964), pp. 443–5.

HAMPSHIRE, S., 'Fallacies in Moral Philosophy,' *Mind*, LVIII (1949), pp. 466–82. Hampshire discusses Hume's view.

HARE, R. M., 'Descriptivism,' *Proceedings of the British Academy*, XLIX (1963). Also in Hudson (ed.).

'The Promising Game,' *Revue Internationale de Philosophie*, XVIII (1964), pp. 398–412. Also in Hudson (ed.) and Foot (ed.).

HAYEK, F. A., 'The Legal and Political Philosophy of David Hume,' A public lecture delivered at the University of Freiburg on July 18, 1963, and published in *Il Politico*, XXVIII (1936). Also in Chappell (ed.).

HELM, PAUL, 'Hume on Exculpation', *Philosophy*, XLII (1967), pp. 265–71.

HOBART, R. E., 'Free Will as Involving Determination and Inconceivable Without It,' *Mind*, XLIII (1934), pp. 1–27. And in Berofsky (ed.).

HOERNLE, R. F. A., 'Broad and Hume on Causation and Volition,' *The Journal of Philosophy*, XXIV (1927), pp. 29–36.

HUDSON, W. D., 'Hume on *Is* and *Ought*,' *The Philosophical Quarterly*, XIV (1964), pp. 246–52. Also in Chappell (ed.) and in Hudson (ed.).

'The " is–ought" Controversy,' *Analysis*, 25 (1964–5), pp. 191–5. Also in Hudson (ed.).

HUNTER, GEOFFREY, 'Hume on "Is" and "Ought",' *Philosophy*, XXXVII (1962), pp. 148–52. Also in Hudson (ed.).

'Reply to Professor Flew,' *Philosophy*, XXXVIII (1963), pp. 182–4. Also in Chappell (ed.) and in Hudson (ed.).

JONES, PETER, 'Another Look at Hume's Views of Aesthetic and Moral Judgments,' *The Philosophical Quarterly*, XX (1970), pp. 53–9.

JORGENSEN, CARL, 'On the Possibility of Deducing What Ought to be from What Is,' *Ethics*, LXVI (1955–6), pp. 271–8.

MACINTYRE, A. C., 'Hume on "Is" and "Ought",' *The Philosophical Review*, LXVIII (1959), pp. 451–68. Also in Hudson (ed.) and Chappell (ed.).

'Determinism,' *Mind*, LXVI (1957), pp. 28–41. And in Berofsky (ed.).

MARCUS, R. I., 'Hume: Reason and Moral Sense,' *Philosophy and Phenomenological Research*, XIII (1952–3), pp. 139–57.

MARSHALL, GEOFFREY, 'David Hume and Political Scepticism,' *The Philosophical Quarterly*, IV (1954), pp. 247–57.

MCCLELLAN, J. E. and KOMISAR, B. P., 'On Deriving "ought" from "is",' *Analysis*, 25 (1964–65), pp. 32–7. Also in Hudson (ed.).

MCCLOSKEY, H. J., 'An Examination of Restricted Utilitarianism,' *The Philosophical Review*, LXVI (1957), pp. 466–85.

MCGILVARY, E. B., 'Altruism in Hume's *Treatise*,' *The Philosophical Review*, XII (1903), pp. 272–98.

MILLER, DAVID L., 'The ought and the is,' *Ethics*, LXVII (1957), pp. 206–7.

MILLER, D. S., 'Hume's Deathblow to Deductivism,' *The Journal of Philosophy*, 46 (1949), pp. 745–62.

MITCHELL, DOROTHY, 'Must We Talk about "Is" and "Ought"?' *Mind*, LXXVII (1968), pp. 543–9.

MOSSNER, ERNEST C., 'The First Answer to Hume's *Treatise*,' *The Journal of the History of Ideas*, XII (1951), pp. 291–4.
'The Continental Reception of Hume's *Treatise*, 1739–41,' *Mind*, LVI (1947), pp. 31–43.

NOWELL-SMITH, P. H., 'Ifs and Cans,' *Theoria*, XXVI (1960), pp. 85–101. And in Berofsky (ed.).

NOXON, JAMES, 'Senses of Identity in Hume's *Treatise*,' *Dialogue*, VIII (1969–70), pp. 367–84.

PERKINS, MORELAND, 'Emotion and Feeling,' *The Philosophical Review*, LXXV (1966), pp. 139–60.
'Emotion and the Concept of Behaviour,' *The American Philosophical Quarterly*, 3 (1966), pp. 291–8.

PHILLIPS, D. Z., 'The Possibilities of Moral Advice,' *Analysis*, 24 (1964–5), pp. 37–41. Also in Hudson (ed.).
and MOUNCE, H. O., 'On Morality's having a point,' *Philosophy*, XL (1965), pp. 308–19. Also in Hudson (ed.).

PIKE, NELSON, 'Hume on Evil,' *The Philosophical Review*, LXXIII (1963), pp. 180–97.

PITCHER, GEORGE, 'On Approval,' *The Philosophical Review*, LXVII (1958), pp. 195–211.
'Emotion,' *Mind*, LXXIV (1965), pp. 326–46.

RAWLS, JOHN, 'Two Concepts of Rules,' *The Philosophical Review*, LXIV (1955), pp. 3–32. Also in Foot (ed.).
'The Sense of Justice,' *The Philosophical Review*, LXXII (1963), pp. 281–305. Also in *Moral Concepts* (ed. Joel Feinberg), Oxford University Press, London, 1969.
'Justice as Fairness,' *The Philosophical Review*, LXVII (1958), pp. 164–94.
'Constitutional Liberty and the Concept of Justice,' *Nomos IV: Justice* (eds. C. J. Friedrich and J. W. Chapman), Atherton Press, New York, 1963.

ROSS, IAN, 'Hutcheson on Hume's Treatise: An Unnoticed Letter,' *Journal of the History of Philosophy*, IV (1966), pp. 69–72.

SCOTT-TAGGART, M. J., 'MacIntyre's Hume,' *The Philosophical Review*, LXX (1961), pp. 239–44.

SEARLE, JOHN R., 'How to Derive "Ought" from "Is",' *The Philosophical Review*, LXXIII (1964), pp. 43–8. Also in

Hudson (ed.) and in Foot (ed.).

'Deriving "ought" from "is" : objections and replies,' in Hudson (ed.).

SEN, AMARTYA K., 'Hume's Law and Hare's Rule,' *Philosophy* XLI (1966), pp. 75–9.

SHARP, F. C., 'Hume's Ethical Theory and its Critics,' *Mind* XXX (1921), pp. 40–56 (I), and pp. 151–71 (II).

SMART, J. J. C., 'Extreme and Restricted Utilitarianism,' *The Philosophical Quarterly*, VI (1956). Also in Foot (ed.).

STEVENSON, C. L., 'Ethical Judgments and Avoidability,' *Mind* XLVII (1938), pp. 45–57.

'Persuasive Definitions,' *Mind*, XLVII (1938), pp. 331–50.

'The Emotive Meaning of Ethical Terms,' *Mind*, XLVI (1937) pp. 14–31.

SWEIGART, JOHN, 'The Distance between Hume and Emotivism,' *The Philosophical Quarterly*, XIV (1964), pp. 229–36 An abstract of this is in *The Journal of Philosophy*, 59 (1962) pp. 671–2.

TAYLOR, GABRIELE, 'Hume's Views of Moral Judgments,' *The Philosophical Quarterly* (1971).

TAYLOR, RICHARD, 'Deliberation and Foreknowledge,' *American Philosophical Quarterly*, I (1964), pp. 73–80. And in Berofsky ed.).

THALBERG, I., 'Emotion and Thought,' *American Philosophical Quarterly*, I (1964), pp. 45–55.

THOMSON, JAMES and JUDITH, 'How not to Derive "Ought" from "Is",' *The Philosophical Review*, LXXIII (1964), pp. 512–16. Also in Hudson (ed.).

TRANOÏ, KNUT ERIK, 'Hume on Morals, Animals, and Men,' *The Journal of Philosophy*, LVI (1959), pp. 94–103.

WALSH, W. H., 'Pride, Shame and Responsibility,' *The Philosophical Quarterly*, XX (1970), pp. 1–13.

WAND, BERNARD, 'Hume's Account of Obligation,' *The Philosophical Quarterly*, VI (1956), pp. 155–68. Also in Chappell (ed.).

'A Note on Sympathy in Hume's Moral Theory,' *The Philosophical Review*, LXIV (1955), pp. 275–79.

'Hume's Non-Utilitarianism,' *Ethics*, LXXII (1961–2), pp. 193–6.

WARNOCK, MARY, and EWING, A. C., 'The Justification of Emotions, A Symposium,' *Proceedings of the Aristotelian Society Supplementary Volume*, XXXI (1957). Mrs. Warnock's paper contains a discussion of Hume.

WILLIAMS, BERNARD, 'The Idea of Equality' in *Philosophy, Politics and Society* (Second Series) (eds. Laslett and Runciman), Blackwell, 1962. Also in 'Moral Concepts,' (ed. Feinberg), Oxford University Press, 1969. (Paper.)

WOLIN, S. S., 'Hume and Conservativism,' *American Political Science Review*, XLVIII (1954), pp. 999–1016.

ZIMMERMAN, M., 'The "is–ought": An unnecessary dualism', *Mind*, LXXI (1962), pp. 53–61. Also in Hudson (ed.).
  'A Note on the "is–ought" barrier,' *Mind*, LXXVI (1967), p. 286. Also in Hudson (ed.).

Critical Books

AARON, RICHARD I., *The Theory of Universals*, The Clarendon Press, Oxford, 1952 (Second edition, 1955). Chapter IV throws considerable light upon Hume's view with regard to meaning.

AIKEN, HENRY D. (ed.), *Hume's Moral and Political Philosophy*, Hafner Publishing Co., New York, 1948. The editor's introduction is interesting and useful.

ÁRDAL, PALL S., *Passion and Value in Hume's Treatise*, Edinburgh University Press, Edinburgh, 1966. Stresses the importance of Book II of the *Treatise* for the interpretation of *Of Morals*.

BASSON, A. H., *David Hume*, Pelican Books, London, 1958. Also published by Dover (New York, 1968) with author as A. P. Cavendish. Does not emphasize Hume's contribution to moral theory.

BEROFSKY, BERNARD (ed.), *Free Will and Determinism*, Harper and Row, New York, 1966. (Paper.) A useful collection of essays and excerpts from books on a topic to which Hume contributed something of permanent importance.

BRANDT, RICHARD B. (ed.), *Social Justice*, Prentice-Hall, Engelwood Cliffs, 1962. (Paper.) This includes articles by Kenneth E. Boulding, William Frankena, Paul A. Freund, Alan Gewirth and Gregory Vlastos.

BROAD, C. D., *Five Types of Ethical Theory*, Routledge & Kegan Paul, London, 1930. The interpretation of Hume's theory is based upon *The Enquiry Concerning the Principles of Morals*.

BROILES, R. DAVID, *The Moral Philosophy of David Hume*, Martinus Nijhoff, The Hague, 1964. A limited discussion, centred round the distinction between exciting and justifying reasons.

BRYSON, GLADYS, *Man and Society: The Scottish Inquiry of the Eighteenth Century*, Princeton University Press, Princeton, New Jersey, 1945. An interesting account of the intellectual climate of Scotland. Valuable background reading.

CHAPPELL, V. C. (ed.), *Hume: A Collection of Critical Essays*, Anchor Books, New York, 1966. (Paper.) A collection of essays, some of which are relevant to Books II and III of the *Treatise*.

D'ENTREVES, A. P., *Natural Law. An Introduction to Legal Philosophy*, Hutchinson's University Library, London, 1951. Traces the history of the concept of natural law. Useful although it places no special emphasis upon Hume's criticism of the concept.

FEINBERG, JOEL (ed.), *Moral Concepts*, ('Oxford Readings in Philosophy'), Oxford University Press, London, 1969 (Paper.)

FOOT, PHILIPPA (ed.), *Theories of Ethics* ('Oxford Readings in Philosophy') Oxford University Press, London, 1967 (Paper.) Both these collections contain a number of articles on topics discussed in Books II and III of Hume's *Treatise*.

FLEW, ANTONY, *Hume's Philosophy of Belief*, Routledge and Kegan Paul, London, 1961. The chapter on liberty and necessity may be of some help to readers of the *Treatise* although this is a commentary on Hume's *First Inquiry*.

GAY, PETER, *The Enlightenment: An Interpretation*, Alfred A. Knopf, New York, 1966. There is considerable attention paid to Hume in this authoritative historical study. It contains a long and erudite bibliographical essay.

GLATHE, ALFRED BOULIGNY, *Hume's Theory of the Passions and of Morals. A Study of Books II and III of the Treatise*, University of California Press, Berkeley, 1950. A sound exposition of Hume's views in Books II and III of the *Treatise*.

GREEN, T. H. and GROSE, T. H. *The Philosophical Works of Hume*. Longmans, Green, London, 1874–75. Green's introduction to the moral part of the *Treatise*, though somewhat unsympathetic, is full of interest. This introduction is now contained in Thomas Hill Green's *Hume and Locke*, Apollo Editions, Thomas Y. Cromwell, Co., New York, 1968. (Paper.)

HEDENIUS, INGEMAR, *Studies in Hume's Ethics*, Almqvist and Wiksells, Uppsala, 1937. Can be recommended to the advanced student of Hume's ethics.

HUDSON, W. D., *Ethical Intuitionism*, Macmillan, London, 1967. (Paper.) Includes a short but lucid discussion of the debate between the adherents of a moral sense theory in the eighteenth century and rationalists, such as William Wollaston.

— (ed.), *The Is/Ought Question*, Macmillan, London, 1969. (Paper.) An excellent collection of essays.

KEMP, J., *Reason, Action and Morality*, Routledge and Kegan Paul, London, 1964. The book begins with a useful discussion of Cudworth, Locke, Clarke, Hume and Kant.

KEMP SMITH, NORMAN, *The Philosophy of David Hume,*

Macmillan, London, 1941. The most detailed comprehensive study of Hume's thought.

KRUSE, L. F. VINDING, *Hume's Philosophy in his Principal Work A Treatise of Human Nature and in His Essays*, translated by P. T. Federspiel, Oxford University Press, London, 1939. A short study. Stresses the similarities and differences between Hume's principal works and is valuable for that reason. There is little philosophical discussion of Hume's views.

KYDD, RACHAEL MARY, *Reason and Conduct in Hume's Treatise*, Oxford University Press, London, 1946. Stresses features of Hume's thought that make him closer to rationalists, such as Spinoza.

LAING, B. M., *David Hume*, Benn, London, 1932. A comprehensive study of modest length of Hume's life and philosophy.

LAIRD, JOHN, *Hume's Philosophy of Human Nature*, Methuen, London, 1932; Archon Books, Hamden, Conn, 1967. Scholarly and reliable. A comprehensive study of Hume's philosophical writings.

LOVEJOY, ARTHUR O., *The Great Chain of Being*, Cambridge, Mass., Harvard University Press, 1936; Harper & Row, New York, 1960 (c 1936). (Paper.) A classic historical study of the ideas behind the world view against which Hume was reacting.

MACNABB, D. G. C., *David Hume, his Theory of Knowledge and and Morality*, Hutchinson's University Library, London, 1951; Second edition, Basil Blackwell, Oxford, 1966; Archon Books, Hamden, Conn., 1966. Best available short introduction to Hume's philosophy.

PASSMORE, J. A., *Hume's Intentions*, Cambridge University Press, Cambridge, 1952; Duckworth, London, 1968. (Paper.) Disentangles various strands in Hume's thought. Not exclusively concerned with Books II and III of the *Treatise*.

PEARS, D. F. (ed.), *David Hume: a symposium*, Macmillan, London, 1963. Short studies by different authors of various aspects of Hume's thought.

PLAMENATZ, JOHN, *Man and Society* (Vol. I, Ch. 8), Longmans, Green, London, 1963. (Paper.) Mainly concerned with Hume's social and political doctrines.

PRIOR, ARTHUR N., *Logic and the Basis of Ethics*, The Clarendon Press, Oxford, 1949. Valuable for the background it gives to some of Hume's doctrines and their subsequent history.

RAPHAEL, D. D., *The Moral Sense*, Oxford University Press, London, 1947. Short discussion of an aspect of Hume's thought. Also discusses the views of some of his contemporaries and immediate predecessors.

ROTWEIN, EUGENE (ed.), *David Hume's Writings on Economics*,

University of Wisconsin Press, Madison, Wisconsin, 1955 The introduction is useful for its discussion of Hume's psychology.

SABINE, GEORGE H., *A History of Political Theory,* Henry Holt & Company, New York, 1937; Third edition, Holt, Rinehart & Winston, 1961. A standard history of political thought that emphasizes Hume's importance as a political and social thinker.

STEPHEN, LESLIE, *History of English Thought in the Eighteenth Century,* 2 vols., ('A Harbinger Book') Rupert Hart-Davis, London; Harcourt, New York, 1962. (Paper.) A classic study in the history of thought. Valuable background reading.

STEWART, JOHN B., *The Moral and Political Philosophy of David Hume,* Columbia University Press, New York and London, 1963. A scholarly work, useful to advanced students of Hume's thought.

WATKINS, FREDERICK (ed.), *Hume: Theory of Politics,* Nelson, Edinburgh and New York, 1951. This selection from Hume's works has a short introduction and is a useful guide to Hume's contribution to political theory.

ZABEEH, FARHANG, *Hume: Precursor of Modern Empiricism,* Martinus Nijhoff, The Hague, 1960. The discussion of Hume's doctrines about meaning may be found helpful in discussing some aspect of Hume's moral theory, such as his account of promises.

Chronological Table

1687 Newton's *Principia*
1690 Locke's *Essay Concerning Human Understanding*
1710 Berkeley's *Principles of Human Knowledge*
1711 Hume born in Edinburgh
1723–5 or 26 At Edinburgh University
1726–34 At Ninewells, studying
1729 Francis Hutcheson appointed Professor of Moral Philosophy at Glasgow
1734–7 In France, principally La Flèche, writing the *Treatise*
1737–9 In London arranging publication
1739 *Treatise*, Books I and II published
1740 The *Abstract* published
    Treatise, Book III, with Appendix, published
1739–45 At Ninewells and Edinburgh
1744 Unsuccessful candidate for Chair of Ethics and Pneumatical Philosophy at Edinburgh
1745–6 Tutor to Marquis of Annandale, near St. Albans
1746–9 Secretary to General St Clair on military expedition to Brittany and diplomatic mission to Vienna and Turin
1748 *Philosophical Essays* (later called *Enquiry*) *Concerning Human Understanding* published
1751 Unsuccessful candidate for Chair of Logic at Glasgow
1751 *Enquiry Concerning the Principles of Morals* published
1752–7 Keeper of Advocates' Library, Edinburgh
    Writing *History of Great Britain*
1763–6 Private Secretary to Lord Hertford
    Secretary and for a time *chargé d'affaires* at the British Embassy in Paris
1766 Returns to London, bringing Rousseau
    Quarrel with Rousseau. Publication of correspondence with Rousseau
1767–9 In London. Under-Secretary of State, Northern Dept., till 1768
1769–76 In Edinburgh
1776 Visits London and Bath
1776 Died August 25th in Edinburgh
1779 *Dialogues Concerning Natural Religion* published

Index

Appendix

Correlation of page numbers in this edition with those in the OUP edition of *A Treatise of Human Nature*, edited by L. A. Selby-Bigge.

Fontana Philosophy Classics

This series of texts and anthologies, with substantial introductions, was originated by G. J. Warnock and is being continued under the editorship of A. M. Quinton.

**The Principles of Human Knowledge and
Three Dialogues Between Hylas and Philonous**
George Berkeley   *Edited by* G. J. Warnock

An Essay Concerning Human Understanding
John Locke   *Edited by* A. D. Woozley

Leviathan
Thomas Hobbes   *Edited by* John Plamenatz

A Treatise of Human Nature
David Hume **Book I**   *Edited by* D. G. C. Macnabb
Books II and III   *Edited by* P. S. Ardal

Hume on Religion
Edited by Richard Wollheim

Russell's Logical Atomism
Edited by David Pears

The Light of Reason
Rationalist Philosophers of the 17th Century
Edited by Martin Hollis

A Guide to the British Moralists
Edited by D. H. Monro

Utilitarianism
Edited by Mary Warnock